Issues in
Diagnostic Research

Issues in
Diagnostic Research

Edited by
CYNTHIA G. LAST
and
MICHEL HERSEN

Western Psychiatric Institute and Clinic
University of Pittsburgh School of Medicine
Pittsburgh, Pennsylvania

PLENUM PRESS • NEW YORK AND LONDON

Library of Congress Cataloging in Publication Data

Issues in diagnostic research.

Includes bibliographies and index.
1. Psychodiagnostics—Research. I. Last, Cynthia G. II. Hersen, Michel. [DNLM: 1.
Mental Disorders—diagnosis. WM 141 I86]
RC469.I87   1987   616.89'075   86-30575
ISBN 0-306-42424-X

© 1987 Plenum Press, New York
A Division of Plenum Publishing Corporation
233 Spring Street, New York, N.Y. 10013

Printed in the United States of America

Contributors

Craig Edelbrock, *Department of Psychiatry, University of Massachusetts Medical School, Worcester, Massachusetts*

Irl L. Extein, *Lake Hospital, Lake Worth, Florida*

John P. Feighner, *Feighner Research Institute, Encinitas, California and Department of of Psychiatry, University of California School of Medicine, San Diego, California*

Mark S. Gold, *Lake Hospital, Lake Worth, Florida*

William Goodpastor, *Department of Psychiatry, Western Psychiatric Institute and Clinic, University of Pittsburgh School of Medicine, Pittsburgh, Pennsylvania*

William M. Grove, *Department of Psychiatry, University of Iowa, Iowa City, Iowa*

James L. Hedlund, *Department of Psychiatry, University of Missouri School of Medicine, St. Louis, Missouri*

Jessica Herbstein, *Feighner Research Institute, Encinitas, California*

Cynthia G. Last, *Department of Psychiatry, Western Psychiatric Institute and Clinic, University of Pittsburgh School of Medicine, Pittsburgh, Pennsylvania*

Ada C. Mezzich, *Department of Psychiatry, Western Psychiatric Institue and Clinic, University of Pittsburgh School of Medicine, Pittsburgh, Pennsylvania*

Juan E. Mezzich, *Department of Psychiatry, Western Psychiatric Institute and Clinic, University of Pittsburgh School of Medicine, Pittsburgh, Pennsylvania*

Theodore Millon, *Department of Psychology, University of Miami, Coral Gables, Florida*

Melinda C. Mullins, *Departments of Behavioral Medicine and Psychiatry and Internal Medicine, West Virginia University Medical Center, Morgantown, West Virginia*

Rosemery O. Nelson, *Department of Psychology, University of North Carolina, Greensboro, North Carolina*

Judith L. Rapoport, *Laboratory of Clinical Science, National Institute of Mental Health, Bethesda, Maryland*

William S. Rea, *Lake Hospital, Lake Worth, Florida*

James M. Stevenson, *Departments of Behavioral Medicine and Psychiatry and Internal Medicine, West Virginia University Medical Center, Morgantown, West Virginia*

W. Douglas Thompson, *Department of Epidemiology and Public Health, Yale University School of Medicine, New Haven, Connecticut*

Bruce W. Viewig, *Department of Psychiatry, University of Missouri School of Medicine, St. Louis, Missouri*

Diane K. Wagener, *Department of Psychiatry, Western Psychiatric Institute and Clinic, University of Pittsburgh School of Medicine, Pittsburgh, Pennsylvania*

Preface

Prior and subsequent to the publication of the third edition of the *Diagnostic and Statistical Manual of Mental Disorders* (DSM-III), we have witnessed a considerable upsurge in the quantity and quality of research concerned with the psychiatric diagnostic process. There are several factors that have contributed to this empirical influx, including improved diagnostic criteria for many psychiatric disorders, increased nosological attention to childhood psychopathology, and development and standardization of several structured diagnostic interview schedules for both adult and child populations.

With the advent of DSM-III-R, and in anticipation of DSM-IV, diagnostic labels and their definitions have been in a state of change, as evinced by the many refinements and modifications currently taking place. However, the basic *purpose* or raison d'être of the nosological scheme has not been altered. Psychiatric diagnosis is the means by which we classify or categorize human psychopathology. And, as is the case in the medical arena, psychiatric diagnosis serves three central functions: *classification, communication,* and *prediction.* As research accumulates, our understanding of psychiatric disorders increases, and we are in a much better position to classify reliably and with validity, as well as to communicate and predict.

Despite periodic changes in the diagnostic system, the basic strategies for conducting diagnostic research (e.g., genetic-family studies, biological markers, follow-up studies, etc.) do not vary appreciably over time. But in over one decade no scholarly book has appeared that tackles the essential research issues involved in upgrading the diagnostic endeavor. Therefore, the primary purpose of our book is to define and clarify the empirical issues involved in conducting psychiatric diagnostic research.

Issues in Diagnostic Research is divided into three parts. In the first part the diagnostic systems in use are examined in detail, as are the general issues of diagnostic reliability and validity. The second part is concerned with the important methodological issues facing the diagnostic researcher for each of the major research approaches to validating psychiatric diagnoses, such as lifetime psychiatric diagnoses, biological markers, genetic factors, and developmental considerations. The issues discussed in this section are of considerable importance in evaluating the utility and validity of our diagnostic categories.

In the third and final part, a number of contemporary topics are reviewed in depth, including multivariate and computer-generated approaches, differential diagnosis of medical and psychiatric disorders, the relationship of DSM-III to behavioral assessment, and the revision of DSM-III as it impacts on child diagnosis.

Many people have contributed their time and effort to this volume. First and foremost we thank our eminent contributors for sharing their expertise with us. Second, we are most appreciative of the technical assistance of Jenifer Brander, Cynthia Lease, Mary Newell, and Kim Sterner. Finally, we thank Eliot Werner, our editor at Plenum, for his support and forbearance in the face of the inevitable delays.

CYNTHIA G. LAST
MICHEL HERSEN

Contents

Part III   Special Topics

General Issues

On the Nature of Taxonomy in Psychopathology

THEODORE MILLON

INTRODUCTION

To recall thoughts expressed some years ago concerning the character of theory (Millon, 1969), I voiced my chagrin that nature was not made to suit our need for a tidy and well-ordered universe. Quite evidently, the complexity and intricacy of the natural world make it difficult not only to establish clearcut relationships among phenomena, but to find simple ways in which these phenomena can be classified or grouped. In our desire to discover the essential order of nature, we find it necessary to concern ourselves with only a few of the infinite number of elements that could be chosen; in this selection we narrow our choice only to those aspects of nature that we believe best enable us to answer the questions we have posed. Moreover, the elements we choose are labeled, transformed, and reassembled in a variety of ways, but we must bear in mind that these labels and transformations are not "realities." The various concepts and categories that we construct as scientists are only optional tools to guide our observation and interpretation of the natural world; different concepts and categories may be formulated as alternative approaches to the understanding of the same subject of inquiry. These tools are especially necessary when the terrain we face is as uncharted as the taxonomy of psychopathology, and the materials of which it is composed are as intractable as they are.

THEODORE MILLON • Department of Psychology, University of Miami, Coral Gables, FL 33124.

With these perspectives and caveats in mind, we may now address the question: How can we best conceptualize and organize the clinical data that comprise psychopathology? Clearly, the mental disorders we observe express themselves in a variety of ways. Not only are they complex, but they can be approached at different levels and can be viewed from many frames of reference. For example, behaviorally, disorders can be conceived and grouped as complicated response patterns to environmental stimuli. At a phenomenological level, they can be understood and classified as personal experiences of discomfort and anguish. Approached physiologically, they can be analyzed and organized as sequences of complex neural and chemical activity. And intrapsychically, they can be inferred and categorized as unconscious processes that defend against anxiety and conflict.

Given these diverse possibilities, we can readily understand why psychopathologic states and processes may be classified in terms of any of several data levels we may wish to focus on, and any of a variety of attributes we may wish to identify and explain. Beyond this, each data level lends itself to a number of specific concepts and categories, the usefulness of which must be gauged by their ability to help solve the particular problems and purposes for which they were created. That the subject matter of psychopathology is inherently diverse and complex is precisely the reason why we must not narrow the clinical data comprising a classification to one level or one approach. Each source and each orientation has a legitimate and potentially fruitful contribution to make. It should be clear from these considerations that no classification in psychopathology today "carves nature at its joints," that is, is an inevitable representation of the "real world." Rather, our classifications are, at best, interim tools for advancing knowledge and facilitating clinical goals. They serve to organize our scientific work in a logical manner, and function as explanatory propositions to give meaning to our clinical experiences.

The subject areas which subdivide the natural world differ in the degree to which their phenomena are inherently differentiated and organized. Some areas are "naturally" more articulated and quantifiable than others. To illustrate: The laws of physics relate to highly probabalistic processes in many of its most recondite spheres, but the features of our everyday physical world are highly ordered and predictable. Theories in this latter realm of physics (e.g., mechanics, electricity) serve largely to *uncover* the lawful relationships that do, in fact, exist in nature; it was the task of turn-of-the-century physicists to fashion a network of constructs that faithfully mirrored the universal nature of the phenomena they studied. By contrast, probabalistic realms of physical analysis (e.g., shortlived elementary particles) or systems of recent evolutionary development (e.g., human interactions) are inherently weakly organized, lacking either articulated or invariant connections among their constituent elements. In knowledge domains that relate to these less ordered spheres of nature (the "softer" sciences), classifiers and theorists find it necessary to *impose* a somewhat arbitrary measure of systematization; in so doing, they construct a degree of clarity and coherence that is not fully consonant with the "naturally" unsettled and indeterminate character of their subject. Rather than equivocate strategically, or succumb to the "futility of it all," noble or pretentious efforts are made to arrange and categorize these inexact and probabalistic elements so that they simulate a degree of precision and order transcending that which they intrinsically possess. To illustrate: In fields such as economics and psychopathology, categories and classifications are, in considerable measure, splendid fictions, compelling notions, or austere formulas devised to give coherence to their *inherently imprecise* subjects.

The logic, substance, and structures created or imposed as a means of giving order to the phenomena of psychopathology will be the principal topic of this chapter. It will be both a pedagogic introduction and a comprehensive review, depending on the starting point of the reader. Coverage will be all too sketchy, and many basic terms and concepts must be explicated to tutor the untutored. It should serve the advanced, as well, in that no other source appears to be available that addresses the subject in as systematic a manner.

WHY CLASSIFY?

Man developed reliable and useful classifications long before the advent of modern scientific thought and methods. Information, skill, and instrumentation were achieved without "science" and its symbolic abstractions and techniques of research. If useful classifications could be acquired by intelligent observation and common sense alone, what special values are derived by applying the complicated and rigorous procedures required in developing explicit criteria, taxonic homogeneity, and diagnostic efficiency? Is rigor, clarity, precision, and experimentation more than a compulsive and picayunish concern for details, more than the pursuit for the honorific title of "science"? Are the labors of differentiating attributes or exploring optimal cutting scores in a systematic fashion worth the time and effort involved?

There is little question in this "age of science" that the answer would be yes. But why? What are the distinguishing virtues of precision in one's terminology, the specification of observable conceptual referents, the analysis of covariant attribute clusters? What sets these procedures apart from everyday methods of categorizing knowledge?

Because the number of ways we can observe, describe, and organize the natural world is infinite, the terms and concepts we create to represent these activities are often confusing and obscure. For example, different words are used to describe the same behavior, and the same word is used for different behaviors. Some terms are narrow in focus, others are broad, and some are difficult to define. Because of the diversity of events to which one can attend, or the lack of precision in the language we employ, different processes are confused and similar events get scattered hodgepodge across a scientific landscape; as a consequence, communication gets bogged down in terminological obscurities and semantic controversies.

One of the goals of formalizing the phenomena comprising a scientific subject is to avoid this morass of confusion. Not all phenomena related to the subject need be attended to at once. Certain elements may be selected from the vast range of possibilities because they seem relevant to the solution of a specific question. And to create a degree of reliability or consistency among those interested in a subject, its elements are defined as precisely as possible and classified according to their core similarities and differences (Dougherty, 1978; Tversky, 1977). In a subject such as psychopathology, these classes or categories are given specific labels which serve to represent them. This process of definition and classification is indispensable for systematizing observation and knowledge.

Is conceptual definition and classification possible in psychopathology? Can these most fundamental of scientific activities be achieved in a subject that is inherently inexact, of only modest levels of intrinsic order, one in which even the very slightest variations in context or antecedent conditions—often of a minor or random character—produce highly divergent outcomes (Bandura, 1982)? Because this "looseness" within the network of variables in psychopathology is unavoidable, are there any grounds for believing that such endeavors could prove more than illusory? Persuasive answers to this question of a more philosophical nature must be bypassed in this all-too-concise chapter; those who wish to pursue this line of analysis would gain much by reading, among others, Pap (1953); Hempel (1965); and Meehl (1978). Let us touch, albeit briefly, on a more tangible and psychologically based rationale for believing that formal classification in psychopathology may prove to be at least a moderately fruitful venture.

There is a clear logic to classifying "syndromes" in medical disorders. Bodily changes wrought by infectious diseases and structural deteriorations repeatedly display themselves in a reasonably uniform pattern of signs and symptoms that "make sense" in terms of how anatomic structures and physiological processes are altered and dysfunction. Moreover, these biological changes provide a foundation not only for identifying the etiology and pathogenesis of these disorders, but also for anticipating their course and prognosis. Logic and fact together enable us to construct a rationale to explain why most medical syndromes express themselves in the signs and symptoms they do, as well as the sequences through which they unfold.

Can the same be said for psychopathological classifications? Is there a logic, perhaps evidence, for believing that certain forms of clinical expression (e.g., behaviors, cognitions, affects, mechanisms) cluster together as do medical syndromes; that is, not only covary frequently, but "make sense" as a coherently organized and reasonably distinctive group of characteristics? Are there theoretical and empirical justifications for believing that the varied features of personality display a configurational unity and expressive consistency over time? Will the careful study of individuals reveal congruency among attributes such as overt behavior, intrapsychic functioning, and biophysical disposition? Is this coherence and stability of psychological functioning a valid phenomenon, that is, not merely imposed upon observed data by virtue of clinical expectation or theoretical bias?

There are reasons to believe that the answer to each of the preceding questions is yes. Stated briefly and simply, the observations of covariant patterns of signs, symptoms, and traits may be traced to the fact that people possess relatively enduring biophysical dispositions which give a consistent coloration to their experience, and that the range of experiences to which people are exposed throughout their lives is both limited and repetitive (Millon, 1969, 1981). Given the limiting and shaping character of these biogenic and psychogenic factors, it should not be surprising that individuals develop clusters of prepotent and deeply ingrained behaviors, cognitions, and affects that clearly distinguish them from others of dissimilar backgrounds. Moreover, once a number of the components of a particular clinical pattern are identified, knowledgeable observers are able to trace the presence of other, unobserved but frequently correlated features comprising that pattern.

If we accept the assumption that most people do display a pattern of internally consistent characteristics, we are led next to the question of whether groups of patients evidence commonality in the patterns they display. The notion of clinical categories rests on the assumption that there are a limited number of such shared covariances, for example, regular groups of diagnostic signs and symptoms which can confidently be used to distinguish certain classes of patients. (It should be noted that because patients can profitably be classified into categories does not negate the fact that patients, so classified, display considerable differences as well, differences we routinely observe with medical diseases.)

Another question that must be addressed concerning the nature of clinical categories may be phrased best as follows: Why does the possession of characteristic A increase the probability, appreciably beyond chance, of also possessing characteristics B, C, and so on? Less abstractly, why do particular behaviors, attitudes, mechanisms, and so on, covary in repetitive and recognizable ways rather than exhibit themselves in a more or less haphazard fashion? And, even more concretely, why do each of the following: behavioral defensiveness, interpersonal provocativeness, cognitive suspicion, affective irascibility, and excessive use of the projection mechanism, co-occur in the same individual, rather than be uncorrelated and randomly distributed among different individuals?

The "answers" are, first, that temperament and early experience simultaneously effect the development and nature of several emerging psychological structures and functions; that is, a wide range of behaviors, attitudes, affects, and mechanisms can be traced to the same origins, leading thereby to their frequently observed covariance. Second, once an individual possesses these initial characteristics, they set in motion a series of derivative life experiences that shape the acquisition of new psychological attributes causally related to the characteristics that preceded them in the sequential chain. Common origins and successive linkages increase the probability that certain psychological characteristics will frequently be found to pair with specific others, resulting thereby in repetitively observed symptom clusters, or what we term "clinical syndromes." Illustrations of these reciprocal covariances and serially unfolding concatenations among longitudinal influences (e.g., etiology) and concurrent attributes (e.g., signs, traits) may be found in Millon (1969, 1981).

Although grievances itemizing the inadequacies of both our current and historic systems of psychopathology have been voiced for years, as are suggestions that endeavors to refine these efforts are fussy and misdirected, if not futile and senseless pretensions that should be abandoned, the presence of categorical systems is both unavoidable—owing to man's linguistic and attribution habits—as well as inevitable—owing to our need to differentiate and to record, at the very least, the most obvious of dissimilarities among the psychologically impaired. Given the fact that one or another set of categories is inevitable, or as Kaplan (1964, p. 279) once phrased it, "it is impossible to wear clothing of no style at all," it would appear both sensible and fitting that we know the explicit basis upon which such distinctions are to be made, rather than have them occur helter-skelter in nonpublic and nonverifiable ways. Further, if psychopathology is to evolve into a true science, its diverse phenomena must be subject to formal identification, differentiation, and quantification procedures. Acts such as diagnosis and assessment presuppose the existence of discernable phenomena that can be recognized and measured. Logic necessitates, therefore, that psychopathologic states and processes be distinguished from one another, being thereby categorizable in some degree *before* they can be subjected to identification and quantification.

The number of categories that can be distinguished in a classification schema will depend in part on the incisiveness with which diagnosticians make their clinical observations and the creative inferences they draw from them. As has been discussed in earlier pages, classification data may legitimately be derived both from concrete observations and abstract inferences.

This chapter will provide a reasonably balanced overview of the alternate and rival methods of psychopathologic classification, but it is the author's bias that "natural" and scientific classifications are best derived from the systematic principles of a theoretical schema (Hempel, 1965). As is well known (Menninger, 1962; Stengel, 1959; Zilboorg & Henry, 1941), classifications have been proposed in psychiatry since time immemorial. Why is it that only a small number of schemas in but a few fields of science endure and prove informative, whereas others are patently useless or fail to withstand the test of time?

In the early stages of knowledge, the categories of a classification rely invariably on observed similarities among phenomena (Tversky, 1977). As knowledge advances, overt similarities are discovered to be an insufficient, if not false basis for cohering categories and imbuing them with scientific meaning (Smith & Medin, 1981). As Hempel (1965) and Quine (1977) have pointed out, it is theory that provides the glue that holds a classification together and gives it both its scientific and its clinical relevance. In his discussion of classificatory concepts, Hempel wrote (1965) that

> the development of a scientific discipline may often be said to proceed from an initial "natural history" stage ... to subsequent more and more "theoretical" stages.... The vocabulary required in the early stages of this development will be largely observational.... The shift toward theoretical systematization is marked by the introduction of new, "theoretical" terms ... more or less removed from the level of directly observable things and events....
>
> These terms have a distinct meaning and function only in the context of a corresponding theory. (pp. 139–140)

Quine makes a parallel case for the use of theories in determining category membership. Noting the usual progression from what he terms an innate, similarity-based conception of classification to a theoretically oriented one, he wrote (1977) that

one's sense of similarity or one's system of kinds develops and changes ... as
one matures. ... And at length standards of similarity set in which are geared
to theoretical science. This development is ... away from the immediate, subjective, animal sense of similarity to the remoter objectivity of a similarity
determined by scientific hypotheses ... and constructs. Things are similar in
the later or theoretical sense to the degree that they are ... revealed by science.
(p. 171)

More will be said in later pages concerning the view that scientific
classifications must *ultimately* be based on theoretically anchored constructs (Wright & Murphy, 1984).

No issue in psychopathology has raised deeper social or thornier
epistemological questions than those related to classification, diagnosis,
and labeling. The present chapter will address a wide range of classificatory questions, but it cannot undertake a thorough examination of
several of the more problematic philosophical and moral issues involved
in categorical labeling. Further, no matter how noble and compelling a
goal it may be, there is no hope that a universal classification system can
be achieved; different purposes (e.g., diagnostic, administrative, statistical) call for different solutions. There is a complex network of purposes
and a correspondingly varied set of contexts and methods, both pragmatic
and theoretical, which will bear on the efficacy and utility of a classification schema. It is hoped that the remainder of this chapter will guide the
reader to recognize more clearly the delicate balance required among
these complexities and alternatives.

TERMINOLOGY

Despite the long history of classification in psychiatry (Menninger,
1962; Stengel, 1959), formal methods of differentiating and denoting psychopathological phenomena are of only recent origin. Moreover, the
scientific study of classification itself, be it of biological species or of mental disorders, is a late, twentieth century development. As a consequence,
the terminology of important aspects of this field may not be familiar to
the reader. Owing also to its recency, the meaning of several key concepts
remains somewhat unclear, resulting in inconsistent usage and diverse
connotations. To reduce these ambiguities and enable the reader to
become increasingly familiar with both the logic and rationale of this
emerging area of study, it may be useful to record the more or less conventional meanings of several frequently employed terms, as well as to refine
distinctions and to introduce new variants of old designations.

First, *classification* itself may be broadly defined as a procedure for
constructing groups or forming categories, as well as for assigning *entities*

(disorders, persons) to these categories on the basis for their shared attributes or relationships. The product of this procedure consists of a nonarbitrary set of categories that are called a *classification system*. The act of assigning previously unallocated entities to their "correct" categories is termed *identification;* in clinical contexts, where entities comprise patterns of clinical attributes, or the patients who possess them, identification is referred to as *diagnosis*.

The term *taxonomy* will be applied to scientific classification systems; it refers to the sorting and arranging of entities of scientific or clinical interest into "natural" categories on the basis of key features they share, or concepts they illustrate in common. The term is employed also to represent the metatheory and scientific study of the classification process itself (Simpson, 1961); in this context, it encompasses the logic, principles, and methods of constructing categorical systems, as well as the procedures and rules by which identifications are made. The adjective *taxonomic* is used to refer to matters which pertain specifically to taxonomies. In clinical realms, the word *nosology* relates to a taxonomy of pathological phenomena (e.g., diseases, disorders); *nomenclature* pertains to the names or labels used to designate the categories of a taxonomy, be it nosological or otherwise.

The major categories of taxonomic (or nosologic) systems are called *taxa* (singular: taxon); they may be differentiated in a number of different ways. What are labeled here as *manifest* taxa involve categories that are based on observable or phenotypic commonalities (e.g., overt behaviors). *Latent* taxa will pertain to categories formed on the basis of abstract mathematical derivations or the propositional deductions of a theory, each of which ostensibly represents the presence of genotypic commonalities (e.g., etiologic origins or intrapsychic similarities). In psychopathology, the principal subject domains of taxa may be differentiated into three sets. *Syndromal* taxa pertain to patterns of clinical signs and symptoms (diseases or disorders) that represent but a partial segment, albeit an important one, of a person's total psychological makeup. The term *personological* taxa will be employed to represent a complex of clinically relevant traits (personality disorders) which have an individual's overall psychological makeup as their focus. Of more recent origin are *situational* taxa, categories that seek to encompass relevant sources of environmental influence (psychosocial stressors). The adjective *taxonic* refers to matters that pertain to taxa. Taxa may comprise elements of broader or lesser scope and abstraction. In a stepwise and ever-widening hierarchy of taxonic tiers there may be broadly encompassing categories that subsume taxa of lesser range, for example, the overarching taxon "personality disorders" is a category of higher rank that embraces and in-

corporates more particular personality types such as borderline and narcissistic, each of which is a taxon in its own right.

There are several overlapping concepts which relate to the composition of nosologic taxa, notably *clinical attributes, defining features,* and
diagnostic criteria. The first represents a broad class of clinically relevant
characteristics of either current psychological functioning (signs, symptoms, traits) or longitudinal relevance (etiology, course, prognosis, treatment response). Each attribute may be differentiated into specific subclasses to represent distinctive psychological properties of clinical import
(e.g., separating traits into those of interpersonal conduct, cognitive style,
and expressive mood). Refining matters further, several variants of each
subclass of clinical attributes may be specified in order to differentiate
and distinguish among a group of comparable nosologic taxa. For example, the trait subclass of "interpersonal conduct" may usefully be subdivided into a series of specific indicators which will not only identify, but
typify and discriminate each personality disorder from the others. These
distinctive and exemplifying qualities are termed a taxon's *defining
features.* To illustrate: Antisocial personalities may be characterized by the
defining feature of "irresponsible" interpersonal conduct; dependents
may be noted by their "submissive" conduct; compulsives may typically
be "respectful" interpersonally; narcissists may be notably "exploitive,"
and so on. A particular set of to-be-included and to-be-excluded defining
features, arranged in accord with specific rules (e.g., monothetic, polythetic), is called the *diagnostic criteria* of the taxon.

The set of defining features which serve as the diagnostic criteria of
taxonic membership may be *extensional* or *intensional.* Taxa based on extensional definitions require that *all* of the possible features of which a
specific taxon is comprised be known prior to the construction of that
taxon, an unattainable goal in fields such as psychopathology. By contrast, intensional definitions comprise rules concerning *how many* and
which defining features must be present to make a diagnosis. Rules may be
either *monothetic* or *polythetic.* In the former case, producing what is
generally referred to as "classical" taxonomies (Cantor & Mischel, 1979;
Rosch, 1978), all of the defining features that comprise a taxon must be in
evidence for a diagnosis to take place, resulting in entirely homogeneous
taxa. Polythetic rules characterize what are known as "prototypal" taxonomies, and require that only a subset of possible diagnostic features be
exhibited; being more open than classical taxa, they permit heterogeneity
through membership diversity. Monothetic rules are fixed and invariant,
whereas polythetic rules may be either inflexible or flexible; in the latter
case, changing combinations of defining features may suffice in different
circumstances to comprise a taxon's diagnostic criteria.

PHILOSOPHICAL CONSIDERATIONS

As noted in previous paragraphs, the metatheoretical logic and scientific study of classification is of recent origin, given its most important impetus in several major works, notably those by Simpson (1961), and by Sokal and Sneath (1963). Both volumes were oriented to the application of quantitative methods in biological taxonomies, setting forth explicit principles and formal procedures to achieve scientific goals such as interjudge reliability and external validity. Of no lesser importance was a seminal paper by Hempel (1961) addressed specifically to psychopathologists; with unerring logic, it served not only to raise conceptual considerations involved in developing productive taxonomies, but to alert clinicians to the key role that should be played by theoretical clarity and synthesis. Prior to these splendid and influential contributions, the history of psychopathologic classification reflected belief systems based on impressionistic clinical similarities; most were not grounded in quantifiable data, employed unrepresentative patient populations, and were devoid of a cohering or systematizing theory.

Psychopathology as a science is an outgrowth of both psychology and medicine. As such, efforts to construct a taxonomy must contend with the goals, assumptions, concepts, and complications inherent in both disciplines (e.g., context moderators, intensity variability, definitional ambiguities, overlapping symptomatologies, criterion unreliabilities, multidimensional attributes, population heterogeneities, feedback interactions, instrument deficits, ethical constraints, to name but a few).

The state of contemporary psychopathologic nosology and diagnosis resembles that of medicine a century ago. Concepts remain overwhelmingly descriptive; to illustrate: The recent DSM-III was not only formulated to be atheoretical, but addressed itself exclusively to observable clinical phenomena. It is not that inferences and theoretical deductions have failed in the past to provide useful knowledge, but that important segments of the mental health profession have not been convinced of their scientific utility, at least not sufficiently so as to employ this knowledge as a basis for a nosology. On the other hand, despite the fact that much observation and experimentation has been done, their products appear either far from satisfactory or lack an adequate consensus as to their significance. Thus, we remain unsure today whether to conceive "depression" to be a taxon (category) or an attribute (symptom), whether to conceive it as a dimension or as a set of discrete types, whether to approach it as a neuroendocrinological disease or as an existential problem of life. Although debates about these issues frequently degenerate into semantic arguments and theoretic hairsplitting, it would be naive to assume that metaphysical verbiage and philosophical word quibbling was all that was involved. Nevertheless, the language we use, and the assumptions and orientations it reflects, are very much a part of our "scientific" disagreements.

In the following brief sketch of a number of philosophical and quasiphilosophical issues, we hope to wet the reader's appetite, at least enough to illustrate one point, namely that philosophical concepts and modes of analysis should be considered in formulating a psychopathologic taxonomy. Arguably, philosophical analysis will not in itself reveal clear resolutions to all nosological quandaries. More likely will be its role in "unsettling" prevailing habits, forcing us thereby to progress, if for no other reason than having had our cherished beliefs and assumptions challenged. Let us begin this philosophical excursion with some relatively simple and homespun considerations.

Pragmatic Matters

The search for an ideal taxonomy rests on the assumption of an intrinsic order in the universe. It would be lovely if a single, unique, and well-defined nosology were found to be isomorphic with the "natural" world. Unfortunately, there may be segments of a subject domain that can never be adequately differentiated. More problematic, at least in a clinical science such as psychopathology, is the multitude of competing and legitimate purposes to which a taxonomy can be put, purposes which cannot be ranked *a priori* as to their intrinsic value. At the very outset, then, psychiatric nosologies must face the task of meeting diverse, if not rival goals. Taxonomic efficacy must be judged, therefore, by the success with which they fulfill the varied and competing ends for which they may have been designed.

What are some of the more noteworthy goals of a psychopathologic nosology?

Perhaps the most universally agreed upon purpose of classification in a clinical science is that of *communication reliability,* the presence of descriptive and identifying terms that can consistently be employed to distinguish patients and to facilitate exchanges of information with optimal clarity. Unfortunately, many descriptive and categorical terms have been misbegotten (dementia praecox), connoting meanings that are long abandoned (hebephrenia), or are reified by the naive (id, ego); this is but one price paid for the illusion of facile clinical discourse (Meehl, 1973).

Of lesser import to clinicians and academics, but not to those who must record or manage their doings, are *statistical* and *administrative* nosologies. For the most part these depend on schemas that permit precise notations of prevalence and incidence data. Here epidemiologists may seek to quantify trends and actuarial risks that will enable them to identify causes and plan interventions. Panzetta noted additional purposes in the realm of economics and public policy (1974):

> Nosology becomes the language which the legislator and the adminis-trator must use in their discharge of policy and management responsibilities.
> What will insurance cover? Who is diagnosed, according to what criteria, and why? What was the mandate to those in the community mental health movement? Who shall be hospitalized against his will? There are an endless number of similar questions which flow from consideration of public policy and management. (p.160)

Optimizing the clinical utility of a nosology is its role in *intervention decisions.* Primitive though our therapeutic science may be, there are grow-ing signs that taxonomic systems may be utilized as a basis for treatment selection (Frances, Clarkin, & Perry, 1985; Klein, Gittelman, Quitkin, & Rifkin, 1980). Another related but perhaps more attainable goal is that of prognosis, specifying the likely response to treatment, as well as the typical course or progression of a disorder.

A fourth major goal of classification, one common to all branches of science, is that of *advancing knowledge.* As Sokal has put it (1974):

> Classifications that describe relationships among objects in nature should generate hypotheses. In fact the principal scientific justification for establish-ing classifications is that they are heuristic (in the traditional meaning of this term as "stimulating interest as a means of furthering investigation") and that they lead to the stating of a hypothesis which can be tested. A classification raises the question of how the perceived order has arisen. (p. 117)

A systematic nosology can provide a useful framework for organizing and retrieving research data. Similarly, to the extent that classificatory concepts are extensions of theory, they can be employed to guide hy-pothesis-oriented investigations, as well as to furnish empirical evidence relevant to its validation.

As evident from the foregoing, it will be difficult indeed to develop a single taxonomy that will meet each of the diverse goals and purposes to which a classification can be put.

Conceptual Issues

What exactly is a clinical attribute, that is, what is it that we wish to in-clude in a taxon and what grounds shall we employ to decide that it exists? To pose this question is not to engage in mere sophistry. For example, a

serious issue demanding the attention of responsible philosophers, physicians, and psychologists (Medin, Altom, Edelson, & Freko, 1982; Smith
& Medin, 1981; Toulmin, 1977) is the very nature of the construct "disease
entity". Noting the complexities inherent in conceiving so universal a concept as disease, Mischel wrote (1977):

> To have a concept of a physical disease is . . . to have a theory about a complex
> course of events, a theory which accounts for the interrelations between
> etiological events; pathogenic mechanisms; morphological, chemical, and
> functional changes, symptoms, and signs and which allows a prognosis of the
> probable outcome of this course of events as well as an understanding of what
> might influence that outcome. (p. 199)

Discussing other ambiguities of the term, Kendell (1975) noted
that

> contemporary writers still make frequent reference to "disease en-
> tities" . . . almost invariably without defining their meaning. Like "disease" it-
> self, "entity" has become one of those dangerous terms which is in general use
> without ever being defined, those who use it fondly assuming that they and
> everyone else knows its meaning. (p. 65)

Feinstein (1977) illustrated the circular nature of many of our definitions in the following:

> The complex situation we have been contemplating can be greatly simplified if
> only we are allowed a bit of circular reasoning. At the root of the difficulty is the
> problem of deciding what is a diagnosis. We can dispose of that difficulty by
> defining a diagnosis as the name for a disease. We are now left with defining
> disease, which we can call a state of abnormal health. Abnormal health is
> readily defined as a departure from normal health. And then, completing the
> circle, normal health can be defined as the absence of disease. (p. 189)

As Feinstein goes on to note, "disease" is an abstract and multifaceted
concept that remains so even if we prefer to represent it with other terms
such as ailment, sickness, illness, or disorder.

Finally, Meehl, in bringing his incisive analytic skills to the taxonic
concept, wrote (1972):

> In analyzing the problem of a *taxonomic entity* (I am not myself the least bit in-
> terested in the label "disease," or . . . whether mental disorder is an "illness"),
> there are . . . questions to be explored if this is to be an intellectually respon-
> sible enterprise rather than the burblings of a cliche-artist.
> Here we (must) struggle with metatheoretical problems concerning contextual
> and "implicit" definition, reduction-sentences, counterfactuals, open con-
> cepts . . . and the like. (pp. 20–21)

Those who have more than a tangential interest in the nature of psychopathologic classification cannot help but be apprehensive over the

profound problems that arise in merely defining its constituents, no less in their specification, criteria, and measurement.

The following paragraphs will survey the extent to which concepts such as "taxa" and "attributes" have tangible empirical referents. The basic issue at hand is whether these concepts are anchored to observable or to inferred phenomena.

Constituents of a nosological classification are represented by a set of terms or labels, that is, a language by which members of a clinical group communicate about a subject. These terms may be seen as serving two functions. First, they possess a value in that they facilitate the manipulation of ideas. Clinical or theoretical concepts are systematically (if implicitly) linked; it is through their interplay that meaningful clinical ideas are formulated and deductive scientific statements are proposed. Second, most concepts possess an empirical significance; that is, they are linked in some way to the observable world. Although some may represent processes or events which are not apparent, they can be defined by or anchored with reference to the explicit and tangible. It is this translatability into the empirical domain that allows the taxonomist to test his schema in the world of "clinical reality "

Ideally, all concepts comprising a nosology should be empirically anchored, that is, correspond to clinical properties in the observable world; this would minimize confusion regarding the attributes of which a taxon is composed. Further, nosologic labels should be more precise than the words of ordinary language; although everyday language has relevance to significant real world events, it gives rise to ambiguity and confusion because of the varied uses to which conventional words are often put. Taxonic concepts should be defined as "precisely" as possible in order to assure that their meaning is clear and specific.

Empirical precision can be achieved only if every defining feature that distinguishes a taxon is anchored to a single observable phenomenon; that is, a different datum would be used for every difference that can be observed in the clinical world. This goal is simply not feasible, nor is it desirable for reasons which will become apparent shortly. Classificatory terms do differ, however, in the extent to which they achieve empirical precision. The following discussion identifies points along a gradation from conceptual specificity to conceptual openness; it may aid the reader to recognize certain features that distinguish among both attributes and taxa.

Certain concepts are defined literally by procedures which measure observable events, possessing no meaning other than the results obtained in this manner. They are akin to what Bridgman (1927) termed *operational definitions.* The meaning of an operationally defined concept is synonymous with how we measure it, not with what we say about it. To illustrate: The concept "anxiety" would involve nothing more than the set of operations by which it is measured; there would be a different concept for anxiety when measured by the score on an anxiety inventory than determined by clinician ratings. The advantage of operational definitions is obvious; taxa and the attributes of which they are composed are unambiguous, and diagnostic identifications associated with these taxons would be translatable directly into the clinical attributes they represent.

Useful as operational definitions may be, they present several problems. Diagnostic terms should be generalizable; that is, they should enable the clinician to include a variety of measures and observations with a taxon. Operational definitions are restrictive; they preclude extensions to new situations that are even slightly different from the original defining condition. Certainly, one of the primary goals of a classification is to integrate diverse observations with a minimum number of terms; a strict operational approach would flood us with an infinite number of attributes and taxa, cluttering thinking with essentially irrelevant distinctions. The major value of operational definitions is cautionary; it alerts the taxonomist to be mindful of the importance of precision and empirical relevance.

Intrapsychic and organismic processes are nebulous and concealed, hidden from the observable world and, hence, only to be inferred. These unobservable mediating structures or processes are not merely useful but necessary elements in constructing a psychopathologic nosology. Owing to their abstract and hypothetical character, these indeterminate and intervening constructs are known as *open concepts* (Pap, 1953). Some are defined by, and largely reducible to, a diverse set of empirical events. For example, the concept *projection* may be determined by observing an individual ascribe his own traits to others, by the presence of certain scores on a psychological test, by a history of litigious actions, and so on. Although the term projection implies a concealed intrapsychic process within the individual that cannot itself be observed, its existence is inferred from a variety of observables.

Many open, fully speculative concepts are formulated without definitive reference to explicit observables. Their failure to be anchored to observable events has led some to question their suitability in scientific contexts. No doubt, clarity gets muddled, and deductions may often be tautological when a diagnosis is "explained" in terms of a series of such constructs. For example, statements such as "in the borderline the mechanisms of the ego disintegrate when libidinous energies overwhelm superego introjections" are, at best, puzzling. Postulating connections between one set of open concepts and another may lead to facile but often confusing diagnostic statements, as any periodic reader of contemporary psychoanalytic literature can attest. Such use results in imprecise formulations that are difficult to decipher because we cannot specify observables by which they can be anchored or evaluated.

Open concepts usually take their meaning with reference to a theoretical network of variables and constructs within which they are embedded. The surplus meaning they derive thereby accounts both for their weaknesses and strengths in constructing and evaluating a taxonomy.

A classification is a human artifact; not every one of its terms need be linked to observable events, especially if its purpose is to extend the generalizability of knowledge (Dougherty, 1978). Unrealistic standards of empirical anchorage, particularly in the early stages of taxonomic construction, may discourage the kind of imaginative speculation necessary to decipher and to integrate elusive phenomena. Vague and risky as open concepts may be, they are often among the most fertile tools available in the development of a productive classification.

Epistemological Perspectives

The polar distinction described in the previous section between operational definitions, at the one end, and open concepts, at the other, represents in part a broader epistemological dichotomy that exists between those who prefer to employ data derived from empirical-practical contexts versus those who prefer to draw their ideas from more causal-theoretical sources. This distinction was first drawn by Aristotle when he sought to contrast the understanding of disease with reference to knowledge of principles—which ostensibly deals with all instances of a disease, however diverse—versus direct empiric knowledge—which deals presumably only with specific and individual instances. To Aristotle, knowledge based on direct, empirical experience alone represented a more primitive type of knowledge than that informed by a conceptual theory which could, through the application of principles, explain not only why a particular disease occurs, but illuminate commonalities among seemingly diverse ailments. This same theme was raised in the writings of the distinguished 19th century neurologist, Hughlings Jackson. For example, Jackson drew a distinction between two kinds of disease classifications, one "scientific," which he termed theoretical, designed to advance the state of knowledge, the other "empirical," which he termed clinical, and was organized for routine or daily practice. Both were seen as necessary, but Jackson asserted that with each elucidation of a contemporary disease there would be an accretion of theory, resulting in the ultimate supplanting of "mere" clinical knowledge.

A more recent and parallel distinction has been drawn between "manifest" and "scientific" images in diagnostic practice (Sellars, 1963). For example, direct encounters between a diagnostician and a patient initially evoke a manifest image; that is, a subjective and sensory impression of their shared experiences in that particular context. Events of this nature are immediate and phenomenological. By contrast, scientific images are a product of a screening process in which events are modified by filters and mental constructs that transform the immediacy of "natural" experience in terms of theory-derived concepts and pre-established objective evidence. Differing from the experiential quality of the manifest world, scientific images may seem remote in that they reflect implicit theoretical formulations, gaining their evidential support from esoteric and arcane sources.

The contrast between manifest and scientific images reflects in part one of philosophy's more perennial problems; namely, the rivalry between opposing views regarding the primary source of knowledge (i.e., the empiricist vs. rationalist epistemologies). Rationalism argues not only that knowledge consists of principles and universals, but that knowledge is what distinguishes the mind from the senses, the latter being capable of apprehending only experiential particulars. In rebuttal, empiricists contend that knowledge must be derived from direct sensory experience first, and only then generalized to broader principles. Rationalists assert in response that it is the logic of reasoning that distinguishes the human from lower species.

Medicine has been rent throughout its history by this empiricist-rationalist dichotomy. Debates between Aristotelian and Galenic rationalist exponents, on the one hand, and Hippocratic and Paracelsian empiricists, on the other, led to repeated, if not consistent, disagreement as to how diseases should be characterized and understood. This very issue continues to face us as we seek to conceptualize and organize psychopathology today. Shall we follow the policy guiding the construction of the DSM-III, an empiricist-clinical approach, or should we assume an orientation more consonant with a rationalist-theoretical formulation? In a later section, we will review contemporary methods of taxonomic construction that reflect these polar differences.

SUBSTANTIVE CHOICES

What raw data from the stream of ongoing clinical events and processes should we select to serve as the basic units of taxa? Should we include only observables, or will inferred processes be permitted? Should they be comprised of behaviors only, or will self-reports, past history, or physiological signs be admissable? What of developmental history, socio-economic or situational factors? Is everything to be grist for the taxonic mill? Should the attributes of diagnostically comparable syndromes be uniform, that is, consist of the same class of data, or will biological indices be included only in some, cognitive processes in others, and so on?

Clinical Attributes

Psychopathology can be studied from many vantage points; it can be observed and conceptualized in legitimately different ways by behaviorists, phenomenologists, psychodynamicists, and biochemists. No point of observation or conceptualization is sufficient to encompass all of the complex and multidimensional features of psychopathology. Clinical processes and events may be described in terms of conditioned habits, reaction formations, cognitive expectancies, or neurochemical dysfunctions. These content domains cannot be arranged in a hierarchy, with one level viewed as reducible to another. Nor can they be compared in terms of some "objective truth value." Alternative substantive levels merely are different; they make possible the observation and conceptualization of different clinical attributes and may lead, therefore, to different taxa. The point to be made is that taxa may be differentially composed in accord with the kinds of clinical data (e.g., etiology, symptoms, treatment response) they comprise as their basic constituents. Choices may be pragmatic, and questions of comparative utility cannot be determined *a priori*. However, irrelevant controversies and needless confusions will be avoided if the class of attributes from which taxa are composed has been specified clearly. When done properly, clinicians and researchers can determine whether two taxonomies are comparable, whether the same syndromic label refers to different clinical phenomena, whether different taxa encompass the same attributes, and so on. As Panzetta stated (1974):

> As one begins to consider the variety of starting-off points then we quickly appreciate that the first step in the nosologic process is inherently arbitrary. I would insist that we begin by acknowledging that the arbitrary focus is not, per se, a deficiency but rather a reality which flows naturally from the tremendous complexity of human behavior. It is useless to try to develop the "correct" initial focus. There is no correct focus, only several alternatives. (p. 155)

Sneath and Sokal (1973) record the endless array of attributes in every subject which could be potentially useful in forming a taxonomy. The task

is that of identifying which will be most relevant and optimally productive. The history of psychopathology provides a number of guidelines
which may be fruitful in our taxonomies. The following sections draw a
well-established and important distinction, that between *longitudinal* and
concurrent attributes, the former representing features discerned by track-
ing the progression of various clinical phenomena across time and cir-
cumstance, the latter addressing diverse ways in which these phenomena
manifest themselves contemporaneously and simultaneously across a
number of expressive dimensions.

Longitudinal Attributes

Can we identify the causal or formative roots of distinctive types of
psychopathology, and can we sort out the sequence of features they exhibit prior to reaching their clinical state? Further, can we trace their
postclinical progression or their characteristic response to specifiable interventions? These questions relate to matters of origin, course, and prognosis, the major time-related taxonic attributes.

Etiology

Employing data concerning causal factors as clinical attributes
would be extremely appealing, were such knowledge only available. Unfortunately, our etiologic data base is scanty and unreliable. Moreover, it
is likely to remain so owing to the obscure, complex, and interactive nature of influences that shape psychopathologic phenomena. In the main,
etiologic attributes are conjectures that rest on tenuous empirical grounds;
most reflect divergent "schools of thought" positing their favorite hypotheses. These speculative notions are best construed as questions that
deserve empirical testing on the basis of taxa formed by less elusive
data.

Among the few etiologic schemas relevant to taxonomic goals is
Zubin's (1968) differentiation of six categories: social-cultural (ecologi-
cal), developmental, learning, genetic, internal environment, and neurophysiological. Systematic and orderly though this model may be, it does
not fully address issues associated with alternate levels of analysis, nor
does it seek to trace the intricate and varied causal chains that unfold ultimately into a clinical state. Commenting on the task of analyzing this interactive and multideterminant process, Panzetta wrote (1974):

> The term etiology, which once suggested isolated variables, is now generally
> thought of in much more comprehensive terms. We now almost routinely think

about "predisposing" factors, "precipitating" factors and "sustaining" factors. And the "placement" of all of these factors may occur at any of the multiple levels of organization from the infracellular to sociocultural.

Whereas depression may have determinant factors operating at a neurochemical level (decreased normetanephrine), it may also have determinant factors operating at the psychological level (inhibition of anger), and at the psychosocial level (loss of an important other), and at the sociocultural level (social expectation of continuing responsibility despite loss of the important other). Which level is more determining of a specific depressed person may not be readily apparent but that all the levels play some part is an axiomatic position. (p. 158)

And beyond the issue of identifying which of several "levels" of an interactive causal system should be selected as etiological attributes, there are questions of a more philosophical and methodological nature concerning what exactly is meant by etiology and in what precise way it may be gauged. Meehl (1972) addressed these issues succinctly:

A metatheoretical taxonomy of causal factors and a metataxonomy of causal relations (such as "necessary but not sufficient condition," "interaction effects," "threshold effects," and the like) are badly needed. In medicine, we recognize several broad etiologic classes, such as deficiency diseases, autoimmunity diseases, disease due to microorganisms, hereditary-degenerative diseases, developmental anomalies, diseases due to trauma.... The concept "specific etiology"... appears to have half a dozen distinguishable and equally defensible meanings (e.g., *sine qua non,* critical threshold, uniformly most powerful factor) that might be useful under various circumstances. (p. 22)

The long and gallant yearning among taxonomists for a neat package of etiologic attributes simply cannot be reconciled with the complex philosophical-methodological issues and difficult-to-disentangle networks of both subtle and random influences that shape our mental disorders (Bandura, 1982). It also makes understandable the action of the DSM-III Task Force in setting etiological variables aside as clinical grist for its taxonic mills.

Course Prognosis

It is to Kraepelin that we give credit for contributing "disease course and prognosis" as factors distinguishing various classes of mental disorder. That the distinctions he drew proved tangential to the disorders he addressed, and that the principles he adduced were inconsistent with well-established tenets of medical logic, is now forgotten, especially in light of his astute clinical descriptions (Kraepelin, 1899). As Zilboorg and Henry have noted (1941):

(His) was a departure from a vital and sound principle of general medicine. One cannot say that because a disease ends in a certain definite way it is a certain definite disease. Kraepelin in himself was apparently unaware of this singular deviation from medical principles. (p. 456)

Nevertheless, there is no *a priori* reason to dismiss the potential contribution that could be made by characterizing the course of an otherwise definable disorder, both prior and subsequent to its manifest clinical state. As Strauss has written (1986):

> A disease is a manifestation of some kind of pathologic process. The nature of the process may be identified and understood by attending to its course and to the variables that influence it. In essence, the principle is that when exploring and trying to understand a mysterious object, one valid approach is to see the way the object responds to a variety of situations and events. If the object changes over time, studying its evolution provides further crucial information about its nature. (p. 258)

Matters of complexity and variability make this goal a difficult one. Course is not a unidimensional phenomenon that can be characterized readily either by salient or reliable features, such as its duration or episodicity (Strauss, Kokes, Carpenter, & Ritzler, 1978). Not only does the contour of "course" encompass a wide and diverse band of time-related dimensions, but it represents a mix of ongoing processes that unfold through an inextricable sequence of interactions. As Strauss (1986) has phrased it, "the course of a disorder might best be viewed as involving several open-linked systems of functioning" (p. 259). The task of unraveling and identifying the constituents of course and prognosis for taxonic purposes may be awesome, but Strauss and his associates (Strauss, Loevsky, Glazer, & Leaf, 1981) have undertaken the challenge in an as yet uncompleted project. Commenting on this work-in-process, Strauss reported (1986) that

> it appears that certain characteristics ('components') of the individual–environment interaction—structure, self-esteem, involvement, and social contact—can be identified . . . for purposes of understanding and ultimately for diagnosis. . . . The subjective experience and interpretations of meaning by the patient . . . can also be incorporated into this conceptual structure. (p. 260)

Encouraging as this report may be in pointing toward indices of clinical course and prognosis, it would appear that much work remains to be done before it achieves the methodological precision, surmounts the philosophical complications, and demonstrates the empirical predictability necessary to confirm or disconfirm Kraepelin's turn-of-the-century assumptions.

Treatment Responses

A useful distinction among future-oriented attributes may be made between the prognosis of a disorder and its response to treatment; the former follows naturally evolving pathogenic processes, whereas the latter is evoked by contrived (and ostensibly beneficial) interventions. Treatment effect is a measurable response to a planful mediation that may furnish sufficiently distinctive information to serve as a clinical datum of taxonic membership. To illustrate, an early paper by Stockings (1945) proposed that certain schizophrenics responded well to insulin coma treatment while others appeared to benefit more from electroconvulsive methods. Suggesting that this differential might signify a relevant distinction among schizophrenic disorders, Stockings proposed that insulin reactors be relabeled "dysglycotics" and electroconvulsive responders termed "dysoxics." Similarly, Overall and his colleagues (1966) demonstrated differential responses among depressives to various pharmacological agents; "anxious" depressives evidenced a favorable response to tranquilizers, "retarded" types gained best results with tricyclics, and "hostile" depressives displayed no better than a placebo response level to all medications.

Logic argues that the nature of a psychiatric disorder should be at least partially revealed by its response to treatment; the data available on this matter, however, provide little that goes beyond rather broad generalizations. This contrasts with the situation in medicine at large, in which a variety of interventions are specific to particular disorders. Also notable in medicine are a variety of "challenge" or "stressor" tasks that serve to identify patient vulnerabilities (e.g., introducing allergens to uncover susceptibilities or to elicit reaction sensitivities). Considerations of ethics and human sensibilities preclude adopting parallel strategies in psychiatry. But even where intent and action are clearly beneficial, as in psychological treatment interventions, the problems encountered in discerning and differentiating optimal clinical attributes are many, for example, the inevitability of spontaneous remissions and unanticipated life events. Even if we could successfully partial out the effects of these "confounding" events, could we identify *the* ingredients that account for beneficial reactions in a heterogeneous patient population? Further, what conclusions could be drawn about a medication whose efficacy is widespread, that is, demonstrable among disorders whose origins and expression are diverse (e.g., aspirin successfully reduces pain in fractures, muscle tensions, cancer, as will chemically different tranquilizers reduce anxiety generated as a consequence of characterological tensions and temporary financial reverses). Complicating matters at the moment is the fact that every school and technique of therapy claims high efficacy across a wide band of sundry diagnostic classes. Conclusion: treatment response, as etiology, course, and prognosis, may prove ultimately to be a useful taxonic attribute; for the present, however, reliable discriminative data are not in hand.

Concurrent Attributes

Inasmuch as longitudinal attributes are problematic, what remains to comprise psychodiagnostic taxa are coexistent attributes of a contemporaneous nature, notably "objective" *signs,* on the other hand, and subjectively reported *symptoms,* on the other. To these two traditional indicators of disorder should be added the essentially inferred attributes of personality *traits.* Information comprising these clinical features are derived from four conceptually and methodologically distinct data sources (Millon, 1982; Millon & Diesenhaus, 1972, namely, the *biophysical, intrapsychic, phenomenological,* and *behavioral.* Clinical signs are drawn almost exclusively from the biophysical and behavioral realm; symptoms originate essentially in reports of phenomenological experience; traits are deduced inferentially, largely from the three psychological domains, intrapsychic, phenomenological, and behavioral.

Signs

These comprise more or less objectively recorded changes in state or function that indicate both the presence and character of clinically relevant processes or events. Two classes of data comprise the main body of clinical signs: *biophysical markers* and *behavioral acts.*

As for the first set, biophysical markers, we find few anatomical, biochemical, and neurophysiological gauges among our standard diagnostic taxa, despite their tangible, objective, and quantitative nature (Millon & Diesenhaus, 1972). This failure is both surprising and disconcerting, given the vast number of psychopathologic studies over the years that have hypothesized and investigated potential biophysical markers obtained from a multitude of measures, such as those of urine or blood, sundry muscle appraisals, skin gauges, cardiac assessments, eye movements, metabolic indices, EEG rhythms, and so on.

That none of these biophysical measures have borne fruit as clinical attributes can be traced to a number of factors. Most do not lend themselves to clearly discriminable categories and, with few exceptions, normative distributions on relevant clinical populations are either unavailable or inconsistent. For many, reliability measures are lacking or indicate high levels of variability over time and across contexts. To complicate interpretive efforts, low intercorrelations exist among measures that ostensibly represent the same basic functions. Finally, the expense of technical equipment is so high, and the availability of needed expertise is often so scarce, as to make many of these procedures essentially out of reach for all but well-funded research investigators.

Turning to explicit *behavioral acts,* the second of the major objective indices, it has been the methodological goal of behavioral "purists" to avoid drawing inferences concering "internal" or "subjective" processes. Hence, they seek to employ techniques which ostensibly bypass explicit dependence on subjective "symptomatic" data. For pedagogic purposes, these "objective" methods may be separated into three subgroups: systematic observation, verbal behavior analyses, and performance measures.

The first, *systematic observation,* includes formal procedures that code and quantify behavior in an organized and standardized manner; among the more systematic of these techniques are various "behavior inventories" and "rating scales" which categorize a variety of potentially useful clinical attributes such as speech mannerisms and social interaction frequencies. The second group of methods, known as *verbal behavioral analyses,* overlooks the content and meaning of what is being communicated by the patient, and focuses intead on features such as grammatical structure and voice characteristics. Notable among these techniques are procedures for identifying and quantifying "paralinguistic phenomena" and recording "word quotients" such as adjective-to-verb ratios. The third set of methods, *performance measures,* comprises objectively tabulated scores based on the efficiency and character with which various well-designed and standardized tasks are executed; included here are scores obtained on assorted psychomotor or skill acquisition exercises.

Rather commonplace activities of potential diagnostic significance have recently come under systematic scrutiny and analysis. Of particular note is the work of Buss and Craik (1983, 1984) and of Livesley (1985a, 1986 a,b). Attempting to provide a descriptive (i.e., non-explanatory) basis for diagnostically relevant features, these investigators construct lists of familiar acts observed in the course of everyday life that may typify certain clinical characteristics. As Buss and Craik describe it (1987):

> The act frequency approach starts by identifying the act subsumed by each syndrome-relevant disposition. Dispositional constructs such as grandiose and exhibitionistic are treated as categories of acts occuring in everyday conduct. For example, "he bragged about his accomplishments" and "she undressed with the curtains opened" were nominated by an undergraduate panel as grandiose and exhibitionistic acts, respectively.... Because single acts rarely are invariantly diagnostic of dispositions or syndromes, act trends or multiple-act criteria become the units of analysis.
>
> Act trends and their dispositional designations are descriptive rather than explanatory. Stating that (a person) is exhibitionistic, for example, does not explain why he streaked nude through the football field, danced on table tops, hung his self-portrait in a public space, or posed for Playgirl magazine. Ex-

planatory accounts of act trends must be marshalled subsequently. (pp. 73–81)

Promising as the observation of behavior may be as a source for clinical attributes, numerous concerns have been registered regarding its utility, not the least of which is its unpredictability: that is, its high variability across situations and times (e.g., the recording of verbal behaviors fails to generate reliable normative data across diverse circumstances). This contrasts with data produced by well-constructed rating instruments. Most are reasonably reliable, succeed in discriminating among relevant patient groups, and possess adequate normative data for differential or comparative purposes. The strategy taken by Buss and Craik and by Livesley in developing lists of familiar, garden-variety activities (signs) that are prototypic of specific clinical taxa are not only promising, but may redeem the behavioral approach. Until these advances, behavioral methods had been long on neat clinical measures of a rather trivial character, having tangential or limited substantive significance in the realm of psychopathologic taxonomy.

Symptoms

In distinction to clinical signs, symptoms are subjective in nature, representing reports by patients of their conscious recollections and recorded experiences (e.g., moods, feelings, perceptions, memories, attitudes, and so on). Together with signs, clinical symptoms focus on phenomenological processes and events that relate directly to diagnostic matters. The psychopathologist has an advantage over the physicist or the biologist, for neither can ask the objects of their study to reflect on their experience, no less communicate it in articulate or meaningful ways. As Strauss framed it (1986):

> The subjective experience of the patient cannot be ignored in attempting to understand the course of disorder and processes of disease and recovery. Descriptive characteristics, such as symptoms ... are important in defining diagnostic categories and are relatively easy to assess reliably. ... To some extent, the field has been discouraged by previous claims and promises regarding the understanding of subjective experiences such as these. Although the claims were often overstated, and the assessment of these processes is complex, neither reason is adequate for avoiding a major attempt to develop creative ways for looking at the role of such subjective experiences in the course of psychopathology and their relevance to diagnosis. (p. 262)

The substantive content of phenomenological symptoms deal with the unseen "private world"; as such, its data are elusive and often unreliable, fraught with philosophical and methodological complexities. Despite these hazards, taxonomists cannot afford the luxury of bypassing them—symptoms lie at the very heart of all psychopathologic inquiries. The events they portray are "real," representing facets of experience far richer in scope and diversity than concrete observables.

Having been studied systematically since their heyday as the material for the "method of introspection" in the first two decades of this century, phenomenological events fell into disrepute following the rise of behaviorism in psychology, and empiricism in philosopy. Nevertheless, the formal study of subjective experience survived as a form of psychological investigation and psychiatric diagnosis "under various aliases," as Boring (1950) once put it. Despite repeated attacks concerning its reliability and unscientific status, the use of discursive symptomatic reports continued unabated, standing as the cornerstone in many quarters of diagnostic psychiatry. Here, the "mental status examination" continued as the essential component of psychiatric evaluations, routinely addressing symptomatic data such as disturbances of consciousness, perception, memory, and feeling, as well as appraising the content of thought and the presence of pathological preoccupations. It is in this realm that symptomatic terms such as distractible, clouded, illusions, apprehensive, despondent, guilt, shame, obsessions, and delusions gained their coinage.

A few words of review may be useful to summarize two formal methods, interview procedures and self-report inventories, that have been developed to systematically investigate this rich source of clinical attributes. Not all of the problems inherent in the subjective reporting of symptoms have been resolved by these methods, but they institute useful correctives to minimize problematic effects.

The first, *interview procedures,* consists of two major techniques, *prearranged interview schedules* and *postinterview content* analyses (Millon & Diesenhaus, 1972). In the former, a fixed list of questions is outlined to ensure that data relevant to a diagnostic assessment are obtained during the interview itself. By organizing the interviewer's attention in advance to a uniform set of topical attributes, the prospects for gathering comparable data from all patients is greatly enhanced. Postinterview content analysis methods code already transcribed verbal communications, focusing most commonly on the manifest or overt content of what has been said rather than its unconscious symbolic meanings. Depending on whether typewritten texts or audio or video transcriptions are used, different facets of the interview may be addressed.

Self-report inventories are a major psychological tool for assessing clinical attributes; most are geared to the appraisal of personality traits, but a number are designed to identify and quantify a variety of single-dimension symptomological characteristics (e.g., depression, anxiety).

What contributes to the utility of symptomatic data is their ease of evocation. Formal appraisal methods, such as interview schedules and self-report inventories, minimize potential sources of distortion. Nevertheless, both methods are subject to quandaries which can invalidate data (e.g., one cannot assume that subjects interpret questions posed to them in the same way, or that they possess sufficient self-knowledge to respond informatively, or that they may not be faking or dissembling).

Traits

Whereas signs represent objective biologic measures or behavioral acts, and symptoms refer to phenomenologically reported recollections and experiences, traits characterize inferred pscyhological habits and stable dispositions of broad generality and diverse expression. This well-established psychological construct has been employed in two ways: first, it encompasses and summarizes various characteristic habits, moods, and attitudes; and second, through inference, it identifies dispositions to act, feel, and think in certain ways. Traits can be conceived as being both more and less than signs and symptoms. Thus, several traits can coalesce to form the expression of a single behavioral sign. On the other hand, several different specific symptoms may be the upshot of a single trait. Moreover, each trait may express itself in diverse signs and symptoms. Evidently, there is no one-to-one correspondence between traits and signs or symptoms.

Traits are inferred rather than observed, generalized rather than specific, and dispositional rather than consequential. They are characterized as enduring and pervasive. However, only a few traits of an individual display this durability and pervasiveness; that is, only a few prove to be resistant to the influences of changing times and circumstances. Other forms of behavior, attitude, and emotion are more transient and malleable. It should be noted that traits exhibiting consistency and stability in one person may not be the same as those doing so in others. The qualities of consistency and stability are most prominent among characteristics that are central to maintaining a person's overall psychological balance and style of functioning. To illustrate: The "interpersonal conduct" trait of significance for some patients is that of being agreeable, never differing or having conflict; for another, it may be interpersonally important to keep one's distance from others so as to avoid rejection or being humiliated; for a third, the influential interpersonal trait may be that of asserting one's will and dominating others.

Each person possesses a small and distinct group of primary traits that persist over time and exhibit a high degree of consistency across situations. These enduring (stable) and pervasive (consistent) traits are the clinical attributes we search for when we consider diagnosing a "personality disorder" taxon.

The sources employed to identify and quantify clinical traits are highly diverse, from methods designed to uncover intrapsychic processes, such as free association, dreams, hypnosis, and projective techniques, to a variety of phenomenological methods such as structured interviews and self-report inventories, as well as to behavioral data obtained via methods of observation and rating, be they systematic or otherwise.

It is no understatement to say that the rich vein of clinical attributes uncovered by intrapsychic methods has been a boon to clinical theory, but a source of perplexity and despair to taxonomists. More than any other data domain, intrapsychic methods produce information that is fraught with complexities and obscurities that can bewilder the most sophisticated of classifiers. Part of the difficulty, of course, stems from the fact that the identification of hidden traits is highly inferential. Because the dispositional structure and functions comprising traits can be only partially observed, as well as taking different manifest forms in different contexts, it is difficult to identify them reliably and, hence, assign them a standard place in a taxonomy. Matters are not made easier by the absence of intrapsychic normative and base rate data, nor by the lack of strong validational support.

Fortunately, there are more reliable sources and methods available to identify personality traits than those designed explicitly to uncover intrapsychic processes. These trait-oriented procedures accept the "reality" of intrapsychic events, but seek to decode or represent them indirectly with reasonably reliable and valid instruments. Of the three methods employed to develop clinically relevant trait attributes—*self-report inventories, prototypic acts,* and *clinical ratings*—the first two have been described previously, albeit briefly.

Trait- or personality-oriented self-report inventories have a long tradition in psychological assessment; few, however, have been designed with clinical attributes or diagnostic taxa in mind. The well-known Minnesota Multiphasic Personality Inventory (MMPI, Hathaway & McKinley, 1943) provides a series of scales to gauge specific clinical disorders, as well as a rich source of information on clinically relevant personality traits. A more recently constructed instrument, the Millon Clinical Multiaxial Inventory (MCMI, Millon, 1977, 1986d), parallels the personality disorders of the DSM-III, as well as providing a variety of trait characteristics that can be employed as explicit attributes for taxonomic classes.

As touched on earlier, the methods developed by Buss and Craik

Table 1. Interpersonal Conduct Attributes for the Personality Disorders

Personality	Interpersonal conduct
1. Schizoid	Aloof: Seems indifferent and remote, rarely responsive to the actions or feelings of others, possessing minimal "human interests; fades into the background, is unobtrusive, has few close relationships and prefers a peripheral role in social, work and family settings.
2. Avoidant	Aversive: Reports extensive history of social pan-anxiety and distrust; seeks acceptance, but maintains distance and privacy to avoid anticipated humiliation and derogation.
3. Dependent	Submissive: Subordinates needs to stronger, nurturing figure, without whom feels anxiously helpless; is compliant, conciliatory, placating, and self-sacrificing.
4. Histrionic	Flirtatious: Actively solicits praise and manipulates others to gain needed reassurance, attention, and approval; is demanding, self-dramatizing, vain and seductively exhibitionistic.
5. Narcissistic	Exploitive: Feels entitled, is unempathic and expects special favors without assuming reciprocal responsibilities; shamelessly takes others for granted and uses them to enhance self and indulge desires.
6A. Antisocial	Irresponsible: Is untrustworthy and unreliable, failing to meet or intentionally negating personal obligations of a marital, parental, employment or financial nature; actively violates established social codes through duplicitous or illegal behaviors.
6B. Aggressive (sadistic)	Intimidating: Reveals satisfaction in competing with, dominating and humiliating others; regularly expresses verbally abusive and derisive social commentary, as well as exhibiting vicious, if not physically brutal behavior.
7. Compulsive	Respectful: Exhibits unusual adherence to social conventions and proprieties; prefers polite, formal and correct personal relationships.
8A. Passive-aggressive	Contrary: Assumes conflicting and changing roles in social relationships, particularly dependent acquiescence and assertive independence; is concurrently or sequentially obstructive and intolerant of others, expressing either negative or incompatible attitudes.
8B. Self-defeating	Deferential: Relates to others in a self-sacrificing, servile and obsequious manner, allowing, if not encouraging others to exploit or take advantage; is self-abasing and solicits condemnation by accepting undeserved blame and courting unjust criticism.
S. Schizotypal	Secretive: Prefers privacy and isolation, with few, highly tentative attachments and personal obligations; has drifted over time into increasingly peripheral vocational roles and clandestine social activities.
C. Borderline	Paradoxical: Although needing attention and affection, is unpredictably contrary, manipulative and volatile, frequently eliciting rejection rather than support; reacts to fears of separa-

Table 1 *(continued)*

Personality	Interpersonal conduct
	tion and isolation in angry, mercurial and often self-damaging ways.
P. Paranoid	Provocative: Displays a quarrelsome, fractious and abrasive attitude; precipitates exasperation and anger by a testing of loyalties and a searching preoccupation with hidden motives.

Note: From "Personality Prototypes and Their Diagnostic Criteria" by T. Millon. In T. Millon and G.L. Klerman (eds.) *Contemporary Directions in Psychopathology,* 1986, Guilford Press. Reprinted by permission.

(1983, 1984) and by Livesley (1985a, b) are based on observable behavioral acts. Both sets of investigators sought to refine procedures to appraise personality-related clinical attributes, as well. In their approach, they focused on prototypical acts that exemplified specific personality traits. These acts were evaluated and refined to eliminate generalities or obscurities and were rated by independent judges for their accuracy in typifying target traits. Each trait accumulated a diverse set of criterion behaviors through these procedures, providing a basis for gauging their salience or degree of presence.

Still under development, a prototypal framework guided the construction of a clinical rating schedule, tentatively entitled the *Millon Diagnostic Personality Schedule* (MDPS). The trait attributes it encompasses go substantially beyond the tangible behavioral acts comprising the Buss-Craik approach. Depending largely on theoretical discriminations and clinical inference, it presents trait descriptions for eight clinical attributes, namely "behavioral presentation," "interpersonal conduct," "cognitive style," "expressive mood," "unconscious mechanism," "self-image," "internalized content," and "intrapsychic organization." Table 1 presents the comparable trait descriptions for one of these clinical attributes, that of interpersonal conduct; a different characterization is presented for each of the 11 personality disorders in DSM-III and for two additional disorders that are likely to appear in the revised edition of DSM-III (DSM-III-R), as well as having been generated in terms of the author's theoretical model (Millon, 1986b, c).

Toward what end shall we organize the various clinical attributes that have been described? This question leads us naturally into our next topic, that pertaining to choices concerning the principal domains of diagnostic interest, as well as their potential covariance.

Taxonomic Domains

Are the substantive clinical attributes we have described used to define "disorders" or the "persons" who exhibit them? The DSM-III asserts that its nosology applies to disorders; others claim that the diagnostic criteria of the DSM-III relate to patients, not disorders (Blashfield, 1984). Clearly, Axes I and II address two different, concurrent domains of psychopathology, what we shall term the syndromic and personologic. And Axis IV focuses on a third realm of diagnostic relevance, situational factors, albeit to assess only their level of severity.

If we put aside the role of longitudinal clinical attributes—etiology, course–prognosis, and treatment response—we may usefully conceptualize the concurrent attributes—signs, symptoms, traits—as fitting a multiaxial schema of expanding contexts or concentric circles (see Figure 1). In this contextual framework, the inner circle of defining features comprises what is known as a "syndrome," a constellation of signs and symptoms that co-occur with sufficient regularity to justify considering it a valid "disorder" taxon. Viewed contextually, this inmost syndromic taxon can be seen as located within a larger matrix of co-occuring characteristics, inhering, if you will, in a "patient" whose broader and more enduring constellation of traits provides a context for it. This patient context,

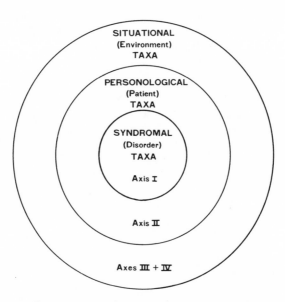

Figure 1. Concentric model of taxonomic domains.

in turn, is itself comprised of an identifiable and predictable cluster of defining features that we have termed "personologic" taxa (Millon, 1986b, c). Enlarging the scope of this contextual framework further allows us to place these personologic taxa in an even broader context of psychosocial factors (e.g., environments, relations, conditions). And the role of these situational determinants can likewise be systematized to represent orderly patterns of influence which impact on clinical states and processes, furnishing thereby what we may term "situational" taxa. A few words on these contextually related classes of taxa may be useful.

Syndromal (Disorder) Taxa

As noted earlier, the concept "syndrome" represents the clustering of a set of signs or symptoms that frequently co-occur or covary. Not all of the signs and symptoms of a taxon are likely to be immediately observed, but the presence of a subset of a syndromic taxon suggests that its other features may be uncovered upon closer examination.

By convention, syndromes do not identify a person, but define a disorder; that is, they represent pathological processes that affect particular and limited structures or functions that are neither synonymous nor coterminous with the person as a whole. As a result of their restricted nature several syndromes may coexist in the same person. Not only do they occupy less "space," so to speak, than does the entire person, but syndromes are usually time-limited in that they possess a circumscribed temporal course. Variations in quantitative severity from person to person and from time to time within a single person also characterize syndromes. Not only is there a waxing and waning in the salience of its component signs and symptoms, but only a few of its typical indices are likely to be manifest at any one time. Owing both to its changeability and partial expression, definitive assignments to a syndromic taxon often require the presence of certain necessary or joint criteria. Rarely, however, are the signs and symptoms comprising these criteria syndromically exclusive (i.e., never found in other syndromes). Given the contextual model of concentric circles described previously, the "meaning" and forms in which syndromic features are expressed are often best understood in terms of the wider personologic taxon within which they are embedded (Millon, 1981).

Personologic (Patient) Taxa

Whereas syndromic taxa represent circumscribed disorders composed of limited sets of covarying signs and symptoms, personologic taxa designate groups of patients who exhibit in common certain preeminent characteristics that distinguish them from other patients. Among major points of differentiation, personologic taxa are conceived as holistic, that is, designed to represent or synthesize the person's total psychological functioning. A major factor that sets personologic taxa apart from syndromic taxa is that their defining features are ostensibly both durable and pervasive (stable over time and consistent across situations). The qualities of holism, stability and consistency have made the "type" construct especially attractive to earlier nosologists and theorists; it is also the basis for developing what we are here terming "personologic" taxa.

More recently, the construct "prototype," to be elaborated shortly, has been introduced as a potentially useful formulation for conceptualizing all forms of taxa, particularly in that it melds the meanings historically given the constructs of both "syndrome" and "type." It seems especially apt in the personologic realm in that it encompasses both the syndromal notion of a constellation of diverse traits with the typal notions of holism, durability, and pervasiveness.

Situational (Environment) Taxa

To ensure a greater recognition of the context-dependent nature of psychopathology, we would advocate that efforts continue toward the end of bringing a more comprehensive "systems" perspective to our taxonomic schema. The advent of both family and community orientations in recent years argues forcefully for a more rigorous and articulated framework of situational taxa than currently exists (e.g., Axis IV). It is an exceptional achievement that the DSM-III instituted even its rudimentary taxonomy of psychosocial stressors. This should be seen, however, only as a beginning, a preparatory step for future DSMs to recognize more fully that behaviors and settings interact as lawful, interdependent systems and, most relevantly, that disorders are expressed differently in different personalities, and that people behave differently in different settings. Serious thought must be given to formulating a taxonomic schema that will provide a systematic framework for sampling clinically relevant psychosocial situations, both stressful and commonplace. To cite an earlier paper (Millon, 1975):

> A rose may be rose, but it is a different rose if it is presented to a loved one in a birthday bouquet than if seen in passing as one among many in a garden. Clinical signs cannot be abstracted from their personological and situational contexts without leading to false equivalences ... Hallucination 1 is simply not the same as hallucination 2 if they are a part of different personality and situational configurations. It is precisely this patterned and multivariate cluster of symptoms, set within comparably delineated personality and situational

contexts, that can best serve as a framework for developing new taxonomies. (p. 461)

STRUCTURAL ALTERNATIVES

Whatever data are incuded to provide the substantive body of a taxonomy, decisions must be made concerning the structural framework into which the taxonomy will be cast, the rules that will govern the taxa into which its clinical attributes and defining features will be placed, and the compositional properties that will characterize these attributes and features. Here we are dealing with the overall architecture of the taxonomy, whether it should be organized horizontally, vertically, or circularly, whether all or only a limited and fixed subset of features should be required for taxonic membership, whether its constituents should be conceived as categories or dimensions, as well as a host of other differentiating characteristics from which one may choose. A number of the more significant of these structural elements, and the choices to be made among them, will be discussed in this section, a task of no simple proportions since there is nothing logically self-evident, nor is there a traditional format or contemporary consensus to guide selections among these alternatives. The sequence to be followed reflects as faithfully as possible the major issues involved in providing a structure for psychopathologic phenomena.

Taxonomic Structure

Shall the various attributes that comprise the substantive data of psychopathology be "strung out" randomly or should they be ordered into a series of logical or functional groups that attempt to mirror the inherent "nature" of psychopathology? Clearly, we would answer, the latter. And toward the end of advancing both the science and the practice of psychopathology, a structure should be selected that serves both research and clinical goals.

Alternate frameworks for structuring psychopathology have been formulated in recent years; they need not be mutually exclusive. Viewed spatially, they can be seen as reflecting either a vertical, horizontal, or circular structure. The vertical, known as the *hierarchical* framework, organizes the various taxa of psychopathology (e.g., depressive disorder, schizophrenic disorder) in a series of echelons in which lower tiers are subsumed as subsets of those assigned higher ranks. The second model,

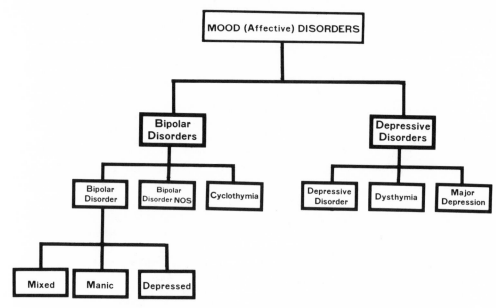

Figure 2. Hierarchic model of mood (affective) disorders.

the horizontal framework, is known as the *multiaxial* schema; it seeks to order different classes of attributes (e.g., symptoms, etiologies) in a series of aligned or parallel categories. The DSM-III encompasses both hierarchical and multiaxial structural forms, albeit with modest logic and success. The third, or circular framework, referred to as the *circumplical* model, has not received official recognition, although it has gained considerable currency among theorists oriented toward the role of interpersonal attributes.

Hierarchical Models

These models are typically arranged in the form of taxonic decision trees (see Figure 2). Hence, once a particular "branch," i.e., higher order diagnosis, has been chosen, subsequent taxonic choices are limited to the several "twigs" which comprise that branch's subdivisions. To illustrate: Once it has been decided in the DSM-III-R that a patient is exhibiting a major mood disorder, the clinician may further differentiate the disturbance as one of either a "biopolar disorder" or a "depressive disorder." Assuming the choice was bipolar, the clinician may move further down the hierarchy to select among "bipolar, mixed," "bipolar manic," "bipolar, depressed," or "cyclothymia."

A prime consequence of so carefully fashioned a sequential chain of categories is that successive taxa in the classification invariably are more specific and convey more precisely differentiated information than those that precede them. This increasing distinctness and exactitude, necessary ingredients in a successful hierarchical schema or decision tree procedure, assures that each successive category possesses authentic clinical features not found in categories previously listed.

Another hierarchical rationale employed in major taxonomies (e.g., ICD-9) is the sequential ordering of categories in accord with diagnostic priority. Hence, the organic mental syndromes classification is arranged so as to precede (not immediately) that of the schizophrenic disorders, which come before the mood disorders, which lead to the anxiety disorders, the adjustment disorders, and so on. In a prioritized hierarchical format the sequence has a clear rationale, albeit one that may be difficult both to justify and implement. Thus, a patient who was discovered to have a major lesion would be labeled with an organic syndrome diagnosis, even if he possessed clear schizophrenic signs. Likewise, a patient exhibiting symptoms sufficient to call for a schizophrenic label would not be otherwise diagnosed, even if he displayed a variety of signs characteristic of disorders that were given a priority status farther down the hierarchy.

Serial patterns of either the decision tree or diagnostic priority type would be a remarkable achievement for any hierarchical nosology, were they "naturally" or logically justified (Millon, 1983, 1986a). Not only is there no inherent structure to psychopathology that permits so rigorous an arrangement, but the International Classification of Diseases, Ninth Revision (ICD-9) and DSM-III, for instance, impose only a modest degree of sequential rigor on its taxonomic organization. For example, the compositional structure of DSM-III diagnostic criteria, which derives from a prototypal model that allows for taxonic heterogeneity, recognizes the inevitable covariation of diverse attributes within single taxa, and acknowledges that no one attribute or pattern of features is either necessary or sufficient to define a taxon. The problems of pursuing a method designed for purposes of differential diagnosis are compounded further by the fact that the DSM-III not only permits but encourages multiple diagnoses, a problem aggravated further by the manual's standard multiaxial framework. Thus, not only does the hierarchical goal of orderly and successive diagnostic choice points run hard against the polythetic character of DSM-III taxa, but its formalism and sequential requirements would be undermined repeatedly by the multidagnostic aims and intrinsic multiaxial schema of the DSM-III.

Multiaxial Models

The multiaxial format, the second of the overarching structural models, encounters few of the logical difficulties and assumptions found in hierarchical systems. The formal adoption of the multiaxial schema in the DSM-III, and in the forthcoming ICD-10, has been hailed as a diagnostic reformulation that approaches the magnitude of a paradigm shift (Millon, 1983, 1986a). It represents a distinct turn from the traditional infectious disease model where the clinician's job is to disentangle "distracting" symptoms and to clear away "confounding" situational problems so as to pinpoint the underlying or "true" pathophysiologic state. By contrast, the multiaxial model (Essen-Moller & Wohlfahrt, 1947; Mezzich, 1979; Williams, 1985a, b) not only recognizes that "distracting" signs and "confounding" circumstances are aspects worthy of attention, but encourages recording them on their own representative axis as part of an interactive complex. In essence, the multiaxial structure aligns as many of the potentially relevant factors that can illuminate the nature of a clinical condition, and provides a means of registering their distinguishing attributes. In contrast to traditional or hierarchical models, where a single class of attributes is differentiated, (e.g., both signs or etiologies), the multiaxial format permits multiple classes of data (e.g., signs and etiologies), encouraging thereby diagnostic formulations comprising several facets of information relevant to clinical decision making. Moreover, each class of attributes can be appraised in a quasi-independent manner, for example, assessing evidence related to symptomatology separately from those suggestive of etiologic factors, decreasing, thereby, the likelihood that convictions concerning etiology contaminate judgments of symptomatology, and vice versa.

The categories that typically comprise multiaxial systems vary somewhat in their composition (Williams, 1985a, b). All include presenting symptomatology or phenomenological states (e.g., DSM-III, Axis I). Many encompass axes for personality traits, patterns, or disorders as a means of representing more longstanding and pervasive features (e.g., DSM-III, Axis II). Others take into account axes such as "social functioning," "course," "severity," and "etiology." A thorough review of these alternatives may be found in Chapter 2 of this volume.

The very richness of the multiaxial model may prove its undoing. Such systems provide a more thorough and comprehensive picture than do schemas comprised of unitary axes. But they are, perforce, more complicated and demanding to implement, requiring a wider band of data and a greater clarity and diversity of judgments than clinicians are accustomed to perform. What the author (Millon, 1983) has stated previously concerning difficulties associated with the painstaking decision-tree procedure applies no less to the searching demands of multiaxial diagnoses. In essence, they impose a procedural complexity on an otherwise facile and expedient process. From a pragmatic view, the expectations of a fully comprehensive multiaxial assessment may be considered an unnecessary encumbrance in routine diagnostic work, impractical for everyday decision making, and abhorrent to clinicians accustomed to the diagnostic habit of "intuitive" synthesis. Should multiaxial models generate significantly greater diagnostic accuracy in the future, or prove useful in deepening clinical understanding, or aid in the selection of efficacious treatment modalities, then it might gain a sufficient following to override the inertia of traditional practice. Failing in these regards, it may become a novel but largely unused conception.

Circumplical Models

These models have been employed in the arrangement of both taxa and attributes. In neither case have they achieved recognition in formal psychopathologic taxonomies, gaining their primary use as a structural tool for ordering interpersonal traits (Benjamin, 1974, 1986; Lorr, 1966, Lorr, Bishop, & McNair, 1965), most notably in conjunction with personality processes and disorders (Kiesler, 1983, 1986; Leary, 1957; Plutchik, 1967; Plutchik & Platman, 1977; Wiggins, 1982).

The circumplical model is structured to permit similar taxa to be located in adjoining or nearby segments of a circle; conversely, taxa located as bipolar opposites on the circle are considered psychologically antithetical. Plutchik and Conte (1985) marshal evidence to the effect that emotions, traits of personality, and personality disorders line up in parallel ways on a circumplex, suggesting that this structure can place diverse concepts in a common framework, leading thereby to the identification of relationships that might otherwise not be recognized.

To illustrate the conceptual utility of circumplical models, Figure 3 arranges the DSM-III-R personality disorders in accord with the author's theoretical schema of primary attributes (1986b,c). Interesting though a formulation such as this may be for organizing conceptual categories, the circumplex appears at present to be an essentially academic tool of theoretic rather than clinical value, despite promising indications favoring the latter, as well (Benjamin, 1986, 1987; Kiesler, 1986).

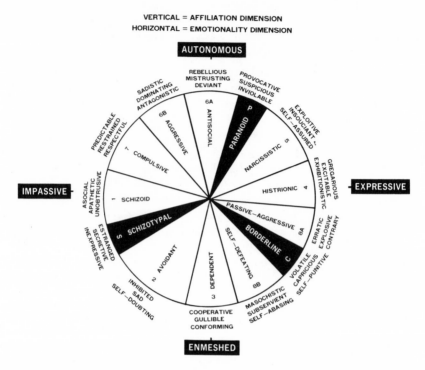

Figure 3. Circumplical model of DSM-III-R personality disorders, arranged in accord with Millon theory.

Taxonic Structure

As noted earlier, taxonic units in psychopathology are defined "intensionally." These definitions may be monothetic or polythetic in structure. In the former, monothetic case, all attributes comprising a taxon must be in evidence for a diagnosis to be correctly made. In the latter, polythetic definition, various and different optional subsets of the full attribute list can suffice to justify a diagnosis.

Classical Taxa

The "classical" form of diagnostic taxa assumes that categories comprise discrete entities that are homogeneous with respect to their defining features; that is, conceived in a restrictive, monothetic format (Cantor & Mischel, 1979; Rosch, 1978). In this classical view, failures to identify all of the attributes of a taxon result from obscuring and confounding conditions, or from deficits in observational technology and skill.

Frances and Widiger (1986) described the major characteristics and difficulties with classical taxa as follows:

> The classical model of categorization conceives of disorders as qualitative, discrete entities and assumes that the defining features are singly necessary and jointly sufficient, that the boundaries between categories are distinct, and that members are homogeneous with respect to the defining features.... Although the classical model works well for abstract categories (e.g., "square"), it fails to do justice to the complexity of naturally occuring taxonomic problems. All squares share the features of having four equal sides joined at right angles [but] .. actual objects, plants, animals, and persons, however, often fail to share a set of singly necessary and jointly sufficient features ... If a classical typology is an inappropriate model for classification of objects, birds, and plants, it is clearly inappropriate for psychiatric diagnosis. (p. 392)

Prototypal Taxa

The more modern, prototypal structure assumes a measure of taxonic heterogeneity and, hence, adheres to a polythetic format. Its open and permissive definition of taxa are more consonant with the natural "fuzziness" of conceptual boundaries (Cantor & Genero, 1986; Osherson & Smith, 1981; Wittgenstein, 1953), as well as the inherent inexactness of "natural reality" (Meehl, 1978).

Horowitz, Post, French, Wallis, and Siegelman (1981) described the prototypal construct succinctly:

> A prototype consists of the most common features or properties of members of a category and thus describes a theoretical ideal or standard against which real people can be evaluated. All of the prototype's properties are assumed to characterize at least some members of the category, but no one property is necessary or sufficient for membership in the category. Therefore, it is possible that no actual person would match the theoretical prototype perfectly. Instead different people would approximate it to different degrees. The more closely a person approximates the ideal, the more the person typifies the concept. (p. 575)

Personologic and syndromic taxa share many qualities, notably the presence of a measure of diversity among the clinical attributes they encompass (polythetic definition), resulting in the not inconsiderable heterogeneity found among similarly diagnosed patients. Albeit implicitly, the prototype model guided the thinking of the DSM-III Task Force in formulating the diagnostic criteria of taxa in both Axis I and Axis II (e.g., the opportunity given in the diagnostic criteria of most taxa to select only a partial subset of the full list of defining features).

As noted earlier, the prototype concept is especially well suited to represent the "typical" pervasive, durable, and holistic features that distinguish personological taxa. In a series of thoughtful papers, Widiger and Frances (1985a,b) have appraised the pros and cons of classical and prototypal structures, especially as they relate to personologic taxa. As expressed in an earlier quote, it is their well-reasoned judgment that the advantages of the polythetic strategy far outweigh those of the more classical, monothetic model. Referring to the classical approach, they write that once patients have been placed in the same taxon there is a tendency to exaggerate their similarities, ignore their differences, and focus on the stereotypic features that distinguish the category, all at the expense of bypassing disconfirming traits and downplaying idiosyncratic behaviors. By contrast, they state that polythetically constructed taxa would inhibit stereotyping, permit diagnostic flexibility, and emphasize within-group variability. On the other hand, no pathognomonic signs would exist, persons similarly diagnosed would vary in their degree of prototypicality, and defining features would differ in their diagnostic efficiency.

Whereas classically structured taxa are fixed and absolute in their monothetic rules, a fact that contributes in part to their inutility in psychopathologic taxonomies, the contrasting openness of polythetically structured prototypal taxa does require the diagnostician to give serious consideration to a number of statistical, ethical, and utilitarian matters (Finn, 1982; Meehl, 1986; Meehl & Rosen, 1955; Widiger, 1983; Widiger, Hurt, Frances, Clarkin, Gilmore, 1984). For example, given the option in a prototypal structure of choosing which attributes to include (and which to exclude), one must weigh the fact that the diagnostic efficiency of an attribute as an indicator of a taxon will vary as a function, not only of that taxon's local base rate, but the rates of other taxa from which it is commonly differentiated. As such, there would be need to obtain local prevalence data, as well as to arrange that cutting scores are flexible, (i.e., dependent on the obtained diagnostic base rate proportions).

Widiger and Frances (1985a) recorded several additional points worth noting:

> Polythetic criteria allow the option of including symptoms that are often but not always present, but are still important to the diagnosis. . . . If the criteria set were to be monothetic, then one could only include symptoms that were always present in every case . . . [and] disagreements among clinicians regarding the presence or absence of any one criterion can result in disagreement regarding the presence or absence of the disorder. . . . In contrast, when polythetic criteria are employed, disagreements over the basis of any single symptom is less likely to affect agreement concerning the presence or absence of the disorder. . . . The reliability of the diagnosis is influenced less by any one criterion. (p. 616)

Categorical versus Dimensional Taxa

We have progressed in this section on structural alternatives from options between three taxonomic configurations (hierarchical vs. multiaxial vs. circumplical) to a selection between two taxonic structures (classical vs. prototypal). In this and the next segment we will continue this progression toward increasing specifics, addressing the choices that need to be made concerning the compositional character of taxa and attributes. Here we will raise the issue of whether taxa and their attributes should be conceived qualitatively (categorically) or quantitatively (dimensionally).

The issue of categorization versus dimensionalization applies to different substantive matters, one related to taxa, the other to the clinical attributes of which they are composed. The greater body of literature is focused on the former.

Among taxa that follow monothetic rules (classical), authors have asked whether clinical syndromes (e.g., dysthymia) should be conceived as qualitatively discrete categories or whether they should be conceived on a quantitative dimension of severity (Frances, 1982). The issue among those who arrange polythetic rules (prototypal) is whether different combinations of defining features can be conceived as forming quantitative variations of the same qualitative category. This latter approach focuses not on the taxa themselves, but on their clinical attributes and defining features. In this variant of the issue, each attribute is conceived as a quantifiable dimension along lines such as salience or severity. What is categorized here is not the taxon, but any of the several variants of a clinical attribute that may have been observed (e.g., if "interpersonal conduct" is a relevant attribute for diagnosing personality disorder taxa, then choices may be made first among the several interpersonal defining feature options: aversive, seductive, secretive). Second, once the interpersonal defining feature options have been chosen (qualitative categorization), each may be given a "score" to represent their degree of salience or severity (quantitative dimensionalization).

Let us briefly discuss the first of the two approaches to the issue, that related to categorical versus dimensional taxa; several literature reviews may provide useful elaborations (Frances, 1982; Strauss, 1973, 1975). A second discussion will follow on the issue as it applies to clinical attributes, where the trend toward prototypal models and polythetic definitions is more central.

The taxonic issue may best be stated in the form of a question: Should taxa be conceived and organized as a series of dimensions that combine to form distinctive profiles for each patient, or should certain characteristics found commonly in clinical populations be selected to exemplify and categorize taxa?

Dimensional conceptions emphasize continua with quantitative gradations among individuals, rather than qualitative, discrete, all-or-none class distinctions. To illustrate: Kendell (1968) conjectured that a single dimension may suffice to represent the continuum he found between neurotic and psychotic depressions. By contrast, and in line with the clear boundaries between taxa to be expected with a categorical schema, Paykel (1971) found minimal overlapping among four classes: those of psychotic, anxious, hostile, and young depressives.

Several advantages to dimensional models should be noted. Most important is that they combine several clinical attributes (or their defining features) in a single configuration. This comprehensiveness results in a minimal loss of information; nor is any one attribute or feature given special significance, as is the case when only a single, albeit distinctive characteristic is brought to the forefront in a typal or syndromal category. Dimensional profiles also permit the assignment of unusual or atypical cases; in categorical formats, the not infrequent "odd" or "mixed" condition is often excluded because it fails to fit the prescribed criteria. Given the diversity and idiosyncratic character of many clinical conditions, a dimensional system permits representation and assignment of "interesting" and unique cases without "forcing" them into procrustean categories for which they are ill-suited. Another advantage of the dimensional model is that the strength of its constituent features is gauged quantitatively, with each characteristic extending into the normal range: As a consequence, normality and abnormality are construed merely as points on a continuum, rather than as distinct and separable phenomena.

Despite these advantages, dimensional taxa have not fared well in the diagnosis of psychopathology. Numerous complications and limitations have been noted in the literature, such as the fact that there is little agreement among theorists concerning the number of dimensions necessary to represent psychopathological phenomena, and these should be recorded. For example, Menninger (1963) contends that a single dimension will suffice; Eysenck (1960) asserts that three are needed, whereas Cattell (1965) claims to have identified as many as 33 and believes there to be many more. It appears, in fact, that theorists invent dimensions in accord with their expectations, rather than "discover" them as if they were intrinsic to nature, merely awaiting scientific detection. The number of dimensions required to assess psychopathology appears not to be determined by the ability of our research to disclose some inherent truth, but rather by our predilections for conceiving and organizing our observations. Another disadvantage is that the process of describing psychopathologic taxa with more than a few dimensions produces complex and intricate schemas that require geometric or algebraic representation. There is nothing intrinsically wrong with such quantitative formats, but they do pose considerable difficulty both in comprehension and in communication among professionals. Apart from matters of convenience and comfort, mathematical representations usually are arranged in groups before the information they contain is communicated. Thus, once a population has been identified as possessing a similar dimensional profile or configuration, it soon becomes a category; although its original composition may have been dimensional, its constituent members are invariably spoken of as if they were a "type." Syntheses such as these can be tolerated for routine clinical purposes, but certain statistical analyses (sensitivity and specificity measures, diagnostic cutting scores) become problematic, if not impossible, with noncategorical dimensional models.

Categorical models have been the traditional form used to represent clinical conditions. There are several reasons for this preference. First, most taxa neither imply nor are constructed to be all-or-none categories, despite assertions to the contrary. Although certain features are given prominence, others are not overlooked but merely assigned lesser significance. It is the assignment of centrality to particular characteristics that distinguishes categorical taxa from those composed of dimensions.

A major reason for the "success" of categorical taxa is the ease with which clinicians can employ them in making rapid diagnoses with numerous patients seen briefly. Although clinical attention here is drawn to only the most salient patient attributes, other, less conspicuous characteristics are often observed, suggested, or inferred. The quality of intimating characteristics beyond the immediately observed is a feature that contributes much to the value of established categorical taxa. This power of extending its scope to a variety of typical "associated attributes" contrasts the categorical approach with the tendency of dimensional schemas to segment, if not fractionate, persons and disorders into separate components. Categories restore and recompose the unity of a patient's pathology by integrating seemingly diverse elements into a single, coordinated configuration. Hence, well-established categorical taxa provide a standard reference for clinicians who would otherwise be faced with reconstructions or *de novo* diagnostic creations.

Objections to the use of categorical taxa should be noted. They contribute to the fallacious belief that psychopathological processes comprise discrete entitities, even medical "diseases," when, in fact, they are merely concepts that help focus and coordinate our observations. Further, categories often fail to identify or include significant aspects of behavior owing to the decision to narrow their list to a set of predetermined characteristics. Of course, the discarding of information if not limited to categories; dimensional schemas also choose certain attributes to the exclusion of others. The problem, however, is that certain categorical schemas, notably syndromal or typal taxa, tend to give primacy only to one or two attributes. An associated criticism is that both the number and diversity of categories in most taxonomies are far less than the clinically significant individual differences observed in everyday practice. Not only are there problems in being able to assign many patients to the limited categories available, but clinicians often claim that the more they know patients, the greater the difficulty they have in fitting them into a category.

Attribute Structures

Many of the advantages and disadvantages noted in the preceding paragraphs have equal relevance to clinical attributes. The possibilities and problems have merely been shifted to observations and inferences of lesser scope; attributes are "the stuff" of which taxa are composed.

Categorical versus Dimensional Attributes

In many ways, issues of categoricality versus dimensionality are more properly the province of attributes than of taxa. For example, the Axis I syndrome (taxon) "depressive disorders" "really" represents a clinical attribute, and distinctions between its two major subcategories, "major depression" and "dysthymia," are essentially a matter of quantitative severity and, hence, dimensional. To illustrate further, the distinction between "bipolar disorders" and "depressive disorders" might be more properly conceived as variations in two clinical attributes, not taxa; the former (which encompasses the latter) reflects the operation of two mood attributes, mania and depression, each of which may vary quantitatively as a single dimension, although both may be found in certain persons (bipolar), whereas only one may be exhibited in others (depression). The fact that some taxa in contemporary nosologies (e.g., DSM-III, ICD-9) are composed essentially of a single clinical attribute, whereas others encompass several distinct attributes, has not only confounded discussions of categoricality versus dimensionality, but has contributed a share of confusion to theory, research and practice, as well.

Skinner (1986) elaborates several "hybrid models" that integrate elements of normally divergent schemas. In what he terms the *class-quantitative* approach, efforts are made to synthesize quantitative dimensions and discrete categories. An endeavor of this nature was described in earlier reports by the author (Millon, 1984, 1986c). Integrating a mixed categorical-dimensional model for personologic taxa, it was noted that an essential step toward this goal was the specification of a distinctive defining feature for each clinical attribute of each personality disorder. To illustrate: If the clinical attribute "interpersonal conduct" is deemed of diagnostic value in assessing personality disorders, then a specific defining feature should be identified to represent the characteristic or distinctive manner in which each personality disorder ostensibly conducts its interpersonal life.

By composing a taxonomic schema that includes all relevant clinical attributes (e.g., behavioral presentation, expressive mood, interpersonal conduct, cognitive style), and specifies a defining feature on every attribute for each of the DSM-III's personality disorders, the proposed format would then be fully comprehensive in its clinical scope and possess directly comparable defining features for its parallel Axis II categories. A schema of this nature would also furnish substance and symmetry to a class-quantitative taxonomy.

To enrich the qualitative categories (the several defining features comprising the clinical range of each attribute) with quantitative discriminations (numerical intensity ratings), clinicians would not only identify which features (e.g., distraught, hostile, labile) of a clinical attribute (e.g., expressive mood) best characterizes a patient, but would record a number (e.g., from 1 to 10) to represent the degree of prominence or pervasiveness of the chosen defining feature(s). Clinicians would be encouraged in a prototypal schema to record and quantify more than one defining feature per clinical attribute (e.g., if suitable, to note both "distraught" and "labile" moods, should their observations and inferences so incline them).

A procedure such as that described in the preceding paragraph illustrates that *categorical* (qualitative distinction) and *dimensional* (quantitative distinction) taxonic models need not be framed in opposition, no less be considered mutually exclusive. Assessments can be formulated, first, to recognize qualitative (categorical) distinctions in what features best characterize a patient, permitting the multiple listing of several such features, and second, to differentiate these features quantitatively (dimensionally) so as to represent their relative degrees of clinical prominence or pervasiveness. To illustrate: On the "interpersonal conduct" attribute, patient A may be appraised as justifying quantitative ratings of 10 on the "aversive" feature, 6 on the "ambivalent" feature, and 4 on the "secretive" feature. Patient B may be assigned a rating of 9 on the "ambivalent" feature, 7 on "aversive" and 2 on "paradoxical." Both patients are charac-

terized by the "aversive"and "ambivalent" defining features, but to differing extents. They are not only distinguishable quantitatively (dimensionally) on two of the same qualitative (categorical) features, but differ as
well on qualitative grounds, one having been judged as exhibiting "secretive," the other "paradoxical" interpersonal conduct.

CONSTRUCTION OPTIONS

How have taxonomies in psychopathology come into being?

For the most part, traditional classifications were the product of a
slowly evolving accretion of clinical experience (Menninger, 1963), fos-
tered and formalized periodically by the systematizing efforts of respected
clinician-scholars such as Kraepelin (1899). One should expect empirical
data or theoretical advances on matters of causality or structure to serve as
the primary heuristic impetus, but such has not been the case. Further, ad-
vocates of competing hypotheses have precluded a consensus favoring the
acceptance of any one viewpoint. With but few exceptions (e.g., the shortlived psychoanalytic "explication" of neurotic disorders, recently ex-
punged as an organizing construct in the DSM-III), theoretically generated or research-grounded taxonomies have fared rather poorly. A more
recent spur to classification has originated in a series of quantitative
methods known as "cluster analyses" (Sneath & Sokal, 1973). Only time
will tell whether these mathematical tools will generate taxa of sufficient
consequence to gain acceptance in the clinical world. In describing taxonomic advances in the biological sciences, Sokal wrote (1974):

> In classification, theory has frequently followed methodology and has been an
> attempt to formalize and justify the classificatory activity of workers in various
> sciences. In other instances, classificatory systems have been set up on *a priori*
> logical or philosophical grounds and the methodology tailored subsequently
> to fit the principles. Both approaches have their advantages and drawbacks;
> modern work tends to reflect an interactive phase in which first one and then
> the other approach is used, but in which neither principles nor methodology
> necessarily dominate. (p. 1115)

Taxonomic methods in psychopathology are less advanced than in
the biological sciences, but they are approaching the threshold at which
some of the same controversies as are found in their biological forerun-
ners will arise (Sneath & Sokal, 1973). Although each of the alternative
construction methods to be discussed shortly may prove fruitful, taxonomists are likely to engage in debates as to which is best. It is important
to recognize at the outset that different methods use different procedures
and focus on different data. There is no "correct" choice, and no rules can

be found in "nature" to tell us which are best or likely to be profitable. To make sense and give order to the taxonomies they employ, clinicians should know what approach to construction was followed and what attributes comprised their data base. With the techniques and building blocks of these methods clearly in mind, clinicians may assess them intelligently and judge their relevance to the questions they pose.

The reader might ask at this point why different construction methods for taxonomies are needed. Cannot one taxonomic approach do the job alone? For the time being, at least, the answer is no. At this stage of our knowledge different methods will serve as instruments to construct psychopathologic data in specific realms rather than provide a fully comprehensive schema. Their alternative efficacy will be determined in time.

To recapitulate briefly, taxonomies differ not only in their attributes, subject domains, and structural models, but also in the manner in which they are put together. Construction approaches and their products can be separated conceptually and methodologically into three types: clinically based disorders, numerically derived clusters, and theoretically deduced constructs.

A few words might be said concerning similarities between methods of taxonomic formation and procedures for developing psychometric tools. Before discussing these parallels, the correspondence between these modes of construction and the distinction between empiricist and rationalist epistemologies should also be noted. For example, methods of formulation that generate taxa directly from clinical data adhere closely to the empiricist's commitment to direct observation and experiential knowledge. Those who deduce taxa by examining the implications of abstract principles and theoretical constructs are following a rationalist epistemology. Numerically derived clusters and factors bridge both empiricist and rationalist philosophies in applying the procedures of abstract mathematical analyses to concrete particulars.

Returning to parallels between the building of taxonomies and the development of psychometric instruments, Skinner (1981, 1986) draws upon the logic outlined by Loevinger (1957) for sequentially validating diagnostic tests and applies it creatively to the composition of taxonomies. The mutually reinforcing strength achieved by a combination of Loevinger's three "validation strategies" may be kept in mind as we elaborate each of the three construction options to be discussed shortly. In the following quote, Skinner progresses from the theoretical to the statistical (internal) to the clinical (external), a sequence especially suitable to the validation of diagnostic tests, and one which both Jackson (1971) and Millon (1977) followed in fashioning their recent psychometric inventories. Our presentation will reverse this sequence to accord with the historical order in which taxonomies have and will continue to be composed. Skinner wrote (1981):

> Basically, the *theory formulation* component involves a precise definition of the typal constructs, a specification of the purpose (e.g., etiological versus descriptive), and a formulation of linkages among types. Second, the *internal validation* component entails the choice of a relevant statistical technique, the development of an empirical taxonomy, and an evaluation of its internal properties (e.g., reliability). Third, the *external validation* component involves a series of studies that address various facets of validity, such as the clinical relevance of the diagnostic categories. All three components interact in a program of research as successive refinements are made to both the operational taxonomy and the underlying theoretical model. This framework is meant to serve as a meta-theory of classification, which should have heuristic value. (p. 69)

Clinically Based Disorders

For the greater part of history (Menninger, 1963; Zilboorg & Henry, 1941), psychiatric taxonomies were formed on the basis of clinical observation, the witnessing of repetitive patterns of behavior and emotion among a small number of carefully studied mental patients. Etiologic hypotheses were generated to give meaning to these patterns of covariance (e.g., Hippocrates anchored differences in observed temperament to his humoral theory, and Kraepelin distinguished two major categories of severe pathology, dementia praecox and manic-depressive disease, in terms of their ostensive divergent prognostic course). The elements comprising these theoretic notions were *post hoc,* however, imposed after the fact on prior observational data, rather than serving as a generative source for taxonomic categories. The most recent example of a clinical taxonomy, one tied explicitly to phenomenal observation and constructed by intention both atheoretically and nonquantitatively, is, of course, the DSM-III. Spitzer, chairperson of the Task Force, stated in the DSM-III manual (APA, 1980) that "clinicians can agree on the identification of mental disorders on the basis of their clinical manifestations without agreeing on how the disturbances came about" (p. 7).

Albeit implicitly, the DSM-III is a product of causal or etiologic speculation. Nevertheless, a major goal of the Task Force was to eschew theoretic or pathogenic notions, adhering to as strict an empiricist philosophy as possible. In doing so, only those attributes that could be readily observed or consensually validated were to be permitted as diagnostic criteria. Numerous derelictions from this epistemology are notable, nevertheless, especially among the personality disorders, where trait ascriptions call for inferences beyond direct sensory inspection.

Not all who seek to render taxa on the basis of clinical data insist on keeping inference to a minimum (Tversky, 1977). And by no means do those who draw their philosophical inspiration from an empiricist mind-set restrict themselves to the mere specification of surface similarities (Medin *et al.*, 1982). It is not only those who employ open concepts and who formulate theoretically generated nosologies who "succumb" to the explanatory power and heuristic value of pathogenic, dynamic, and structural inferences. Feinstein (1977) a distinguished internist, provides an apt illustration of how one man's factual observations may be another's inference. As Feinstein put it:

> In choosing an anchor or focus for taxonomy, we can engage in two distinctly different types of nosologic reasoning. The first is to form names, designations or denominations for the observed evidence, and to confine ourselves exclusively to what has actually been observed. The second is to draw inferences from the observed evidence, arriving at inferential titles respresenting entitities that have not actually been observed. For example, if a patient says "I have substantial chest pain, provoked by exertion, and relieved by rest," I, as an internist, perform a denomination if I designate this observed entity as *angina pectoris*. If I call it *coronary artery disease*, however, I perform an inference, since I have not actually observed coronary artery disease. If a radiologist looking at a coronary arteriogram or a pathologist cutting open the coronary vasculature uses the diagnosis *coronary artery disease*, the decision is a denomination. If the radiologist or pathologist decides that the coronary disease was caused by cigarette smoking or by a high fat diet, the etiologic diagnosis is an inference unless simultaneous evidence exists that the patient did indeed smoke or use a high fat diet. (p. 192)

In large measure, clinically based taxa gain their import and prominence by virtue of consensus and authority. Cumulative experience and habit are crystallized and subsequently confirmed by offical bodies (Millon, 1986a). Specified criteria are denoted and articulated, acquiring definitional, if not stipulative powers, at least in the eyes of those who come to accept the attributes selected as infallible taxonic indicators.

Numerically Derived Factors and Clusters

Inasmuch as clinically based categories stem from the observations and inferences of diagnosticians, they comprise, in circular fashion, the very qualities that clinicians are likely to see and deduce. Categories so constructed will not only direct future clinicians to focus on and to mirror these same taxa in their patients, but they may lead future nosologists away from potentially more useful tools with which to fathom less obvious patterns of attribute covariation. It is toward the end of penetrating beneath the sensory domain to more "latent" commonalities that taxonomists have turned either to numerical methods or to theoretical principles. It is the former to which our attention will be directed in this section.

Andreasen and Grove (1982) enumerated the advantages of what are variously termed in the literature as empirical and numerical methods of computing patient similarities:

> First, the empirical method gives an opportunity for the observed characteristics of the subjects to determine the classification and perhaps to lead to a classification that the clinician was unable to perceive using clinical judgment alone. Second, the empirical method allows a great deal of information on the subjects to enter into the genesis of the classifications; human beings can keep in mind only a relatively small number of details concerning a case at any given time, but the empirical approach can process very large sets of measurements. Third, empirical or numerical approaches can combine cases in more subtle ways than can clinicians; combinations of features too complex to grasp intuitively may yield better classifications than simple combinations. (p. 45)

There has been a rapid proliferation of new and powerful mathematical techniques both for analyzing and synthesizing vast bodies of clinical data. This expansion has been accelerated by the ready availablilty of inexpensive computer hardware and software programs. Unfortunately, such mushrooming has progressed more rapidly than its fruits can be digested. As a consequence, to quote Kendell (1975) early in its development, "most clinicians ... have tended to oscillate uneasily between two equally unsatisfactory postures of ignoring investigations based on these techniques, or accepting their confident conclusions at face value" (p. 106).

There are numerous purposes to which this growing and diverse body of quantitative methods can be put, of which only a small number are relevant to the goal of aiding in taxonomic construction. Other statistical techniques relate to the validation of existent nosologies (e.g., discriminant analyses), rather than to their creation. Among those used to facilitate taxonomic development, some focus on clinical attributes as their basic units, whereas patients themselves are the point of attention of others. For example, *factor analysis* condenses sets of clinical attributes and organizes them into syndromic taxa. *Cluster analysis,* by contrast, is most suitable for sorting patients on the basis of their similarities into personologic taxa. A brief review of these two numerical techniques is appropriate in the present context; other mathematical procedures employed in taxonomic construction and evaluation, such as latent class, log-linear, discriminant analysis, and **MANOVA**, may be examined in a number of useful publications (Blashfield, 1984; Everitt, 1980; Grove & Andreasen, 1986; Harman, 1976; Hartigan, 1975; Kendell, 1975).

Factor Analytic Methods

As noted, factorial techniques are designed to represent relationships among attributes (signs, symptoms) and have their primary value in identifying core dimensions in the development of syndromic taxa. Despite efforts to apply them to other realms, their statistical properties render them unsuitable to the task of uncovering personal similarities or to optimally classify individuals (Torgerson, 1968; Zubin, 1968).

The notion that the presence of covarying symptoms might signify "disease entities" can be traced to the seventeenth-century writings of Thomas Syndenham. In connecting this notion to factor analytic techniques, Blashfield (1984) commented:

> Sydenham, who promoted the concept of *syndrome* . . . argued that a careful observer of patients could note that certain sets of symptoms tended to co-occur. If these co-occurring sets of symptoms were seen repeatedly across a number of patients, this observance would suggest that the syndrome may represent more than a chance collection of symptoms. Instead, the consistent appearance of a syndrome would suggest a disease with a common etiology and a common treatment.
>
> Factor analysis . . . can be thought of as a statistical tool used to isolate syndromes of co-occurring symptoms. . . . In addition, factor analysis provides a statistical estimate of the "underlying factor" that explains the association among a collection of related symptoms. (pp. 169–170)

The designation "factor analysis" is a generic term encompassing a variety of numerical procedures which serve to achieve different goals.

In the method of *principal components,* the aim is to reduce a set of correlated attributes into a smaller number of uncorrelated components. Each component is generated mathematically and selected sequentially such that the first accounts for the maximum variance of a correlational matrix, and each succeeding component explains successively lesser amounts. In psychological domains, the first 4 to 6 components usually cover most of the variance. This method essentially transforms what would be a substantial number of diverse attributes into a few distinct and uncorrelated factors, without the loss of much information.

Whereas principal component analysis is concerned primarily with variance and aims to reduce the diverse attributes, it includes, initially to a minimum, a number of uncorrelated components. *Factor analysis* is concerned primarily with covariance, and seeks to reveal the underlying structure of its attributes by identifying factors which account for their covariation. Toward this end, linear combinations of the attributes are sequentially chosen to cumulate as much variance as possible. Factors derived in this manner are often "rotated" after their initial mathematical solution in order to increase their psychological meaning.

Although optimally suited to forming clinical attribute categories, both methods are unsuitable for classifying persons. To achieve this latter goal, Overall and Hollister (1964) introduced the method of *inverted factor* or *Q analysis* in their search for a psychiatric taxonomy. Kendell (1975) described this technique as follows:

> The original matrix is composed of correlations between pairs of individuals across all tests or ratings, instead of, as in normal (factor) analysis, correlations between ratings across all members of the population. *Q* correlations are in fact measures of the similarity between two individuals rather than of the degree of association between two variables. In *Q* analysis, the number of factors found is taken to indicate the number of types or subpopulations present, and each type is built up by assigning to it those individuals whose largest factor loadings are on the corresponding factor. (p. 110)

Q-correlation methods have proven problematic and have been criticized on several grounds, as have both principal components and normal factor analysis. Not only has the *Q* technique been shown to be a poor gauge of person similarities, in that it often produces uninterpretable findings (Everitt, 1980; Fleiss, 1972), but several of its assumptions are usually unsupportable and it sets restrictive limits on the number of derivable categories. Other problems of factorial techniques are summarized in the following brief quotes. Kendell (1975) reported that skepticism in the field remains high,

> largely because of the variety of different factor solutions that can be obtained from a single set of data and the lack of any satisfactory objective criterion for preferring one of these to the others. The number of factors obtained and their loadings are often affected considerably by relatively small changes in the size or composition of the subject sample, or in the range of tests employed. (p. 108)

And Sprock and Blashfield (1984) concluded that

> deciding when to stop the process of selecting the number of factors, rotating the solutions, and interpreting the factors are all highly subjective and at the discretion of the user. Therefore, many distrust the results. (p. 108)

In addition to these methodological caveats, a number of conceptual forewarnings must be kept in mind regarding the structural implications of a factorial approach. As is known among those involved in the development of psychometric instruments (Loevinger, 1957; Millon, 1977, 1986d), a reasonable degree of "fidelity" should exist between the pattern of relationships among the scales of a test and its structural model of psychopathology. For the same reasons, taxa should conform in their pattern of relationships to their taxonomy's structural conception (Smith & Medin, 1981). For example, assume that a model of psychopathology posits its taxa as both monothetic and independent, that is, each containing exclusive and uncorrelated attributes. If that is how psychopathology has been conceived, then a factorial structure would fit it handsomely: the attributes comprising each taxa would not only intercorrelate positively, but correlate negatively with all of the other taxa comprising the nosology. Factors would exhibit fidelity to such a psychopathologic model. However, despite its popularity with many a distinguished psychometrician, factorial structures are far from universally accepted. Not only do few psychopathological entities give evidence of factorial "purity" or attribute independence, but factorial solutions are antithetical to the predominant polythetic structure and overlapping relationships that exist among clinical conditions (Millon, 1981). Neither personologic nor syndromic taxa consist of entirely homogeneous and discrete clinical attributes. Rather, taxa are comprised of diffuse and complex characteristics that share many attributes in common.

The need to ensure an *optimal* level of taxonic homogeneity is justified, though not to the extent of the overzealous requirements of factorial models. To accept the inevitability of attribute overlap, yet achieve taxonically meaningful levels of covariation, attributes comprising each taxon should exhibit a strong, but not necessarily unique, association with that taxon. There are structural, as well as clinical and empirical, reasons to expect that certain attributes would correlate secondarily with taxa other than the one for which they are most consonant. For example, an attribute selected for the "dysthymic" taxon may, in measures of sensitivity, show a base rate of .60 among persons assigned that taxon, and .35 among those assigned an "anxiety" taxon; this modes level of redundancy would be considered clinically acceptable and structurally congruent. However, if the dysthymic attribute were to achieve a sensitivity base rate of .50 with its own taxon, and .40 among those assigned an incongruent "impulse disorder" taxon, serious reservations about including the attribute in either taxon might be called for.

To summarize, factorial methods of taxonic construction appear to rest on a model that fails to accord with the "intrinsic nature" of covariations that characterize the structure of psychopathology. Despite these caveats, factor analytic methods may still prove helpful as a tool to identify and clarify the more central attributes that comprise syndromic taxa.

Cluster Analytic Methods

This body of mathematical techniques comprises measures of similarity designed to sort apparently heterogeneous populations into subsets of relatively homogeneous types. Patient clusters, alike in the configuration or profile of their clinical attributes, are formed thereby. More suitable than factor analytic procedures for creating personologic taxa, cluster analysis approaches the task of classifying patients in their full complexity. Whereas factorial methods focus on part structures or dimensions, cluster methods address similarities among overall patterns or configurations. This is not to say that cluster analysis cannot be applied to the construction of dimensions or syndromes, for they most assuredly have been. Rather, it is our view that their most suitable application, as yet unrealized, is in the assignment of patients to personologic taxa, or as a means of validating taxonomies generated on clinical or theoretical grounds.

Most cluster algorithms are structured to follow the hierarchical "tree" model. Grove and Andreasen (1986) described the structure and procedure of cluster analysis as follows:

> Such trees define a hierarchy, and they can be produced by either agglomerative or divisive methods. Agglomerative methods form the tree from the bottom up by successively fusing individuals or groups together. Divisive methods form trees by taking the whole sample at the outset and dividing it on some measure of dissimilarity. One of the two groups thus formed is then redivided, and so on until N individuals are left at the bottom of the tree. Divisive methods have not found much favor among numerical taxonomists, as they tend to make an initial erroneous division from which they are unable to recover. Even within the group of agglomerative hierarchical methods there are many different algorithms. (p. 350)

Given the number of cluster methods available to the taxonomist, one may rightly ask whether a single procedure has proven empirically most useful or valid. In response we must note that early studies carried out by McKeon (1967), Forgy (1968), and Strauss, Bartko, and Carpenter (1973) were rather discouraging, having demonstrated dismaying facts, such as finding that clusters would be generated from a single, multivariate normal distribution, which should yield no distinctions, or that totally different clusters routinely are obtained from ostensibly comparable algorithms, and that none or only one even resembled known population distinctions. Although a more recent review by Milligan (1981) indicates that all clustering methods fail to construct accurate categories when analyzing complex and mixed patient groups, two techniques stood out as reliably successful—the average-linkage and Ward's methods—when dealing with clearly discernable populations.

Although cluster algorithms of reasonable reliability have begun to mirror broad clinically based diagnostic populations, these slender advances do not answer the question of whether cluster analysis produces categories that resemble the "natural" structure of psychopathology any better than those of our more traditional or clinically based nosologies; nor is there any evidence that they provide more accurate predictions of such nonstructural concerns as prognosis and treatment response.

Two brief quotes nicely summarize the current state of affairs, as well as addressing problems that are likely to persist in the use of numerical construction procedures. Skinner and Blashfield wrote (1982):

> Clinicians have at best given only a lukewarm reception to such classifications. They have been skeptical about the value of clustering methods to identify "naturally" occurring subgroups. Furthermore, the classifications generated by these methods have not seemed particularly meaningful or relevant to everyday clinical practice. (p. 727)

In his usual perspicacious manner, Kendell's comment of more than a decade ago (1975), upon reviewing the preceding 20-year period, is, rather sadly, no less apt today as then:

> Looking back on the various studies published in the last twenty years it is clear that many investigators, clinicians and statisticians, have had a naive, almost Baconian, attitude to the statistical techniques they were employing, putting in all the data at their disposal on the assumption that the computer would sort out the relevant from the irrelevant and expose the underlying principles and regularities, and assuming all that was required of them was to collect the data assiduously beforehand.
>
> Moreover, any statistician worth his salt is likely to be able, by judicious choice of patients and items, and of factoring or clustering procedures, to produce more or less what he wants to. (p. 118)

Theoretically Deduced Constructs

Whereas the biases of statisticians in shaping data are likely to be implicit or arcane, those of taxonomic theorists are explicit and straightforward. For the most part, the concepts and orientations of theorists are stated as plainly as their subject permits, although their propositions and the deductions they derive therefrom are rarely as empirically clear as one might wish. Also, "taxonomic" theories are usually less difficult to grasp than the theories of "etiology" or "dynamics" one encounters in the literature, where jargon often flourishes and where the task of concretizing and verifying hypothetical processes is most formidable indeed.

A few words should be said about the role of theoretical constructs in generating taxonomies. As noted earlier, distinguished philosophers such as Hempel (1965) and Quine (1977) consider that mature sciences progress from an observationally based stage to one that is characterized by abstract concepts and theoretical systemizations. It is their judgment that classification alone does not make a scientific taxonomy, and that similarity among attributes does not necessarily comprise a scientific category (Smith & Medin, 1981). The card catalog of the library or an accountant's ledger sheet, for example, are well-organized classifications, but hardly to be viewed as a system of science. The characteristic which distinguishes a scientific classification, or what we term a latent as contrasted to a manifest taxonomy, is its success in grouping its elements according to theoretically consonant explanatory propositions. These propositions are formed when certain attributes which have been isolated and categorized have been shown or have been hypothesized to be logically or causally related to other attributes or categories. The latent taxa comprising a scientific nosology are not, therefore, mere collections of overtly similar attributes or categories, but a linked or unified pattern of known or presumed relationships among them. This theoretically grounded pattern of relationships is the foundation of a scientific taxonomy.

Certain benefits derive from systematizing clinical data in a theoretical fashion that are not readily available either from clinical or numerical procedures (Wright & Murphy, 1984). Given the countless ways of observing and analyzing a set of data, a system of explanatory propositions becomes a useful guide to clinicians as they sort through and seek to comprehend the stream of amorphous signs and chaotic symptoms they normally encounter. Rather than shifting from one aspect of behavior, thought, or emotion to another, according to momentary and uncertain impressions of importance, theoretically guided clinicians may be led to pursue in a logical and perhaps more penetrating manner only those aspects which are likely to be related, and to experience thereby a sense of meaningful order (Dougherty, 1978). In addition to furnishing this guidance, a theoretically anchored taxonomy may enable diagnosticians to deduce hypotheses about clinical relationships they may not have observed before. It enlarges the sensitivity and scope of knowledge of observers by alerting them to previously unseen relationships among attributes, and then guides these new observations into a coherent body of knowledge.

Systematization leads to another advantage of a theoretically deduced taxonomy. Because of its scope and generality, clinical observers from diverse settings and orientations are given an opportunity to examine and verify its utility and validity. Erroneous speculations and spheres of inapplicability are readily exposed by comprehensive scrutiny.

This exposure assures that the theory's propositions must be supported by public evidence and consensual validation.

Despite their value as ultimate goals, taxonomic theories need be neither fully comprehensive nor extensively supported to inspire and guide the early phases of taxonomic development. Addressing these points in discussing his concept of the schizoid taxon, Meehl wrote (1972):

> I would not require that a genuinely integrated theory explain *everything* about schizophrenia, a preposterous demand, which we do not customarily make of any theory in the biological or social sciences. At this stage of our knowledge, it is probably bad strategy to spend time theorizing about small effects, low correlations, minor discrepancies between studies and the like.
>
> Being a neo-Popperian in the philosophy of science, I am myself quite comfortable engaging in speculative formulations completely unsubstantiated by data. To "justify" concocting a theory, all one needs is a problem, plus a notion (I use a weak word advisedly) of how one might test one's theory (subject it to the danger of refutation). (p. 11)

The reader may be taken aback by Meehl's seemingy tolerant views, and be disposed to assert that theory leads to scientific irresponsibility, justifying thereby the taking of a rigorous atheoretical stance. As we have stated previously, however, the belief that one can take positions that are free of theoretical bias is naive, if not nonsensical (Heelan, 1977; Hempel, 1965; Leahey, 1980; Weimer, 1979). Those who claim to have eschewed theory have (unknowingly) subscribed to a position that gives primacy to experience-near data, such as overt behaviors and biological signs, as opposed to experience-distant data that require a greater measure of inference. The positivist (empiricist) position once held sway in philosophy, as it still does in some psychiatric and psychological quarters, but it would be difficult, as Meehl (1978) has noted, "to name a single logician or a philosopher (or historian) of science who today defends strict operationism in the sense that some psychologists claim to believe in it" (p. 815).

What distinguishes a true theoretically deduced taxonomy from one that provides a mere explanatory summary of known observations and inferences?

Simply stated, the answer lies in its power to *generate* attributes or taxa other than those used to construct it. This generative power is what Hempel (1965) terms the "systematic import" of a scientific clasification. In contrasting what are familiarly known as "natural" (theoretically guided, deductively based) and "artifical" (conceptually barren, similarity-based) classifications, Hempel wrote (1965):

> Distinctions between "natural" and "artificial" classifications may well be explicated as referring to the difference between classifications that are scien-

tifically fruitful and those that are not: in a classification of the former kind, those characteristics of the elements which serve as criteria of membership in a given class are associated, universally or with high probability, with more or less extensive clusters of other characteristics.

Classification of this sort should be viewed as somehow having objective existence in nature, as "carving nature at the joints" in contradistinction of "artificial" classifications, in which the defining characteristics have few explanatory or predictive connections with other traits.

In the course of scientific development, classifications defined by reference to manifest, observable characteristics will tend to give way to systems based on theoretical concepts. (pp. 146–148)

As noted earlier, theoretical concepts employed in psychopathologic taxonomies can be differentiated, albeit roughly, into three subject domains: etiology, dynamics, and structure. Notable here is that each of these refer to attributes that are not directly visible in a patient's behavior or environment. Rather, they pertain to properties and processes that must either be uncovered or inferred. It is not their experience-distant quality that is central, however, but rather the fact that they are integral to a theoretical system. As Bower's (1977) has phrased it, they contribute to "a deeper seeing, a more penetrating vision that goes beyond superficial appearances to the order underlying them" (p. 127).

The first theoretical domain, that of etiology, draws its distinctions on the basis of ostensive causal or sustaining agents that give taxonic shape to a variety of pathologic phenomena (e.g., analytic developmental conceptions that account for libidinal character types, or social learning principles that explain the form and sphere of expression of reinforcement-contingent compulsions). The second, the dynamic domain, construes its categories as the product of an active interplay among unremitting emotional forces and counterbalancing homeostatic processes, such as conflicts and defense mechanisms, resulting in a series of "neurotic resolutions" (e.g., phobic avoidance, hysterical conversion). The third, or structural domain, employs the character and congruence among quasi-permanent substrates and dispositions within the individual to give shape to its taxonic forms. As described elsewhere (Millon, 1986c):

These [quasi-permanent] attributes represent a deeply embedded and relatively enduring template of imprinted memories, attitudes, needs, fears, conflicts, and so on, which guide the experience and transform the nature of ongoing life events. Psychic structures have an orienting and preemptive effect in that they alter the character of action and the impact of subsequent experiences in line with preformed inclinations and expectancies. By selectively lowering thresholds for transactions that are consonant with either constitutional proclivities or early learning, future events are often experienced as variations of the past. (p. 683)

The configuration and cohesion of these structured residuals establish relatively enduring and pervasive "styles" of coping, behaving, thinking, emoting, and the like, creating thereby a foundation for a wide range of personality or character types (e.g., narcissistic, borderline, avoidant).

In his recent proposals favoring the integration of classifications and theory, Skinner (1981, 1986) summarizes a number of current formulations employed in both the construction and confirmation of taxonomies. Traditional theories should not be overlooked however, for they also have been a productive source of nosological taxa. Notable here are psychoanalytic conceptions that satisfy the key criterion of a "natural" classification, that of *generating* taxa *de novo* from theoretical principles or propositions. To illustrate: The analytic thesis of psychosexual development spawned taxa such as oral and anal character types. Similarly, the conception of intrapsychic conflict resolution led to productive taxonic proposals such as phobias and conversions.

Impressive concepts with taxonic implications have recently been generated by contemporary "interpersonal theorists," notably among those structuring their dimensions in a circumplical model. Worthy of record here is the work of Wiggins (1982), Kiesler (1983, 1986), and Conte and Plutchik (1981). Perhaps the most inventive of this group is Benjamin (1974, 1986, 1987), who has formed a twofold circumplex that considers the balance and interplay between "self" and "other" processes.

Figure 3, presented earlier in the chapter, portrays a circumplex model of DSM-III-R personality disorders arranged in accord with concepts drawn from the author's theoretical notions. Although similar to those of the interpersonal school, their circumplical frameworks typically employ the dimensional polarities of affiliation and control. The contrasting horizontal and vertical poles they posit are characterized usually by terms such as love versus hate, on the horizontal, dominance versus submission, on the vertical. A thoughtful and comprehensive review of the major interpersonal theorists, as well as the taxonomic possibilities inherent in their approach, may be found in Wiggins (1982).

Refreshing and inventive as they are, it remains unclear as to whether the conceptual paradigms of the interpersonal group possess the "systematic import" that Hempel considers essential to a "natural" classification, or whether they have simply portrayed established taxa in a clinically interesting format (Widiger & Frances, 1985b). Both Kiesler's and Benjamin's complex and richly detailed formulations appear to give the most promise of adding new features to our established DSM-III taxonomy.

The author's biosocial-learning theory (Millon, 1969, 1981, 1986b) is a model that has generated several of the new personality taxa in DSM-III (Kernberg, 1984). Drawing upon a threefod polarity framework—pain-pleasure, self-other, active-passive—a series of eight personality "prototypes" and three severe variants were deduced (two additional types have subsequently been generated), of which several proved to be "original" derivations in the sense that they had never been formulated as categories in prior psychiatric nosologies (e.g., portraying and coining the avoidant personality designation, Millon, 1969). Progressive research will determine if the network of concepts comprising this theory provides an optimal structure for a comprehensive taxonomy of personality pathology. At the very least, it contributes to the view that formal theory can lead to the deduction of *new* taxa worthy of consensual verification.

Although theorists of taxonomy are skilled at *a priori* reasoning, for the most part their formulations are rarely tarnished by the realities of everyday clinical practice. The "real job" that faces most theorists is that of keeping their conceptions simple and generalizable enough to provide useful insights to the practicing clinician, while at the same time maintaining sufficient distance not to "fall in love" with their own formulations, as if they embodied some ultimate "truth." It is this latter concern which leads us quite naturally to our next topic.

EVALUATION STANDARDS AND PROCEDURES

As Feinstein (1977) has commented, classification systems "can be a product of sheer speculation or arbitrary caprice" (p. 196). Hence, once a taxonomy has been constructed, be it comprehensive in scope, such as the DSM-III or the ICD-9, or circumscribed in focus, such as Freud's unifying conception of the neurotic disorders or Millon's theoretical schema for personality prototypes, it behooves clinicians and scientists to evaluate each taxonomy as a whole, its constituent taxa, and the specific attributes and defining features that comprise each taxon. To assure a minimum of "sheer" speculation and caprice, developers of taxonomies should keep in mind several guiding principles or "standards" that may optimize both the validity and utility of their "creations." These guidelines may prove especially useful in the formulation and construction phases of a taxonomy, serving to orient developers in ways that may enhance their system's ultimate efficacy. Also presented will be a number of empirical and statistical procedures relevant to taxonic construction and evaluation.

Appraising Taxa and Taxonomies

Earlier literatures on classifications and their validation will not conform readily to distinctions made in the following sections. For purposes of pedagogic clarity, divisions will be drawn between optimal standards and validation procedures, separating thereby what is pragmatically desirable from that which can be empirically evaluated; judgments on both matters are necessary, of course. Further, a separation will be made between a taxonomy and its component taxa, as well as between taxa and the attributes and diagnostic features of which they are comprised. Here, again, matters of clinical pragmatics are often not readily subject to statistical analysis, yet both are important evaluative ingredients. Owing to the fact that this is but one chapter of a book, albeit a lengthy one, taxonomy and taxa will be treated together.

Optimal Taxonomic Standards

Blashfield and Draguns (1976) concluded their excellent early review of evaluative criteria for psychiatric classifications by noting such prosaic, yet prudent and sensible suggestions as:

> [a taxonomy] should be simple in its structure, the diagnostic rules for identifying patients as members of particular categories should be easy for clinicians to use, and the characteristics on which the classification is based should be those which are most frequently analyzed in standard clinical practice. When considering the purpose of communication, it is obvious that the final judgment on the value of a classification will be made by the clinicians for whose use the system is designed. If clinicians ... are dissatisfied with a classification system, then the classification will never enter their linguistic practices, and the classification will fail. (p. 147)

Stated simply, unless a taxonomy is easy to understand and use, it is quite unlikely to gain adherents in the clinical world, no matter how well-formulated and scientifically sound it might otherwise be. In the following paragraphs a number of principles or standards to guide both the construction and evaluation of both taxonomies and their taxa will be elaborated. A different perspective concerning more general properties desirable in a taxonomic system will be found in Sneath and Sokal (1973), especially as they relate to numerically derived classifications.

Clinical Relevance. A number of taxonomies are shrouded in a dense cloak of words and concepts. Their structure is so opaque that assumptions may be concealed, principles may be difficult to extract, and consistent connections to the clinical world may be impossible to establish. In short, the structure and language of the taxonomy and its taxa are formulated more complexly and obscurely than necessary.

Relevance and simplicity suggest that a taxonomy depend on a minimum number of assumptions and a minimum number of concepts. Alone, these standards neither eliminate taxonomic opaqueness nor verify the clinical utility of a taxonomy's derivations: They merely suggest that excess baggage be eliminated so that the central features of clinical relevance in the system be seen more clearly. Taxonomists, be they clinicians, statisticians, or theorists, who formulate their ideas in a complex network of concepts and assumptions, must anticipate the added burden of overcoming the resistance of less-than-convinced professional colleagues. Excess baggage invites only confusion and trouble.

Diagnostic Reliability. In their review some 25 years ago, Zigler and Phillips (1961) noted that the reliability of diagnostic judgments among clinicians "has been a matter of continuing concern" (p. 610). Although Matarrazo's (1983) more recent appraisal of clinician agreement is more sanguine, the problem remains an ongoing one as new taxonomies continue to appear on the scene.

Despite the advent of reasonably explicit diagnostic criteria in the DSM-III, a step taken to enhance interjudge reliability, the levels of agreement achieved in appraising Axis II disorders as a whole was quite modest, averaging in the vicinity of .60, with the antisocial disorder attaining an impressive .80 level, and that the passive-aggressive diagnosis evidencing a dismaying less-than-chance *negative* coefficient. Not only is satisfactory reliability an essential ingredient in achieving one of the prime purposes of a taxonomy, that of unambiguous communication among clinicians and researchers, but it is, in large measure, a prerequisite for advancing other, more scientific goals.

Poor levels of diagnostic reliability result from clinicians differing in their competence, their sources of information, and the attributes they focus on. Beyond these personal, informational, and observational sources of variance are a number of aspects of the taxonomy itself which contribute to diagnostic disagreements, such as failing to specify the defining features of taxa in as explicit a manner as possible, or overlooking inclusion or exclusion features of infrequent prevalence. Complications such as these are especially problematic when proceeding from broad, inclusive groups (e.g., mood or affective disorders), to narrower, more focal ones (e.g., bipolar disorder, mixed).

It may be of interest to record what Zigler and Phillips (1961) had to say years ago; it remains apt today:

While certain extraclassificatory factors, e.g., proficiency of the clinicians, biases of the particular clinical settings, etc., may influence it, reliability is primarily related to the precision with which classes of schema are defined. Since the defining characteristic of most classes in psychiatric diagnosis is the occurrence of symptoms in particular combinations, the reliability of the system mirrors the specificity with which the various combinations of symptoms (syndromes) have been spelled out. It is mandatory for a classificatory system to be reliable since reliability refers to the definiteness with which phenomena can be ordered to classes. If a system does not allow for such a division of phenomena, it can make no pretense of being a classificatory schema. (p. 610)

Representative Scope. If a taxonomy is too narrow in its range of applicability, failing to encompass the broad variety of disorders for which clinicians have diagnostic responsibility, then its level of utility and acceptance will be markedly diminished. Ideally, the number of taxa and attributes to which a taxonomy applies should not be limited. So comprehensive a requirement is, of course, neither feasible nor possible, except in official nosologies such as DSM-III or ICD-9. Nevertheless, many clinically and scientifically derived taxonomies are constructed to cover only the very limited data and concepts from which they were initially generated. This early stage formulation may restrict its long-range or potential applicability. It is preferable, therefore, that the taxa of a classification be sufficiently numerous to encompass future refinements and new clinical conditions, should such elaborations be justified.

Implicit in the standard of representative scope is the suggestion that the value of a taxonomy may be gauged by its ability to generate or to subsume new observations after its initial formulation. Despite the importance of this criterion, it is wise to recognize that a disparity wil exist between the *potential* range of a taxonomy's applicability and its *actual* range of empirical support. Failure to keep this disparity in mind can lead only to erroneous generalizations.

Another, somewhat related problem often arises in attempts to balance the twin standards of reliability and of scope, at least with regard to taxa, if not taxonomies. Blashfield and Draguns (1976) related the problem as follows:

Classifiers are faced with an apparent paradox. If categories (taxa) are precisely defined, the reliability of the classificaiton will be relatively good, but the coverage will be poor. On the other hand, if the categories have vague general definitions, then complete coverage will be possible, but reliability will suffer. Since coverage and reliability are both important criteria if a classification is to be used for communication, this apparent paradox is quite important. (p. 145)

Illustrating this issue with reference to the precise defining features and the highly reliable manner with which the DSM-III antisocial personality taxon is judged, Widiger and Trull (1987) write:

> The DSM-III diagnostic criteria for the antisocial personality disorder have been faulted for being too narrowly focused on criminal and delinquent behavior. The criteria set has achieved high levels of reliability but there is more to the construct of psychopathy-sociopathy than criminal behavior.... These constructs are difficult to measure, but an inaccurate measure of sociopathy may be more useful to a clinician than a measure of the tendency to be arrested. Even if clinicians disagree in their diagnoses they may be more accurate in assessing sociopathy than the readily verifiable DSM-III criteria.

Concurrent Robustness. As commented on previously, prescientific taxonomies draw their data and organize their taxa on the basis of patterns of covariation observed among clinical symptoms and signs. Categories formed in accord with monothetic rules exhibit high measures of homogeneity within taxa, that is, substantial phenotypic similarity among its constituent members. A question arises as to whether taxonic groupings so formed are robust; that is, retain their membership composition under new conditions and with attributes other than those used to construct them initially. Thus, monothetic (homogeneous) taxa based on a single source of data (e.g., test scores), or one type of attribute (e.g., interpersonal conduct), or one class of patients (e.g., inpatients) may fail to cross-generalize, that is, to remain stable, distinct, and uniform when based on parallel, yet unidentical sources of data (e.g., structured interviews), attributes (e.g., cognitive style), or populations (e.g., outpatients).

Among the ostensive attractions of "scientific" taxa (i.e., based on numerical derivations or theoretical deductions), is that their coherence represents "fundamental" or genotypic processes and, hence, would presumably be sustained across diverse measures, conditions, and persons (Wright & Murphy, 1984). Appealing as this prospect may be, little work has been carried out comparing the robustness or concurrent equivalence of taxa based on different data sources (observation, psychological tests, interviews, biological indices, social history), divergent clinical attributes (interpersonal, behavioral, cognitive, intrapsychic, affective), or population samples (outpatients, inpatients, admission units, public hospitals, drug rehabilitation centers). Nor has any evidence been adduced to argue convincingly that substantial robustness is achieved with theoretically and numerically developed taxonomies.

The concepts and methodologies termed "convergent and discriminant validity," formulated initially in the research design writings of

Campbell and Fiske (1959), are especially pertinent to the issue of concurrent robustness. Skinner (1981) summarized these concepts as follows:

> Convergent validity involves the extent to which individuals are classified according to the same type across alternative measures, such as behavioral observations, symptoms, personality characteristics, and social history. Discriminant validity addresses the distinctiveness among types across alternative measures. Poor discriminant validity would be evidenced by the finding that the differentiation among types based on one assessment mode (e.g., self-report data) was largely lost when the classification is attempted with a parallel set of measures (e.g., clinical ratings). (p. 77)

Longitudinal Matching. Whereas the standard of concurrent robustness addresses the extent to which the categories of a taxonomy remain stable (if polythetically arranged), or distinct and homogeneous (if monothetically arranged) across diverse data sources, attributes, and populations, the standard of longitudinal matching relates to the accuracy with which taxonic categories correspond to a variety of typically nontaxonic data of an essentially biographic and prognostic nature.

Longitudinal matching transcends the validational significance of concurrent robustness in that evidence of the latter type demonstrates, as in the case of correlations among psychological tests, that the elements being compared merely produce similar results, and nothing more. If concurrent measures fail to correlate there is no way of knowing which of the compared measures is the worse and which the better, if either is of any value at all. By contrast, gauges of longitudinal matching demonstrate either a factual correspondence to known prior events, or a predictive power to anticipate future ones. Evidence leading to correct retrospective deductions concerning biographic history, or to the forecasting of prognostic course or treatment response is, in the last analysis, the most potent gauge of a taxonomy's validity.

Care must be taken to guard against the temptation to make "retrodictions" or "predictions" after the facts have been recorded. Such "facts" may be dressed up into an acceptable propositional form, and then presented as verification of a taxonomy's accuracy, when contradictory results might also have been successfully "explained." The need for caution is clear: confidence in a taxonomy's validity must be restrained until its empirical consequences are unequivocal and genuinely retrodictive or predictive.

Taxonomic Validation Procedures

This section will briefly address a few of the more empirically oriented procedures employed to appraise existent taxonomies. The standards described in previous pages have played a small role in evaluating classifications for two principal reasons. First, historic and contemporary nosologies are almost invariably of the prescientific or clinically based sort, rarely conceived with considerations of logic and methodology in mind. Second, the standards that have been set forth are quite demanding, likely to be achieved with difficulty, but only among the more advanced biological taxonomies, where data are tangible, quantitative, and manipulable. Lamenting the difficulties of psychopathologic classification, Feinstein noted (1977):

> The opportunity to perform an external validation is both the greatest strength and the greatest weakness of inferential classificaitons. The strength arises because we check against something that is outside our own intellectual machinations. This kind of external check provides the kind of fundamental scientific assurance that people seek in the form of objective proof. The main weakness of the external validation is its requirement for something that is both external and acceptable to validate against. . . . Almost none of them is susceptible, within the limitations of human reality, to tests by methods that would be clinically practical as well as scientifically acceptable. (p. 197)

Two matters of taxonomic interest have been subjected to regular empirical evaluation: those of interjudge reliability and those of compositional resemblance. In the former, statistical procedures gauge the extent to which clinicians agree in their diagnostic ascriptions. In the latter, numerical procedures examine consonance among diagnostic structures.

Interdiagnostician Agreement. Although it would appear a straightforward matter, the simple calculation of diagnostic agreement among clinicians proves to be a problematic statistic. Some difficulties arise from the fact that agreement percents can be affected both by disorder base rates and diagnostician assignment rates. To obviate confounding factors such as these, Cohen (1960) introduced what is termed the *Kappa* statistic, calculated as the percentage of observed agreement, less chance agreement. Analogous in its numerical distribution to intraclass correlation, it provides comparability across samples with base rate differences. Maxwell (1977) noted that the Kappa statistic assumes that clinicians engage in random diagnostic choices, a position he contends cannot be sustained. Asserting that diagnosticians choose in a systematically biased manner, Maxwell proposed a statistical correction that obviates the randomness assumption, terming it the "random error coefficient." Following up this debate, Janes (1979) found that Cohen and Maxwell's measures obtain comparable levels of agreement where disorder base rates approximate equivalence; where base rate divergences are substantial, however, the measures lead often to appreciably different results.

Compositional Resemblance. Statistical methods to appraise profile and configurational correspondence among ostensively comparable taxonomies are rather new. Moreover, there is little agreement, or clarity for that matter, on what notions such as resemblance or homogeneity might mean in polythetic taxa, no less how to gauge them statistically. In addition to factor and cluster methods, which lend themselves to evaluation as well as construction purposes, the following procedures also are employed as taxonomic evaluative measures.

Multivariate analyses of variance (MANOVA), a widely applied statistic, provides a useful means of simultaneously comparing both the magnitude and configuration of attribute scores among taxonic groups. With the severity level and symptom pattern calculated for two or more disorders (e.g., major depression, dysthymia, bipolar disorder), MANOVA will enable a researcher to determine whether their profile elevations (illness severity) are comparable and, controlling for elevation, whether their profile shapes (symptom pattern) are commensurable. The elevation statistic is a test of severity comparability, whereas the profile statistic is a test of attribute similarity.

Beginning with several populations that meet the criteria of established taxa, the method of *discriminant analysis* selects the optimal combination of attributes to accurately allocate patients. In contrast to MANOVA, which aims to increase between-group differences, discriminant analysis identifies and assigns attribute weights to produce the greatest number of "correct" taxonic placements. The success rate of discriminant analysis is often "incestuous," however, that is, its quantitative results are based on the same population used in its initial development, producing thereby impressively high (and inflated) "hit rates." Unless cross-validated with a fresh population in settings comprising different disorder base rates, the commendable initial results may prove to be largely spurious (Grove & Andreasen, 1986).

Appraising Clinical Attributes

In his excellent review of issues associated with psychiatric diagnosis, Kendell (1975) refered to the following, all-too-common problem:

> The information that the subjects of a particular study had all been diagnosed as schizophrenic or hysterics often tells us remarkably little about them, certainly not enough for us to be able to assemble another group of patients with any confidence that they would be comparable. (p. 137)

In a chapter by the author on the history of the DSM-III, the virtues of specifying clear criteria for defining the features of patients assigned the same diagnostic taxon are noted as follows (Millon, 1986a):

> It is this very precision in articulating specific and uniform rules of definition, originally and significantly termed *operational criteria*, that makes the DSM-III so serviceable and potentially fruitful also as a research tool. Not only do the criteria delineate the components that will enable reasonably homogeneous group assignments, but its application as a standard national (and it is hoped, international) gauge will ensure at least a modicum of reliability and comparability among studies undertaken at diverse research settings. (p. 52)

It is not only when contradictory research findings result that one wonders if the problem of taxonic unreliability stems from the use of dissimilar clinical attributes. Common also are communication disagreements among practicing clinicians. Unless they agree on the attributes they employ to identify a diagnostic taxon, it may be impossible to determine whether they are dealing with different patients or simply talking about different clinical entities.

Complicating matters further is the statistical fact that enhanced reliability may not only fail to contribute to enhanced validity (Carey & Gottesman, 1978), but that defining features which achieve the highest levels of reliability are often neither useful nor especially efficient diagnostically. For example, the explicit criteria of the antisocial disorder reliably identifies "criminal behaviors" at the expense of overlooking broader and diagnostically more useful "sociopathic" characteristics (Widiger, Hurt, Frances, Clarkin, & Gilmore, 1984).

Despite these limits, it would appear reasonable to assume that explicit diagnostic criteria, such as found in the DSM-III, would lead to improved interdiagnostician reliability, as well as greater patient comparability among research studies. There are, however, substantive deficits in the DSM-III criteria that deserve continued attention. As the author has noted previously (Millon, 1983, 1984), the DSM-III criteria offer no more than a promise and inspiration. Interjudge reliability data were obtained during the field trials, and these are encouraging in the main, especially when compared to prior studies of earlier classifications. Nevertheless, most DSM-III criteria (as will be those of DSM-III-R, for that matter) lack empirical support. Some are inadequately explicit or, conversely, are overly concrete in their operational referents. Many are internally redundant, simply restating the same defining feature in different words or illustrative examples. Others are insufficiently comprehensive in taxonic scope, are not comparable in their attributes, or display a lack of symmetry among parallel taxa. At best, then, the diagnostic criteria of the

DSM-III represent a significant *conceptual* step toward a future goal when clinical attributes of appropriate relevance and breadth will provide reliable, valid, and diagnostically efficient indices for identifying major taxonic classes.

In their seminal paper on diagnostic efficiency, Widiger *et al.* (1984) suggested numerous steps that can further improve the auspicious beginnings of DSM-III. They wrote:

> Psychodiagnosis may be improved further and made more specific, however, by developing methods for weighting the diagnostic criteria differentially, rather than assuming that all criteria are equally important, by considering the diagnostic efficiency of combinations of symptoms as well as single symptoms, and by using the overlap among diagnoses to the diagnostician's advantage. (p. 1005)

Optimal Attribute Standards

If we put aside for the present the more general concerns registered about DSM-III criteria, we may proceed to ask whether certain properties of clinical attributes would enable them to serve optimally as a source of diagnostic criteria. Several are worth noting.

Feature Comparability. One step toward the goal of refining diagnostic comparisons is to spell out a series of defining features for every relevant clinical attribute associated with a set of parallel diagnostic taxa. For example, if the clinical attribute "interpersonal conduct" is deemed of diagnostic value in identifying and differentiating personality disorder taxa, then a distinctive description should be written to represent *the* characteristic or singular manner in which each personality disorder "conducts its interpersonal life."

The notion that clinical attributes be arranged in parallel and comparable form is known as the concept of "homology" in biological taxonomies. As Sneath and Sokal (1973) have phrased it:

> If we are to compare "apples and oranges", we must compare them over a set of characteristics applicable to both of them.
>
> Homology may be loosely described as compositional and structural correspondence. By *compositional correspondence* we mean a qualitative resemblance in biological or chemical constituents; by *structual correspondence* we refer to similarity in terms of arrangements of parts. (pp. 75, 77)

Others have referred to schemas composed of comparable constituents as "attributive matching" or "relational matching" (Jardine & Jardine, 1969). By composing a taxonomy that includes all relevant clinical attributes (e.g., behavioral presentation, mood expression, cognitive sytle), and specifies a distinctive defining feature on every attribute for each of a set of parallel taxa (e.g., the 11 personality disorders in DSM-III), the resulting classification would be both fully comprehensive in clinical scope, and possess directly comparable constituents among its diagnostic features. Table 1 (p. 32) illustrated a set of comparable defining features on the "interpersonal conduct" attribute for each of the 13 personality disorders derived from the author's biosocial theory (Millon, 1969, 1986b, 1986c). A directly comparable format of this nature furnishes symmetry among the taxa comprising a taxonomy, enabling investigators thereby to systematically compare each taxon's diagnostic validity (e.g., sensitivity, specificity), as well as each attribute's relative diagnostic efficiency (e.g., positive and negative predictive power).

Empirical Reference. The expectation that taxonic attributes be well-defined and verifiable is stated by Hempel (1965) as follows:

> If a classificatory scheme is to be used with a high degree of uniformity by different investigators, the concepts determining its various subclasses will have to possess clear criteria of application that can be stated in terms of publically ascertainable characteristics. (p. 144)

As noted previously, attributes that depend on intricate, higher-order inferences are major factors contributing to diagnostic unreliability. Clinicians agree more readily on observations of concrete behavior, such as "he slams his fist repeatedly," than on a complex intrapsychic inference, such as "his object-related structures exhibit a dedifferentiated configuration." Lest it appear that simple or lower-order inferences assure interjudge consistency, one can quickly be disabused of this belief by reflecting on case conference staff disagreements concerning mini-diagnostic attributions, such as whether a patient is "anxious," "distressed," "depressed," or "melancholic." To quote Hempel (1965) further:

> While the formulation of more reliable criteria of applicaiton is certainly very desirable, it is not, I am sure, always an easy task. . . . It would therefore be unreasonable and self-defeating to insist on the highest standards of precision from the beginning; but it is important to aim at increasingly reliable criteria. (p. 145)

Where feasible, the defining features that comprise diagnostic criteria should be assigned properties in the observable world. A problem arises when one attempts to balance the desire for generality or openness among attributes with the standard of empirical precision. As discussed with regard to the problem of balancing the taxonic standards of reliability and scope, can we achieve empirical relevance among attributes, and thereby minimize ambiguity in language, while simultaneously freeing them to encompass a wide range of phenomena?

The use of open concepts, discussed earlier in this chapter, encourages the view that taxonomies progress by enabling their attributes to be defined by a variety of different empirical phenomena. Allowing diverse yet related clinical events to serve as indicators or illustrations of an attribute permits taxonomists to achieve an optimal compromise between generality and empirical reference.

There are open concepts, however, that do not meet empirical standards; nevertheless, they may be extremely valuable in representing hidden or elusive phenomena of considerable taxonic relevance. For example, the explication of the crucial role played by unconscious processes may be entirely impossible or extremely difficult to articulate without them (e.g., defense mechanisms, intrapsychic organization). Ultimately, and where feasible, these "hypothetical" constructs should be coordinated to the empirical domain by extending them gradually to encompass their more concrete and observable correlates.

Certain defining features of clinical attributes may undermine the integrity of a taxon, specifically those which "beg questions" for which the taxon should seek answers. To illustrate, if a defining feature embedded in the schizophrenic taxon calls for a genetic inference, then the inference suggests a conclusion to an etiologic question that the taxon may be called upon to answer. It is not the inference per se that is problematic, but the assumption of a fact that may be not only unwarranted, but may deserve future study on the basis of that taxon.

Several proposals have been made through the years to increase the referential precision of clinical attributes, beginning with suggestions by Lazarsfeld (1950), to the effect that complex features such as traits and attitudes be subdivided into smaller and more explicit components. We previously discussed several recent methods designed to enhance the empirical basis of inferred traits, notably Buss and Craik's (1983, 1984) and Livesley's (1985a, 1985b) procedures for selecting "prototypal acts." A thoughtful review of this and comparable procedures will be found in Widiger and Frances (1985a,b); similarly, a "debate" in the *Journal of Personality Disorders* on the theme of explicit versus inferential diagnostic criteria highlights the respective advantages and disadvantages of these methods.

Quantitative Range. Most psychopathological features express themselves as a matter of degree rather than simple presence or absence (e.g., severity of depression, level of anxiety). Hence, it would be useful if the clinical attributes that comprise taxa would permit the registration of a wide range of intensity or frequency differences. This psychometric property of quantitative gradation is one of the major strengths of psychologocial tests, but it is not limited to them. For example, in a recent series of investigations carried out by the author and his research associates, clinical judges were asked not only to identify whether certain defining features characterized a patient, but also to record a number (from 1 to 10) to represent the degree of prominence or pervasiveness of each of the defining features that were present. As indicated in our earlier discussion concerning categorical versus dimensional attribute compositions, judges were encouraged to record and quantify not only one defining feature, but several per clinical attribute, permitting both the multiple listing of a number of different defining features and differentiating them quantitatively as to their relative *degrees* of clinical prominence or pervasiveness.

Cumulative "scores" obtained on several clinical attributes composed of multiple defining features will no doubt result in complex configurations that may require simplification for routine use. Diagnostic profiles such as these will provide, however, a clinically rich and insightful portrayal of patients, as well as usefully detailed information for research investigations. Not to be overlooked is its potential for therapeutic decisions, such as identifying which attribute might best serve as the initial focus of treatment (e.g., deciding to address a defining feature of the interpersonal conduct attribute that has been shown to benefit from "group or family techniques," pinpointing an expressive mood attribute especially responsive to "pharmacotherapy," and so on).

Diagnostic Accuracy. As suggested previously, a host of diverse clinical attributes (e.g., interpersonal conduct, cognitive style) should be drawn upon to identify the specific defining features (e.g., hostile or labile among the "expressive mood" attribute) that best characterize a taxon. The diagnostic accuracy (Meehl & Rosen, 1955) of a defining feature is usually gauged by its ability to correctly detect cases known to fit a specific taxon (true-positive rate), relative to its level of incorrect ascriptions (false-positive rate).

In monothetic taxa, all of a taxon's defining features must be present to achieve a correct diagnosis; hence, all defining features have the same true-positive rate, that of 100%; differences in diagnostic accuracy occur only if defining features differ in their false-positive rate.

Matters are more complicated in polythetic taxa since diagnostic membership can be determined in multiple ways, and defining features differ both in their true- and false-positive rates. Given that the defining features are neither singly necessary nor jointly sufficient, diagnostic accuracy among polythetic taxa is entirely probabalistic. Each feature of each attribute must be calculated separately and empirically with an appropriate (i.e., reasonably generalizable) clinical population. These obsessive steps are complicated further by the fact that diagnostic accuracy varies with clinical population base rates (e.g., inpatient admissions ward versus family therapy centers), as well as the specific clinical groups one may seek to differentiate (e.g., a defining feature may be highly accurate in differentiating histrionic from schizoid personalities, but poor in distinguishing histrionics from narcissists). Other considerations to be kept in mind in appraising the efficiency of defining features are noted by Frances and Widiger (1986) in the following example:

> It is also important to consider its efficiency when in various combinations with the other definitional features. A feature with low efficiency when present alone might become quite important in combination with certain other features. A localized headache is not especially diagnostic by itself, but in combination with certain other symptoms (e.g., contralateral sensory impairments) it can become highly suggestive. Personality disorders are typically conceptualized as being a constellation of features, and it would be misleading to dismiss a feature based on its diagnostic efficiency when it is considered by itself, ignoring its efficiency when it is combined with other features. (p. 394)

Attribute Validation Procedures

The following statistical terminology, developed first by Yerushalmy (1947), and recently applied by Baldessarini *et al.* (1983) and Widiger *et al.* (1984), relate to the probabalistic, covariant relationships between attributes (specific symptoms) and taxa (specific disorders). As in the early pages of this chapter, a number of concepts will be employed that may not be familiar to the reader. Some terms will be defined in the following paragraphs; certain relationships among them are summarized in Table 2.

Sensitivity and Specificity. The statistic termed *sensitivity,* also known as the true-positive rate, is the proportion of persons with a diagnosed dis-

Table 2. Taxonic Validity and Attribute Efficiency Terminology

Attribute presence	Actual diagnosis[a]	
	Positive	Negative
Positive	True-positives (a)	False-positives (b)
Negative	False-negatives (c)	True-negatives (d)
Total	Total positives (a+c)	Total negatives (b+d)

Note. From "The Predictive Power of Diagnostic Tests and the Effect of Prevalence of Illness" by R. Baldessarini, S. Finkelstein, and G. Arana, 1983, *Archives of General Psychiatry, 40,* p. 570, and "Diagnostic Efficiency and DSM-III" by T. A. Widiger, W. W. Hurt, A. Frances, J. F. Clarkin, and M. Gilmore, 1984, *Archives of General Psychiatry, 41,* p. 1006. Adapted by permission.
[a]Base rate = (a+c) / (a+b+c+d); sensitivity or true-positive rate = a/ (a+c); specificity or true-negative rate = d/ (b+d); negative predictive power = d/ (c+d); positive predictive power = a/(a+b).

order who manifest a particular attribute (symptom, sign, trait, etiology); it is also the "conditional probability" of possessing a particular attribute given that one has a particular disorder. The *specificity* statistic, otherwise referred to as the true-negative rate, is the proportion of persons without a particular disorder who do not manifest a particular attribute. It also represents the conditional probability of not having the attribute, given that one does not have a disorder. We will refer to both sensitivity and specificity as measures of *taxonic validity* in that they reflect a taxon's differential diagnostic accuracy in corresponding to the attributes (defining features) of which it ostensibly is composed.

Whereas true-positive rate (sensitivity) and true-negative rate (specificity) are essential to the evaluation of the diagnostic validity of taxonic attributes, Widiger *et al.* (1984) convincingly argued that these measures do not provide as complete and useful a picture as possible. They illustrate that in certain instances both sensitivity and specificity statistics may prove misleading (e.g., base rate conditions in which both measures of an attribute are high, but where diagnostic assignments will be more incorrect than correct).

Positive and Negative Predictive Power. The *positive predictive power (PPP)* statistic represents the proportion of persons with a particular attribute who have a particular disorder; it equals the conditional probability of possessing the disorder, given that one possesses the attribute. *Negative predictive power (NPP),* in contrast, represents the proportion of persons without a particular attribute who do not have a particular disorder. We will refer to both positive and negative predictive power as measures of *attribute efficiency* in that they reflect an attribute's differential diagnostic accuracy in corresponding to the taxon of which it ostensibly is a defining feature.

The value of these efficiency measures can be seen readily by contrasting the information they provide to that furnished by the sensitivity and specificity statistics. Whereas sensitivity generates a probability figure indicating the percentage of patients with a particular disorder (e.g., histrionic personality) who are likely to exhibit a particular attribute (e.g., exaggerated emotionality), it may be equally (if not more) useful clinically to estimate the percentage of patients who possess a particular disorder on the basis of having exhibited a particular attribute. In *PPP* or *NPP,* the predictive relationship of the sensitivity and specificity measures is reversed, that is, the probability of a diagnosis (histrionic) is gauged by the presence of a defining feature (exaggerated emotionality). *PPP* furnishes the other side of the sensitivity coin; similarly, *NPP* provides the reverse side of the specificity statistic.

SUMMARY

Long as the chapter has been, it is but a brief and inadequate sketch of a burgeoning field. It is hoped that the chapter will have tempted the reader to plunge more deeply into the subject, having tested its waters ever so lightly.

A point worthy of being made in conclusion pertains to the multitude of intellectual fronts open in taxonomic study to the clinically and academically curious. There are no unequivocal answers to the many questions posed in psychopathologic taxonomy, be it the matter of selecting attributes, choosing structures, or opting for one construction method or another.

In saying the foregoing, we do not mean to imply that the philosophies and techniques of today are irrelevant, or that the theoretical or diagnostic underpinnings of contemporary practice are valueless. Rather, we wish to raise a caveat to the effect that both taxonomic and diagnostic conceptualizers would do well to step back and reflect on established techniques and formulations, while at the same time restrain themselves from imposing newer methodologies or clever theories, without substantive data. We must keep our distance from the twin foibles of traditionalism and faddism. Otherwise, taxonomics will degenerate into forms that reduce the richness of the natural clinical world into a playing field for competing and abstruse speculations, on the one hand, and passive receptacles that are shaped by the dehumanized and arcane methods of mathematical analysis, on the other. Protected from neither convention, vogue, presumption, or cabalism, taxonomic psychopathology could become dogmatic, trivial, or formalistic, as well as devoid of a substantive life of its own. Prevailing frameworks are to be challenged, and imaginative alternatives stimulated—yet always with the realities of the clinic and its patients in prime focus.

REFERENCES

American Psychiatric Association. (1980). *Diagnostic and statistical manual of mental disorders (3rd ed.).* Washington DC: Author.

Andreasen, N., & Grove, W. (1982). The classification of depression: A comparison of traditional and mathematically derived approaches. *American Journal of Psychiatry, 139,* 45–52.

Baldessarini, R. Finkelstein, S., Arana, G. (1983). The predictive power of diagnostic tests and the effect of prevalence of illness. *Archives of General Psychiatry, 40,* 569–573.

80   THEODORE MILLON

Bandura, A. (1982). The psychology of chance encounters and life paths. *American Psychologist, 37,* 747–755.
Benjamin, L. S. (1974). Structural analysis of social behavior. *Psychological Review, 81,* 392–425.
Benjamin, L. S. (1986). Adding social and intrapsychic descriptors to Axis I of DSM-III. In T. Millon & G. L. Klerman (Eds.), *Contemporary directions in psychopathology: Towards the DSM-IV.* New York: Guilford.
Benjamin, L. S. (1987). Use of the SASB dimensional model to develop treatment plans for personality disorders: I. Narcissism. *Journal of Personality Disorders, 1,* 43–47.
Blashfield, R. K. (1984). *The classification of psychopathology.* New York: Plenum Press.
Blashfield R. K., & Draguns, J. G. (1976). Evaluative criteria for psychiatric classification. *Journal of Abnormal Psychology, 85,* 140–150.
Boring, E. G. (1950). *A history of experimental psychology* (2nd ed.). New York: Appleton-Century-Crofts.
Bowers, K. S. (1977). There's more to Iago than meets the eye: A clinical account of personal consistency. In D. Magnusson & N. S. Endler (eds.)*Personality at the crossroads.* Hillsdale, NJ: Erlbaum.
Bridgman, P. W. (1927). *The logic of modern physics.* New York: Macmillan.
Buss, D. M., & Craik, K. H. (1983). The act frequency approach to personality. *Psychological Review, 90,* 105–126.
Buss, D. M., & Craik, K. H. (1984). Acts, dispositions and personality. In B. Maher & W. Maher (Eds.) *Progress in experimental personality research* (Vol. 13). New York: Academic Press.
Buss, D. M., & Craik, K. H. (1987). Act criteria for the diagnosis of personality disorders. *Journal of Personality Disorders, 1 (1)* 73–81.
Campbell, D. T., & Fiske, D. W. (1959). Convergent and discriminant validation by the multitrait-multimethod matrix. *Psychological Bulletin, 56,* 81–105.
Cantor, N., & Genero, N. (1986). Psychiatric diagnosis and natural categorization: A close analogy. In T. Millon, & G.L. Klerman (Eds.), *Contemporary directions in psychopathology: Towards the DSM-IV.* New York: Guilford.
Cantor, N. & Mischel, W. (1979). Prototypes in person perception. In L. Berkowitz (Ed.), *Advances in experimental social psychology* (Vol. 12) New York: Academic Press.
Carey, G., & Gottesman, I. (1978). Reliability and validity in binary ratings. *Archives of General Psychiatry, 35,* 1454–1459.
Cattell, R. B. (1965). *The scientific analysis of personality.* Chicago: Aldine.
Conte, H., & Plutchik, R. (1981). A complex model for interpersonal personality traits. *Journal of Personality and Social Psychology, 40,* 701–711.
Dougherty, J. W. D. (1978). Salience and relatively in classification. *American Ethnologist, 5,* 66–80.
Essen-Möller, E., & Wohlfahrt, S. (1947). Suggestions for the amendment of the official Swedish classification of mental disorders. *Acta Psychiatrica Scandinavia Supplement, 47,* 551–555.
Everitt, B. S. (1980). *Cluster analysis* (2nd ed.). London: Halstead Press.
Eysenck, H. J. (1960). *The structure of human personality.* London: Routledge & Kegan Paul.
Feinstein, A. R. (1977). A critical overview of diagnosis in psychiatry. In V. M. Rakoff, H. C. Stancer, & H. B. Kedward (Eds.), *Psychiatric diagnosis.* New York: Brunner/Mazel.
Finn, S. E. (1982). Base rates, utilities, and DSM-III. Shortcomings of fixed-rate systems of psychodiagnosis. *Journal of Abnormal Psychology, 91,* 294–302.
Fleiss, J. L. (1972). Classification of the depressive disorders by numerical typology. *Journal of Psychiatric Research, 9,* 141–153.

Forgy, E. W. (1968). Discussant's remarks. In M. M. Katz, J. O. Cole, & W. E. Barton (Eds.), *Classification in psychiatry and psychopathology.* Washington D.C.: Public Health Service Publications.

Frances, A. (1982). Categorical and dimensional systems of personality diagnosis: A comparison. *Comprehensive Psychiatry, 23,* 516–527.

Frances, A., & Widiger, T. A. (1986). Methodological issues in pesonality disorder diagnosis. In T. Millon & G. L. Klerman (Eds.), *Contemporary directions in psychopathology: Towards the DSM-IV.* New York: Guilford.

Frances, A., Clarkin, J. & Perry, S. (1985). *Differential therapeutics in psychology.* New York: Brunner/Mazel.

Grove, W. M., Andreasen, N. C. (1986). Multivariate statistical analysis in psychopathology. In T. Millon & G. L. Klerman (Eds.), *Contemporary directions in psychopathology: Towards the DSM-IV.* New York: Guilford.

Harman, H. H. (1976). *Modern factor analysis* (3rd ed.). Chicago: University of Chicago Press.

Hartigan, J. A. (1975). *Clustering algorithms.* New York: Wiley.

Hathaway, S. R., & McKinley, J. C. (1943). *Manual for the Minnesota Multiphasic Personality Inventory.* New York: Psychological Corporation.

Heelan, P. A. (1977). The nature of clinical science. *Journal of Medicine and Philosophy, 2,* 20–32.

Hempel, C. G. (1961). Introduction to problems of taxonomy. In J. Zubin (Ed.), *Field studies in the mental disorders* (pp. 3-22). New York: Grune & Stratton.

Hempel, C. G. (1965). *Aspects of scientific explanation.* New York: Free Press.

Horowitz, L., Post, D., French, R., Wallis, K., & Siegelman, E. (1981). The prototype as a construct in abnormal psychology: 2. Clarifying disagreement in psychiatric judgments. *Journal of Abnormal Psychology, 90,* 575–585.

Jackson, D. W. (1971). The dynamics of structured personality tests. *Psychological Review, 78,* 229–248.

Janes, C. L. (1979). Agreement measurement and the judgment process. *Journal of Nervous and Mental Disease, 167,* 343–347.

Jardine, N. & Jardine, C. J. (1969). Is there a concept of homology common to several sciences? *Classification Society Bulletin, 2,* 12–18.

Kaplan, A. (1964). *The conduct of inquiry.* San Francisco: Chandler.

Kendell, R. E. (1968). *The classification of depressive illness.* London: Oxford University Press.

Kendell, R. E. (1975). *The role of diagnosis in psychiatry..* Oxford: Blackwell.

Kernberg, O. (1984). *Severe personality disorders.* New Haven: Yale University Press.

Kiesler, D. J. (1983). The 1982 interpersonal circle: A taxonomy for complementarity in human transactions. *Psychological Review, 90,* 185–214.

Kiesler, D. J. (1986). The 1982 interpersonal circle: An analysis of DSM-III personality disorders. In T. Millon & G. L. Klerman (Eds.), *Contemporary directions of psychopathology: Towards the DSM-IV.* New York: Guilford.

Klein, D. F., Gittelman, R., Quitkin, F., & Rifkin, A. (1980). *Diagnosis and drug treatment and psychiatric disorders* (2nd ed.). Baltimore: Williams & Wilkins.

Kraepelin, E. (1899). *Psychiatrie: Ein lehrbuch* (6th ed.). Leipzig: Barth.

Lazarsfeld, P. F. (1950). The logical and mathematical foundation of latent structure analysis. In S. A. Stouffer (Ed.), *Measurement and prediction.* Princeton, N.J.: Princeton University Press.

Leahey, T. (1980). The myth of operationism. *Journal of Mind and Behavior, 1,* 127–143.

Leary, T. (1957). *Interpersonal diagnosis and personality.* New York: Ronald Press.

Livesley, W. J. (1985a). The classification of personality disorder: 1. The choice of category concept. *Canadian Journal of Psychiatry, 30,* 353–358.

Livesley, W. J. (1985b). The classification of personality disorder: 2. The problem of diagnostic criteria. *Canadian Journal of Psychiatry, 30,* 359–362.

Livesley, W. J. (1986a). Trait and behavior prototypes of personality disorder. *American Journal of Psychiatry, 43,* 1018–1022.

Livesley, W. J. (1986b). Theoretical and empirical issues in the selection of criteria to diagnose personality disorders. *Journal of Personality Disorders, 1,* 88–94.

Loevinger, J. (1957). Objective tests as measurements of psychological theory. *Psychological Reports, 3,* 635–694.

Lorr, M. (1966). *Explorations in typing and psychotics.* New York: Pergamon Press.

Lorr, M., Bishop, P. F., & McNair, D. M. (1965). Interpersonal types among psychiatric patients. *Journal of Abnormal Psychology, 70,* 468–472.

Matarazzo, J. D. (1983) The reliability of psychiatric and psychological diagnosis. *Clinical Psychological Review, 3,* 103–145.

Maxwell, A. E. (1977). Coefficients of agreement between observers and their interpretation. *British Journal of Psychiatry, 67,* 30–42.

McKeon, J. J. (1967). *Hierarchical cluster analysis.* Washington, DC: George Washington University Biometrics Laboratory.

Medin, D. L., Altom, M. W., Edelson, S. M., & Freko, D. (1982). Correlated symptoms and simulated medical classification. *Journal of Experimental Psychology: Learning, Memory and Cognition, 8,* 37–50.

Meehl, P. E. (1972) Specific genetic etiology, psychodynamics, and therapeutic nihilism. *International Journal of Mental Health, 1,* 10–27.

Meehl, P. E. (1973). Why I do not attend case conferences. In P. E. Meehl (Ed.), *Psychodiagnosis: Selected papers.* Minneapolis: University of Minnesota Press.

Meehl, P. E. (1978). Theoretical risks and tabular asterisks: Sir Karl, Sir Ronald, and the slow progress of soft psychology. *Journal of Consulting and Clinical Psychology, 46,* 806–834.

Meehl, P. E. (1986). Diagnostic tests as open concepts: Metatheoretical and statistical questions about reliability and construct validity in the grand stategy of nosological revision. In T. Millon & G. Klerman (Eds.), *Contemporary directions in Psychopathology: Towards the DSM-IV.* New York: Guilford.

Meehl, P. E., & Rosen, A. (1955). Antecedent probability and the efficiency of psychometric signs, patterns or cutting scores. *Psychological Bulletin, 52,* 194–216.

Menninger, K. (1963). *The vital balance.* New York: Viking.

Mezzich, J. E. (1979). Patterns and issues in the multiaxial psychiatric diagnosis. *Psychological Medicine, 9,* 125–137.

Milligan, G. W. (1981). A review of Monte Carlo tests of cluster analysis. *Multivariate Behavioral Research, 16,* 379–407.

Millon, T. (1969). *Modern psychopathology: A biosocial approach to maladaptive learning and functioning.* Philadelphia: Saunders.

Millon, T. (1975). Reflections on Rosenhan's "On being sane in insane places." *Journal of Abnormal Psychology, 84,* 456–461.

Millon, T. (1977). *Millon clinical multiaxial inventory Manual.* Minneapolis: National Computer Systems.

Millon, T. (1981). *Disorders of personality: DSM-III, Axis II.* New York: Wiley.

Millon, T. (1982). *Theories of personality and psychopathology.* New York: Holt, Rinehart & Winston.

Millon, T. (1983). The DSM-III: An insider's perspective. *American Psychologist, 38,* 804–814.

Millon, T. (1984). On the renaissance of personality assessment and personality theory. *Journal of Personality Assessment, 48,* 450–466.

Millon, T. (1986a). On the past and future of the DSM-III: Personal recollections and projections. In T. Millon & G. L. Klerman (Eds.), *Contemporary directions and psychopathology: Towards the DSM-IV.* New York: Guilford.

Millon, T. (1986b). A theoretical derivation of pathological personalties. In T. Millon & G. L. Klerman (Eds.), *Contemporary directions in psychopathology: Towards the DSM-IV.* New York: Guilford.

Millon, T. (1986c). Personality prototypes and their diagnostic criteria. In T. Millon & G. L. Klerman (Eds.), *Contemporary directions in psychopathology: Towards the DSM-IV.* New York: Guilford.

Millon, T. (1987). *Millon clinical multiaxial inventory II Manual.* Minneapolis: National Computer Systems.

Millon, T., & Diesenhaus, H. I. (1972). *Research methods in psychopathology.* New York: Wiley.

Mischel, T. (1977). The concept of mental health and disease: An analysis of the controversy between behavioral and psychodynamic approaches. *Journal of Medicine and Philosophy, 2,* 197–220.

Osherson, D. N. and Smith, E. E. (1981). On the adequacy of prototype theory as a theory of concepts. *Cognition, 9,* 35–58.

Overall, J. E. & Hollister, L. E. (1964). Computer procedures for psychiatric classification. *Journal of the American Medical Association, 187,* 583–588.

Overall, J. E., Hollister, L. E., Johnson, M., & Pennington, V. (1966). Nosology of depression and differential response to drugs. *Journal of the American Medical Association, 195,* 946–948.

Panzetta, A. F. (1974). Towards a scientific psychiatric nosology: Conceptual and pragmatic issues. *Archives of General Psychiatry, 30,* 154–161.

Pap, A. (1953). Reduction-sentences and open concepts. *Methods, 5,* 3–30.

Paykel, E. S. (1971). Classification of depressed patients: A cluster analysis derived grouping. *British Journal of Psychiatry, 118,* 275–288.

Plutchik, R. (1967). The affective differential: Emotional profiles implied by diagnostic concepts. *Psychological Reports, 20,* 19–25.

Plutchik, R. & Conte, H. R. (1985). Quantitative assessment of personality disorders. In J. O. Cavenar (Ed.), *Psychiatry* (Vol. I). Philadelphia: Lippincott.

Plutchik, R., & Platman, S. R. (1977). Personality connotations of psychiatric diagnoses: Implications for a similarity model. *Journal of Nervous and Mental Diseases, 165,* 418–422.

Quine, W. V. O. (1961). *From a logical point of view* (2nd. ed.). New York: Harper & Row.

Quine, W. V. O. (1977). Natural kinds. In S. P. Schwartz (Ed.) *Naming, necessity and natural groups.* Ithaca: Cornell University Press.

Rosch, E. (1978). Principles of categorization. In E. Rosch & D. B. Lloyd (Eds.), *Cognition and categorization.* Hillsdale, N.J.: Erlbaum.

Sellars, W. (1963). *Science, perception and reality.* New York: Humanities Press.

Simpson, G. G. (1961). *Principles of animal taxonomy.* New York: Columbia University Press.

Skinner, H. (1981). Towards the integration of classification theory and methods. *Journal of Abnormal Psychology, 90,* 68–87.

Skinner, H. (1986). Construct validation approach to psychiatric classification. In T. Millon & G. L. Klerman (Eds.), *Contemporary directions in psychopathology: Towards the DSM-IV,* New York: Guilford.

Skinner, H. & Blashfield, R. (1982). Increasing the impact of cluster analysis research: the case of psychiatric classification. *Journal of Consulting and Clinical Psychology, 50,* 727–735.

Smith, E. E., & Medin, D. L. (1981). *Categories and concepts.* Cambridge, MA: Harvard University Press.

Sneath, P. H. A., & Sokal, R. R. (1973). *Numerical taxonomy.* San Francisco: Freeman.

Sokal, R. R. (1974). Classification: Purposes, principles, progress, prospects. *Science, 185,* 1115–1123.

Sokal, R. R. & Sneath, P. H. A. (1963). *Principles of numerical taxonomy.* San Francisco: Freeman.

Sprock, J., & Blashfield, R. K. (1984). Classification and nosology. In M. Hersen, A. E. Kazdin, & A. S. Bellack (Eds.), *The clinical psychology handbook.* New York: Pergamon Press.

Stengel, E. (1959). Classification of mental disorders. *Bulletin of the World Health Organization, 21,* 601–663.

Stockings, G. T. (1945). Schizophrenia in military psychiatric practice. *Journal of Mental Science, 91,* 110–112.

Strauss, J. S. (1973). Diagnostic models and the nature of psychiatric disorder. *Archives of General Psychiatry, 29,* 445–449.

Strauss, J. S. (1975). A comprehensive approach to psychiatric diagnoses. *American Journal of Psychiatry, 132,* 1193–1197.

Strauss, J. S. (1986). Psychiatric diagnoses: A reconsideration based on longitudinal processes. In T. Millon & G. L. Klerman (Eds.), *Contemporary directions in psychopathology: Towards the DSM-IV.* New York: Guilford.

Strauss, J. S., Bartko, J. J., & Carpenter, W. T. (1973). The use of clustering techniques for the classification of psychiatric patients. *British Journal of Psychiatry, 122,* 531–540.

Strauss, J. S., Kokes, R. F., Carpenter, W. T. & Ritzler, B. (1978). The course of schizoprhenia as a developmental process. In L. C. Wynne, R. L. Cromwell, & S. Matthysse (Eds.), *Nature of schizophrenia.* New York: Wiley.

Strauss, J. S., Loevsky, L., Glazer, W., & Leaf, P. (1981). Organizing the complexities of schizophrenia. *Journal of Nervous and Mental Disease, 169,* 120–126.

Strober, M., Green, J., & Carlson, G. (1981). Reliability of psychiatraic diagnosis in hospitalized adolescents. *Archives of General Psychiatry, 38,* 141–145.

Torgerson, W. W. (1968). Multidimensional representation of similarity structures. In M. M. Katz, J. O. Cole, & W. E. Barton (Eds.), *Classification in psychiatry and psychopathology.* Washington, DC: Public Health Service Publications.

Tversky, A. (1977). Features of similarity. *Psychological Review, 84,* 327–352.

Weimer, W. (1979). *Notes on the methodology of scientific research.* Hillsdale, N.J.: Erlbaum.

Widiger, T. A. (1983). Utilities and fixed diagnostic rules: Comments on Finn. *Journal of Abnormal Psychology, 92,* 495–498.

Widiger, T. A., & Frances, A. (1985a). Axis II personality disorders: Diagnostic and treatment issues. *Hospital and Community Psychiatry, 36,* 619–627.

Widiger, T. A. & Frances, A. (1985b). The DSM-III personality disorders: Perspectives from psychology. *Archives of General Psychiatry, 42,* 615–623.

Widiger, T. A., & Trull, T. J. (1987). Behavioral indications, hypothetical constructs, and personality disorders. *Journal of Personality Disorders, 1,* 82–87.

Widiger, T. A., Hurt, W. W., Frances, A., Clarkin, J. F., & Gilmore, M. (1984). Diagnostic efficiency and DSM-III. *Archives of General Psychiatry, 41,* 1005–1012.

Wiggins, J. S. (1982). Circumplex models of interpersonal behavior in clinical psychology. In P. C. Kendall & J. N. Butcher (Eds.), *Handbook of research methods in clinical psychology.* New York: Wiley.

Williams, J. B. W. (1985a). The multiaxial system of DSM-III: Where did it come from and where should it go? I. Its origins and critiques. *Archives of General Psychiatry, 42,* 175–180.

Williams, J. B. W. (1985b). The multiaxial system of the DSM-III: Where did it come from and where should it go? II. Empirical studies, innovations, and recommendations. *Archives of General Psychiatry, 42,* 181–186.

Wittgenstein, L. (1953). *Philosophical investigations.* Oxford: Blackwell.

Wright, J. C., & Murphy, G. L. (1984). The utility of theories in intuitive statistics: The robustness of theory-based judgments. *Journal of Experimental Psychology: General, 113,* 301–322.

Yerushalmy, J. (1947). Statistical problems in assessing methods of medical diagnosis, with special reference to X-ray techniques. *Public Health Reports, 62,* 1432–1449.

Zigler, E., & Phillips, L. (1961). Psychiatric diagnosis: A critique. *Journal of Abnormal and Social Psychology, 63,* 607–618.

Zilboorg, G., & Henry, G. W. (1941). *A history of medical psychology.* New York: W. W. Norton.

Zubin, J. (1968). Biometric assessment of mental patients. In M. M. Katz, J. O. Cole, & W. E. Barton (Eds.), *Classification in psychiatry and psychopathology.* Washington, DC: Public Health Service Publications.

2

Structural Issues in Diagnosis

JUAN E. MEZZICH, WILLIAM GOODPASTOR, and ADA C. MEZZICH

INTRODUCTION

A diagnostic judgment typically involves much more than determining whether the individual under examination has a given disorder or not. A number of issues pertinent to the conceptual and methodological structures used for describing the condition of the patient need to be considered as they crucially influence the content, format, and implications of the diagnostic judgment and its formulation.

One of these issues involves diagnostic definitions and refers to the problem faced by the clinician when several sets of diagnostic criteria are available for the same disorder. In response to this situation, the so-termed poly-diagnostic approach has been proposed (Berner, Katschnig, & Lenz, 1982), which involves the formulation of a diagnostic judgment according to each of the diagnostic criteria.

Another structural issue refers to the exclusion in the diagnostic formulation of certain disorders by the presence of another. This typically reflects a hierarchial arrangement of psychopathological syndromes on the basis of either etiological assumptions or differential symptomatogical pervasiveness (the symptomatology of one disorder encompassing the symptomatology of another).

A third issue refers to the formulation of multiple diagnoses, which arises when the diagnostic definitions or criteria for several disorders are met. How are these disorders to be listed? What are the implications of such a formulation for treatment and prognosis?

JUAN E. MEZZICH, WILLIAM GOODPASTOR, and ADA C. MEZZICH • Western Psychiatric Institute and Clinic, Pittsburgh, PA 15213.

Finally, in response to the need for doing greater justice to the complexity of the clinical condition and for preparing a reasonably comprehensive treatment plan, the multiaxial diagnostic approach has been proposed. This evaluative approach involves the systematic consideration of several parameters of illness and requires the establishment of an appropriate scale, typological, or dimensional, for each parameter or axis.

Each of these issues will be discussed in the course of this chapter.

THE POLY-DIAGNOSTIC APPROACH

The poly-diagnostic approach, as presented by Berner (1982), consists of a data recording system which yields a set of diagnostic judgments based on information reflecting various diagnostic systems. This approach has been developed as an alternative to the so called "compromise" method, as represented by International Classification of Diseases, 9th Revision (ICD-9) and DSM-III (Berner & Katschnig, 1983), where the diagnostic system has been established on the basis of consensus and has involved compromise or sacrifice of certain elements of particular diagnostic models.

The poly-diagnostic approach offers a procedure which allows for comparability between various models of diagnosis and for more insight into their predictive value. This approach might be of particular value in research, as comparability of results from several research centers would be enhanced and results from previous studies could be replicated or refuted. Additionally, the identification of more homogeneous groups, with respect to course and treatment response may be more likely. Thirdly, this approach might serve as a "mental exercise" by forcing the diagnostician to think concurrently in terms of different diagnostic systems.

In recent years, various tools have been developed, resulting in better descriptions of symptoms and the introduction of exclusion criteria for delineating diagnostic categories. Thus, as pointed out by Berner, *et al* (1982), "the different elements used for diagnostic assignment have become explicit and understandable in the same sense by all" (p. 245). Diagnostic concepts, however, remain divergent and can be broadly termed "theory-oriented" or "pragmatic."

An example of this classification of concepts can be found in the "theory-oriented" and "pragmatic-oriented" classifications of the functional psychoses. Bleuler (1908), who is considered one of the first of the "theory-oriented" proponents, relied on theoretical concepts of the illness process which led him to the establishment of a symptoms hierarchy. An example of the "pragmatic" approach can be found in the formulation of Schneider's first-rank symptoms (Schneider, 1959). Hybrid systems also exist, the criteria developed by Taylor and Abrams (1975) being an example of this.

An illustration of the use of the poly-diagnostic approach is offered by Berner, et al (1982) in their study of diagnosis of schizophrenia. When utilizing different diagnostic criteria in examining patients, the frequency of a diagnosis such as schizophrenia will vary according to the specified criteria. One might expect a high degree of correlation between the assignment of this diagnosis according to Bleuler's (1908) and Schneider's (1959) criteria. This was in fact seen with a more than 77% concordance. One would not expect to see such a high degree of correlation between, for example, Schneider's criteria and those of the Research Diagnostic Criteria (Spitzer, Endicott, & Robins, 1978), which again was empirically confirmed utilizing the poly-diagnostic approach.

Associations between different diagnosed and external criteria in a patient population suffering from "endogenous depression" have been studied by Katschnig, Brandle-Nebehay, Fuchs-Robetine, Selig, Eichbergher, and Strobb (1981). They showed, utilizing the poly-diagnostic approach, that external criteria such as life events have different relationships to subtypes of depression depending upon the classification system utilized for diagnosis.

This type of diagnostic exercise has merits apart from its usefulness for a specific research project. It can be the starting point for a "comparative nosology" (Katschnig & Berner, 1985), which may lead, in turn, to a clearer understanding of different diagnostic systems used around the world. The demonstration of incongruencies forces one to give more thought to the different definitions of a diagnostic category, in terms of theory, logical structure, and content.

In summary, the poly-diagnostic system offers a diagnostic approach which allows for increasing comparability of results obtained in different research centers by divergent diagnostic systems. This system (1) makes replication of studies more frequently possible. (2) could potentially aid in the establishment of more homogenous diagnostic groups. (3) may lead to further identification of nosological entities, and (4) might encourage clinical diagnosticians to consider various diagnostic systems in the application of pertinent criteria. On the other hand, the implementation of this approach may be quite difficult in busy clinical settings or when applied to more than a few categories at a time.

HIERARCHIAL RELATIONSHIPS

A diagnostic hierarchy, recognized clearly by Jaspers (1963), may be described as the arrangement according to which diagnostic categories are ranked in such a way that patients with a wide range of symptoms can be assigned to a single diagnostic category. A diagnosis would exclude symptoms of high members of the hierarchy and would include symptoms of lower members. Such a hierarchy implies that the presence of any disorder may be associated with manifestations of a disorder lower in the hierarchy. Such a hierarchy corresponds to the idea that, with regard to a disease entity, one expects that no more than one illness can be diagnosed in any one person (Jaspers, 1963).

Historically, this assumption has not been limited to psychiatry, but has been applied to other fields of medicine as well. Jaspers's diagnostic hierarchy is implicit in Kräpelin's classification. It involves the following ordering of mental disorders (1) organic mental disorders; (2) schizophrenia; (3) manic-depressive illness; and (4) neurotic illness. As Surtees and Kendell (1979) point out, this hierarchical conceptualization is also present in the current ICD and in the CATEGO diagnostic computer program. (Wing, Cooper, & Sartorius, 1974).

Another illustration of this model would be Schneider's "symptoms of first rank" considered as pathognomonic of schizophrenia "except in the presence of coarse brain disease" (Schneider, 1959). The organic psychoses would, therefore, be placed uppermost within this hierarchy and would determine the diagnosis irrespective of the presence of other psychotic or neurotic symptoms. Schizophrenia would be listed next, those symptoms accepted as diagnostic of schizophrenia being utilized in the diagnosis. The manic-depressive disorder would occupy the following diagnostic step, and neurotic illness the next.

Foulds and Bedford published seminal concepts and research on diagnostic hierarchies in 1975. Fould's hierarchy considered delusions of disintegration at the top of the ranked list, followed by other delusions (grandeur, contrition, and persecution), neurotic symptoms (conversion, dissociative, phobic, compulsive, and ruminative symptoms) and dysthymic states (anxiety, depression, and elation) (Foulds, 1976). This hierarchy focuses on symptoms, rather than on syndromes as Jaspers did, and differs from DSM-III regarding the ranking of affective disorders. DSM-III places these disorders higher than obsessive-compulsive disorders, while in Foulds' hierarchy they share a low level.

Subsequent to the formulation of his symptomatological hierarchy, Foulds (1976) developed the Delusion-Symptoms-States Inventory which gathers information on symptom levels arranged in accordance with his theory. He found in his investigations that the existence of symptoms listed anywhere in the hierarchy, such as delusions, implies the presence of at least two lower-rank symptoms such as neurotic and anxiety or affective ones. Sturt, in 1981, reviewed Foulds's and other studies in which Foulds's hierarchic theory had been applied. She concluded that Foulds's theory could be interpreted as a manifestation of a more general principle which postulates that subjects who present symptoms of a high class would also have the tendency to show symptoms that belong to a lower class. This principle was derived from her analysis of data from the Present State Examination (PSE) (Wing *et al.*, 1974) which showed that subjects who have rare PSE syndromes tended to have high total symptom scores and every symptom had a significant association with the total symptom score.

Exclusion criteria can be found in nosological systems preceding the DSM-III, like the Feighner Criteria (Feighner *et al.*, 1972) and the Research Diagnostic Criteria (Spitzer *et al.* 1978). The 1984 report of Boyd *et al.* regarding the co-occurrence of hierarchy-free syndromes revealed that if two disorders were related to each other (according to DSM-III exclusion criteria) then the presence of a "dominant" disorder greatly increased the odds of the "excluded" disorder being present. A general tendency toward co-occurrence was also reported in that the presence of any disorder increased the likelihood of having almost any other disorder. This applied even if DSM-III did not list it as a related disorder. The authors concluded that further study is indicated concerning the use of exclusion criteria in DSM-III. They also outlined a form that such studies of diagnostic hierarchies might take, stating that "one disorder can be said to be 'due to' another disorder if the two disorders have the same prognosis, if they wax and wane together, and if the excluded disorder has different risk factors and responds to different treatment than it would if it occurred in the absence of the dominant disorder" (p. 989).

Classification systems have been noted to serve the unrelated needs of "different matters" including biologic researchers (Boyd *et al.* 1984). As a means of helping to ensure a homogeneous patient population with respect to the disorder in question, exclusion criteria are desirable. For example, elimination from consideration of questionable or even atypical cases, as well as those having a different disorder, can be facilitated via use of exclusion criteria. It has been further noted that for purposes of epidemiological and nosological research, it is important to assess everyone in a population and to assign multiple diagnoses, if present. In particular, a clinical classification system is desirable and useful if it aids in prognosis and the choice of therapy, as well as serving various accounting purposes (Boyd *et al.* 1984).

MULTIPLE DIAGNOSES

The phenomenon of multiple diagnoses refers to the description of an individual's condition in a certain domain through the use of more than one category of illness. For example, the description of the psychopathological condition of a subject may include three diagnoses: dysthymic disorder, phobic disorder, and alcohol abuse. Fundamental questions arise with regard to such a formulation.

Concern has been expressed about the way patients with multiple diagnoses are judged and dealt with in clinical and research settings. The patient may be treated as if each of his or her diagnoses were independent of the others. Are such disorders really distinct from each other, with separate and distinguishable courses? Are they significantly interrelated? Do they reflect an amorphous illness with epiphenomenal variations? One of the ways of approaching this quandary is related to the topic discussed in the preceding section and involves the classification of the patient according to a hierarchial system. In such an arrangement, the patient is assigned to the dominant diagnostic category and the other syndromes are relegated to a subsidary status. For example, the hierarchical diagnostic criteria of Feighner *et al.* (1972) will exclude the formulation of concomitant diagnoses, such as axorexia nervosa, when there is a preexisting history of depressive illness.

It appears that researach needs to be placed on the elucidation of fundamental associations between disorders which are candidates for multiple listing. An example of this situation is given by the possible association between the diagnoses of alcohol abuse and affective disorder. Attention to the premorbid and postrecovery affective status of a patient with a diagnosis of alcohol abuse may have clarifying values in this regard.

One of the longest controversies regarding dual or multiple diagnosis involves the consideration of an anxiety disorder and depression. Leckman, Merikangas, Pauls, Prusoff, and Weissman (1983), in their review of 133 patients with a diagnosis of major depression, found that 30 had anxiety disorders that were temporally separate from episodes of major depression, and 51 warranted an anxiety disorder diagnosis although their anxiety symptoms were temporally associated with depressive episodes. Overall, 58% of their population displayed anxiety symptoms that met DSM-III criteria for agoraphobia, panic disorder, or generalized anxiety disorder.

Ianzito, Cadoret, and Pugh (1972), concerned with the formulation of multiple diagnoses, developed a method for displaying diagnostic combinations to facilitate grouping of categories and coding for data analysis.

Their format offers options for combining or separating subject with single and multiple diagnoses and those with definite and probable diagnoses. The method involves a combination of a diagnostic hierarchy and a double grid display. The first column of the format contains a list of possible "priority" diagnoses. The first grid, adjacent to the priority column, is for those additional diagnoses that had been made with a high degree of certitude by using the most rigorous exclusion criteria. These, as well as the "priority" diagnoses, were considered as "definite." When a diagnosis was based on fewer criteria it was qualified as "probable" and represented on the second grid. Thus, three diagnoses, two definite and one probable, could be represented in the table by indicating their presence in the priority diagnosis column and at the appropriate intersects on the two grids. Because of space constrains, this format accommodates only a limited number of diagnostic categories, that is, those 11 considered to have adequate validity at their academic institution.

Another method for formulating multiple diagnoses is contained in the semistructured Initial Evaluation Form (Mezzich, Dow, Rich, Costello, & Himmelhoch, 1981). Its diagnostic summary format provides a layout for the formulation of diagnoses along all axes of DSM-III, plus a current functioning axis. For each typological axis, it contains, first, a main formulation section with slots for an ordered listing of several diagnostic categories and their qualification as principal or provisional diagnoses whenever needed, and an adjacent section with slots for additional or alternatives categories to be ruled out. The use of this format with 1,111 consecutive patients who presented themselves for care at a comprehensive psychiatric facility showed, for example, that substance-use disorders were most frequently listed as second, third, or fourth diagnoses (Mezzich, Coffman, & Goodpastor, 1982).

The use of multiple diagnoses also poses challenges to the assessment of diagnostic reliability. Most of the reliability indices have been developed for the case of single diagnoses. Mezzich, Kramer, Worthington, and Coffman (1981) dealt with the issue of inter-rater agreement among several raters formulating multiple typological diagnoses. They described three techniques which are extensions of unweighted kappa (Cohen, 1960). Their proportional overlap and the intraclass correlation procedures are pertinent to the situation in which the multiple diagnosis involves a list of non-ordered categories. Their rank correlation procedure is appropriate when the order of the categories is important. This methodology was employed in a study of the reliabilities of DSM-III and DSM-II using 27 child psychiatric cases, for most of which multiple diagnoses had been made (Mezzich, Mezzich, & Coffman, 1985)

MULTIAXIAL DIAGNOSIS

The multiaxial diagnostic approach attempts to present a comprehensive view of the patient's condition by articulating several parameters of illness and using various scaling arrangements. It involves the systematic formulation of the patient's condition and its associated factors through several variables or aspects, which are termed axes.

These axes are treated as quasi-independent from each other, and, from a scaling viewpoint, they are classified as typological or dimensional. A typological axis describes a patient's condition through the use of items of a catalog of diagnostic categories, that is, it is measured on a nominal scale. It may allow for the listing of multiple diagnoses, as in the case of Axis I of DSM-III. A dimensional axis describes patients by their standing on an interval scale (e.g., IQ, in some multiaxial systems for child psychiatry) or a rank scale (e.g., DSM-III Axis IV on psychosocial stressor severity).

The diagnostic criteria employed in a typological axis may include exclusion rules which typically reflect hierarchical relationships among diagnostic entities. In this case, the presence of a disorder high in the hierarchy will exclude the listing of a disorder lower in the hierarchy when both coexist or overlap. For example, most psychopathological nosologies have organic mental conditions at the top of the hierarchies; thus, the coexistence of such a condition with any other syndrome would exclude the latter from consideration in the diagnostic formulation.

The determination of the most appropriate number of axes in a multiaxial system would depend on the scope of clinical information required to reach a comprehensive diagnosis of the patient. At the same time consideration should be given to the ease of use of the system, that is, its applicability.

Two studies, one involving a review of the literature and the other an international survey of expert diagnosticians, indicated that the model number of axes most often used in clinical and research work was five (followed by four and three) (Mezzich, 1979; Mezzich, Fabrega, & Mezzich, 1985).

In terms of content, there are certain axes which tend to be included in most multiaxial systems as they are considered useful and essential for general purposes. Included in this group are psychiatric syndromes, personality disorders, physical disorders, and course of illness. Also included with some frequency are axes on specific psychosocial stressors, adaptive funtioning, psychoticism, etiology, and intellectual level or mental retardation.

DIAGNOSTIC SUMMARY

I. Clinical psychiatric syndromes *(Instructions and codes on back of pages 6 and 7)*

Main Formulation:	Codes	Alternatives to be ruled out	Codes
1.			
2.			
3.			
4.			

II Personality and specific developmental disorders *(Instructions and codes on back of pages 6 and 7)*

Main Formulation:	Codes	Alternatives to be ruled out:	Codes
1.			
2.			

III. Physical Disorders *(Instructions on back of page 7)*

Main Formulation:	Codes	Alternatives to be ruled out:	Codes
1.			
2.			
3.			
4.			

IV. Psychosocial stressors *(Instructions on back of this page)*   Codes

A. Ranked list: 1.
2.
3.
4.

B. Overall stressor severity:	1 None	2 Minimal	3 Mild	4 Moderate	5 Severe	6 Extreme	7 Catastrophic	0 Unspecified

V. Highest level of adaptive functioning during the past year *(Instructions on back of this page)*

	1 Superior	2 Very Good	3 Good	4 Fair	5 Poor	6 Very Poor	7 Grossly Impaired	0 Unspecified

VI. Current functioning: *(Instructions on back of this page)*

		Superior	Adequate	Slightly Impaired	Moderately Impaired	Markedly Impaired	Unspecified
	A. Occupational	1	2	3	4	5	0
	B. With family	1	2	3	4	5	0
	C. With other indiv. & groups	1	2	3	4	5	0

Figure 1. Expanded DSM-III Multiaxial Diagnostic Format contained in the Initial Evaluation Form.

In order to maintain manageability of a system, subaxes are sometimes included to add more detailed information without increasing the number of axes. Using this approach as well as extended coding schemas, severity, course of illness, and etiology could be used to complement the axis on psychiatric syndromes (Mezzich & Sharfstein, 1985; Mezzich, Fabrega, & Mezzich, in press).

In reviewing multiaxial issues, Strauss and Helmchen (1982) pointed out the need to improve the definitions and scaling of diagnostic axes in order to ensure the reliability of multiaxial systems. A similar concern was expressed by the diagnosticians who participated in the international survey on multiaxial diagnosis carried out by Mezzich, Fabrega, and Mezzich (1985). In addition to the remarks made earlier in this paper regarding the reliability of typological axes, it should be noted that the reliability of dimensional axes also needs to be assessed. Mezzich, Mezzich, and Coffman (1985) in their study of the reliability of DSM-III in child psychiatry, used the intraclass correlation procedures described by Shrout and Fleiss (1979) for the evaluation of dimensional axes.

Regarding the prospects for data-based improvement of the categorization of syndromes in typological axes, the possibility of using statistical techniques such as cluster analysis should be mentioned. However, given the tentative status of these approaches, they must be considered exploratory in nature and should be used in interaction with clinical experience and judgement (Mezzich, 1984).

As a final consideration in respect to multiaxial diagnosis, the need for a format to facilitate the completion and recording of multiaxial formulations should be mentioned. Figure 1 presents the diagnostic summary format contained in the most recent version of the Initial Evaluation Form (Mezzich, Slayton, Dow, Costello, & Himmelhoch, 1983) This format provides a structure for an expanded DSM-III multiaxial diagnostic formulation.

SUMMARY

This paper has reviewed several issues relevant to the structure of diagnostic systems. It has specifically considered (1) the poly-diagnostic approach, which articulates the concurrent use of alternative sets of diagnostic criteria; (2) hierarchical relations among psychopathological syndromes, which express themselves through the use of exclusion rules in differential diagnosis; (3) the use of multiple diagnoses for systematizing the description of complex psychopathological pictures with several categories of illness; and (4) the multiaxial approach to comprehensive diagnostic formulation, using several variables of typological and dimensional scaling. Consideration of these issues should help in the design of improved diagnostic systems useful for both clinical care and scientific investigation.

REFERENCES

Berner, P., & Katschnig, H. (1983). Principles of "multiaxial" classification in psychiatry as a basis of modern methodology. In T. Helgason (Ed.), *Methodology in evaluation of psychiatric treatment.* Cambridge, England: Cambridge University Press.
Berner, P., Katschnig, H., & Lenz, G. (1982). Poly-diagnostic approach: A method to clarify incongruencies among the classification of the functional psychoses. *The Psychiatric Journal of the University of Ottawa, 7,* 244–248.
Bleuler, E. (1908). Die prognose der dementia praecox schizophrenic gruppe. *Allgemeine Zeitschrift von Psychiatrie, 65,* 436–464.

Boyd, J.H., Burke, J.D., Gruen, E., Jr., Holzer, III, C.E., Rae, D.S., & George, L.K. (1984). Exclusion criteria of DSM-III. *Archives of General Psychiatry, 41,* 983–989.

Carney, M. W. P., & Sheffield, B. F. (1965). Depression and the Newcastle scale: Their relationship to Hamilton's scale. *British Journal of Psychiatry, 121,* 35–40.

Cohen, J. (1960). A coefficient of agreement for nominal scales. *Educational and Psychological Measurement, 20,* 37–46.

Feighner, J. P., Robins, E., Guze, S. B., Woodruff, R. A. Winokur, G., & Munoz, R. (1972). Diagnostic criteria for use in psychiatric research. *Archives of General Psychiatry, 26,* 57–63.

Foulds, G. A. & Bedford, A. (1975). Hierarchy of classes of personal illness. *Psychological Medicine, 5,* 181–192.

Foulds, G. A. (1976). *The hierarchical nature of personal illness.* New York: Academic Press.

Ianzito, B. M., Cadoret, R. J., & Pugh, D. D. (1972). A Research technique for organizing multiple pychiatric diagnoses. *Comprehensive Psychiatry 13,* 73–78.

Jaspers, K. (1963). *General psychopathology.* Manchester, England: The Univeristy of Manchester Press.

Katschnig, J., & Berner, P. (1985). The poly-diagnostic approach in psychiatric research. In WHO & ADAMHA, *Mental disorders, alcohol and drug-related problems: International perspectives on their diagnostic and classification.* Amsterdam: Elsevier Science Publishers.

Katschnig, H., Brandle-Nebehay, A., Fuchs-Robetine, C., Seelig, P., Eichberger, G., & Strobl, R. (1981). Lebensverändernd Ereignnisse, psychosoziale Dispositionen und depressive Verstimmungszuszustände. Deutsche Forschungsgemeinschaft. Research Report, Wein University, Vienna, Austria.

Leckman, J.F., Merikangas, K.R., Pauls, D.L. Prusoff, B.A., & Weissman, N.M. (1983). Anxiety disorders associated with episodes of depression: Family study data contradict DSM-III convention. *American Journal of Psychiatry, 140,*880–882.

Mezzich, A.C., Mezzich, J.E., & Coffman, G.A. (1985). Reliability of DSM-III vs. DSM-II in child psychopathology. *Journal of the American Academy of Child Psychiatry, 24,* 273–280.

Mezzich, J.E. (1979). Patterns and issues in multiaxial psychiatric diagnosis. *Psychological Medicine, 9,* 125–137.

Mezzich, J.E. (1983). New developments in multiaxial psychiatric diagnosis. *Psychiatric Annals, 13,* 793–807.

Mezzich, J.E. (1984). Multiaxial diagnostic systems in psychiatry. In H.I. Kaplan, B.J. Sadock (Eds.), *Comprehensive textbook of psychiatry (4th ed.).*Baltimore: Williams & Wilkins.

Mezzich, J.E., & Sharfstein, S.S. (1985). Severity of illness and diagnostic formulation: Classifying patients for prospective payment systems. *Hospital and Community Psychiatry, 36,* 770–772.

Mezzich, J.E., Dow, J.T., Rich, C.L., Costello, A.J., & Himmelhoch, J.M. (1981). Developing an efficient clinical information system for a comprehensive psychiatric institute: II. Initial Evaluation Form. *Behavioral Research Methods and Instrumentation, 13,* 464–478.

Mezzich, J.E., Kraemer, H.C., Worthington, D.R.L., & Coffman, G.A. (1981). Assessment of agreement among several raters formulating multiple diagnoses. *Journal of Psychiatric Research, 16,* 29–39.

Mezzich, J.E., Coffman, G.A., & Goodpastor, S.M. (1982). A format for DSM-III diagnostic formulation: Experience with 1,111 consecutive patients. *American Journal of Psychiatry, 139,* 591–596.

Mezzich, J.E., Slayton, R.I. Dow, J.T., Costello, A.J. & Himmelhoch, J.M. (1983). A semistructured psychiatric evaluation procedure. Paper presented at the 136th Annual Meeting of the American Psychiatric Association, New York, May 1983.

Mezzich, J.E., Fabrega, H., Jr., & Mezzich, A.C. (1985). An international consultation on multiaxial diagnosis. In P. Pichot, P. Berner, R Wolfe, & K. Thau (Eds.), *Psychiatry: The state of the art:* Vol. 1. Clinical psychopathology and nomenclature and classification. London: Plenum Press.

Mezzich, J.E., Fabrega, H., Jr., & Mezzich, A.C. (in press). On the clinical utility of multiaxial diagnosis: Experience and perspectives. In G. Tischler (Ed.), *Diagnosis and classification.* Cambridge, England: Cambridge University Press.

Schneider, K. (1959). *Clinical Psychopathology.* Translated by M.W. Hamilton. New York: Grune & Stratton.

Shrout, P.E., & Fleiss, J.L. (1979). Intraclass correlation: Uses in assessing rater reliability. *Psychological Bulletin, 38,* 420–428.

Spitzer, R.L., Endicott, J., & Robins, E. (1978). Research diagnostic criteria. *Archives of General Psychiatry, 35,* 773–82.

Strauss, J.S., & Helmchen, H. (1982). Review paper on multiaxial diagnosis. Presented at the World Health Organization Conference on the Diagnosis and Classification of Mental Disorders, Alcohol and Drug-Related Problems. Copenhagen, Denmark.

Sturt, E. (1981). Hierarchial patterns in the distribution of psychiatric symptoms. *Psychological Medicine, 11,* 783–794.

Surtees, P.G., & Kendell, R.E. (1979). The hierarchy model of psychiatric symptomatology: An investigation based on Present State Examination ratings. *British Journal of Psychiatry, 135,* 438–443.

Taylor, M.A., & Abrams, R.A. (1975). A critique of the St. Louis research criteria for schizophrenia. *American Journal of Psychiatry, 132,* 1276–1280.

Wing, J.K., Cooper, J.E., & Sartorius, N. (1974). *The measurement and classification of psychiatric symptoms.* Cambridge, England: Cambridge University Press.

The Reliability of Psychiatric Diagnosis

WILLIAM M. GROVE

INTRODUCTION

In science, one needs to be able to understand and repeat another's work. In psychopathology this is difficult, since our descriptions of patients are often ambiguous and idiosyncratic (Elkin, 1947). Measurement research in psychopathology corresponds to the development of laboratory tests in clinical medicine; it is often tedious but indispensable. This chapter first surveys some methodological and statistical problems that arise in diagnostic reliability research. Recent developments in the statistics of diagnostic reliability are reviewed. The outcomes of studies of diagnostic reliability are then surveyed. Ongoing studies related to diagnosis are touched on. The reader is cautioned against overoptimism about the attainable certainty of psychiatric diagnosis.

At the outset, one must realize that reliability of diagnoses is a joint function of the diagnostic scheme and the diagnosticians. For example, Helzer and Coryell (1983) have recently told how one of them was unable to confirm findings of another investigator using the dexamethasone suppression test as an indicator of melancholia. After some detective work, the failure to replicate was attributed to variance in how the agreed-on DSM-III (American Psychiatric Association, 1980) diagnostic rules were being interpreted. Diagnostic reliability studies correspond to the calibration of a new laboratory's assay procedures and reagent preparations.

WILLIAM M. GROVE • Department of Psychiatry University of Iowa, Iowa City, IA 52242.

HOW UNRELIABILITY CONSTRAINS VALIDITY

Three independent quantities are sufficient to describe any procedure that yields a dichotomous diagnosis (Galen & Gambino, 1975). The first quantity, P, is the prevalence of the disorder in question. The second and third parameters, sensitivity and specificity, denoted by Se and Sp, respectively, capture the accuracy of the diagnostic process. Sensitivity is the probability that a truly ill person is correctly labeled by the diagnostic process, and specificity is the probability that a truly well person is correctly labeled. If we denote the complement of the prevalance, $1 - P$, by Q, it is easy to prove that

$$\hat{P} = P\,Se + Q\,(1 - Sp) \tag{1}$$

which shows that the prevalance of a disorder is not even unbiasedly estimated by the apparent prevalence $\hat{P}$ (the frequency with which the disorder is diagnosed by an imperfect rater). If two imperfect interchangeable raters with stable diagnostic habits, making diagnostic errors independently, jointly diagnose patients, their expected percentage agreement is

$$p_o = P\,Se^2 + Q\,(1 - Sp)^2 + P\,(1 - Se)^2 + Q\,Sp^2 \tag{2}$$

This forbidding-looking expression says that the probability of two raters agreeing on the presence or absence of an illness is composed of two parts, agreement on presence of illness and agreement on absence. Each of these, in turn, comprises cases on which both raters judge correctly and cases on which both err. All reliability coefficients in common use depend on p_o and thus on P as well. It is due to the complexity of Equation (2) that the interpretation of reliability coefficients as constraints on validity is so tortuous.

The dictum that "reliability constrains validity" originally formulated for continuous mental test scores holds *in a certain way* for dichotomous diagnoses as well. For example, imagine an instance of a common kind of study in psychopathology, in which a diagnostic group is compared with other patients or normal controls, on some characteristic related to etiology, outcome, or treatment response. Now, some members of the diagnostic group and some controls will be misclassified when study subjects are selected. In fact, ignoring sampling error, a proportion equal to

$$PPV = \frac{P\,Se}{P\,Se = Q\,(1 - Sp)} \tag{3}$$

of the subjects in the diagnostic group actually have the illness, and similarly a proportion equal to

$$NPV = \frac{Q\,Sp}{P\,(1 - Se) + Q\,Sp} \qquad (4)$$

of the controls actually do not have the illness. These two quantities, *PPV* and *NPV,* are called the positive predictive value and negative predictive value, respectively.

Consider an example. Suppose that the true prevalence of an illness in a hospital is 30%, the sensitivity of the diagnostic process is 50% and the specificity is 75%. One is interested in studying suicide risk in patients versus controls. If the rate of suicide in the truly ill group is $r_1 = 15\%$ and is $r_2 = 1\%$ in controls, the true relative risk is 15. However, in our example *PPV* = .4615 and *NPV* = .7778, which means that just 46% of all study cases truly have the disorder and only about three quarters of the controls are really controls. With such contamination of samples, the estimated relative suicide risk is $[r_1 PPV + r_2 (1 - PPV)] / [r_1 (1 - NPV) + r_2 NPV] = 7.5\%/4\% = 1.8$, approximately. This difference could easily escape detection, and we might conclude that the rates of suicide were identical in the two groups, in the face of a true fifteen-fold difference. On the other hand, if another study were conducted in the same hospital with better diagnoses (say *Se* = .8; *Sp* = .9), then the relative suicide risk would be about 12%/2% or 5.3. This figure, while still a drastic underestimate, is much more accurate and is more likely to be discovered in a small-sample study. Please note that these examples are optimistic because they ignore sampling error; the situation will be worse, on the average, in any real study.

Carey and Gottesman (1978) have pointed out that, because prevalences vary from clinic to clinic, two raters with stable diagnostic habits will experience changes in diagnostic reliability as they move from clinic to clinic. If errors of commission matter and errors of omission do not, it can happen that the less reliable diagnois is more valid. Real studies often proceed by choosing just the definitely ill and comparing them to certain noncases, such as medical-surgical controls. In such a situation, kappa may not index the decrement in validity caused by diagnostic errors since only specificity matters: incorrect labeling of some patients as noncases does not decrease validity.

COLLECTING DATA FOR RELIABILITY STUDIES

Determining the reliability of diagnoses involves the study of rater agreement or consistency. If we make the testable assumptions that our raters are equally skilled and that their habits do not change, we may make certain predictions. First, if two (or more) raters each examine separate series of patients and if specific patients are assigned to specific raters only by chance factors, then the raters should agree, within sampling error, in their frequencies for specific diagnoses. For example, if patients are sent to one of several wards in a hospital solely by the availability of an empty bed, and if doctors are rotated among wards, then the frequency of chart-diagnosed schizophrenia should be the same across wards. Also, in the absence of a change in catchment populations or referral patterns, the frequency of diagnosed schizophrenia should be stable over time. Clearly, the latter assumptions are stronger than the former, making studies of diagnostic frequency over time riskier than the comparison of rates between wards or between hospitals. Both these procedures were once used to test diagnostic reliability, but such methods have been superseded.

Agreement in diagnostic frequencies for independently diagnosed patient series is necessary but not sufficient for proving diagnoses reliable. Two raters could see patients together, each call 20% of them schizophrenic, and never agree on a solitary diagnosis of schizophrenia. Therefore, one would prefer to examine agreement between diagnosticians on a single patient series.

One can employ any of several methods to obtain multiple diagnoses on a series of patients. Several raters can read a series of patient charts or prepared clinical vignettes. This may not be a stringent test of reliability, but it allows one to identify problems in interpreting chart material and points up ambiguities in diagnostic criteria. Alternatively, raters can diagnose recorded interviews. In videotape or audiotape studies, the original interviewer may be counted as a rater for reliability purposes or not, depending on whether he or she could have noticed diagnostically important patient behavior not captured on tape. This design is well suited to intercenter or international reliability studies.

A rigorous method is to conduct joint reliability interviews. Two or more raters can sit in, each interviewing some of the patients (to average out interviewer effects). With live interviews, subtle behavior can be noticed by all, perhaps making diagnoses more reliable. However, it is difficult for a taped or observed interviewer to follow any but the most rigidly structured interview schedule without giving coraters diagnostic cues, biasing agreement upwards. Interviews with optional questions which may be skipped are especially problematic.

Test–retest reliability studies offer a stringent test of agreement. Here one avoids accidental cueing of fellow raters, offering a high methodological hurdle. However, such studies are no panacea. Only two or three raters can see each patient. A problem with a short- or medium-term retest study is that the patient may recall the previous interview, perhaps reciting remembered answers and inflating interrater agreement. This can only be avoided by using a longer followup, but then the patient's condition may change. Cloninger, Miller, Wette, Martin, and Guze (1979) have treated the analysis of diagnostic stability over time, under a restrictive assumption that various causal factors linearly influence diagnostic status over the long term. The best (but expensive) solution is to combine test–retest and simultaneous rating designs, preferably with short-term and long-term retest intervals. In this way the various reliabilities, interrater and test–retest, can be computed and compared.

One innovation in test–retest studies deserves special mention. It may be impossible to have each of several raters interview every patient. If one can have each possible pair (or triplet) of raters in a study occur with an equal number of patients, one has a balanced incomplete blocks design (Fleiss, 1981). This was first employed by Rosenzweig, Vandenburg, Moore, and Dukay (1961), but they used the wrong analysis for their design. More recently, the Iowa 500 Study and the National Institute of Mental Health Clinical Research Branch Collaborative Depression Study (Katz, Secunda, Hirschfeld, & Koslow, 1979) have used this design. It requires many fewer interviews per patient than full rater-by-subject designs in order to get reliability estimates.

MEASURING DIAGNOSTIC AGREEMENT

Given a series of patients, each diagnosed at least twice, one wishes to quantify diagnostic agreement. The simplest statistic is the observed percentage agreement, but this has undesirable statistical properties. When the prevalence of a given disorder is low, agreement could be made high by calling each patient well. One would prefer an index not subject to inflation by such extraneous factors, but all indices of rater agreement are affected by the true prevalence. One can, however, use statistics that correct for the apparent prevalence, which is as close as one can ordinarily come to knowing the prevalence anyway. An important class of such statistics is exemplified by kappa (Cohen, 1960), defined as

$$K = \frac{p_o - p_c}{1 - p_c} \tag{5}$$

where p_o is the observed percentage agreement and p_c is the agreement expected if raters assigned diagnoses to patients randomly, each rater having his or her own frequency of making the diagnosis. Cohen's original proposal was that chance agreement would occur as follows. If rater A made $p_1 = 40\%$ positive diagnoses while rater B made a $p_2 = 30\%$ and if each rater assigned diagnoses at random, then they would agree by chance $(.4)(.3) + (1 - .4)(1 - .3) = 54\%$ of the time. Cohen therefore defined chance agreement for dichotomous diagnoses as

$$p_c = p_1 p_2 + (1 - p_1)(1 - p_2) \tag{6}$$

This makes K a chance-corrected index of interrater agreement, and it also makes K independent of the observed rater "prevalences." However, it cannot make K independent of the true prevalence (Kraemer, 1978).

Kappa is therefore an exceptionally useful statistic, and it has several nice algebraic properties. For a large class of agreement statistics denoted by t_o, the quantity

$$T = \frac{t_o - t_c}{1 - t_c} \tag{7}$$

is equal to K, provided only that t_c is computed under the assumption that raters assign diagnoses at random so as to obtain their observed frequencies of positive diagnosis. Many reliability indices reduce to K once chance agreement is allowed for. A very useful fact is that K is almost exactly equal to an intraclass correlation coefficient computed on two raters' dichotomous diagnostic data, coded 1 for a positive diagnosis, 0 otherwise (Fleiss & Cohen, 1973).

Kappa depends on P (for fixed Se and Sp) and yet P is conceptually irrelevant to diagnostic agreement. To get around this problem, which is serious with the low base rates seen in epidemiological studies, an agreement index originally proposed by Yule has been studied in some detail by Spitznagel and Helzer (1985). This index is

$$Y = \frac{p_{00}\, p_{11}\, /\, p_{01}\, p_{10} - 1}{p_{00}\, p_{11}\, /\, p_{01}\, p_{10} + 1} \tag{8}$$

where p_{00} is the agreement on negative diagnoses, p_{11} is the agreement on positive diagnoses, and p_{01} and p_{10} are the disagreement cells. This index agrees closely with kappa for base rates above .4 when diagnoses are of reasonable quality, but is much less sensitive to declining prevalence than kappa (i.e., as P approaches zero). It may be that this is bought at the cost of Y's insensitivity to declining agreement as well. However, this index deserves statistical study, and shows promise for use in epidemiological work.

Analysis becomes complicated for studies with multiple raters. One needs to define agreement when more than two raters diagnose a case. One could define it as pairwise agreement (proportion of all possible rater pairs who agree), majority agreement, or total agreement (all raters agree). It turns out to be simplest to use pairwise agreement.

The definition of a kappa-type statistic for pairwise agreement in complex designs has been discussed by Fleiss and Cuzick (1979), who provided a kappa-type statistic useful when different and varying numbers of raters examine each patient; it is assumed that each patient is seen by a separate set of raters. Uebersax (1983) gave a kappa-type statistic for the general case in which the number of raters per patient varies, but raters may overlap in the patients they see.

I prefer the general approach of Landis and Koch (1977) to that of deriving special kappas. They proposed to bypass the computation of chance agreement, instead computing an intraclass correlation coefficient for the diagnostic "score" coded 1 if present, 0 otherwise. As mentioned above, when two raters see a series of patients together, K is essentially identical to an intraclass correlation coefficient. The intraclass correlation is a "signal" to "signal plus noise" ratio, and assesses the proportion of measurement variance accounted for by systematic patient differences. One can use intraclass correlations for any reliability design whatsoever; they do not require that raters be the same for all patients or be different for each patient, and do not require that the number of raters per patient be constant. All one needs to compute them is a good analysis of variance program. Intraclass correlations are the only approach presently available for analyzing the results of balanced incomplete blocks designs. I employed the method of Landis and Koch (1977) to define a kappa-type agreement statistic wherever possible in this review, in reanalyzing old reliability data. The price paid for this flexible approach is that different components of measurement variability must be estimated in different situations, so that no one simply defined statistic indexes agreement in all instances.

The derivation of standard errors for kappas can be difficult. It is usually not very important to test the hypothesis $K = 0$, as it is implausible that agreement is no better than chance. One would prefer to obtain a confidence interval for the true intraclass correlation or kappa. Unfortunately, this is an area where often no exact or even approximate results are available. Often one must be satisfied with an estimate of kappa without a standard error. Landis and Koch (1977) gave a method for deriving approximate standard errors which is generally applicable to all sorts of designs, but it requries complex and expensive computation. Uebersax (1983) gave another method which is likewise general but very expensive and only approximate.

The study designs and statistics discussed above have all seen employment by investigators interested in diagnostic reliability. Over the last fifty years, there has been a gradual increase in the methodological sophistication of reliability studies. Early studies compared rates of various diagnoses between wards or hospitals, but in the 1950's investigators became interested in simultaneous rating and test–retest studies of diagnosis. In the 1960's kappa and structured diagnostic interviews were first used in reliability studies, and in the 1970's diagnostic criteria and balanced incomplete blocks designs were introduced. To these studies we now turn. First I will discuss older studies which calculated, or allow one to calculate, chance-corrected agreement.

Studies of Reliability Antedating Specified Diagnostic Criteria

Table 1 gives results of many important older studies giving kappas or allowing a kappa to be computed. There is enormous variation in methodology between these studies, and many had small samples. Only a few studies require comment. Masserman and Carmichael (1938) followed up patients for a year, showing some diagnostic inconsistency for each category studied. They did not distinguish between changes in patients' conditions and discrepancies due to better histories available at follow-up. Norris (1959) studied the agreement between observation unit diagnoses in general hospitals and later diagnoses after transfer to psychiatric hospitals in London. This comparison is hampered by patient changes due to the natural history of disorders and to a longer observation period in hospital. The simultaneous rating and test–retest studies control for these problems. The best of these studies were by Schmidt and Fonda (1956), Beck, Ward, Mendelson, Mock, and Erbaugh (1962), and Sandifer, Pettus, and Quade (1964).

Schmidt and Fonda (1956) examined the agreement between diagnoses made by psychiatric residents and staff physicians, a design which causes two problems. The resident's history was a major source of staff diagnoses; this would push agreement up. On the other hand, the staff doctor had access to ward observations the resident did not; this would tend to lower kappa. These biases may not offset each other.

Ward et al. (1962) asked raters, who interviewed patients in a test–retest design, why they disagreed on diagnoses when they disagreed. It

Table 1. Interrater Reliability of Non-Criterion-Oriented Diagnoses[a]

Study	M[b]	N	Sc	Mn	D[c]	PD	(ASPD)	Nr	Comment
Masserman & Carmichael (1938)	F-U[b]	101	.62		.59[c]		(.52)	.53	One year
Foulds (1955)	T-RT	18	.61		.44[c]			.47	Resident vs. staff
Schmidt & Fonda (1956)	T-RT	426	.77		.32[c,d]	.63[e]			Hospital transfers
Norris (1950)	F-U	6263	.53		.53				Mostly outpatients
Kreitman et al. (1961)	T-RT	90			.82[c]			.51	Outpatients
Beck et al. (1962)	T-RT	153	.42		.47	.33	(.53)	.45	10 judges
Sandifer et al. (1964)	SR	91		.68[d]	.42[c,d]	.56[d]		.58[d]	
Kendell et al. (1971)									
American	SR	8	.25						Filmed interviews
British	SR	8	.59			.71			Many judges
World Health Organization (1973)									
	SR	190	.81		.70	.77			Intracenter
	T-RT	51	.67			.70	.77		Intracenter
Spitzer et al. (1975)	SR	120	.48	.37	.07-.25[f]	.06	.42[f]		Median for specific disorders
Standage (1979)	SR	81				.66			Laotians' case records
Westermeyer & Sines (1979)	SR	35			.36[f]				
Johnson et al. (1980)	SR	30			Overall K = .45				Lay judges
	T-RT	35			Overall K = .56				Lay versus clinician

[a] In this and the following tables: M = Method; N = Sample size; Sc = Schizophrenia; Mn = Mania; D = Manic Depressive illness, Depressed, Psychotic Depression, Involutional Depression, Depressive Reaction; PD = Personality Disorder; ASPD = Antisocial Personality; Nr = Neurosis.

[b] T-RT = Test-retest; SR = Simultaneous rating; F-U = Followup.

[c] Affective disorder.

[d] Estimated from incomplete data.

[e] Personality disorder.

[f] Agreement on specific diagnoses.

turned out that a majority of disagreements occurred because raters used different criteria for diagnosis, or because raters found the diagnostic criteria in *DSM-I* called for impossibly fine distinctions. This suggests that a clear, minimally inferential set of criteria, agreed on by all raters beforehand, would lead to much higher diagnostic reliability. Sandifer *et al.* (1964), using a simultaneous-rating design with 10 judges, obtained distinctly higher reliability for schizophrenia and personality disorder than did Beck *et al.* This may be due to design differences (simultaneous rater vs. test–retest).

Two other studies in Table 1 deserve comment. The investigators of the World Health Organization's International Pilot Study of Schizophrenia (World Health Organization, 1973) conducted reliability exercises within each of their nine world-wide study centers. Both simultaneous-rating and test–retest studies were done, using the Present State Examination (PSE; Wing, Birley, Cooper, Graham, & Isaacs, 1967) as their structured interview, but diagnosing patients without specific rules. The reliabilities for schizophrenic and affective disorder diagnoses were higher than most in Table 3, suggesting that reducing interviewer variability increased reliability. Unfortunately, almost no intercenter reliability data were gathered, and none reported. This was perhaps unavoidable given the vast distances separating many centers. Clearly, intracenter agreement and intercenter agreement can differ.

Spitzer, Endicott, Robins, Kuriansky, and Gurland (1975), involved in designing psychiatric interviews for many years, studied the reliability of diagnosing case records, mostly oriented toward the diagnosis of schizophrenia. The results, based on *DSM-II* (American Psychiatric Association, 1968) diagnoses, were disappointing. This may be partly due to the deficiencies of case records as the sole source of diagnostic information.

Reliability of Criteria-Based Diagnoses

Not satisified with this state of affairs, and as part of piloting the NIMH Clinical Research Branch Collaborative Program on the Psychobiology of Depression (CDS), Spitzer, Endicott, and Robins (1978) developed the Research Diagnostic Criteria (RDC). These criteria showed the influences of Eli Robins and colleagues at Washington University, who developed the Feighner (or St. Louis group) criteria, and also of Spitzer and colleagues' experiences in designing interviews. With collaborators, these investigators conducted a 150-patient pilot study for the CDS, allowing the "debugging" of the RDC under field conditions. While the St.

Louis group criteria considerably antedate the RDC, reliability studies of the former postdate the RDC, so I will discuss the RDC first.

The Spitzer *et al.* (1975) study cited above, which showed poor reliability of *DSM-II* diagnoses, was also a study of the reliability of an early draft of the RDC. Using the same case records as for the test of *DSM-II* reliability, but comparing Spitzer to a research assistant when both used RDC definitions of illnesses, much higher reliabilities for all RDC diagnoses studied were obtained. However, this could be due to their developing a private consensus about how to diagnose difficult cases. In that case other investigators would not replicate these results.

Table 2 shows that this did not happen. To obtain pooled figures that would allow generalization, I made weighted averages of kappas in the table (by Fisher z-transformation). The mean reliability for schizophrenia is .79, for mania or bipolar I .92, for major depression .85, and for alcoholism .94 (drug abuse, essentially 1.0). Several facts are noteworthy. First, investigators not identified with developing the RDC obtained results as good as those of Spitzer *et al.* Second, there is a modest positive correlation between sample size and the reliability obtained; this argues against a hypothesis that small studies relied on handpicked patients who are easy to diagnose. Similarly, it is not just handpicked raters who gave good reliability. Analyses of data for all 36 raters active in the CDS study (Andreasen, McDonald-Scott, Grove, Keller, Shapiro, & Hirschfeld, 1982) showed that within broad limits rater experience made no observable difference to reliability. Test–retest studies show reliabilities equal to, or little worse than, simultaneous-rating studies. Lifetime or past diagnoses are as reliable as current diagnoses (almost all studies looking at other than current diagnoses used lifetime diagnoses). This latter finding is hard to fathom, since subjects have to rely on their memories to answer questions about past illnesses. A last conclusion: schizophrenia may have benefited least from the advent of RDC and structured interviews.

Table 3 shows studies of St. Louis group criteria. One smaller study used lay judges and a highly structured interview (Coryell, Cloninger, & Reich, 1978), and is not comparable in aim to the other studies. Helzer, Clayton, Pambakian, Reich, Woodruff, and Revely (1977) looked at the test–retest stability of several diagnoses using a checklist developed at Washington Univeristy to record interview data. Helzer and colleagues have been very interested in substituting lay interviewers for psychiatrists, and have made comparisons between them. They used a newer interview schedule, the Renard Diagnostic Interview (RDI; Helzer, Robins, Croughan, & Welner, 1981). The results are complex, and their interpretation depends heavily on the assumption that the psychiatrist is a highly accurate judge. Helzer *et al.* (1981) found that lay judges were more sensitive

Table 2. Interrater Reliability of RDC Diagnoses[a]

Study	M	N	Sc	Mn	MD	ASPD	Nr[b]	Alc (Drug)	Comment
Andreasen et al. (1981)	T-RT	50		1.00[c]	.87			.94	5 centers; lifetime diagnosis
	T-RT	Same		.88[c]	.75			.72	Same day 6 month
Andreasen et al. (1982)	SR	8		.68	.84				5 centers; many raters Videotape SADS-L vs. DIS
Hesselbrock et al. (1982)	T-RT	42			.72			1.00	3-4 days; present diagnosis
	T-RT	Same			.74			1.00	3-4 days; past diagnosis
Hostetter et al. (1983)	SR	120		.86	.95				Consensus v. expert Case material
Keller et al. (1981a)	T-RT	25	.52	.72	.85				Present diagnosis Same day
Keller et al. (1981b)	T-RT	25	.60	.52	.82			.67	Past diagnosis Same day
Mazure & Gershon (1979)	T-RT	47		1.00[c]	.88			1.00	6 months
Rounsaville et al. (1980)	SR	15			Specific category K's .64–1.00				Drug abusers
	T-RT	11			Major depression = .62, other K's = .30–1.00				3-10 days

Study	Method	N							
Rounsaville et al. (1982)	T-RT	117			.47	.52	.71		6 months
Spitzer et al. (1974)	T-RT	100	.78	.59[c]					< 1 week
	T-RT	Same	.65	.45[e]					< 1-3 months
									See text
Spitzer et al. (1978)									
Study A	SR	68	.80	.82	.88			.86(0.76)	Present episode
	SR	Same	.75	.89	.97			.88(0.89)	Lifetime diagnosis
Study B	SR	150	.91	.98	.90			.97(0.95)	Present episode
	SR	Same		.93	.91	1.00		.98(1.00)	Lifetime diagnosis
Study C	T-RT	60	.65	.82	.90			1.00(0.92)	Present episode; 1-2 days
	T-RT	Same	.73	.77	.71			.95(0.73)	Lifetime diagnosis
Study D	SR	49			.85				Past diagnosis; 1½-2 years
Study E	T-RT	29		.85	.76		.78–1.00	1.00	Lifetime diagnosis; 1-2 days
Spitzer et al. (1975)	SR	120	.78-.84	.76-.92	.66-.74	.66	.39-.66	.66-1.00 (1.00)	Case records

[a]Headings for this and following tables: MD = Major Depression; AD = Affective Disorder (MD or Mn); Alc = Alcoholism; Drug = Abuse.
[b]Phobic, Panic, Obsessive-Compulsive or Generalized Anxiety Disorder.
[c]Bipolar
[d]Unipolar
[e]Major Depression or Mania.

Table 3. Reliability of St. Louis Group Criteria Diagnoses

Study	M	N	Sc	Mn	D	ASPD	Nr[a]	Alc(Drug)	Comment
Helzer et al. (1977)									
	T-RT	101	.58	.82	.55	.81	.72-.78	.74(.84)	1 day
Coryell et al. (1978)									
	SR	34			.57		.74	1.00(.91)	Lay judges
Martin et al. (1979)									Female felons
	F-U	66				.65	.45-.47	.47(.76)	5 years
Helzer et al. (1981)									
Lay-lay	T-RT	31	.43		.64		.52	.89	See text
MD-MD	T-RT	26	.26		.62		.51	.70	1-3 days
Lay-MD	T-RT	42	.84		.51		.53	.73	Same
Pooled	T-RT	99	.52		.58		.53	.77	Same

[a]Headings in this table: Anxiety, Phobic, Obsessional Disorder, or Briquet's Syndrome.

than psychiatrists, who in turn tended to show higher specificity. But these trends were not strong and the two classes of interviewer usually agreed quite closely.

Table 4 gives results of reliability studies using *DSM-III* criteria. Originally there was no interview associated with the *DSM-III*, and studies used case summaries (Hyler, Williams, & Spitzer, 1982), structured interviews created for other purposes, or unstructured interviews (Spitzer, Forman, & Nee, 1979). In the reliability field trials of *DSM-III*, special efforts were made to involve many psychiatrists, so that these studies are certainly among the most representative of any done using specified diagnostic criteria: the raters are far from handpicked, though many were expert diagnosticians. The results of the field trials were analyzed in two separate phases: an initial report (Spitzer, *et al.*, 1979), and a separate study comparing the reliability of diagnoses based on case vignettes to those based on interviews (Hyler, *et al.*, 1982). The former report suggests that *DSM-III*, when used by clinicians, may be about as reliable as the RDC in the hands of research interviewers. Case record diagnoses of *DSM-III* disorders always tended to be a little less reliable than interview diagnoses, making chart review studies suspect.

The studies by Helzer, Stoltzman, Farmer, Brockington, Plesons, Singerman, and Works (1985), Helzer, Robins, McEvoy, Spitznagel, Stoltzman, Farmer, and Brockington (1985), Robins, Helzer, Ratcliff, and Seyfried (1982) and by Burman, Karno, Hough, Escobar, and Forsythe (1983) were conducted as part of the NIMH Epidemiological Catchment Area program (ECA; Regier, Myers, Kramer, Robins, Blazer, Hough, Eaton & Locke, 1984). This multicenter collaborative program aims to interview 20,000 individuals in the community to determine prevalence of *DSM-III*-defined psychiatric disorders and risk factors for these disorders. The Diagnostic Interview Schedule (DIS; Robins, Helzer, Croughan, & Ratcliff, 1981) was developed for the ECA to allow lay interviewers to diagnose *DSM-III* (as well as St Louis group and RDC) disorders without much clinical judgment; practically every word the interviewer says is spelled out, and follow-up to almost every possible interviewee answer is dictated as well. This is perhaps not ideal for clinical research settings, but that remains to be seen. Reliability of diagnoses in the community based on the DIS will soon be published; the studies in Table 4 are based on lay or psychiatric interiewers examining identified patients. The reliability of the diagnoses appears satisfactory, though perhaps not quite as high as for the RDC. A most important finding is that the Spanish-language DIS reported on by Burman *et al.* (1983) gives comparable reliability to the English-language version, and yields nearly identical results when used to interview bilingual subjects twice.

Table 4. Reliability of DSM-III Diagnoses

Study	M	N	Sc	Mn	MD	PD	ASPD	Nr	Alc(Drug)	Comment
Spitzer et al. (1979)										
	SR	150	.82		.70[a]				.90[b]	DSM-III field trials
	T-RT	131	.82		.65[a]			.74	.74[b]	Interval not stated; a few days
Hyler et al. (1982)										
	SR	46	.54		.59[a]				.69[b]	DSM-III field trials
	SR	46	.69		.55[a]			.83	.95[b]	Case records Live
Mellsop et al. (1982)										
	T-RT	74				-.05-49[c]	.49			1-2 days; median .23; See text
Burman et al.(1983)										
Both Spanish	T-RT	61	.66		.49		.92	.45-51[c]	.63	
Spanish-English	T-RT	90	.48		.61		.69	.40-47[c]	.86	
DiNardo et al.(1983)										
	T-RT	60	.60	.65	.57			.66-85[c]		Anxiety clinic patients 1-9 weeks
Robins et al.(1983)										
	T-RT	216			.63		.63	.40-67[c]	.86(.73)	Lay vs. M.D. Interval not stated; a few days
Helzer et al.(Note 2)										
Kappa	T-RT	370		.21	.50		.56	.24-49[c]	.68(.52)	Lay vs. M.D. 3 weeks
Yule's Y	Same	Same		.55	.60		.74	.49-64[c]	.74(.72)	Same

[a] Major affective disorder.
[b] Substance abuse or dependence.
[c] Agreement on specific diagnosis.

A large number of studies have reported reliabilities for specific diagnoses, as opposed to the reliability of sets of criteria for multiple disorders. Some of these were reliability checks, or study patient inclusion for large studies following up patients over time or investigating the genetics of major psychiatric disorders. These are useful for judging how exacting the inclusion process was in various studies, but their bearing on the reliability of diagnoses may be limited by circumstances. This is because almost all studies examined selected patients for whom the diagnostic decision was artificially confined to one or a few possibilities. Since the patients and their diagnoses are often not randomly sampled from any meaningful population, it is hard to decide whether the special circumstances of a given study would bias reliability up (by reducing diagnostic choices) or down. For example, selecting patients who are all deluded makes the diagnosis schizophrenia-not schizophrenia less reliable, by excluding those in whom schizophrenia cannot even be suspected by any rater. Some studies have also recently looked at comparative reliabilities for differing definitions of some disorders, (e.g., borderline or schizotypal personality disorders or schizophrenia). One can collect a large number of such one- or two-diagnosis studies, but since they are not comparable to studies reviewed above, I shall not cover them here.

What Does the Future Hold?

It would appear that many diagnoses have been made more understandable and more reliable by introducing specified diagnostic criteria and structured interviews. Some still-difficult diagnoses can probably be made more reliably. Interviews for personality disorders (Stangl, Pfohl, Zimmerman, Bowers & Corenthal, 1985) and anxiety disorders (DiNardo, O'Brien, Barlow, Waddell & Blanchard, 1983) are being developed. Such efforts have already resulted in interim revisions of a number of *DSM-III* criteria. A burgeoning area is the diagnosis of psychiatric disorders in the community; the NIMH ECA is producing much data relevant to the reliability of diagnoses in persons not currently in treatment. Such data are critical for interpreting the meaning of "case finding" in psychiatric epidemiology. Last, the emergence of cross-national diagnostic interviews, which started with the PSE, has continued with the Spanish version of the DIS and with subsequent interviews as well. Wittchen and colleagues in Munich are working on a German translation of the DIS (Helzer, 1984), while a collaborative group of World Health Organization and Alcoholism, Drug Abuse, and Mental Health Administration personnel are developing a WHO-ADAMHA Comprehensive International Diagnostic Interview. Wittchen has recently completed a physician re-examination study of both DIS and CIDI using his German translations. Spitzer and colleagues are working on a clinician interview for the making of *DSM-III* diagnoses, the Structured Clinical Interview for *DSM-III* (Spitzer, 1983). While these developments pertain most directly to the information-gathering phase of diagnosis, the development of structured interviews has already enlarged our knowledge of diagnostic reliability. Future developments will clarify whether diagnostic concepts which have proved reliable in Anglo-American psychiatry travel well to other cultures, and to what degree skilled clinical judgment is necessary for reliable diagnosis.

Readers might feel rather comfortable about psychiatric diagnosis at this point. They should not. Many people becme overconfident of diagnostic accuracy when they read of high reliability. One has to remind oneself that while unreliability constrains validity in a general way, raising reliability is no panacea. High reliability can always be bought by gerrymandering diagnostic definitions, or by local agreements on minutiae of interpretation of specified criteria. Therefore, reliability studies can never be more than a necessary first step in diagnostic research. Given the amorphous and overlapping nature of many psychiatric syndromes, one must be suspicious of highly reliable diagnoses until they are proven to be highly valid, too.

REFERENCES

American Psychiatric Association. (1968). *Diagnostic and Statistical Manual of Mental Disorders*, 2nd edition. Washington, DC: Author.

American Psychiatric Association. (1980). *Diagnostic and Statistical Manual of Mental Disorders*, 3rd edition. Washington, DC: Author.

Andreasen, N.C., McDonald-Scott, P., Grove, W.M., Keller, M.D., Shapiro, R.W., & Hirschfeld, R.M.A. (1982). Assessment of reliability in multi-center collaborative research using a videotape approach. *American Journal of Psychiatry, 139,* 876–882.

Andreasen, N.C., Grove, W.M., Shapiro, R.W., Keller, M.B., Hirschfeld, R.M.A., & McDonald-Scott, P. (1981). Reliability of lifetime diagnosis: A multicenter collaborative perspective. *Archives of General Psychiatry, 38,* 400–405.

Beck, A.T., Ward, C.H., Mendelson, M., Mock, J.E., & Erbaugh, J.K. (1962). Reliability of psychiatric diagnoses: 2. A study of consistency of clinical judgements and ratings. *American Journal of Psychiatry, 119,* 351–357.

Burman, M.A., Karno, M., Hough, R.L., Escobar, J.I., & Forsythe, A.B. (1983). The Spanish Diagnostic Interview Schedule: Reliability and comparison with clinical diagnoses. *Archives of General Psychiatry, 40,* 1189–1195.

Carey, G., & Gottesman, I.I. (1978). Reliability and validity in binary ratings: Areas of common misunderstanding in diagnosis and symptom ratings. *Archives of General Psychiatry, 35,* 1454–1459.

Cloninger, C.R., Miller, J.P., Wette, R., Martin, R.I., & Guze, S.B. (1979). The evaluation of diagnostic concordance in follow-up studies: 1. A general model of causal analysis and a methodological critique. *Journal of Psychiatric Research, 15*, 85–106.

Cohen, J. (1960). A coefficient of agreement for nominal scales. *Educational and Psychological Measurement, 20*, 37–46.

Coryell, W., Cloninger, C.R., & Reich, T. (1978) Clinical assessment: Use of nonphysician interviewers. *Journal of Nervous and Mental Disease, 166*, 599–606.

DiNardo, P.A., O'Brien, G.T., Barlow, D.H., Waddell, M.T., & Blanchard, E.B. (1983). Reliability of *DSM-III* anxiety disorder categories using a new structured interview. *Archives of General Psychiatry, 40*, 1170–1078.

Elkin, F. (1947). Specialists interpret the case of Harold Holzer. *Journal of Abnormal and Social Psychology, 44*, 272–276.

Fleiss, J.L. (1981) Balanced incomplete block designs for interrater reliability studies. *Applied Psychological Measurement, 5*, 105–112.

Fleiss, J.L., & Cohen, J. (1973). The equivalence of weighted kappa and the intraclass correlation coefficient as measures of reliability. *Educational and Psychological Measurement, 33*, 613–619.

Fleiss, J.L., & Cuzick, J. (1979). The reliability of dichotomous judgments: Unequal numbers of judges per subject. *Applied Psychological Measurement, 3*, 537–542.

Foulds, G.A. (1955). The reliability of psychiatric, and the validity of psychological, diagnoses. *Journal of Mental Science, 101*, 851–862.

Galen, G.S., & Gambino, S.R. (1975). *Beyond normality: The predictive value and efficiency of medical diagnoses.* New York: Wiley.

Helzer, J.E., & Coryell, W. (1983). More on *DSM-III:* How consistent are precise criteria? (Editorial) *Biological Psychiatry, 18*, 1201–1203.

Helzer, J.E., Clayton, P.J., Pambakian, R., Reich, T., Woodruff, R.A., Jr., & Reveley, M.A. (1977). Reliability of psychiatric diagnosis: II. The test/retest reliability of diagnostic classification. *Archives of General Psychiatry, 34*, 136–141.

Helzer, J.E., Robins, L.N., Croughan, J.L., & Welner, A. (1981). Renard Diagnostic Interview: Its reliability and procedural validity with physicians and lay interviewers. *Archives of General Psychiatry, 38*, 393–398.

Helzer, J.E., Robins, L.N., McEvoy, L.T., Spitznagel, E.L., Stoltzman, R.K., Farmer, A.L., & Brockington, I.F. (1985). Results of the St. Louis ECA physician reexamination study of the Diagnostic Interview Schedule. *Archives of General Psychiatry, 42*, 657–666.

Helzer, J.E., Stoltzman, R.K., Farmer, A., Brockington, I.F., Plesons, D., Singerman, B., & Works, J. (1985) Comparison with a DIS/*DSM-III* based physician reevaluation in St. Louis. In W.W. Eaton & L.G. Kessler (Eds.), *Epidemiologic field methods in psychiatry: The NIMH Epidemiologic Catchment Area program.* New York: Academic Press.

Hesselbrock, V., Stabenau, J., Hesselbrock, M., Mirkin, P., & Meyer, R. (1982). A comparison of two interview schedules: The Schedule for Affective Disorders and Schizophrenia-Lifetime and the National Institute for Mental Health Diagnostic Interview Schedule. *Archives of General Psychiatry, 39*, 674–677.

Hostetter, A.M., Egeland, J.A., & Endicott, J. (1983). Amish Study, II: Consensus diagnoses and reliability results. *American Journal of Psychiatry, 140*, 62–71.

Hyler, S.E., Williams, J.B.W., & Spitzer, R.L. (1982). Reliability in the *DSM-III* field trials: Interview v. case summary. *Archives of General Psychiatry, 39*, 1275–1278.

Johnson, J.H., Klingler, D.E., Giannetti, R.A., & Williams, T.A (1980). The reliability of diagnoses by technician, computer, and algorithm. *Journal of Clinical Psychology, 36*, 447–451.

Katz, M.M., Secunda, S.K., Hirschfeld, R.M.A., Jr. & Koslow, S.R. (1979). NIMH Clinical Research Branch Collaborative Program on the Psychobiology of Depression. *Archives of General Psychiatry, 36,* 765-771.

Keller, M.B., Lavori, P.W., Andreasen, N.C., Grove, W.M., Shapiro, R.W., Sheftner, W., & McDonald-Scott, P. (1981a). Test-retest reliability of assessing psychiatrically ill patients in a multi-center design. *Journal of Psychiatric Research, 16,* 213-227.

Keller, M.B., Lavori, P., McDonald-Scott, P., Scheftner, W.A., Andreasen, N.C., Shapiro, R.W., & Croughan, J. (1981b). Reliability of lifetime diagnoses and symptoms in patients with a current psychiatric disorder. *Journal of Psychiatric Research, 16,* 229-240.

Kendell, R.E., Cooper, J.E., Gourlay, A.J., Copeland, J.R.M., Sharpe, L., & Gurland, B.J. (1971). Diagnostic criteria of American and British psychiatrists. *Archives of General Psychiatry, 25,* 123-130.

Kraemer, H.C. (1978). Ramifications of a population model for K as a coefficient of reliability. *Psychometrika, 44,* 461-472.

Kreitman, N., Sainsbury, P., Morrissey, J., Towers, J., & Scrivener, J. (1961). The reliability of psychiatric assessment: An analysis. *Journal of Mental Science, 107,* 876-886.

Landis, J.R., & Koch, G.G. (1977). A one-way components of variance model for categorical data. *Biometrics, 33,* 671-679.

Martin, R.L., Cloninger, C.R., & Guze, S.B. (1979). The evaluation of diagnostic concordance in follow-up studies: II. A blind, prospective follow-up of female criminals. *Journal of Psychiatric Research, 15,* 107-125.

Masserman, J.H., & Carmichael, H.T. (1938). Diagnosis and prognosis in psychiatry: With a follow-up study of the results of short-term general hospital therapy of psychiatric cases. *Journal of Mental Science, 84,* 893-946.

Mazure, C., & Gershon, E.S. (1979). Blindness and reliability in lifetime psychiatric diagnosis. *Archives of General Psychiatry, 36,* 521-525.

Mellsop, G., Varghese, F., Joshua, S., & Hicks, A. (1982). The reliability of Axis II of *DSM-III:* A report of a clinical study. *American Journal of Psychiatry, 139,* 1360-1361.

Norris, V. (1959). *Mental illness in London.* London: Chapman & Hall.

Regier, D.A., Myers, J.K., Kramer, M., Robins, L.N., Blazer, D.G., Hough, R.L., Eaton, W.W., & Locke, B.Z. (1984). The NIMH Epidemiologic Catchment Area Program. *Archives of General Psychiatry, 41,* 934-941.

Robins, L.N., Helzer, J.E., Croughan, J., & Ratcliff, K.S. (1981). National Institute of Mental Health Diagnostic Interview Schedule: Its history, characteristics, and validity. *Archives of General Psychiatry, 38,* 381-389.

Robins, L.N., Helzer, J.E., Ratcliff, K.S., & Seyfried, W. (1982). Reliability and validity of the Diagnostic Interview Schedule, Version II: *DSM-III* diagnoses. *Psychological Medicine, 12,* 855-870.

Rosenzweig, N., Vandenberg, S.G., Moore, K., & Dukay, A. (1961). A study of the reliability of the mental status examination. *American Journal of Psychiatry, 117,* 1102-1108.

Rounsaville, B.J., Cacciola, J., Weissman, M.M., & Kleber, H.D. (1982). Diagnostic concordance in a follow-up study of opiate addicts. *Journal of Psychiatric Research, 16,* 191-201.

Rounsaville, B.J., Rosenberger, P., Wilber, C., Weissman, M.M., & Kleber, H.D. (1980). A comparison of the SADS/RDC and the *DSM-III:* Diagnosing drug abusers. *Journal of Nervous and Mental Disease, 168,* 90-97.

Sandifer, M.G., Jr., Pettus, C., & Quade, D. (1964). A study of psychiatric diagnosis. *Journal of Nervous and Mental Disease, 39,* 350-356.

Schmidt, H.O., & Fonda, C.P. (1956). The reliability of psychiatric diagnosis: A new look. *Journal of Abnormal and Social Psychology, 52,* 262-267.

Spitzer, R.L. (1983). Psychiatric diagnosis: Are clinicians still necessary? *Comprehensive Psychiatry, 24,* 399–411.

Spitzer, R.L., Endicott, J., Cohen, J., & Fleiss, J.L. (1974). Constraints on the validity of computer diagnosis. *Archives of General Psychiatry, 31,* 197–203.

Spitzer, R.L., Endicott, J., Robins, E., Kuriansky, J., & Gurland, B. (1975). Preliminary report of the reliability of Research Diagnostic Criteria applied to psychiatric case records. In A. Sudilovsky, S. Gershon, & B. Beer (Eds.), *Predictability in psychopharmacology: Preclinical and clinical correlations* (pp. 1–47). New York: Raven.

Spitzer, R.L., Endicott, J., & Robins, E. (1978). Research Diagnostic Criteria: Rationale and reliability. *Archives of General Psychiatry, 35,* 773–782.

Spitzer, R.L., Forman, J.B.W., & Nee, J. (1979). *DSM-III* field trials: I. Initial interrater diagnostic reliability. *American Journal of Psychiatry, 136,* 815–817.

Spitznagel, E.L., & Helzer, J.E. (1985). A proposed solution to the base rate problem in the kappa statistics. *Archives of General Psychiatry, 42,* 725–728.

Standage, K.R. (1979). The use of Schneider's typology for the diagnosis of personality disorders—An examination of reliability. *British Journal of Psychiatry, 135,* 238–242.

Stangl, D., Pfohl, B., Zimmerman, M., Bowers, W., & Corenthal, C. (1986). A structured interview for the DSM-III personality disorders: A preliminary study. *Archives of General Psychiatry, 42,* 591–596.

Uebersax, J.S. (1983). A design-independent method for measuring the reliability of psychiatric diagnosis. *Journal of Psychiatric Research, 4,* 335–342.

Ward, C.H., Beck, A.T., Mendelson, M., Mock, J.E., & Erbaugh, J.K. (1962). The psychiatric nomenclature: Reasons for diagnostic disagreement. *Archives of General Psychiatry, 7,* 198–205.

Westermeyer, J., & Sines, L. (1979). Reliability of cross-cultural psychiatric diagnosis with an assessment of two rating contexts. *Journal of Psychiatric Research, 15,* 199–213.

Wing, J.K., Birley, J.L.T., Cooper, J.E., Graham, P., & Isaacs, A.D. (1967). Reliability of a procedure for measuring and classifying "present psychiatric state." *British Journal of Psychiatry, 113,* 499–515.

World Health Organization. (1973). *International Pilot Study of Schizophrenia, Vol. I.* Geneva: Author.

4

Diagnostic Validity

JOHN P. FEIGHNER and JESSICA HERBSTEIN

INTRODUCTION

Reliability and validity are basic concepts by which we measure the accuracy and usefulness of nosological or diagnostic processes. Reliability refers to both interrater agreement as to whether the criteria that define a disorder occur in a patient population, and to the consistency with which any particular diagnosis is made over time. Validity refers to the accuracy with which these criteria define and differentiate a disease from other diseases.

Nosology is the foundation of clinical practice and research in psychiatry. In so far as its accuracy and the consistency with which it is applied determine the success of treatment, these are of the utmost importance both to the clinician and the researcher interested in extending empirically tested boundaries. This chapter discusses the history and changes in diagnostic approach that have led to current classificatory systems, procedures for establishing diagnostic validity, instrumentation and measurement techniques, issues in measurement and symptom identification, issues in classification, and future directions for research.

HISTORY OF MODERN NOSOLOGY

Interest in descriptive classification is generally considered to date back to German psychiatry at the end of the nineteenth century. At that time Hecker (1871) and Kahlbaum (1874) described the categories of hebephrenia and catatonia in schizophrenic patients labeling what they

JOHN P. FEIGHNER and JESSICA HERBSTEIN • Feighner Research Institute, Encinitas, CA 92024.

presumed to be separate disease entities. Kraepelin 1909 further established categorization in psychiatry when he classified patients as suffering from manic-depressive illness, dementia praecox, or psychopathy on the basis of clearly observable criteria, which included age and type of onset, course of illness, and clusters of clinical symptoms that were specific to each disorder and differentiated them from each other.

However, Kraepelin could not find a biological basis for these disorders, nor could he offer specific biological treatment for them. As a result, his influence and the interest in classification as a basis for diagnosis waned as psychoanalytic explanation came to the fore at the beginning of this century. Freud (1953) had attempted a neurophysiological theory of consciousness but failed, subsequently developing a purely psychological approach involving consideration of a dynamic unconscious and intrapsychic conflicts as a basis for illness. Psychoanalysis divided mental illness into the neuroses, which were treatable by the analytic method, and the psychoses, which were not.

Because of this broad division and because it concentrated on intrapersonal processes rather than disease entities, the Freudian method made accurate and refined diagnoses to a large extent unnecessary. In this country Adolph Meyer (1908) saw schizophrenia as a disorder of living and social interaction, and under him antidiagnostic sentiment grew, leading to a rejection of the diagnostic process by a large majority of the psychiatric and mental health community. It was argued that because psychiatric illness was the result of distorted human interaction, diagnoses were at best unstable and at worst did more harm than good in that they labelled patients in a way that had lasting negative social and personal consequences for them.

Antinosological approaches dominated mental health until the psychopharmacological revolution of the 1950s, when it was discovered that affective disorders could be successfully chemically controlled by treatment with the monoamine oxidase inhibitors, the tricyclic antidepressants, and lithium, and that schizophrenia was best treated with neuroleptics. Improved specificity in treatment methodology demanded greater specificity in diagnosis. In the late 1960s a systematic, data-oriented program using structured interviews and a strictly phenomenological approach was developed at Washington University, St. Louis. Its objective was to increase reliability of diagnosis by establishing clearly observable inclusion criteria by which a disease could be recognized and exclusion criteria that differentiated it from other diseases. This work resulted in the publication of the Feighner Research Criteria (Feighner, Robins, Guze, Woodruff, & Winokur, 1972) which, following further investigation, were expanded by Spitzer, Endicott, and Robins (1975) into the Research

Diagnostic Criteria (RDC). In 1980 the third edition of the American Psychiatric Association's *Diagnostic and Statistical Manual of Mental Disorders* (DSM-III) represented a further expansion on the previous criteria, and included a number of refinements aimed at increasing diagnostic acuity and allowing for additional systematization of material obtained in the clinical interview. In particular, a multiaxial system for evaluation was added to improve treatment planning and prediction of outcome. It specified separate axes for recording two classes of mental disorders, personality and specific developmental disorders (Axis II) and all other mental disorders (Axis I), physical disorders (Axis III) and related biosocial factors (severity of psychosocial stressors and highest level of adaptive functioning, Axes IV and V) of outcome.

PARAMETERS IN ESTABLISHING DIAGNOSTIC VALIDITY

Nosology in psychiatry involves a complex interaction of psychobiological issues, and its validity can be determined only by adopting a systematic approach with rigorous attention to detail. In order to systematize observation and enhance the validation process we have suggested (1982) a six-stage diagnostic model that includes guidelines for both cross-sectional and longitudinal observation and recording of data. These include:

1. *Clinical description and delimitation of syndromes from each other.* This provides a cross-sectional view of a given disorder that involves objective description of signs and symptoms of both the psychological and physical nature and also includes demographic and psychosocial factors such as age, sex, race, and precipitating events. Clinical description must consider not only what the positive signs for a diagnosis are but also examine exclusion criteria, which differentiate between syndromes that share some but not all signs and symptoms.

2. *Natural history.* Retrospective and prospective studies examine longitudinal factors that characterize a disease and thus play an important part in diagnostic validation. The follow-up study indicates whether individual patients are suffering from the disorder originally diagnosed and in research confirms or negates the accuracy of the diagnostic categories examined. If at follow-up the original patients show symptoms that indicate a different disorder, or the group that forms the sample displays a significant heterogeneity in its symptomatology, it is more than likely that the diagnostic criteria are invalid and need further refinement. This does not mean that the appearance of new symptoms over time necessarily negates validity, but only that the pattern of such symptoms

must vary systematically in different phases of the disease. Such changes in the pattern of symptoms is rather well demonstrated by the course of senile dementia Alzheimer's type, in which there is memory impairment and depressive symptomatology in the prodromal phase, but the individual remains neat, well groomed, and socially appropriate, while in the middle stage, behavior and personality change radically, with the patient sometimes appearing psychotic and sometimes becoming violent. Then, in the final stage, the patient lapses into mutism and inability to cope with even basic needs. Similarly, observation of systmatic changes in the pattern of the symptoms in episodes of mania and depression was a key factor that led Kraepelin to set up the distinction between manic-depressive disorder and schizophrenia.

Retrospective studies are more susceptible to observer bias than prospective studies and therefore, in general, provide less reliable and valid data. However, follow-up study sometimes becomes impossible because of sample instability and attenuation, and in these situations retrospective research may be the only way to identify antecedents of a given disorder. In addition, certain types of variables can be measured quite reliably on a retrospective basis. In particular, demographic data concerning age and sex, prodromal and presenting symptoms, course in terms of number of hospitalizations and previous diagnosis, can usually be documented.

3. *Treatment outcome studies.* Treatment outcome studies can be useful in validating existing diagnostic subtypes and in identifying new subtypes with greater specificity. Whenever possible it is important to use placebo control groups to enhance assessment of treatment-related change. Even when the natural course of a disorder is known, it is difficult to separate nonspecific factors such as life events and independently occurring medical conditions from treatment-related factors.

Recent technological advances have made it possible to produce drugs with highly controlled and specific activities in the CNS. A predicted response by the patient may thus help elucidate a neurophysiological aspect of the disorder that the compound was developed to relieve. It can also help identify new biological subtypes. At this time, greater specificity of action is seen in drugs developed for the treatment of depression. Highly specific anxiolytics now are also being tested and should be of use in differentiating subtypes of depression and anxiety states. With the advent of more specific interventions this phase of diagnostic validation assumes increasing importance. However, even though it is now possible to eliminate many treatment-related factors such as wide dosage range, therapeutic windows, and side effects that have confounded research in the past, detailed records of clinical observations remains essential, both to rule out random features and to allow for the possibility of locating new subtypes by combining treatment outcome with clinical detail.

4. *Family studies.* Family or pedigree studies demonstrate that most psychiatric disorders occur with greater frequency in family members than in the general population. Family studies by themselves can enhance diagnostic validation, but do not allow for etiological specificity, particularly in nature versus nurture issues. When, however, they are combined with twin, half-sibling, and adoptee investigations, a much clearer picture can be obtained with regard to these issues.

Familial specificity of response to pharmacological treatment has been proposed for the affective disorders by Cooper and Magnus (1984) and, with technological advances allowing for highly specific treatment, this area of research may assume greater importance in both diagnostic and treatment-related issues.

5. *Physical and neurological factors.* At this time these factors refer primarily to neuroanatomical or neurophysiological changes seen with disorders such as temporal lobe epilepsy or the senile dementias. Development of potent technological methods—such as CAT scans, PET scans, and MRI—offer increased opportunity for identifying such changes and therefore confirming diagnoses in which they are relevant parameters.

In addition, the capacity to evaluate structural changes at minute levels opens whole new areas of research, and when combined with the ability to measure functional changes adds a magnitude of diagnostic capability that is potentially far greater than anything previously achieved in psychiatry.

6. *Laboratory studies and psychodiagnostic evaluation.* The usefulness of biological markers and psychological measurement in validating nosological systems depends on the precision with which they delineate homogeneous populations. These will be discussed in greater detail in the second and third parts of the following section.

INSTRUMENTATION AND MEASUREMENT TECHNIQUES

Structured Clinical Interviews

In the last two decades a number of structured interviews have been developed for use in large-scale epidemiological studies in this country and also for cross-national comparison purposes. In England the Present State Examination (PSE), developed by Wing and colleagues (1974, 1983), related to diagnostic ideas codified in the computerized diagnostic system (CATEGO), and was used in the International Pilot Study of Schizophrenia (SADS) and the Diagnostic Interview Schedule (DIS) were developed to enable examiners to gather clinical data necessary for making diagnoses according to the Feighner criteria, the Research Diagnostic Criteria (RDC), and DSM-III.

The Composite International Diagnostic Interview (CIDI) combines the British PSE and the DIS and aims at providing a single instrument that can be used by lay or clinical examiners to make diagnoses according to DSM-III or ICD-9 as classified by CATEGO. The availability of such interviews facilitates data collection, which should enhance our ability to evaluate the validity of various nosological systems.

Biological Markers

Specific disease types are often accompanied by changes in neurochemical and neurophysiological functioning, as well as by neuroendocrinological variation. Numerous attempts have been made to use measures of these changes to distinguish between disease entities and subtypes, and thus provide evidence of construct validity of clinical diagnostic categories.

Research on the biological markers has been most highly developed in the area of the major affective disorders, with the biophysiological measures used including the dexamethasone suppression test (DST), the thyrotropin-releasing hormone (TRH) determination—thyroid-stimulating hormone (TSH) response test, and measures of growth hormone (GH) responsiveness to amphetamine, desmethylimipramine, clonidine, and insulin-induced hypoglycemia.

Chemical parameters investigated include measures of monoamines and their metabolites—such as urinary methoxy-hydroxy-phenyl glycol (MHPG)—and other metabolites of norepinephrine. The RBC/lithium ratio (the ratio of the concentration of lithium in the red blood cell to that in the plasma) has also been investigated as a possible means of discriminating between bipolar and unipolar disorders.

Electrophysiological methods have concentrated on identifying specific deviation in sleep patterns, such as in rapid eye movement (REM) latency and REM density, as correlates of depressive disorder.

Finally, receptor research has concentrated on the relationship between the number of imipramine platelet binding sites and decreases in cerebral spinal fluid (CSF) concentrations of 5-HT and 5-HIAA, on the one hand, and such behavioral measures as aggression, impulsivity, and suicide on the other. Among other sites investigated are opioid receptors, the alpha-1 and alpha-2 adrenoceptors, the H-1 and H-2 histamine receptors, and the serotonergic, benzoidiazepine, and muscarinic/cholinergic receptors (Huang & Maas, 1985; Rubin & Marder, 1983).

Studies on schizophrenic patients have involved the dopamine (DA) system, platelet monoamine oxidase activity, creatine phosphokinase (CPK), and endorphin, and enkephalin activity. Anatomical studies have investigated ventricular morphology and electorencephalographic abnormalities (Huang & Maas, 1985; Rubin & Marder, 1983).

Results of this research have been ambiguous. For instance, the most intensively investigated marker, cortisol nonsuppression as measured by the DST, has been shown to average only a 50% success rate in indicating endogenous depression. On the other hand those patients who have a positive reaction, that is, nonsuppression, to the administration of dexamethasone, exhibit a consistent and predictable response to therapy, with strong correlation between increased cortisol suppression and improved clinical status. In addition, a strong association has been found between DST nonsuppression and familial pure depressive disease (FPDD) versus depressive spectrum disease (DSD), with the former sample having a significantly higher percentage of nonsuppression than the latter. However, nonsuppression with the DST has also been found in nonendogenous depression, panic disorders, schizoaffective disorders, organic brain syndrome, obsessive-compulsive disorders, and at a lesser rate in normal subjects, thus seriously compromising the diagnostic validity of the DST. (Huang & Maas, 1985; Rubin & Marder, 1983).

Research on other biological markers, similarly has given inconsistent results, which means that they still cannot be used as more than adjuncts to diagnosis in the clinical setting. However, their high reliability, and the fact that in selected groups where a correlation is found between clinical status and response on a biological marker they consistently behave in an expected manner, makes them valuable tools in follow-up research. In addition, the fact that they do not neatly fit the DSM-III categories may bring about a situation in which the latter are ultimately refined to include groups delimited by the biological tests. Hays (1985) has suggested that clinical observation and recording should go beyond what is demanded for formal classification according to any of the accepted systems, and in this way provide necessary data for differentiating between groups that do and do not correlate positively with biological tests. This would encourage the emergence of new subtypes that are otherwise unlikely to be recognized.

Rating Scales and Observer Measurement

Rating scales measure the severity of illness in individual patients, and are used both in sample selection and to document changes over time that will confirm or negate the original diagnosis and allow for assessment of treatment response.

Global rating methods, which require an overall judgment as to the condition of the patient at various times prior to and during treatment, are attractive because they reflect traditional clinical practice, which has always used global impressions for making clinical judgments. In addition, they require less time to complete than more complex rating scales, which deal with many variables. On the negative side, it might be expected that both reliability and validity would be low when no indication is given as to what the basis for such a global rating should be. Nevertheless, correlations as high as .82, for instance, have been found between global ratings and ratings made on more differentiated scales such as the Hamilton Depression Scale (1960) and the Beck Depression Inventory (1961).

With regard to accuracy and sensitivity, there is no clear answer as to which type of scale performs better. The reason for this is probably that differentiated scales have to make a choice of variables to be covered by the scale with inadequate knowledge of the weights that these should be given. Therefore, it is best to use both global evaluation and specific scales to properly assess change for comprehensive evaluation.

The issue of item selection also affects the validity of self-rating measures. These on the whole correlate inconsistently with observer ratings and are less sensitive and less valid than the latter. One reason is that the range of items in this type of scale is more restricted. Patients are often unable to judge medical aspects of what is wrong with them and, in addition, are often not in a condition to complete complicated and lengthy forms and therefore cannot be relied upon to do so in an adequate manner. In general, self-rating scales have been shown to be more useful in detecting the presence of symptoms than in quantitating them (Carroll, Fielding & Blashki, 1973; Prushoff, Klerman, & Paykel, 1972).

Psychological Tests

The majority of psychological tests currently used for psychiatric diagnosis were developed prior to the appearance of DSM-III and designed to predict criteria other than those that make up the DSM-III diagnostic categories. As a result, their usefulness as diagnostic indicators varies according to the purposes for which they are administered and the type of test used.

The area of psychodiagnostic testing that is most seriously compromised of differences in predictive criteria is that of personality testing. Even an inventory such as the MMPI, which was developed to distinguish between normals and persons with diagnosed psychiatric disorders, and has scales with names similar to those of DSM-III disorders, in fact uses earlier definitions of those disorders (Marks, Seeman, & Haller, 1979). This makes translation of scale elevations into DSM-III terminology unreliable. While this can be corrected in a clinical situation by combining MMPI results with other test and background data (such as family history and history of illness), similar correction cannot be made in research because of the subjective nature of much of the additional material.

In contrast to the rather unsatisfactory status of personality testing for psychiatric diagnosis, neuropsychological methods have considerable diagnostic value when used in a neurological, educational, or gerontological psychiatric setting. In these contexts neuropsychological testing has been particularly valuable in the identification and investigation of learning disabilities in school children and of other specific brain dysfunctions at all ages. In addition to discriminating between psychiatric and neurologic conditions, neuropsychological tests are also useful in distinguishing between different neurological conditions and in providing behavioral data for localizing sites of lesions.

New developments in computerized tomography and magnetic resonance imaging of brain-damaged areas can be expected to stimulate further research in neuropsychology, and increased interaction between the two fields could do much to refine diagnosis and understanding of a variety of organic conditions (Golden, Moses, Zelazowski, Graber, Zatz, Horvath, & Berger 1980).

ISSUES IN MEASUREMENT AND SYMPTOM IDENTIFICATION

Trait and State Characteristics in Diagnosis and Measurement

Diagnostic criteria presently in use emphasize a cross-sectional view of the patient at the time the clinician makes a diagnosis. However, whether the symptoms observed are trait (longitudinally based) or state (cross-sectional) characteristics frequently cannot be determined without consideration of such factors as family history, age of onset, and previous history. Awareness of the distinction between these two characteristics is extremely important for purposes of differential diagnosis. Delusions and hallucinations, for instance, occur in schizophrenia, mania, and agitated depression, and without recourse to history, differentiation is often impossible. Similarly, in the elderly differentiation of senile dementia from major depression unrelated to organic factors is highly dependent on the presence of previous symptoms in the patient and examination of illness in the family. Failure to make this type of distinction frequently leads to the accusation that certain psychometric scales and tests are unreliable because of test–retest discrepancy, whereas in fact this situation may indicate high sensitivity, resulting from the fact that the instrument is loaded with items measuring state characteristics that should show change as the patient's condition improves. Alternatively, failure to take trait–state differences into account when selecting items for test construction may sometimes confound results obtained from tests where this has occurred.

Factors in Symptom Identification

A systematic approach to symptom identification is critical for a predominantly clinical field such as psychiatry. Failure to standardize data collection at this level has led to considerable discrepancy in reports on both incidence and prevalence in epidemiologic studies.

The manner in which psychiatric illness (or indeed any illness) is expressed varies with different social, ethnic, and age factors (Ziborowski, 1952; Twaddle, 1979). Sophisticated and upper-middle-class patients, for instance, accept psychiatric explanations more easily than lower-class patients, who are more likely to underplay mental symptoms and emphasize somatic ones. Adolescents may act out depression by delinquent behavior or truancy.

In addition, diagnosis may be confounded by disagreement between clinicians not only as to the criteria for a particular diagnosis but also as to when to score symptoms as positive. In order to overcome this difficulty we have previously (1982) suggested the following criteria for scoring symptoms as positive:

1. The patient saw a physician (includes chiropractor, naturopath, healer, etc.) for the symptom.

2. The symptom was disabling enough to interfere with the patient's routine.

3. The patient took medicine for the symptom on more than one occasion.

4. The examining physician believes the symptom should be scored positive because of its clinical importance, even though the aforemen-

tioned criteria are not met. Examples include a spell of blindness lasting a few minutes, or hallucinations or delusions that the patient does not report as pathological and that do not disrupt the patient's routine.

5. Symptoms are not scored positive if they can be explained by a known medical disease of the patient. (This does not apply to organic brain disease and mental retardation.)

ISSUES IN CLASSIFICATION

The descriptive, atheoretical, data-oriented approach to diagnosis that culminated in DSM-III has reduced disagreement between practitioners and in this sense has increased reliability of diagnosis. However, a number of important conceptual nosological issues still remain unresolved. Questions that have been a source of controversy for some time refer to the following:

1. Do mental disorders form discrete entities to be categorized as such, or, alternatively, do they represent a continuum ranging from normal to neurotic and psychotic conditions?

2. Are different disorders mutually exclusive or can they exist simultaneously in the same individual?

3. How do cross-cultural factors in the expression of disease affect diagnostic validity?

4. What is the effect of treatability and prognosis on diagnostic categorization?

5. Can national traditions in classification of disease be reconciled?

6. Can a diagnostic system that excludes etiology as a basis for defining most of its categories be valid?

The Categorical versus Dimensional Controversy

The dimensional approach to diagnosis derives from psychologists and statisticians experienced in multivariate statistical techniques who criticize categorical approaches on the basis that they have been set up in an arbitrary fashion and that there are, in fact, no clear boundaries between normal and abnormal conditions. Proponents of the dimensional approach claim that many symptoms, such as anxiety and depression, which are treated categorically and considered as separate disorders by current psychiatric research criteria, are simply extensions of normal phenomena. For example, Kendell and others (Kendell, 1968: Kendell & Gourlay, 1970) studied the distribution of depressed patients' scores using a psychotic/neurotic factor and discriminant function analysis and found this to be unimodal rather than bimodal. From this they concluded that depressive illness forms a continuum with severe or psychotic forms at one end, and mild and chronic forms at the other, and no precise boundaries to warrant categorization between the extremes.

The categorical approach as exemplified by the Feighner criteria, RDC, and DSM-III, accepts that the dimensional approach may provide a more accurate picture of mental disorder, particularly of disorders such as personality disorders, which do not represent discrete syndromes, but claims that its complexity disregards the pragmatism needed in the real world of research. Although less precise, categorical classification satisfies the researcher's need for that simplicity which allows for extraction of essential features from a mass of confusing information and the definition of required research populations. In contrast to the dimensional approach, it is most successful in classification of disorders that present as discrete entities such as the various subtypes of depression, but is less successful in conditions such as personality disorders where the natural boundaries between normality and disturbance are nebulous.

Frances (1982) has pointed out that dimensional and categorical approaches should be seen as complementary rather than mutually exclusive, with their application dependent on the nature of the condition being studied.

Multiple Diagnoses

DSM-III allows for recording of multiple diagnoses on the individual patient when this is necessary to describe the patient's condition. This applies particularly to Axis I, in which, for example, an individual may be noted to have both a substance abuse disorder and an affective disorder, or even multiple diagnoses within the same class, such as a major depression superimposed on a dysthymic disorder. In some classes such as schizophrenic disorders, however, each of the subtypes is mutually exclusive.

Axis II diagnoses can be used for listing personality disorders for adults and specific developmental disorders for children and adolescents and in some cases for adults. The remaining disorders and conditions are included in categories noted in Axis I. This separation is intended to insure that consideration is given to the possible presence of disorders that are frequently overlooked when attention is directed to the usually more florid Axis I disorders. Axis II also calls for listing of personality features such as compulsive traits even when no personality disorder exists.

Axis III permits the clinician to indicate any current physical disorder or condition that is potentially relevant to the understanding or management of the individual. In some instances the physical disorder may be etiologically significant. In others, the relationship may be psychologically significant (for example, diabetes in a child diagnosed as having a conduct disorder), and in yet others, the clinican may wish to note significant associated physical findings such as "soft neurological signs."

Although the use of multiple diagnoses may reflect the natural condition most accurately and parallels diagnostic practice in other branches of medicine (a patient may, for instance, have both cancer and pneumonia), it presents a number of problems in both treatment and research settings. These relate mainly to the difficulty in determining what the predominant diagnosis should be, and whether patients with more than one, and differing secondary, diagnoses should be considered as forming a homogeneous sample for research purposes. DSM-III instructs that when an individual receives more than one diagnosis, the "principal" diagnosis is the condition that was chiefly responsible for occasioning the evaluation or admission to clinical care. It goes on to say that in most cases this condition will be the main focus of attention or treatment. However, as features that occasion admission often fit a number of diagnoses—for example, Axis I: 305.0, Alcohol Abuse; Axis II: 301.70, Antisocial Personality Disorder (one criteria of which is repeated drunkenness or substance abuse with onset before age 15 in individuals 18 years or more)—this, in fact, is of little help in deciding which the predominant diagnosis should be. In fact, predominant diagnosis is probably more often made on the basis of what can be treated, that is, illness for which medication or other effective treatment is available, than on theoretical grounds.

One attempt to overcome this difficulty has been widely investigated in relation to affective disorders. A distinction between primary and secondary depression is made on the basis of natural history. Primary depression is defined as a depressive syndrome occurring in a patient with no prior history of any other psychiatric or physical illness, and is always treated as the principal diagnosis. Secondary depression is defined as a depressive syndrome occurring in a patient who has had an antecedent illness, and may require a different type of treatment than primary depression (Woodruff, Murphy, & Herjanic, 1967; Guze, Woodruff, & Clayton, 1971). Where depression is considered to be secondary, antecedent diagnoses wil be more significant in determining treatment. As, however, Andreasen (1982) has pointed out, in the case of depression there is a danger that antecedent disorders may be so broadly defined that nearly all depressions will be classified as secondary unless, as in Feighner et al. (1972)

and Spitzer, *et al.* (1975), antecedent diagnoses are limited to those defined by the research criteria.

Another problem that has been noted by Andreason (1982) occurs when an illness such as alcoholism comes between an initial and a later episode of affective disorder. Under these conditions patients are primary for the first affective episode and secondary for the second, but difficult to classify on a lifetime basis. One solution to this problem suggested by Wood, Othmer, Reich, Viesselman, and Rutt, (1977) is to introduce the concept of primary complicated affective disorder to describe such cases and prevent contamination of more homogenous groups by excluding them from the research sample. Alternatively, they could be used for investigations on affective disorders, but studied separately with particular reference to individual complicating factors. Distinguishing these complicating factors may, for instance, assist in better understanding of differential prognosis and response to treatment as discussed by Weissman *et al* (1977).

Another method of determining predominance is by study of psychiatric illness in first degree relatives. However, here again results have been equivocal (Andreasen & Winokur, 1979; Akiskal, Djenderedjian, Bolinger, Bitar, Khani, & Haykak, 1978; Andreasen, 1982), and further study is needed to determine the validity of using this distinction as a means of deciding what a principal diagnosis should be.

Cultural Factors and Diagnostic Validity

As no two peoples are culturally identical, no two classificatory systems coming from different countries are exactly comparable. At times, the differences seem so extreme—as for instance, the DHAT syndrome in Indian and African and South American brain fag and possession syndromes (Wig, 1983), that they appear to be undiagnosable by DSM-III or ICD-9 criteria.

This may require addition of further types of disease categories to those categorized in the current diagnostic systems, or they may ultimately turn out to be subsumable under present categories and indeed enrich understanding of them. In either case, decisions will have to be based on careful examination, description, and identification of core symptoms of prototypical cases which, when further studied, may result in change in the definition of these categories.

Treatability and Prognosis in Determining Diagnostic Boundaries

Additional factors that enter diagnostic decision and the definition of diagnostic categories are treatability and prognosis. Andreasen (1982) has again pointed out that we do better to err in the direction of overdiagnosing treatable diseases and underdiagnosing untreatable illnesses as this minimizes the risks involved in diagnostic mistakes. As a result, diseases with less positive prognoses become narrowed in definition, in the sense that more stringent demands are made for their diagnosis, and those more susceptible to therapeutic control become more inclusive. For instance, the requirement made by the DSM-III criteria that a patient must have evidenced psychotic symptoms at some time in order for schizophrenia to be diagnosed both narrows the concept and reduces the range of patients to whom it can be applied. In addition, the exclusion of prominent affective symptoms, and the stipulations that psychotic symptoms should have developed before the age of 45 and persisted for more than six months, are limiting factors in categorizing patients as suffering from schizophrenia. On the other hand, the conceptualization of affective disorders, which have become increasingly treatable since the introduction of lithium and the antidepressants, has been considerably extended. Today it includes conditions in which delusions and hallucinations occur, as well as a variety of disorders that form a continuum of severity and may differ in course but are linked by the fact that they involve a disorder of mood or affect.

Negative side effects of available treatments may have similar influence on conceptualization of different disorders. Tardive dyskinesia, for example, which can result from treatment of schizophrenic patients with neuroleptics, frequently makes the "cure" appear as bad as the disease, and schizophrenia an undesirable diagnosis.

Finally, the patient who has an affective disorder, but is misdiagnosed in the first place as suffering from schizophrenia and treated for an extended period with phenothiazines, will develop changes in affect and Parkinsonian-like symptoms that are likely to reinforce the misdiagnosis. This will result in further inappropriate treatment and possible chronic institutionalization, which the narrower conceptualization may help to avoid.

National Traditions in Validity of Classificatory Systems

To date, diagnostic classifications have differed from country to country because they have evolved out of what has appeared to be useful on an intuitive basis in clinical practice in those countries. American psychiatry emphasizes symptoms, course, and family history, as well as secondarily using levels of social function and stress evaluation. In nosology its approach has been essentially pragmatic, empirical, operational, dualistic, inductive, and antiphilosophical. French psychiatry, on the other hand, delineates diagnostic groups on the basis of the organization or disorganization of the psychic life of the individual. Symptoms are significant only insofar as they indicate psychic being. Swedish psychiatrists are interested in the detailed course of an episode on a day-to-day basis. Even two approaches, DSM-III and ICD-9, which both claim to be descriptive, vary sufficiently in their definitions of subtypes so that in the United States a decision was made to modify the ICD-9 in a way that would provide greater specificity and bring it into closer agreement with the DSM-III classification. The revised version is the ICD-9-CM, and is used in this country for record of all "diseases, injuries, impairments and deaths" needed for international purposes.

The likelihood of reconciling such disparate views of mental illness appears small. However, polydiagnostic research, particularly that using videotape, which enables the same patients to be evaluated according to different systems, may indicate areas of agreement and in this way provide a consensus as to what is under study.

Etiology and Validity

"Etiology unknown" has been called both the "hallmark" and the "bane" of psychiatry (Goodwin & Guze, 1979). Knowing the necessary and sufficient causes of an illness is the ultimate aim of all branches of medicine. However, this degree of knowledge is, in fact, lacking in most medical illnesses. Even in infectious disease, where the virus or bacteria that results in the symptoms can be isolated, some individuals develop the illness while others do not. The fact that illness cannot always be predicted does not, however, remove the responsibility for attempting to reach this ideal goal. The approach that diseases are conventions that may not fit anything in nature at all (Goodwin & Guze, 1979) is extreme. A more positive approach is that taken by the authors of DSM-III in their statement that, while they have temporarily adopted an atheoretical approach with regard to etiology in order to make their manual usable by clinicians of varying theoretical orientation, they nevertheless anticipate some of the disorders ultimately being found to have specific biological etiologies, others to have specific psychological causes, and still others to result from a particular interplay of psychological, social, and biological factors.

CONCLUSIONS

The technological revolution has brought about a significant change in diagnostic potential in the field of psychiatric research. The availability of computers to rapidly process data and to assist in identifying important diagnostic and treatment correlates has greatly augmented our investigative resources. The development of new diagnostic approaches utilizing CT scans, PET scans, MRI, computerized EEG analyses, and combined brain imaging techniques, allow researchers to investigate human brain structure and function in vivo in a manner not previously possible.

In addition the development of new generations of pharmacological treatments that are selective for single neurotransmitter and neuromodulator systems, combined with greater understanding of enzymatic activity and single-membrane transfer systems, have brought a hitherto unparalleled degree of exactitude to psychiatric measurement that will play a significant role, not only in sharpening definition of current diagnostic subtypes, but also in defining new ones.

The utilization of biological markers for diagnostic and treatment purposes began 17 years ago and has unfortunately not progressed at the anticipated rate. To date, for reasons that are unclear, the results tend to be confusing and unreliable. Although, on the one hand, conflicting findings may be the consequence of lack of specificity and sophistication in the test procedures, on the other, the clinical and research criteria by which we try to validate the biological markers may be at fault. In either case, intensive research on all aspects is needed to clarify these issues and determine whether the biological markers can, in fact, fulfill their initial promise as aids to understanding and improving diagnostic classification. In the meantime the employment of the currently available biological markers on a state-of-the-art basis should help us in subtyping diagnoses and enhancing predictability. We clearly need further refinements in measurement techniques for neuroendocrine substances, receptor densities, membrane permeability, and serum and spinal fluid levels of relevant biochemical products.

The effectiveness of psychometric tests in diagnostic research is mixed, and varies according to the context in which the tests are administered and the type of test used. Neuropsychological methods have helped considerably to improve identification and understanding of learning disabilities in school children and of other specific brain dysfunctions in all age groups. On the other hand, personality testing has been less adequately developed and is not, on the whole, well suited to current diagnostic approaches represented by the Feighner criteria, RDC, and DSM-III. Available self and observer rating scales developed for use in the clinical setting are also inadequate to properly evaluate new pharmacological treatments or to define diagnostic subtypes. Thus, while neuropsychological testing is likely to continue to make valuable contributions to the diagnosis and understanding of organic conditions, in the latter areas there is a real need for new psychometric techniques that will relate more directly to current psychiatraic diagnostic practice.

It is extremely seductive to believe that the new technological advances in a wide range of neuropsychiatric/psychometric endeavors will bring about rapid improvements in diagnostic capabilities. It is more likely that change will take place by careful, systematic investigation and integration of all areas of the nosological process rather than as the result of a sudden change in the ability to measure any specific parameter discussed here. It may be hoped that as our knowledge in each area grows, cross-validation and the combined use of old and newly developed research and measurement techniques will provide a more precise (if possibly somewhat revised) picture of the nature of the conditions under study, and the effectiveness of the instruments used to identify and define them.

REFERENCES

Akiskal, H.S., Djenderedjian, A.H., Bolinger, J.M., Bitar, A.H., Khani, M.K. & Haykal, R.F. (1978). The joint use of clinical and biological criteria for psychiatric diagnosis II. Their application in identifying subaffective forms of bipolar illness. In H.S. Akiskal and W.L. Webb (Eds.), *Psychiatric diagnosis: Exploration of biological predictors.* New York: Spectrum Publications.

Andreasen, N.C. (1982). Concepts, diagnosis and classification. In E.S. Peykel (Ed.), *Handbook of Affective Disorders.* New York: Guilford Press.

Andreasen, N.C., & Winokur, G. (1979). Secondary depression: Familial, clinical and research perspectives. *American Journal of Psychiatry, 136,* 62–66.

Beck, A.T., Ward, C.H., Mendelson, M., Mock, J., & Erbaugh, J. (1961). An inventory for measuring depression. *Archives of General Psychiatry, 4,* 561–571.

Carroll, B.J., Fielding, J.M., & Blashki, T.G. (1973). Depression rating scales: A critical review. *Archives of General Psychiatry, 28,* 361–366.

Cooper, A.J., & Magnus, R.V. (1984). Strategies for the drug treatment of depression. *Canadian Medical Association Journal, 130,* 383–390.

Endicott, J., & Spitzer, R.L. (1978). A diagnostic interview: The Schedule for Affective Disorders and Schizophrenia. *Archives of General Psychiatry, 35,* 837–844.

Feighner, J.P. (1982). Nosology and diagnostic criteria in psychiatric research. In E.I. Burdock, A. Sudilovsky, & S. Gershon (Eds.), *The behavior of psychiatric patients: Quantitative techniques for evaluation.* New York: Marcel Dekker.

Feighner, J.P., Robins, E., Guze, J.B., Woodruff, R.A., & Winokur, G. (1972). Diagnostic criteria for use in psychiatric research. *Archives of General Psychiatry, 26,* 57–73.

Frances, A. (1982). Categorical and dimensional systems of personality diagnosis: A comparison. *Comprehensive Psychiatry, 23,* 516–527.

Freud, S. (1953) Analysis terminable and interminable. In J. Strachey (Ed.), *The standard edition of the complete psychological works of Sigmund Freud* (Vol. 23). London: Hogarth Press.

Golden, C.J., Moses, J.A., Zelazowski, R., Graber, B., Zatz, L.M., Horvath, T.B., & Berger, P.A. (1980). Cerebral ventricular size and neuropsychological impairment in young chronic schizophrenics: Measurement by the standardized Luria-Nebraska neuropsychological battery. *Archives of General Psychiatry, 37*, 619–623.

Goodwin, D.W., & Guze, S.B. (1979). *Psychiatric Diagnoses.* New York: Oxford University Press.

Guze, S.B., Woodruff, R.A., & Clayton, P.J. (1971). Secondary affective disorder: A study of 95 cases. *Psychiatric Medicine, 1*, 426–428.

Hamilton, M. (1960). A rating scale for depression. *Journal of Neurological and Neurosurgical Psychiatry, 23*, 56–62.

Hays, P. (1985). Clinical features of affective disorders II: Enhancing the productivity of pharmacotherapeutic and biochemical research. In W.G. Dewhurst, and G.B. Baker (Eds.), *Pharmacotherapy of affective disorders: Theory and practice.* New York: New York University Press.

Hecker, E. (1871), Die Hebephrenie (1871). *Virchows Archiv für Pathologische Anatomie und Physiologie und für Klinische Medizin, 52*, 394–429.

Huang, L.G., & Maas, J.W. (1985). Biological markers in affective disorders. In W.G. Dewhurst, & G.B. Baker (Eds.), *Pharmacotherapy of affective disorders: Theory and practice.* New York: New York University Press.

Kahlbaum, K.L. (1874). Die Katonie oder das Spannungsirresein. Berlin: Hirschwald.

Kendell, R.E. (1968). *A classification of depressive illness.* London: Oxford University Press.

Kendell, R.E., & Gourlay, J. (1970). The clinical distinction between psychotic and neurotic depressions. *British Journal of Psychiatry, 117*, 257–266.

Kraepelin, E. (1909). *Psychiatrie ein Lehrbuch fur Studierende und Arzte* (6th ed.). Leipzig: Barth.

Marks, P.A., Seeman, W., & Haller, D.L. (1979). *The actuarial use of the MMPI in adolescents and adults.* New York: Oxford University Press.

Meyer, A. (1908). The life chart and the obligation of specifying positive data in psychopathological diagnosis. In E.E. Winters (Ed.), *The collected papers of Adolph Meyer,* (Vol. III). Baltimore: Johns Hopkins Press.

Prusoff, B.A., Klerman, G.L., & Paykel, E.S. (1972). Concordance between clinical assessments and patients' self-report in depression. *Archives of General Psychiatry, 26*, 546–552.

Rubin, R.T., & Marder, S.R. (1983). Biological markers in affective and schizophrenic disorders: A review of contemporary research. In M.R. Zales (Ed.), *Affective and schizophrenic disorders: New approaches to diagnosis and treatment.* New York: Bruner-Mazel.

Spitzer, R.L., Endicott, J., & Robins E. (1975). *Research diagnostic criteria for a selected group of functional disorders* (2nd ed.). New York: Biometrics Research Division, New York State Psychiatric Institute.

Twaddle, A.C. (1979). *Sickness behavior and the sick role.* Boston: G.K. Hall.

Weissman, M.M., Pottenger, M., Kleber, H., Rubin, H.L., Williams, D., & Thompson, W.D. (1977). Symptom patterns in primary and secondary depression. *Archives of General Psychiatry, 34*, 854–862.

Wig, N.N. (1983). A perspective from the third world. In R.C. Spitzer, J.B. Williams, & A.E. Skodol, *International perspectives on DSM-III.* Washington, D.C.: American Psychiatric Press.

Wing, J.K., Cooper, J.E., & Sartorius, N. (1974). *The measurement and classification of psychiatric symptoms.* London: Cambridge University Press.

Wing, J.K. (1983). The use and misuse of the PSE. *British Journal of Psychiatry, 143*, 111–117.

Wood, D., Othmer, S., Reich, T., Viesselman, J., & Rutt, C. (1977). Primary and secondary affective disorder: I. Past social history and current episodes in 92 depressed patients. *Comprehensive Psychiatry. 18*, 201–210.

Woodruff, R.A., Murphy, G.E., & Herjanic, M. (1967). The natural history of affective disorders: I. Symptoms of 72 patients at the time of indesc hospital admission. *Journal of Psychiatric Research, 5,* 255–263.

World Health Organization (1973). *The international pilot study of schizophrenia* (Vol. 1). Geneva: Author.

World Health Organization (1977), *International statistical classification of diseases, injuries and causes of death* (9th rev.). Geneva: Author.

Ziborowski, M. (1952). Cultural components in response to pain. *Journal of Sociological Issues, 8,* 16–30.

II

Methodological Issues

Lifetime Psychiatric Diagnoses

W. DOUGLAS THOMPSON

INTRODUCTION

Clinicians and researchers often have occasion to classify individuals as ever or as never having had a particular psychiatric disorder. Because of the recurring nature of many disorders, information on an individual patient's lifetime diagnoses is obviously useful for assessing the present constellation of symptoms and for planning treatment. For research on the etiology of disorders, pragmatic considerations often dictate the use of lifetime diagnoses. The proportion developing a particular psychiatric disorder over a restricted time period is small, even in high risk populations. Consequently, despite conceptual difficulties, potential biases, and the likely inferior quality of information, the cumulative experience of study subjects typically is examined for the occurrence of diagnosable psychiatric disorders.

The purpose of this chapter is to review the current state of knowledge concerning the quantification of lifetime risk and the validity of available techniques for obtaining the requisite information. Particular emphasis will be given to strategies for making optimal use of imperfect data and to the frequent need for cautious interpretation of results. Emphasis is placed on measures of validity, rather than measures of reliability, because of the dependence of measures such as kappa on the frequency of disorder, rather than only on the quality of the diagnostic classification (Grove, Andreasen, McDonald-Scott, Keller, & Shapiro, 1981; Kraemer, 1979; Spitznagel & Helzer, 1985).

W. DOUGLAS THOMPSON • Department of Epidemiology and Public Health, Yale University School of Medicine, New Haven, CT 06510.

INCIDENCE AND PREVALENCE

Two common measures of disease frequency in a population are incidence and prevalence. Lifetime risk is related to both but generally equivalent to neither. An incidence rate is defined as the rate of occurrence of new disorder in unaffected individuals. Although in practice one estimates incidence rates by using information that has been accumulated over a period of time, the underlying concept is an instantaneous one. A fitting analogy is the speed of an automobile. One may estimate speed by observing the distance traveled in a particular period of time, but the actual speed is something instantaneous that may change from moment to moment. An incidence rate is an instantaneous rate of change or transition from an unaffected status to an affected status, and therefore is the most readily interpretable measure of disease frequency for studies of etiology. By contrast, information on the prevalence of a disorder does not permit calculation of a rate of change. Prevalence, as generally used, denotes only the current state of affairs, and the term "prevalence rate" is thus inappropriate (Elandt-Johnson, 1975). Information on the prevalence of a disorder is expressed as the proportion of the population that *currently* meets specified criteria for the disorder.

Data on the prevalence of a disorder present problems of interpretation that data on incidence do not. Prevalence depends in part on the incidence of a disorder, but it also depends on its duration and course. Consequently, when data on prevalence are employed, those factors predictive of the onset of a disorder cannot be disentangled from those factors predictive of its duration and sequelae.

Thompson and Weissman (1981) have reviewed the relation of lifetime risk to both incidence and prevalence. Lifetime risk bears no direct relationship to prevalence when the latter is defined as the proportion that currently has the disorder. However, one may also consider *lifetime prevalence,* that is, the proportion of surviving members of the population or of the study group that has the disorder currently or at any time in the past. This particular quantity may be interpreted as the lifetime risk only if the occurrence of the disorder has no effect on mortality rates or on other factors (such as migration) that would remove persons from the population studied. If, for example, the onset of the disorder is associated with increased mortality, then the proportion of surviving members of the population having a history of the disorder would be an underestimate of the lifetime risk. As Thompson and Weissman (1981) have described in more formal terms, lifetime risk is most appropriately viewed as an accumulation across the age-specific incidence rates that are operative over the course of an individual's life. Simple summation of age-specific incidence rate is not valid, however, because of removal from the population at risk once the disorder has developed. If age-specific incidence rates are available for individual years of age, then the lifetime risk is approximately:

$$1 - e^{-T}$$

where e is the base of the natural logarithm (2.71828) and T is the following total:

Age-specific incidence per person per year in the first year of life
+ Age-specific incidence per person per year in the second year of life
+ Age-specific incidence per person per year in the third year of life
.
.
.

The above equation leads to the exact value for the lifetime risk if time is divided up not into years but into arbitrarily small units. For example, if information were available on a daily basis, then a more accurate value of T would be obtained by accumulating the following sum:

Age-specific incidence per person per day in the first day of life
+ Age-specific incidence per person per day in the second day of life
+ Age-specific incidence per person per day in the third day of life
.
.
.

Lifetime risk depends only on age-specific incidence and not on what happens to someone subsequent to first onset of the disorder. When accumulating age-specific incidence rates in practice, the availability of data will dictate whether it is feasible to calculate risk through age 60, 70, 80 or some other upper limit. In general, however, the calculation will be truncated, and extending consideration to older ages will increase the numeric value of the estimate of lifetime risk unless there is a critical period after which the age-specific incidence becomes essentially zero. Consequently, the term lifetime risk generally requires the qualifier *as of some specific age.*

ESTIMATION OF RISK

A number of approaches to the estimation of lifetime risk have been proposed. All require cohort-type data (collected either prospectively or retrospectively) in order to avoid the problems of interpretation posed by prevalence data and survival. Several of these approaches involve taking a ratio of the following type:

$$\frac{A}{p_1 A + p_2 B}$$

where A = the number of persons who have ever had the disorder, B = the number of persons who have never had the disorder, and p_1 and p_2 are selected so as to take appropriate account of the period of time in which affected and unaffected individuals are, respectively, at risk for developing the disorder. Estimation techniques differ primarily in terms of the methods for obtaining p_1 and p_2. Perhaps the most frequently used technique, which was suggested by Stromgren (1938) and described later by Slater and Cowie (1971), sets p_1 at unity and p_2 at the average proportion of the total risk to which unaffected individuals are subjected while under observation. As Larsson and Sjogren (1954) have pointed out, these values for p_1 and p_2 lead to systematic underestimation of the lifetime risk. More recently Risch (1983) has advocated a return to the original Stromgren estimator (Stromgren, 1935), which employs the same value for p_2 as does the modified version proposed in 1938, but which sets p_1 not at unity but at the average proportion of the total risk to which affected individuals have been subjected at the time of last observation. However, this method is also biased, except in the special case when mortality and other losses occur at the same rate among affected and unaffected individuals.

Thompson and Weissman (1981) have demonstrated that an unbiased estimate of lifetime risk would be obtained by setting p_1 at unity and p_2 at the average relative odds of developing the disorder while under observation. Although the average relative odds cannot be estimated directly, the authors showed that the appropriate value of p_2 is implicitly employed when one applies the biostatistical techniques known collectively as survival analysis (Gross & Clark, 1975; Kalbfleisch & Prentice, 1980; Lee, 1980).

Application of survival analysis to data on lifetime psychiatric diagnosis also renders somewhat academic the calculation of lifetime risk per se. For example, the proportional hazards modeling technique for survival analysis (Cox, 1972) makes it possible to use data on lifetime diagnoses to estimate the relative magnitude of the incidence rates for subgroups of the population. Such ratios of incidence rates can often be estimated using this technique with far greater precision than can the relative magnitudes of lifetime risks. In recent studies, in fact, methods of survival analysis and closely related techniques have largely supplanted calculation of lifetime, or "morbidity," risks (e.g., Klerman, Lavori, Rice, Reich, Endicott, Andreasen, Keller, & Hirschfield, 1985; Leckman, Weissman, Merikangas, Pauls, & Prusoff, 1983). Estimates of lifetime risk are of some additional potential usefulness in the context of family-genetic studies, where the magnitude of lifetime risk in relatives may support or refute a particular mode of inheritance. However, as mentioned earlier, for many psychiatric disorders there is no critical age period after which age-specific incidence becomes essentially zero, and, consequently, lifetime risk can only be calculated as of some particular age. It thereby underestimates the proportion of the study group that would eventually develop the disorder in the absence of deaths due to other causes and in the absence of other losses.

Regardless of whether data on lifetime diagnoses are used to estimate lifetime risk *per se* or to estimate the relative magnitudes of incidence rates, careful selection of groups for study is critical to the validity of diagnostic procedures. Diagnostic procedures must be applied not simply to persons who are currently alive and available at the time of the data collection, but instead to all members both living and dead (or otherwise unavailable) from identifiable cohorts in the population. Failure to adhere to this principle would tend to lead to a confusion of those factors related to incidence and those related to the sequelae of the disorder.

SOURCES OF DATA

Medical records, even ones of excellent quality, are of only limited use for the assessment of lifetime psychiatric diagnoses for research purposes. Nosology has changed substantially over time, and only rather recently have uniform sets of operationalized diagnostic criteria been widely applied (Weissman & Klerman, 1978). Furthermore, simple enumeration of the facilities at which an individual has been treated over his or her lifetime can be difficult, especially when the person is unavailable for direct interview. Consequently, the major source of data on lifetime psychiatric diagnosis is the diagnostic interviews. When the person is available, direct interview regarding lifetime history of psychiatric symptoms is generally preferable to all other means for collecting data. Supplementation with information from relatives may be useful, particularly for such aspects of behavior as consumption of alcohol. If a member of the study cohort is unavailable for direct interview, then the investigation must often rely only on information provided by relatives.

The validity of lifetime psychiatric diagnoses based on currently available instruments for direct interview of subjects remains uncertain. A major reason for this uncertainty derives from the lack of a uniformly accepted criterion against which to validate the instruments. Clinical classification by psychiatrists is often used as a criterion, but since psychiatrists disagree among themselves (Spitzer & Fleiss, 1974), they constitute an imperfect criterion. Recent studies have focused particularly on the quality of diagnoses based on lay diagnostic interviews of the type that can be feasibly conducted in large samples from the general population. Results from a recent validation study of the Diagnostic Interview Schedule (DIS) are given in Table 1. For this methodologic study (Helzer, Robins, McEvoy, Spitznagel, Stoltzman, Farmer, & Brockington, 1985), 370 of the 3004 participants in an epidemiologic survey were reinterviewed by a physician and classified according to DSM-III diagnoses. The diagnoses made on the basis of the original lay interviews using the DIS were then compared to this criterion. The table gives the values for sensitivity (the percentage of affected individuals who were appropriately classified as affected from the lay interview) and for specificity (the percentage of the unaffected individuals who were appropriately classified as unaffected from the lay interview). Selection of 370 subjects for the methodologic study was stratified by initial DIS diagnosis so as to include adequate numbers of affected persons in the major diagnostic groups. However, the numbers used to calculate sensitivity and specificity have been weighted in such a way that the results reflect accurately how the DIS is likely to perform in the general population. Values for sensitivity range from 0.14 to 0.74, whereas specificity is consistently 0.94 or above. Although an appreciable proportion of some psychiatric disorders is missed by the lay DIS interview, only a very small proportion of those whom a physician classifies as free of a disorder is falsely classified as having the disorder from the lay DIS interview.

The implications of the results in Table 1 for the validity and utility of lay DIS lifetime diagnoses are difficult to judge. A given level of specificity, although close to unity, is unacceptable in some circumstances. For rare disorders, less than perfect specificity can swamp the small number of true positives with a relatively large number of false positives. If, for example, only 1% of the population truly has a particular disorder, and specificity is 0.95, then less than 17% of those placed in the affected category will in fact have the disorder, even when sensitivity is 1.00. Another major concern is the validity of the physician's diagnoses. Part of the correspondence between these diagnoses and those based on the lay

Table 1. Sensitivity and Specificity for Lay Diagnostic Interview Schedule Evaluated Against Physicians' Diagnoses

Lifetime diagnosis	Sensitivity (%)	Specificity (%)
Drug abuse or dependence	46	98
Alcohol abuse or dependence	74	94
Antisocial personality	43	98
Somatization	15	99
Panic	27	99
Mania	23	99
Major depression	22	98
Agoraphobia	27	97
Social phobia	19	97
Simple phobia	15	94
Obsessive-compulsive disorder	14	98

Note. From "A Comparison of Clinical and Diagnostic Interview Schedule
Diagnoses" by J.E. Helzer, L.N. Robins, L.T. McEvoy, E.L. Spitznagel, R.K.
Stolzman, A. Farmer & I.F. Brockington, 1985, *Archives of General Psychiatry 42,*
pp. 657–666. Copyright 1985 by the American Medical Association. Reprinted
by permission.

DIS interview may merely represent identical errors of classification
made by both the physicians and the lay interviewers. Since the same
study subjects provide information on symptoms to both the interviewer
and the physician, denial of symptoms or overreporting of them are likely
to affect both sets of diagnoses.

Because of the long-term recall required to provide retrospective information over one's lifetime, assessments of validity may be strengthened
by a longitudinal design in which retrospective information is validated
against the criterion of information that was collected closer to the time of
the actual episodes. The relatively recent development of standardized
diagnostic schemes and lay interviews renders this approach one for the
future. Furthermore, recent data on the apparently poor validity of
diagnoses of current rather than lifetime psychiatric disorders (Anthony,
Folstein, Romanoski, Von Korff, Nestadt, Chahal, Merchant, Brown,
Shapiro, Kramer, & Gruenberg, 1985) suggest that issues of recall may not,
in fact, be the most important threat to the validity of lifetime diagnoses.

Turning now to the second major source of information on lifetime
psychiatric diagnoses, namely reports provided by family members, the
usual method of validation is against the criterion of diagnoses based on
direct interview of the person about whom the family history information
is collected. Table 2 gives estimates of sensitivity and specificity for the information provided by four types of relatives (Thompson, Orvaschel,
Prusoff, & Kidd, 1982), with application of the Research Diagnostic

Table 2. Sensitivity and Specificity of Family History Data According to Relationship of Informant[a]

Diagnostic category	Parent		Sibling		Spouse		Offspring	
	Sensitivity (%)	Specificity (%)	Sensitivity (%)	Specificity (%)	Sensitivity (%)	Specificity (%)	Sensitivity (%)	Specificity (%)
Major depression	33	98	58	95	70	93	69	93
Alcoholism	24	99	30	97	45	97	57	96
Generalized anxiety	7	99	0	98	17	96	0	98
Drug abuse	22	99	16	99	0	100	—	100
Phobia	15	99	10	99	10	99	13	100
Depressive personality	6	98	0	98	0	98	0	98
Hyperthymic personality	0	100	0	99	0	99	0	99

Note. From "An Evaluation of the Family History for Ascertaining Psychiatric Disorders" by W.D. Thompson, H. Orvaschel, B.A. Prusoff & K.K. Kidd, 1985, *Archives of General Psychiatry, 39*, pp. 53–58. Copyright 1985 by the American Medical Association. Reprinted by Permission.
[a]Diagnoses based on family history data are compared with the criterion of Research Diagnostic Criteria diagnoses based on a direct interview with the Schedule of Affective Disorder and Schizophrenia–Lifetime Version.

Table 3. Sensitivity as Specificity of Family History Data on Major Depression, according to Diagnostic Status of Informant[a]

Lifetime diagnosis of major depression in informant	Sensitivity	Specificity
Present	38/74 = 51%	126/146 = 86%
Absent	71/129 = 55%	340/347 = 98%

[a]Diagnosis based on family history data are compared with the criterion of Research Diagnostic Criteria diagnoses based on a direct interview with the Schedule of Affective Disorders and Schizophrenia—Lifetime Version. Major depression is classified as present or absent in informants on the basis of direct interview.

Criteria (Spitzer, Endicott, & Robins, 1978). Sensitivity tended to be lower than the values given in Table 1 for the validity of direct interview. The specificity of the information provided by relatives is high, nevertheless, and the values given are probably underestimates in light of the manner in which the subjects were selected for inclusion. The authors also found that spouses and offspring generally had higher sensitivity than did parents and siblings.

Reliance on family history data concerning lifetime psychiatric diagnoses poses particular problems of interpretation for epidemiologic-genetic studies of familial aggregation. Sackett (1979) has given the term "family information bias" to the tendency for affected family members to be more likely to report disorder in relatives than are unaffected family members. Because many family studies rely heavily on probands to provide information on the lifetime diagnoses of family members, case–control comparisons between the families of affected and unaffected probands may lead to inflated or entirely spurious indices of the magnitude of familial aggregation. Sackett's description of family information bias suggests that it consists primarily of an increased sensitivity among affected informants relative to unaffected informants. He provides empirical evidence of the operation of such a bias in the study of rheumatoid arthritis.

The methodologic study by Thompson *et al.* (1982) provides data concerning the possible operation of such a bias in the lifetime diagnosis of major depression. Table 3 gives these results. From the data are calculated separate estimates of sensitivity and specificity for the lifetime family history diagnoses, based on informants who have themselves either been depressed or not depressed during their lifetimes. The findings, which are based on small numbers, suggest that the diagnostic status of the informant has little impact on the sensitivitiy of the information concerning depression in family members (0.51 and 0.55 for depressed versus nondepressed informants, respectively), but that specificity is lower for depressed informants than for nondepressed informants (0.86 versus 0.98). These findings suggest the possibility of substantially biased estimates of familial aggregation when family history is used as the basis for lifetime diagnoses in relatives. If the frequency of depression in the relatives of the affected and unaffected informants is defined strictly in terms of direct interview, then calculation of the relative risk indicates a 35% increase in depression among the relatives of affected informants. If the family history data provided by the informants are used instead of the direct interviews of the relatives, then there is an apparent increase of 83% in depression among the relatives of affected as opposed to unaffected informants.

The type of reporting bias suggested by these data is rather different from the notion of family information bias as conceptualized by Sackett (1979). Sackett's concept implies greater sensitivity among affected informants than among unaffected informants since the occurrence of the disorder in the informant would presumably lead to the acquisition of more complete information on the occurrence of disorder in relatives. However, the data in Table 3 suggest that the bias may involve increased false positive reports of depression concerning the unaffected relatives of depressed informants. Perhaps persons with a history of depression have some tendency to project their problems onto other family members. It is also possible that affected individuals tend to regard their disorder as transmitted within families by some genetic or social mechanism, and therefore overinterpret normal mood swings in relatives. Another explanation may be that some of the apparent false positives are in fact true positives, and that the direct interview of the relative has failed to detect disorder that is in fact present. For this explanation to accommodate the findings, however, one would have to postulate that persons with affected relatives are less likely than those without affected relatives to report their own depressive symptomatology during a direct interview.

All of these possible explanations are speculative, and further methodologic studies are certainly warranted in order to attempt to replicate these results and to elucidate further the nature of such biases. Nevertheless, the results dramatically illustrate the potential problems of interpretation which arise when the sensitivity and/or specificity of family history data differ according to whether the informant is affected. Such biases clearly have their most serious consequences in studies of familial aggregation. In studies of nonfamilial risk factors, sensitivity and specificity still may be less than perfect but would be more likely to be of equal magnitude across the groups compared. The bias resulting from such nondifferential misclassification would have the undesirable effect of reducing the apparent magnitude of association (Copeland, Checkoway, McMichael, & Holbrook, 1977), but would not produce the more serious

Table 4. Adjusted Odds Ratios for Nonbipolar Depression Among
First Degree Relatives in a Family-Genetic Study

Comparison	Adjusted odds ratio
Proband group	
Nonhospitalized vs. normal	2.34
Hospitalized vs. normal	2.62
Sex of relative	
Female vs. male	2.69
Age of relative	
30–44 vs. under 30	1.18
45+ vs. under 30	1.18
Source of information on relative	
Proband and others vs. proband only	2.25
Direct interviews vs. proband only	4.64

Note. From "Variability in Rates of Affective Disorders in Relatives of Depressed and Normal Probands" by M.M. Weissman, K.K. Kidd, & B.A. Prusoff, 1985, *Archives of General Psychiatry, 39,* pp. 1397–1403. Copyright 1985, by the American Medical Association. Reprinted by permission.

problems of exaggerated associations that can result from differential misclassification. However, regardless of what possible etiologic factor is being examined, there is a potential for differential misclassification, and thus spuriously high associations, whenever the groups being compared differ in terms of the proportion of diagnostic information obtained via family history rather than direct interview. One possible remedy for this bias would be to include source of diagnostic information as a covariate in a multivariable analysis (Thompson *et al.,* 1982). Weissman, Kidd and Prusoff (1982) used this approach in their analysis of a family-genetic study. Some of the results of this analysis are given in Table 4. Logistic regression was used to calculate adjusted odds ratios for the independent effects of age, sex, proband group, and source of information as they related to a lifetime diagnosis of nonbipolar depression in first-degree relatives. Note that the effects for source of information are as large as the effects for the variables of greater substantive interest. However, because source of information has been included in the analysis simultaneously with the other variables, the values of the adjusted odds ratios for these other variables should not be biased by misclassification on lifetime diagnoses of different proportions of subgroups having information from the various sources.

Based on consideration of some specific numerical examples, Greenland and Robins (1985) have recently questioned the advisability of this strategy of including an indicator of source or quality of information as a covariate. They point out that the inclusion of such a covariate can increase rather than reduce the bias in the estimate of the odds ratio for the effects of other variables. Although the bias may in fact be increased, this bias is always in the direction of shifting the values of the measure of association closer to its null value. Because control for source of information frequently has the effect of eliminating a spurious association, the conservative bias that may be introduced in certain circumstances would seem to be quite an acceptable price to pay in the interest of avoiding falsely positive conclusions about factors associated with lifetime risk of psychiatric disorder.

MULTIPLE INFORMANTS

Whatever their source, lifetime diagnoses are clearly imperfect. Researchers must therefore make the fullest use possible of available information. If data on symptomatology are available from several sources, then an important practical concern is how to go about synthesizing this information into a single diagnostic categorization. Two major approaches to this process of synthesis have been suggested. The first entails making separate diagnostic judgments regarding the information available from each of the multiple sources and then combining these ratings according to a specific rule or set of rules. The second approach involves simultaneous review of all available materials. Thompson *et al.* (1982) used the first approach to obtain lifetime diagnoses for persons whose psychiatric symptoms were described by two close relatives. The family-history data provided by one relative about a given individual was evaluated in total isolation from the data provided by the other relative. RDC diagnoses were made separately. The resulting diagnoses were then combined in a mechanical manner by counting as present any disorder that was present according to the diagnoses based on the reports from *either* of the two relatives. When evaluated against the criterion of diagnoses based on direct interview of the subject, this method of combining information from two informants proved to be a useful one. The accuracy of the diagnostic classification was generally better using this method for combining two family-history reports than when the classification was based on a single family-history report. Table 5 gives results for combining information from reports of parents and siblings concerning major depression, alcoholism, generalized anxiety, drug abuse, and

Table 5. Sensitivity and Specificity of Family History Data When Information is Available from Both Parent and Sibling[a]

Diagnostic category	Sensitivity (%)			Specificity (%)		
	Parent	Sibling	Both	Parent	Sibling	Both
Major depression	28	55	61	98	95	93
Alcoholism	25	28	41	99	96	96
Generalized anxiety	10	0	10	100	99	99
Drug abuse	15	19	27	99	99	98
Phobia	17	8	17	100	100	100

Note. From "An Evaluation of the Family History Method for Ascertaining Psychiatric Disorders" by W.D. Thompson, H. Orvaschel, B.A. Prusoff & K.K. Kidd, 1982, *Archives of General Psychiatry, 39*, pp. 53–58. Copyright 1982 by the American Medical Association. Reprinted by Permission.
[a]Diagnoses based on family history data are compared with the criterion of Research Diagnostic Criteria diagnoses based on a direct interview with the Schedule of Affective Disorder and Schizophrenia—Lifetime Version.

phobias. In the columns labelled "both," persons are classified as having the disorder if the diagnosis was made based on information from either the parent or the sibling. For major depression, alcoholism, and drug abuse, the sensitivity of the diagnostic classification was enhanced using this approach. As would be anticipated, application of this liberal definition of which individuals would be classified as having a disorder resulted in a certain number of diagnoses that were falsely positive when evaluated against the criterion of judgments made from direct interviews. However, it can be seen from the table that there are not enough false positive diagnoses to reduce substantially the specificity of the classification.

Recently, Marshall and Graham (1984) have addressed the issue of how best to combine multiple sources of information on the presence or absence of a given characteristic. Based on theoretical and numerical considerations, the authors recommended discarding from the analysis any subjects for whom the two sources of information disagree. Such an approach generally would improve the purity of the negative and positive groups, but the exclusion of the so called "discordant" subjects would reduce the statistical power of one's study.

It has been shown (Kelsey, Thompson, & Evans, 1986; Thompson, 1984) that the exclusion of discordant observations is especially detrimental when sensitivity is low but specificity is high. For example, the authors showed that for a sensitivity of 20% and a specificity of 99%, the mean-squared error of the estimate of the association between the disorder and an etiological factor can be more than five times greater when the procedure of Marshall and Graham is used than when all subjects are retained and a liberal definition of affected status is employed. Because

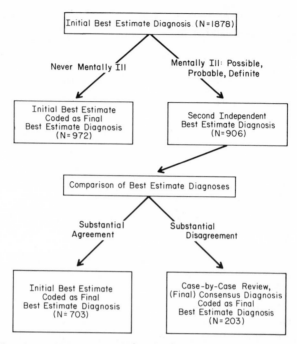

Figure 1. Flowsheet of procedure used to reach final best estimate diagnosis in a family-genetic study. From: "Best Estimate of Lifetime Psychiatric Diagnosis" by J.F. Leckman, D. Sholomskas, W.D. Thompson, A. Belanger, and M.M. Weisman, 1975, *Archives of General Psychiatry 39*, 879–883. Copyright 1985 by the American Medical Association. Reprinted by permission.

information from relatives seems to lack sensitivity rather than specificity, a liberal definition of affected status frequently would be the preferred type of rule to apply to two or more independently classified family history reports.

The second major approach to the synthesis of lifetime psychiatric data concerning a given individual, namely, simultaneous review of all available materials, has been described by Leckman, Sholomskas, Thompson, Belanger, & Weissman (1982). Figure 1 illustrates the procedure used by those investigators. Direct interviews were obtained from 40% of the total group, and more than 50% had family-history information from at least three relatives. Medical records were obtained for 64% of individuals who had been treated for psychological problems. All available information on a given individual was first reviewed by one of two diagnosticians. If no information was present that in any way was suggestive of mental illness, then the first diagnostician classified the person as never mentally ill and no further review of the materials was routinely conducted. However, for each individual with some information suggestive of possible mental illness, the second diagnostician reviewed all available materials. This second review was conducted blindly with respect to the specific diagnoses made by the first diagnostician. The diagnoses made by the two diagnosticians were then compared. If any important disagreement was found, then the materials were reviewed again and a final consensus diagnosis was made. The second diagnostician also blindly reviewed a random subgroup of those individuals for whom the first diagnostician had found no evidence of possible mental illness.

Such simultaneous review of all available information has some clear advantages in that it permits the diagnostician to make a "best estimate" diagnosis that is a judgmental rather than mechanical synthesis, and allows for the direct evaluation of possibly contradictory information. On the other hand, simultaneous review precludes systematic evaluation of the consistency of the information obtained from the multiple sources. Obviously, however, with the use of multiple diagnosticians working independently, it is possible to reap the benefits of both of these approaches to the synthesis of data on lifetime diagnoses.

CONCLUSION

Caution clearly is warranted in the interpretation of data on lifetime psychiatric diagnosis. As has been stressed in this review, the validity of available methods for the diagnosis of disorders long after their clinical manifestations have subsided remains uncertain. Nevertheless, continuing advances in the development of structured diagnostic interviews and of clearly operationalized diagnostic criteria will further reduce this uncertainty. Simultaneously, these advances in instrumentation increase the feasibility of conducting large prospective epidemiologic studies that will provide incidence data requiring recall of symptoms over a period of months rather than over a lifetime. It seems unlikely, however, that the assessment of lifetime diagnoses of psychiatric disorders will become unnecessary in the foreseeable future. Even in prospective studies of incidence, it is important to evaluate the prior occurrence of psychiatric disorders at the beginning of the study, in order to distinguish between first onset and recurrent disorder during the follow-up period. For certain types of studies, such as those of familial aggregation, use of lifetime diagnoses cannot be avoided, since prospective studies of multiple generations would be impractical. An other area of research in which lifetime diagnoses will clearly remain important concerns the relationships among various disorders. To avoid studies that require literally decades to complete, one of the disorders must generally be assessed on a lifetime basis, even if the other can be studied prospectively.

Continued methodologic studies of lifetime psychiatric diagnosis will provide additional insight into the circumstances under which lifetime diagnoses are of acceptable accuracy. Particular attention should be paid to diagnoses made in the absence of direct interview of the study subject. Nevertheless, a critical unanswered question concerns the relevant criteria that should be applied for deciding whether a given system for making lifetime diagnoses is of acceptable accuracy.

SUMMARY

Lifetime diagnosis of psychiatric disorder has an important place in clinical and epidemiologic research. From an assessment of lifetime history of a particular disorder in defined cohorts, it is possible to estimate lifetime risk through a specified age. A number of methods for quantification have been proposed, but for comparison among groups, multivariable methods of survival analysis permit relatively precise estimation of ratios of incidence rates. Direct interview is generally the preferred method for obtaining information on lifetime diagnosis, but good estimates of the accuracy of retrospective information of this type can be obtained only through long-term prospective validation studies. The frequent unavailability of subjects for direct interview necessitates the use of information provided by family members. Although diagnoses based on family history often do not correspond to those based on direct interview, the appropriate synthesis of information from multiple informants can enhance the accuracy of the diagnoses made.

REFERENCES

Anthony, J.C., Folstein, M., Romanoski, A.J., Von Korff, M.R., Nestadt, G.R., Chahal, R., Merchant, A., Brown, H., Shapiro, S., Kramer, M., & Gruenberg, E.M. (1985). Comparison of the lay Diagnostic Interview Schedule and a standardized psychiatric diagnosis. *Archives of General Psychiatry, 42,* 667–675.
Copeland, K.T., Checkoway, H., McMichael, A.J., & Holbrook, R.H. (1977). Bias due to misclassification in the estimation of relative risk. *American Journal of Epidemiology, 105,* 488–495.
Cox, D.R. (1972). Regression models and life-tables (with discussion). *Journal of the Royal Statistical Society, 34,* 187–220.
Elandt-Johnson, R. C. (1975). Definitions of rates: Some remarks on their use and misuse. *American Journal of Epidemiology, 102,* 267–271.

Greenland, S., & Robins, J. M. (1985). Confounding and misclassification. *American Journal of Epidemiology, 122,* 495-506.

Gross, A. J., & Clark, V. A. (1975). *Survival distributions: reliability applications in the biomedical sciences.* New York: Wiley.

Grove, W. M., Andreasen, N. C., McDonald-Scott, P., Keller, M. B., & Shapiro, R. W. (1981). Reliability studies of psychiatric diagnosis. *Archives of General Psychiatry, 38,* 408-413.

Helzer, J. E., Robins, L. N., McEvoy, L. T., Spitznagel, E. L., Stoltzman, R. K., Farmer, A., & Brockington, I. F. (1985). A comparison of clinical and Diagnostic Interview Schedule diagnoses. *Archives of General Psychiatry, 42,* 657-666.

Kalbfleisch, J., & Prentice, R. I. (1980). *The statistical analysis of failure time data.* New York: Wiley.

Kelsey, J. L., Thompson, W. D., & Evans, A. S. (1986). *Methods in observational epidemiology.* New York: Oxford University Press.

Klerman, G. L., Lavori, P. W., Rice, J., Reich, T., Endicott, J., Andreasen, N. C., Keller, M. B., & Hirschfield, R. M. A. (1985). Birth-cohort trends in rates of major depressive disorder among relatives of patients with affective disorder. *Archives of General Psychiatry, 42,* 689-693.

Kraemer, H. C. (1979). Ramifications of a population model for kappa as a coefficient of reliability. *Psychometrika, 44,* 461-472.

Larsson, T., & Sjogren, T. (1954). A methodological psychiatric and statistical study of a large Swedish rural population. *Acta Psychiatrica et Neurologica Scandinavica (Supplementum) 89,* 40-54.

Leckman, J. F., Sholomskas, D., Thompson, W. D., Belanger, A., & Weissman, M. M. (1982). Best estimate of lifetime psychiatric diagnosis: A methodologic study. *Archives of General Psychiatry, 39,* 879-883.

Leckman, J. F., Weissman, M. M., Merikangas, K. R., Pauls, D. L., & Prusoff, B. A. (1983). Panic and major depression: Increased risk of depression, alcoholism, panic, and phobic disorders in families of depressed probands with panic disorders. *Archives of General Psychiatry, 40,* 1055-1060.

Lee, E. T. (1980). *Statistical methods for survival analysis.* Belmont: Lifetime Learning Publications.

Marshall, J. R. & Graham, S. (1984). Use of dual responses to increase validity of case-control studies. *Journal of Chronic Diseases, 37,* 125-136.

Risch, N. (1983). Estimating morbidity risks with variable age of onset: Review of methods and a maximum likelihood approach. *Biometrics, 39,* 929-939.

Sackett, D. L. (1979). Bias in analytic research. *Journal of Chronic Diseases, 32,* 51-63.

Slater, E., & Cowie, V. (1971). *The genetics of mental disorders.* London: Oxford University Press.

Spitzer, R. L., & Fleiss, J. L. (1974). A re-analysis of the reliability of psychiatric diagnosis. *British Journal of Psychiatry, 125,* 341-347.

Spitzer, R. L., Endicott, J., & Robins, E. (1978). Research Diagnostic Criteria: Rationale and reliability. *Archives of General Psychiatry, 35,* 773-782.

Spitznagel, E. L., & Helzer, J. E. (1985). A proposed solution to the base rate problem in the kappa statistic. *Archives of General Psychiatry, 42,* 725-728.

Stromgren, E. (1935). Zum Ersatz des Weinbergschen 'abgekurzten Verfahrens' zugleich ein Beitrag zur Frage von der Erblichkeit des Erkrankungsalters bei der Schizophrenie. *Zeitschrift für die gesamte Neurologie und Psychiatrie, 153,* 784-797.

Stromgren, E. (1938). Beitrage zur psychiatrischen Erblehre auf Grund von Untersuchungen an einer Inselbevolkerung. *Acta Psychiatrica et Neurologica Scandinavica (Supplementum), 19,* 1-257.

Thompson, W. D. (1984). *Multiple measurements and the improvement of estimates of exposure-disease associations.* Paper presented at the Seventeenth Annual Meeting of the Society for Epidemiologic Research, Houston, TX.

Thompson, W. D., & Weissman, M. M. (1981). Quantifying lifetime risk of psychiatric disorder. *Journal of Psychiatric Research, 16,* 113–126.

Thompson, W. D., Orvaschel, H., Prusoff, B. A., & Kidd, K. K. (1982). An evaluation of the family history method for ascertaining psychiatric disorders. *Archives of General Psychiatry, 39,* 53–58.

Weissman, M. M. & Klerman, G. L. (1978). Epidemiology of mental disorders: Emerging trends in the United States. *Archives of General Psychiatry, 35,* 705–712.

Weissman, M. M., Kidd, K. K., & Prusoff, B. A. (1982). Variability in rates of affective disorders in relatives of depressed and normal probands. *Archives of General Psychiatry, 39,* 1397–1403.

6

Biological Markers

WILLIAM S. REA, IRL L. EXTEIN, and MARK S. GOLD

INTRODUCTION

Much of the history of scientific psychiatry may be seen as a struggle to progressively identify the reasons why some of us may be afflicted with a disorder of thinking, feeling, or behavior while others will go through life without such a disruption. Our hope is that, by elucidating the differences between the state of an individual when suffering an acute mental illness and the state of the same individual when healthy, we may better learn effective techniques to ameliorate these conditions. An even more desirable result would be for the knowledge from our research to lead to ways of preventing the emergence of the illness from the very beginning.

Over the past decades there has been an enormous exploration underway of the biological underpinnings to the major psychiatric illnesses, with results that have begun to clarify the functioning of the brain in health and illness and that have led to treatments of unprecedented efficacy. Major depressions with a previously terrible morbidity and mortality may now be resolved in a matter of weeks.

Some of the more clinically applicable biological research in psychiatry has arisen from the observation that patients with the syndrome characteristic of a major depressive disorder (DSM-III) show evidence of both affective and "hypothalamic" symptoms. The affective symptoms often include depressed mood, anxiety, helplessness, hopelessness, and negativism. The hypothalamic symptoms, often referred to as neurovegetative, may include appetite and sleep disturbances, anger, decreased

---

WILLIAM S. REA, IRL L. EXTEIN, AND MARK S. GOLD • Lake Hospital, Lake Worth, FL 33460.

libido, psychomotor retardation or agitation, and diurnal variation of symptoms.

The association of the neurovegetative signs with depressive symptoms has led to a fruitful search for hypothalamic disturbance in active depression. The state of major depression has been linked with an increased probability of abnormal hypothalamic regulation of the adrenal and thyroid axes. With remission of the depression, these hypothalamic abnormalities also tend to remit. In this way neuroendocrine testing of hypothalamic function has become a tool for measuring a marker of active illness that may be as valuable in its own way as cardiac isoenzymes or an electrocardiogram is in myocardial infraction.

It is important to distinguish between "state" and "trait" markers. A "trait" marker is one that indicates a diathesis toward an illness and is present no matter what the current state of the organism may be, ill or well. A "state" marker is present only during the active clinical illness.

Most of the biological tests in current use in psychiatry today are state-dependent tests. Some of the most researched are the diurnal cortisol test, the dexamethasone suppression test, the TRH stimulation test, and urinary MHPG levels. A possible trait-dependent test is platelet monoamine oxidase level.

In reviewing any test it is important to distinguish between sensitivity, specificity, and predictive value. Sensitivity is defined as the percentage of patients with a condition (e.g., major depression) who have a positive test. Specificity is defined as the percentage of patients without the condition who have a negative test. Predictive value, or diagnostic confidence, is the percentage of subjects with a positive test result who have the condition.

Patients with major depressive disorder have been reported to have several neuroendocrine abnormalities. They have a diminished growth hormone (GH) response to a number of provocative stimuli, including insulin (Sachar, Finkelstein, & Hellman, 1971), L-dopa (Sachar, Altman, Gruen, Glassman et al. 1975), clonidine (Matussek, Ackenheil, Hippins, 1980), and amphetamine (Langer, Heinze, Reim, 1976) and an increased growth hormone response to TRH (Gold, Pottash, Extein, 1981).

Other neuroendocrine abnormalities that have been reported in major depression include increased prolactin (PRL) secretion, decreased PRL response to opioids (Extein, Pottash, Gold, Sweeney, Martin & Goodwin, 1980c) decreased luteinizing hormone (LH) (Robins & Guze, 1970), decreased LH response to gonadtropin releasing hormone (LHRH) (Brambilla, Smeraldi, & Sacchetti, 1978), increased cortisol secretion (Sachar, Hellman, & Roffwarg, Halperni, Fukushima, & Gallagher, 1971), failure to suppress cortisol production on the dexamethasone suppression test (DST) (Carroll, Feinberg, Greden, Iarika, Albala, Haskett, James,

Krowfa, Lohr, Steiner, Devisne, & Young, 1981), decreased cortisol secretion in response to dextroamphetamine (Sacher, Halbreich, Asnis, Nathan, Halpern, & Ostow, 1981), and decreased thyroid-stimulating hormone (TSH) and PRL response to TRH (Prange, Lara, Wilson, Alltop & Breese, 1972; Kastin, Ehrensing, Schalch, & Anderson, 1972; Extein, Pottash, & Gold, 1981a; Loosen & Prange, 1982; Loosen, Prange, & Wilson *et al.* 1982).

DIURNAL CORTISOL TEST

The single most commonly noted endocrine abnormality in depression is hyperactivity of the hypothalamic-pituitary-adrenal (HPA) axis, often manifest by hypersecretion of cortisol (Sacher, Hellman, Roffwars, Halpern, Fukushima & Gallagher, 1973). The diurnal cortisol test is one which simply measures plasma levels of cortisol by radio immunoassay, as frequently as possible over a twenty-four hour period. For this test to be valid, medical causes of elevated cortisol (endogenous or exogenous Cushing's syndrome) or reduced cortisol (Addison's disease) must be ruled out. For some patients with depressive symptoms, these diagnoses may be suggested by the pattern of text results. Some authors have suggested that the boundaries between Cushing's syndrome and depression with hypercortisol secretion are not distinct, and that these two entities may share a common pathophysiology as well as symptoms (Reus, 1985).

The normal secretion of cortisol by the adrenal gland is stimulated by the pituitary hormone adrenocorticotropic hormone (ACTH). ACTH is produced by cleavage of a larger hormone, pro-opiocortin, which affects both adrenal and endogenous opioid regulation (Guillemin, Vargo, Rossier, Minick, Ling, Rivier, Vale & Bloom, 1977; Adler, 1980). The production of ACTH is under the control of corticotrophin-releasing hormone from the hypothalamus. This hypothalamic-pituitary-adrenal "cascade" shows inhibitory feedback control (Martin, Reichlin, & Brown, 1977).

On measurement of cortisol plasma levels at multiple time points, normals show diurnal variation with lows in the middle of the night (<6 μg/100 ml) and higher levels at 8:00A.M. (10–25 μg/100 ml) and 4:00 P.M. (> 14 μg/100 ml). This results in a characteristic V-shaped pattern on plotting (see Figure 1).

For some patients with major depression, there are increased coritsol production rates and plasma cortisol level throughout the 24-hour period

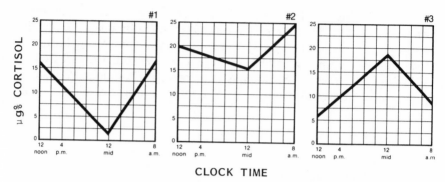

CLOCK TIME

Figure 1. Diurnal cortisol patterns, #1 normal diurnality, no hypersecretion; #2, cortisol hypersecretion (e.g., primary affective disease; Cushing's disease); #3, loss of diurnality; cortisol hypersecretion.

(see Figure 1), with a marked increase in total cortisol secreted. This results in elevation of the V-shape on graphing and may be an indicator for primary depressive illness, if medical causes of hypercortisolemia are ruled out (e.g., pituitary microadenoma, primary adrenal tumor). In some other patients with major depression, there is a reversal of the diurnality, with peak values occuring during the night (see Figure 1). Hypercortisol production can also be measured by sampling a three-hour time span (1:00–4:00 P.M. has been suggested) or by measuring 24-hour urinary free cortisol.

Overall flattening and lowering of the diurnal cortisol test suggest that the patient's depressive symptomatology may be secondary to Addison's disease. There is a subgroup of opioid abusers who have the anhedonic affective symptomatology of a "protracted withdrawal state." The mechanism is thought to be either opioid-induced inhibition of the production of pro-opiocortin with resultant decrease in ACTH, or primary adrenal "burnout" (Gold & Rea, 1983).

DEXAMETHASONE SUPPRESSION TEST

Given the fact that many patients suffering from major depression have elevated plasma cortisol levels, it is of interest whether the primary area of dysregulation is at the hypothalamic-pituitary or adrenal region. As it is not practicable to directly measure the neurotransmitters involved in HPA axis regulation, it was necessary to find an indirect means of evaluating the system—a "window into the brain." The dexamethasone suppression test (DST) is one such means.

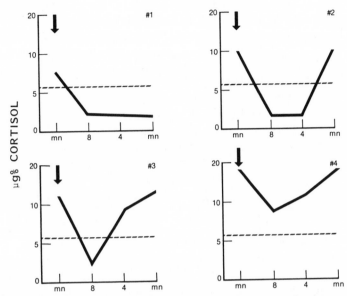

Figure 2. Patterns of response to dexamethasone, #1, normal response; #2, abnormal (late escape); #3, abnormal response (inadequate suppression); #4, abnormal (no suppression); mn, midnight.

The test takes advantage of the inhibitory control which cortisol has over the release of corticotropin releasing factor (CRF). The test is based on the ability of dexamethasone, a potent synthetic corticosteroid, to bind to brain receptors and mimic the action of cortisol.

The standardized DST involves administration of 1 mg of dexamethasone orally to the patient at 11:00 P.M. Cortisol levels are then drawn the next day at 4:00 P.M. and 11:00 P.M. (Carroll, Feinberg, Greden, Iarika, Albala, Haskett, James, Krowfa, Lohr, Steiner, deVisne, & Young, 1981). The dexamethasone binds to intracerebral receptors which register an "excess" of cortisol and hence suppress cortisol secretion for at least 24 hours. Nonsuppression is identified as a plasma level of cortisol greater than 5.0 µg/100 ml. It is important that the laboratory assay be accurate in the low range of cortisol levels (1–10 µg/100 ml) necessary for this test (see Figure 2).

When normal volunteers are compared with patients with major depression on this test, a striking finding emerges. Only about 4%–10% of normal volunteers fail to suppress (a low false positive rate). However, about 45% of patients suffering from major depression fail to suppress (Gold, Pottash, Extein & Sweeney, 1981; Brown & Shuey, 1980; Schlesser,

Winoker, & Sherman, 1980; Greden, Albala, Haskett, James, Goodman, Steiner, & Carroll, 1980; Carroll, Curtis, & Mendels, 1976).

There has been some controversy and confusion about the DST, as reviewed by Carroll (1985). In particular, the specificity has been challenged. Nonetheless, the basic findings remain.

Carroll *et al.* (1981) have reported the diagnostic confidence level of an abnormal DST in the diagnosis of a melancholic subgroup of major depression in a mixed population of psychiatric patients to be approximately 95%. This means that in such a population the failure to suppress on the DST identifies a patient with melancholic major depression 95% of the time. One must keep in mind that the diagnostic confidence (or predictive value) of the DST, like any diagnostic test, will vary depending on the prevalance of the illness in question in the population tested (Galen & Gambino, 1975).

Extein, Pottash, & Gold (1985a) reasoned that, given the pulsatile nature of cortisol secretion, increasing the number of sampling times might help the sensitivity of the test for major depression. They found that using a conventional two-point DST 4:00 P.M. and 12:00 midnight, 5% of 20 normal volunteers, 8% of 13 inpatients with non major depressions, and 31% of 65 inpatients with primary major depression failed to suppress. Using six post-dexamethasone points (8:00 A.M., 12:00 noon, 4:00 P.M., 10:00 P.M., 12:00 midnight), the respective percentages were 10%, 15%, and 44%. The additional points increased the sensitivity by 42%, mostly by identifying more major depressives with a "late escape" pattern. If a clinician is using the DST to establish a marker for major depression that can be repeated to monitor response to treatment and likelihood of relapse, then perhaps the increased sensitivity of the six-point DST would be helpful despite modest decrease in specificity from 94% to 88%.

Certain factors that can affect the validity of the DST must be taken into account in screening psychiatric patients for DST administration (Carroll *et al.,* 1981). For example, while usual therapeutic does of benzodiazepines, neuroleptics, tricyclics, and lithium do not affect the DST, other medications can. Barbituates, phenytoin, carbamazepine, and other medications that induce hepatic enzymes and, hence, speed the metabolism of dexamethasone, can cause false positives.

Failure to suppress on the DST and hypercortisol secretion are dissociated in some patients (Gold, *et al.*, 1981; Sternbach, Extein, & Gold, 1982). In other words, some major depressives have elevated diurnal cortisol levels while showing normal suppression on the DST, and some do not suppress on the DST despite normal diurnal cortisols. More research is needed to explain this dissociation. However, a practical implication of the finding is that measurement of diurnal cortisol may complement the DST as a measure of HPA axis hyperactivity.

As compared to many other laboratory tests in medicine, the DST can be a useful test. The specificity of an abnormal DST in the diagnosis of major depression is 90% to 96%: that is, the failure to suppress on the DST is rare in other psychiatric disorders, with a false positive rate of 5% to 10%. Gold, et al., (1981) found no nonsuppression among 15 schizophrenics, for example. A report by Brown, Keitner, Qualis, and Haier (1985) suggested that a 2-mg DST would markedly increase specificity even further. The sensitivity is approximately 50% to 67%, partially depending on the total number of time-points used in the protocol and depressive subgroup. A positive DST (lack of suppression) is of considerable practical usefulness in diagnosis and treatment. Preliminary studies with patients with borderline personality disorders and depression suggest the DST may help identify the borderline patient with major depressive disease (Sternbach, Fleming, & Extein, 1983). It is a test with unusual diagnosis and predict treatment outcome. A recent study (Shrivastava, Schwimmer, Brown, & Arato, 1985) of major depression found that DST nonsuppression predicted poor response to placebos, consistent with the notion that DST nonsuppression identifies patients with a genuine biological illness.

Normalization of the DST after successful treatment has been reported in many studies. Interestingly, depressed patients who show apparent clinical recovery, but whose DST remains abnormal, are at serious risk for early relapse (Greden, et al., 1980). In such cases, continued DST abnormalities may indicate need for alternative antidepressant treatment, or ECT, or at the minimum, continued somatic treatment and observation. Some clinicians successfully use normalization of the DST as a guide to when to discontinue treatments in a course of electroconvulsive therapy. Other clinicians have suggested the DST returns to normal before clinical response to antidepressants in patients who are on their way to recovery.

Dackis, Bailey, Pottash, Stuckey, Extein, and Gold (1984) looked at the value of the dexamethasone suppression test in the evaluation of alcoholics. After excluding alcoholic patients with hepatic disease or major depression, they found that 20% of the alcoholics failed to suppress during their alcohol withdrawal syndrome, but that after three weeks of sobriety there were no DST abnormalities in the 32 chronic alcoholics examined in this study. These results suggest that, after the alcohol withdrawal syndrome is resolved, the DST may be a useful laboratory adjunct in the diagnosis of depression in alcoholics.

Dackis, Pottash, Gold, and Annitto (1984) conducted a similar investigation on a population of 42 opioid addicts. The patients included 27 heroin-dependent and 15 methadone-dependent patients. Within three days of the DST each patient was administered a SADS-C (Endicott &

Spitzer, 1978). Testing was undertaken two weeks after detoxification. RDC major depression was present in 15 (36%) of the opioid patients, 12 of whom failed to suppress on the DST. Only two of the 27 addicts without major depression failed to suppress.

The DST provided a sensitivity of 80% and a specificity of 93% for major depression in this population. These sensitivity and specificity figures are similar to those found for major depression using the DST as a marker in a nonaddict population. It is remarkable that, given the complexities of assessing depression in the postdetoxified opioid addict patient, the DST seems to be a sensitive and specific laboratory test for major depression in this population.

The DST has been found to be abnormal in anorexia nervosa (Gerner & Swirtsman, 1981), but also in malnutrition due to other causes (Rao, Srikantia, & Gopalan, 1968; Smith, Bledsoe, & Chetri, 1975), making this a test of limited clinical utility in this disorder. The DST is normal in mild to moderate Alzheimer's disease, but abnormal in severe disease (Jenike & Albert, 1984).

In summary, there is incontrovertible evidence of disturbance of the regulation of the hypothalamic-pituitary-adrenal axis, as shown by non-suppression on the dexamethasone suppression test, in a large proportion of major depressive patients.

That the DST is a test whose abnormalities are reflective of the biological state of depression rather than a diathesis or trait, is shown by return of the DST to normal on successful treatment for depression in most cases. It is also of note that alcoholism and drug addiction disorders, which may be genetically linked to an affective diathesis, do not seem to be associated in and of themselves to a higher rate of DST abnormalities in the absence of depression.

THYROTROPIN-RELEASING HORMONE (TRH) TEST

TRH is a tripeptide found in the hypothalamus which, when released, causes secretion of thyroid-stimulating hormone (TSH) from the anterior pituitary gland. TSH then acts directly on the thyroid gland. Endocrinologists have long used the TRH test as a measurement of the responsiveness of this system (Martin, *et al.,* 1977). Five hundred µg of synthetic TRH is administered intravenously to the patient at bedrest after an overnight fast. Samples for TSH are taken at baseline, and at several time points after TRH administration via an indwelling venous catheter. TRH is measured by RIA. Delta TSH (ΔTSH) is the maximum TSH response, derived by subtracting the baseline TSH level from the peak. The peak is usually between 15 and 45 minutes. Subjective response to TRH infusion is limited to mild transient autonomic symptoms, such as the urge to urinate.

TSH is decreased in patients on cortiocosteroids and certain other drugs, although tricyclics, neuroleptics, and benzodiazepines do not appear to influence the TRH test (Kirkegaard, Bjorum, Cohn, Fabear, Lauridsen, & Nekup, 1977). Delta TSH is also reduced in cases of hyperthyroidism and alcoholism, as well as in males over 60. In hypothyroidism exaggerated TSH responses to TRH are seen > 25 µIU/ml. Another factor that can augment the TSH response to TRH is use of lithium, which has antithyroid properties.

In their response to the TRH infusion, enthyroid patients with primary unipolar depressive disorder often show a reduced release of TSH (Prange, et al., 1972; Takahashi, Kondo, Yoshimura, 1972; Hollister, Kenneth, & Berger, 1976; Loosen, et al., 1977; Brambilla, et al., 1978; Extein, Pottash, Gold, Cadet, Sweeney, Davies, Martin, 1980a).

We have found the definition of ΔTSH $\leqslant 7.0$ µIU/ml as a blunted TSH response to TRH useful in discriminating subgroups of depression, although others have suggested a more conservative cutoff of 5.0 µIU/ml. In 20 normal volunteer subjects tested by our laboratory the mean Δ TSH was 13.4$\pm$ 1.0 µIU/ml. In one study (Extein et al., 1981) we administered the TRH test to 105 consecutive patients with major unipolar subtype and to 40 patients with nonmajor (minor or intermittent) depression. All patients met DSM-III criteria for dysthymic disorder, adjustment reaction, or personality disorder. Patients with alcohol or drug abuse, addiction, or use of lithium in the previous six months were excluded from this study. The enrolled patients were free of all medications except acetaminophen and flurazepam for at least three days prior to the TRH test. All were euthyroid, based on physical examination, clinical assessment, and normal results for thyroxine (T4), triiodothyronine (T3) uptake, and baseline TSH. The mean Δ TSH of 7.3 $\pm$.5 µIU/ml in the 105 unipolar patients was significantly lower ($P<.01$ by t test) than that of 10.9 $\pm$ .7 µIU/ml in the 40 patients with non major depressions. Sixty of the unipolar depressed patients, but only four of the non major depressed patients and none of the controls, showed a ΔTSH <7.0 µIU/ml. These intergroup differences were significant ($P<.01$ by chi-square test).

With a ΔTSH <7.0 µIU/ml used to identify patients with a clinical diagnosis of major unipolar depression, in this group of patients and controls, sensitivity was 56%, specificity 93%, and the diagnostic confidence level 91% (Galen & Gambino, 1975). Obviously, the diagnostic confidence level and specificity would be lower in a population with a lesser proportion of patients with major depression or with diagnostic groups other than major depression that may have blunted responses on the TRH test.

We have also found that manic patients tend to have a blunted TSH response to TRH, whereas schizophrenic patients tend to have a normal response (Extein, Pottash, Gold, & Cowdry, 1982; Extein, Pottash, Gold, Sweeney, Martin, Goodwin, 1980c). We administered the TRH test to 30 consecutive euthyroid, nonalcoholic admitted patients who met RDC for mania, and to 30 consecutive euthyroid, nonalcoholic patients who met RDC for schizophrenia, undifferentiated subtype. All the schizophrenic patients were actively psychotic. None of the 60 patients had been treated with lithium within the previous six months. The mean ΔTSH of 6.4 $\pm$ 0.5 µIU/ml in the manic patients was lower than that of 10.2 $\pm$ 0.8 µIU/ml in the schizophrenic patients and that of 13.4 < 1.0 µIU/ml in the 20 normal controls ($p < .05$ by chi-square test). With a ΔTSH < 7.0 µIU/ml used as a marker for mania in this group, sensitivity was 60%, specificity 8.4%, and diagnostic confidence 69%.

Similarly, Targum (1983) reported that abnormalties on the TRH test can be used to characterize those patients with schizophreniform disorder (ill for less than 6 months) who have a good outcome and may have a variant of affective illness.

In the differential diagnosis of depression a blunting of the TSH response to TRH may help distinguish patients with major depressive disorder from those with minor depressions. This distinction is important because patients with major depressions are more likely to require and benefit from antidepressant medications than patients with minor depressions.

In hypothyroid patients, the ΔTSH is markedly increased, greater than 25 or 30 µIU/ml. This occurs at any time of relatively reduced circulating thyroid hormone, because the pituitary is starting to produce extra TSH reserve to enable the individual to compensate for the decrease in thyroid hormones. Although resting TSH levels may be normal, the pituitary gland's TRH receptors are exceptionally responsive to the TRH stimulation (Snyder & Utiger, 1972; Saberi & Utiger, 1975; Vagenakis, Rapoport, & Axixi, 1974).

Grades of hypothyroidism exist and can be identified using the TRH test. The early or "subclinical" stages of a failing thyroid gland may have behavioral presentation such as depression and anergia and can be diagnosed only by waiting until the patient is overtly hypothyroid, or doing a TRH test. Grade 1 (overt) rarely presents to the psychiatrist and is roughly equivalent to classical myedema. All thyroid tests are abnormal (e.g., thyroid hormones decreased, TSH increased, ΔTSH increased). Grade 2, or mild hypothyroidism, while sometimes treatable with thyroid replacement, is more subtle than Grade 1. Patients with Grade 2 may present to the psychiatrist complaining of depression, problems with concentration and memory, or lack of energy. Basal thyroid hormone levels are normal, TSH is elevated, and ΔTSH is markedly increased. Of "depressed" patients, 3% to 4% are grade 2 hypothyroid. Grade 3 patients may have a predominantly psychiatric syndrome with the only evidence of thyroid change being TSH response to TRH pathologically elevated. About two-thirds of such patients have anti-thyroid antibodies indicating the presence of autoimmune thyroiditis. Two to five percent of depressed patients are Grade 3 hypothyroid. In our experience thyroid hormone, TSH, and TRH testing identify those hypothyroid patients who are misdiagnosed by descriptive criteria and labelled as psychiatric. Such patients may be thyroid hormone responders, or require thyroid hormone potentiation of antidepressants (Extein, Pottash, & Gold, 1985b).

For depressed patients without hypothyroidism TRH testing may be of use in predicting relapse. Patients with apparent clinical recovery who nonetheless continue to show abnormal results on the TRH infusion are at greater risk for relapse (Kirkegaard, Bjorum, Cohn, Fabear, Lauridsen, & Nekup, 1977).

Reviewing the TRH test as a diagnostic test for major unipolar depression in this and some other studies, sensitivity often ranges from 60% to 77% and specificity from 77% to 97%. Similar results, with slightly lower specificity, can be seen when the TRH test is used in the differential diagnosis of mania and schizophrenia.

Further use of the TRH test in depression was undertaken by Krogmeyer and her associates (Krog-meyer, Kirkegaard, Kigne, Lumholtz, Smith, Lykke-Oleson, & Bjorum, 1984). This group undertook a double-blind perspective study of patients with unipolar depression who recovered after ECT. TRH tests were performed before and after the ECT. The patients were divided into three groups on the basis of their altered TSH response. Group 1 was composed of patients who had improved their delta TSH greater than 2 micro units per milliliter and Group 2 who had improved their delta TSH less than 2 micro units per milliliter. These were called respectively the good prognosis and the poor prognosis groups. The poor prognosis group was divided in half with half of the patients receiving placebo and the other half receiving amitriptyline for six months. Fewer relapses occured in the first group with good prognosis, and in the second poor prognosis group, which received amitriptyline. In fact, the poor prognosis group on amitriptyline had outcomes similar to the good prognosis group on placebo. This showed that relapse could be predicted

172

by the TRH test and prevented by amitriptyline. There are some data which suggests that bipoloar depressed patients have an increased response to TRH infusion, which can be useful in distinguishing them from unipolar patients (Gold, Pottash, Davies, Ryan, & Sweeney, 1979; Gold, Pottash, Ryan, Sweeney, Davies, & Martin, 1980).

The TRH test was also examined in alcoholic patients without major depression (Dackis, Bailey, *et al.* 1984). The mean delta TSH during withdrawal of 7.3 micro units per ml was significantly lower than that of 9.6 micro units per ml after detoxification. Of the 15 patients with alcohol withdrawal syndrome at admission, 8 had blunted TSH response to TRH when using the cutoff criteria of 7.0 micro units per ml. Five of the 15 had a blunted TRH response when using the more conservative and less sensitive criteria of 5.0 micro units per ml to define an abnormal TSH response. Eight (25%) of the 32 patients tested during week four after detoxification showed a TSH response of less than 7.0 micro units per ml.

The TRH test, as opposed to the DST, therefore, does not seem to have potential as a specific laboratory adjunct in the diagnosis of depression in alcoholics. Loosen and Prange (1980) suggested, however, that a blunted delta TSH response to TRH may be a trait marker for alcoholism.

24-HOUR URINARY MHPG TEST

The major urinary metabolite of brain norepinephrine is 3-methoxy 4 hydroxyphenylglycol (MHPG). Norepinephrine has been reported to be low in some subgroups of major depressed patients, particularly the bipolar group. These findings, however, have been disputed. Some clinicians found measurement of pre-treatment urinary MHPG to be of assistance in the prediction of a response to specific noradrenergic augmenting antidepressant medications.

There has been some disagreement about the percentage of urinary MHPG that is derived from brain as opposed to peripheral sources. However, even peripheral norepinephrine metabolism may reflect central control. Many studies, including the national collaborative study on depression, found that urinary MHPG levels correlate with response to noradrenergic medication such as imiprimine, desipramine, and maprotiline (Maas, Koslow, Katz, Bowden, Gibbons, Stokes, Robins, & Davis, 1984; Schatzberg, Rosenbaum, & Orsulak, 1981). Patients with low MHPG were more likely to respond to such medications than patients with high MHPG. As such, MHPG may be the only well-validated pre-treatment prognostic indicator.

Though most studies have employed a low monoamine diet for at least two days prior to urine collection, there is little hard evidence to suggest that diet is a significant source of variance in urinary MHPG. Patients should be off psychoactive drugs for at least one week prior to the test. Urinary creatinine and total urinary volume are measured at the same time as MHPG to rule out incomplete collection. In patients who are candidates for treatment with antidepressants, demonstration of low pretreatment MHPG levels (less than 1000 µg/24 h) predicts favorable response to the antidepressants affecting noradrenergic nervous systems listed above.

MULTIPLE NEUROENDOCRINE TEST BATTERIES

It is of note that the TRH test and the DST may be complementary in the biological evaluation of the depressed patient. Extein, *et al.* (1981) looked at the results of the TRH test and dexamethasone suppression test in 50 patients with unipolar depression. They found that dexamethasone suppression tests were abnormal in about 50% and that TRH tests results were abnormal in 64%. There was random overlap where some patients had both tests results abnormal (30%). Twenty percent of the patients could be identified by the DST only, and 34% by the TRH test only. Only 16% of the patients with unipolar depression in this study showed both tests results normal.

The use of the TRH test and dexamethasone suppression test in conjunction, therefore, may identify up to 84% of the patients suffering from unipolar depression. Preliminary findings suggest that patients with abnormalities on both tests are more likely to need ECT, and may represent a more ill subgroup. Studies employing two or more neuroendocrine tests in the same patient have suggested increased diagnostic specificity for major depression utilizing a criteria of more than one test abnormality (Bank, Arato, Papp, Rihmer, & Kovacs, 1986; Sternbach, Fleming, Extein, Pottash, & Gold, 1983).

DISCUSSION

It can be readily seen from the above results that there are some major psychiatric disorders which have very clear biological markers associated with them. The prototype of this disorder is unipolar depression. In the overwhelming majority of unipolar depressives, there will be a neuroendocrine abnormality in the form of either an early release of cortisol after administration of dexamethasone or in the form of a blunted release of TSH after administration of TRH. Other affective disorders, including bipolar manic and bipolar depressed, patients will also show abnormalities on this neuroendocrine testing. These abnormalities seem to be related entirely to the overall neuroendrocrine state of the organism at the time of testing and most often return to normal with appropriate treatment and recovery from the active illness. The DST and TRH infusion therefore are useful state dependent markers in the evaluation of affective disorders.

These findings have enormous implications for research and clinical treatment. It may be possible to further hone our diagnostic categories by examining the differences between unipolar depressives who have normal and those who have abnormal neuroendocrine testing. In the presence of positive biological markers (DST/TRH) authorities suggest the patient is a candidate for organic therapy (medications, ECT), without pointing in the direction of a specific medication choice. Research may show that patients with specific biological abnormalities need specific antidepressants or specific forms of potentiation of antidepressants before they are able to recover from the illness.

Along with theoretical significance, the TRH test and dexamethasone suppression test have enormous diagnostic utility. They permit a more exact diagnosis of patients whose symptoms are sufficiently non specific to potentially fall into two diagnostic categories—for example non-major depression, such as seen in character disorders or adjustment reaction, versus major depression, and schizophrenia versus mania. The increased diagnostic sophistication afforded by these tests, when used properly, cannot help but lead to more effective and humane treatment of major psychiatric disorders.

The economic savings afforded by these tests may also be helpful. If the presence of a neuroendocrine abnormality on testing of an inpatient, for example, leads to more rapid effective treatment and shortens the hospital stay by even one or two days, the financial benefit is great, not only for the individual patient care, but also for the mental health care system in general.

Another potential benefit of biologic markers such as these is to increase our sensitivity to the presence of dual illnesses in certain patients. For example, it appears that depression may be relatively undiagnosed in opiate addicts, who nonetheless show clear neuroendocrine disturbance and satisfy DSM-III criteria and RDC criteria for unipolar depression. Although the etiology of this depression in these patients is uncertain, with it possibly being a substance induced abnormality and perhaps reflecting a separate depressive diathesis, it is nonetheless clinically significant that treatment of these patients with tricyclic antidepressants may help lower their relapse rate to opiates.

The usefulness of the dexamethasone suppression test and the TRH test in monitoring treatment may become the most practical application. There is good evidence as noted above, that patients whose tests remain abnormal despite apparent clinical recovery, are at greater risk for relapse in the future. There is a good clinical rationale, for this reason, for utilizing the dexamethasone test or the TRH test sequentially in major affective disorder in the same way that chest X-rays or pulmonary function tests might be utilized to monitor the clinical improvement of a patient with pulmonary disorder. The identification of a subgroup of patients who have increased potential for a relapse allows clinicians to focus more intensive treatments on them with more frequent follow-up, careful attention to therapeutic dosages or blood levels, or possible use of potentiators of the antidepressants in order to improve response.

Finally, the use of the 24-hour urinary MHPG level to try to separate these patients who have a nonadrenergic rather than serotonergic depression may lead to improved treatment response, using various tricyclic antidepressants, which tend to have a preferential effect on one of these two neurochemical systems.

There is much exciting research going on in the field of biological psychiatry and many other biological markers may be identified in the future. It is possible that soon we will be able to test the endorphinergic and other neuromodulator systems with the sophistication with which we can now look at neuroendocrine and monoamine systems. Without removing the human element from the compassionate treatment of patients suffering from emotional disorder, the ready availability of testing for biological markers or psychiatric illness offers opportunities to markedly increase our efficacy in treating these debilitating illnesses.

REFERENCES

Adler, M. W. (1980). Opioid peptides. *Life Science, 26,* 947.

Banki, C. M., Arato, M., Papp, Z., Rihmer, Z., & Kovacs, Z. (1986) Associations among dexamethasone nonsuppression and TRH-induced hormonal responses: Increased specificity for melancholia? *Psychoneuroendocrinology, 11,* 205–211.

Brambilla, F., Smeraldi, E. & Sacchetti, E. (1978). Deranged anterior pituitary responsiveness to hypothalamic hormones in depressed patients. *Archives of General Psychiatry, 35,* 1231–1238.

Brown, W.A., & Shuey, I. (1980). Response to dexamethasone and subtype of depression. *Archives of General Psychiatry, 37,* 747–751.

Brown, W. A., Keitner, G., Qaulis, C. B. & Haier, R. (1985). The dexamethasone suppression test and pituitary-adrenocortical function. *Archives of General Psychiatry, 42,* 121–123.

Carroll, B. J. (1985). Dexamethasone suppression test: a review of contemporary confusion. *Journal of Clinical Psychiatry, 46,* 13–24.

Carroll, B. J., Curtis, G. C., & Mendels, J. (1976). Neuroendocrine regulation in depression: II. Discrimination of depressed from non-depressed patients. *Archives of General Psychiatry, 33,* 1051–1058.

Carroll, B. J., Feinberg, M., Greden, J. F., Iarika, J., Albala, A. A., Haskett, R. F., James, W. M., Krowfol, Z., Lohr, N., Steiner, M., deVisne, J. P., & Young, E. (1981). A specific laboratory test for the diagnosis of melancholia; standardization, validation, and clinical utility. *Archives of General Psychiatry, 38,* 15–22.

Dackis, C. A., Bailey, J., Pottash, A. L. C., Stuckey, R. F., Extein, I. E., & Gold, M. S. (1984). Specificity of the DST and TRH test for major depression among opiate addicts. *American Journal of Psychiatry, 141,* 680–683.

Dackis, C. A., Pottash, A. L. C., Gold, M. S., & Annitto, W. (1984). The dexamethasone suppression test for major depression among opiate addicts. *American Journal of Psychiatry, 141,* 810–811.

Endicott, J., & Spitzer, R. L. (1978). A diagnostic interview: The schedule for affective disorders and schizophrenia. *Archives of General Psychiatry, 35,* 837–844.

Extein, I. E., Pottash, A. L. C., Gold, M. S., Cadet, J., Sweeney, D. R., Davies R. K., & Martin, D. M. (1980a). The thyroid-stimulating hormone response to thyrotropin-releasing hormone in mania and bipolar depression. *Psychiatry Research, 2,* 199–204.

Extein, I. E., Pottash, A. L. C., Gold, M. S., & Martin, D. M. (1980b). Differentiating mania from schizophrenia by the TRH test. *American Journal of Psychiatry, 137,* 981–982.

Extein, I. E., Pottash, A. L. C., Gold M. S., Sweeney, D. R., Martin, D. M., & Goodwin, F. K. (1980c). Deficient prolactin response to morphine in depression. *American Journal of Psychiatry, 137,* 845–846.

Extein, I. E., Pottash, A. L. C., & Gold, M. S. (1981). The thyrotropin-releasing hormone test in the diagnosis of unipolar depression. *Psychiatry Research, 5,* 311–316.

Extein, I. E., Pottash, A. L. C., Gold, M. S., & Cowdry, R. N. (1982). Using the protirelin test to distinguish mania from schizophrenia. *Archives of General Psychiatry, 39,* 77–81.

Extein, I. E., Pottash, A. L. C., & Gold, M. S. (1986a). Number of cortisol time-points and dexamethasone suppression test sensitivity for major depression. *Psychoneuroendocrinology, 10*(3), 281–288.

Extein, I. E., Pottash, A. L. C., & Gold, M. S. (1986b). Thyroid tests as predictors of treatment response and prognosis in psychiatry. *The Psychiatric Hospital, 16,* 127–130.

Galen, R. S., & Gambino, S. R. (1975). *The predictive value and efficiency of medical diagnosis.* New York: John Wiley.

Gerner, R. N., & Swirtsman, H. E. (1981). Abnormalities of dexamethasone suppression test and urinary MHPG in anorexia nervosa. *American Journal of Psychiatry, 138,* 650–653.

Gold, M. S., Pottash, A. L. C., Davis, R. K., Ryan, N., & Sweeney, D. R. (1979). Distinguishing unipolar and bipolar depression by thyrotropin release test. *Lancet, 2,* 411–413.

Gold, M. S., Pottash, A. L. C., Ryan, N., Sweeney, D. R., Davies, R. K., & Martin, D. M. (1980). TRH-induced response in unipolar, bipolar, and secondary depressions; possible utility in clinical assessment and differential diagnosis. *Psychoneuroendocrinology, 5,* 147–155.

Gold, M. S., Pottash, A. L. C., & Extein, I. E. (1981). Hypothyroidism and depression: evidence from complete thyroid function evaluation. *Journal of the American Medical Association, 245,* 1919–1922.

Gold, M. S., Pottash, A. L. C., Extein, I. E., & Sweeney, Dr. R. (1981). Diagnosis of depression in the 1980's. *Journal of the American Medical Association, 245,* 1562–1564.

Gold, M. S., & Rea, W. S. (1983). The role of endorphins in opiate addiction, opiate withdrawal, and recovery, *Psychiatric Clinics of North America, 6,* 489–520.

Greden, J. G., Albala, A. A., Haskett, R. F., James, N. M., Goodman, L., Steiner, M., & Carroll, B. J. (1980). Normalization of dexamethasone suppression test: A laboratory index of recovery from endogenous depression. *Biological Psychiatry, 15,* 449–458.

Guillemin, R., Vargo, T., Rossier, J., Minick, S., Ling, N., Rivier, C., Vale, W., & Bloom, F. (1977). Beta-endorphin and adrenocorticotropin are secreted concomitantly by the pituitary gland. *Science, 197,* 1367–1369.

Hollister, L. E., Kenneth, L. D., & Berger, P. A. (1976). Pituitary response to thyrotropin-releasing hormone in depression. *Archives of General Psychiatry, 33,* 1393–1396.

Jenike, M. A., & Albert, M. S. (1984). The dexamethasone suppression test in patients with presenile and senile dementia of the Alzheimer's type. *Journal of the American Geriatric Society, 32,* 441–444.

Kastin, A. J., Ehrensing, D. S., Schalch, D. S., Anderson, M. S. (1972). Improvement in mental depression with decreased thyrotropin response after administration of thyrotropin-releasing hormone. *Lancet, 2* 740–742.

Kirkegaard, C., Bjorum, N., Cohn, D., Fabear, J., Lauridsen, U. B., & Nekup, J. (1977). Studies on the influence of biogenic amines and psychoactive drugs on the prognostic value of the TRH stimulation test in endogenous depression. *Psychoneuroendocrinology, 2,* 131–136.

Kirkegaard, C., Bjorum, N., Cohn, D. & Lauridsen, U. B. (1978). Thyrotropin-releasing hormone stimulation test in manic depressive illness. *Archives of General Psychiatry, 35,* 1917–1021.

Krog-Meyer, I., Kirkegaard, C., Kijne, B., Lumholtz, B., Smith, E., Lykke-Olesen, L., & Bjorum, N. (1984). Prediction of relapse with the TRH test and prophylactic amitriptylin in 39 patients with endogenous depression. *American Journal of Psychiatry, 141,* 945–948.

Langer, G., Heinze, G., Reim, B. (1976). Reduced growth hormone responses to amphetamine in endogenous depressive patients. *Archives of General Psychiatry, 33,* 1471–1475.

Loosen, P. T., Prange, A. J. (1980). Thyrotropin releasing hormone (TRH): a useful tool for psychoneuroendocrine investigation. *Psychoneuroendocrinology, 5,* 63–80.

Loosen, P. T., Prange, A. J., Jr., Wilson, I. C., Lara, P. P., & Pettus, C. (1977). Thyroid stimulating hormone response after thyrotropin-releasing hormone in depressed, schizophrenic and normal women. *Psychoneuroendocrinology, 2,* 137–148.

Loosen, P. T., & Prange, A. J. (1982). Serum thyrotropin response to thyrotropin-releasing hormone in psychiatric patients: a review. *American Journal of Psychiatry, 139,* 405–416.

Maas, J. W., Koslow, S. N., Katz, M. M., Bowden, C. W., Gibbons, R. L., Stokes, P. E., Robins, E., & Davis, J. M. (1984). Pre-treatment neurotransmitter metabolite levels and response to tricyclic antidepressant drugs. *American Journal of Psychiatry, 141,* 1159–1171.

Martin, J. B., Reichlin, S., & Brown, G. M. (1977). Clinical Neuroendocrinology. *Contemporary Neurological Service, 14,* 3–394.

Matussek, N., Ackenheil, M., Hippins, H. (1980). Effect of clonidine on growth hormone release in psychiatric patients and controls. *Psychiatry Research, 2,* 25–36.

Prange, A. J., Jr., Lara, P. P., Wilson, I. C., Alltop, L. B., & Breese, G. R. (1972). Effects of thyrotropin-releasing hormone in depression. *Lancet, 2,* 999–1002.

Rao, K. S., Srikantia, S. G., & Gopalan, C. (1968). Plasma cortisol levels in protein-calorie malnutrition. *Archives of Disease in Childhood, 43,* 367–367.

Reus, V. I. (1985). Pituitary-adrenal dysfunction in psychiatric illness. *Continuing Medical Education Syllabus and Scientific Proceedings in Summary Form.* The 138th Annual Meeting of the American Psychiatric Association, Dallas, TX.

Robins, E., & Guze, S. B. (1970). Establishment of diagnostic validity in psychiatric illness: Its application to schizophrenia. *American Journal of Psychiatry, 126,* 983–987.

Saberi, M., & Utiger, R. D. (1975). Augmentation of thyrotropin responses to thyrotropin-releasing hormone following small decreases in serum thyroid hormone concentrations. *Journal of Clinical Endocrinology and Metabolism, 40,* 435.

Sachar, E. J., Finkelstein, J., & Hellman, L. (1971). Growth hormone response in depressive illness; I: response to insulin tolerance test. *Archvies of General Psychiatry, 25,* 263–269.

Sachar, E. J., Hellman, L., Roffwarg, H. P., Halpern, F. S., Fukushima, D. K. & Gallagher, T. F. (1973). Disrupted 24-hour patterns of cortisol secretion in psychotic depression. *Archives of General Psychiatry, 28,* 19–24.

Sachar, E. J., Altman, N., Gruen, P. H., Glassman, A., Halpern, F. S., & Sassin, J. (1975). Human growth hormone response to levodopa. *Archives of General Psychiatry, 35,* 502–503.

Sachar, E. J., Halbraiech, U., Asnis, G. M., Nathan, R. S., Halpern, F. S., Ostrow, L. (1981). Paradoxical cortisol responses to dextroampheta in endogenous depression. *Archives of General Psychiatry, 10,* 1113–1117.

Schatzberg, A. F., Rosenbaum, A. H., & Orsulak, P. J. (1981). Toward a biochemical classification of depressive disorders: III. Pretreatment urinary MHPG levels as a predictor of response to treatment with maprotiline. *Psychopharmacology, 73,* 34–38.

Schlesser, M., Winokur, G., & Sherman, G. M. (1980). Hypothalamic-pituitary-adrenal axis-activity in depressive illness. *Archives of General Psychiatry, 37,* 737–743.

Smith, S. R., Bledsoe, T., & Chetri, M. K. (1975). Cortisol metabolism and the pituitary-adrenal axis in adults with protein-calorie malnutrition. *Journal of Clinical Endocrinology and Metabolism, 40,* 43–52.

Snyder, P. J., & Utiger, R. D. (1972). Inhibition of thyrotropin response to thyrotropin-releasing hormome by small quantities of thyroid hormones. *Journal of Clinical Investigation, 51,* 2077.

Sternbach, H., Extein, I. E., & Gold, M. S. (1982). Diurnal cortisol: DST and TRH tests in depression. *Continuing Medical Education Syllabus and Scientific Proceedings in Summary Form.* 135th annual meeting of the American Psychiatric Association, Toronto.

Sternbach, H. A., Fleming, J., Extein, I., Pottash, A. L., & Gold, M. S. (1983). The dexamethasone suppression and thyrotropin-releasing hormone test is depressed borderline patients. *Psychoneuroendocrinology, 8,* 459–462.

Takahashi, S., Kondo, H., Yoshimura, M., Kondo, H., & Yoshimura, M., & Ochi, Y. (1972). Antidepressant effect of thyrotropin-releasing hormone (TRH) and the plasma thyrotropin levels in depression. *Folia Psychiatric Neurology, 27,* 305–314.

Vagenakis, A., Rapoport, B., Axixi, F. (1974). Hyper-response to thyrotropin-releasing hormone accompanying small decreases in serum thyroid hormone concentrations. *Journal of Clinical Investigations, 54,* 913.

7

Genetic Research Designs
Strategies in Psychiatric Research

DIANE K. WAGENER

INTRODUCTION

Research involving diagnostic issues in psychiatry has used families largely to define diagnostic groups or to impart validity to a diagnosis. History has led us almost full circle in this endeavor. The occurrence of disorders in relatives of the patients has been used as a partial reason for splitting diagnoses (e.g., unipolar versus bipolar disorders). Now the occurrence of disorders is being used to argue the continuity of diagnoses as variants on a single dimension of vulnerability (e.g., Gershon et al., 1982). Indeed, using morbidity among family members, it can be argued that there is evidence for homogeneity of major depression and bipolar affective disorder (Stancer, Persad, Wagener, & Jorna, 1985). In fact, relatives may not be the best resource for the search of validity of diagnoses for at least two reasons. Most of the diagnoses in psychiatry and psychology are age and sex dependent. Therefore, the comparison between families of patients or controls is not straightforward (Baldessarini, Gershon, Weissman, Kidd & Prusoff, 1984). Further, generally there is variability in the expression of symptoms. Any ambiguity in diagnoses in the index patients is only compounded by studying relatives in whom the symptoms may not only be fewer, but also less well-defined.

The aim of this chapter is to lead the reader from the formulation of questions which are appropriate for family research to the relevant research designs and analytic tools. We will adopt an informal approach,

DIANE K. WAGENER • Department of Psychiatry, Western Psychiatric Institute and Clinic, University of Pittsburgh School of Medicine, Pittsburgh, PA 15213.

discussing the techniques, sample selection issues, and analytic procedures, preferring to direct the reader elsewhere for details. We will also attempt to refer the reader to recent descriptive publications which should help identify the technical publications relevant to the specific area of interest. The orientation here will be toward the problems more commonly encountered in psychiatric research.

The organization of this review, therefore, will be by the types of questions that one might reasonably ask regarding the occurrence of a disease or a trait in family members. Genetic epidemiology is the study of family-related sampling strategies and their analyses for the purpose of asking questions about the processes affecting expression of a disorder, be they genetic or environmental. There are four broad questions which might be asked regarding the disease in an individual and how its occurence relates to other family members.

1. Is the trait familial? That is, are family members more similar to the index than is expected based on the frequency of the trait in the general population? Does the trait cluster in families?

2. To what extent can the familiality be explained by genetic factors? Another way of saying this is to what extent is the variation of this trait in the population due to genetic variation between individuals (i.e., heritability)? Often these studies emphasize similarities within families, but it is important to realize that the analyses of these studies are based on the *variation between* individuals. A corollary to this question is whether the trait under study is in fact heterogeneous, that is, has several different etiologies. If such is the case, the trait should be redefined and reanalyzed, as most of the research designs are not robust to this complication.

3. What are the natures of the genetic influences? That is, can the genetic influences be described as single genes, polygenes, and so forth? What is the mode of inheritance?

4. What are the relationships between other traits or environmental stresses and the trait under study? Are these related to the trait in a necessary and/or sufficient way? Given an environmental stressor, does this affect the expression of the trait in an individual who is genetically vulnerable to the trait?

THE SEARCH FOR FAMILIALITY

The demonstration that a trait (disorder) tends to cluster in family members of the affected index individual is the *sine qua non* to further research into the nature of that familial clustering. Of course, a trait may cluster in a family for a variety of reasons: shared genes, shared life experiences, shared life style.

Case-Control Family History Studies

The first observations of familiality are usually the result of case-control studies which include assessments of family history (i.e., percentage family history positive). However, these studies are subject to many sources of error. Thompson (Chapter 5) discusses the biases and errors inherent in the use of family history versus family interview data. Additional errors arise if the controls have not been matched on age and family structure to the patients. This is usually difficult to achieve. But variables affecting the life experience of patients and their relatives include adoption status, half-siblings, and the extent to which the family is intact. The sex distribution in the families will affect the observed frequencies of sex-influenced traits. There are many factors which account for the differences in the proportion of cases with affected relatives versus the proportion of controls with affected relatives. Most of these have been ignored either in the research design or analysis of family-related diagnostic research.

Prevalence Studies

The actual frequency (lifetime prevalence) of a trait in the relatives can only be estimated by directly assessing the individuals. For physiological determinants this requirement of direct observation is obvious. But this is true also for diagnostic purposes. The objective of these studies is the determination of whether the prevalence of a trait is increased (significantly?) among family members of cases as compared to family members of controls. However, there are several epidemiological considerations pertinent to the correction of these data before the families can be compared.

Age correction is necessary for any trait which is variably expressed over different ages. In the psychiatric literature such corrections have been referred to as the calculation of the "Bezugziffern," the equivalent population size. This includes the information inherent in the at-risk population as well as the affected individuals. The most appropriate method commonly used is the modified Stromgren method (Slater & Cowie, 1971), which utilizes age of onset distributions for the trait to determine the amount of information available from the unaffected relatives. Appropriate distributions should either be obtained from independent samples of the same population or be adjusted so as to be population independent. Baron, Risch, and Mendlewicz (1983) discuss their attempts at correcting for the demographics of their source population. Risch (1983) has also proposed another method for estimating the equivalent population size, which not only estimates the amount of information available from unaffected family members, but also uses the ages of onset in the patients to estimate the bias in the patient sample due to the selection procedure. To date, most of the population demographic and age corrections have not been done separately for women and for men. However, because of the clear sex effects of most of the disorders, this practice should be changed. To do that, appropriate age- and sex-specific lifetime prevalence rates need to be made available (Sturt, Kumakura, & Der, 1984).

Of course, these family studies depend on the selection of an appropriate control sample whose families are also interviewed with regard to diagnoses. Alternatively, the expected number of affected relatives can be calculated using age- and sex-specific lifetime prevalence data from similarly interviewed populations (Williams, 1984). The expected number of affected relatives depends on age, sex, and cohort specific information of lifetime prevalence. A chi-square test can be formulated to determine whether there is a significant increase in morbidity among relatives. This can also be done to compare between groups of families defined by proband characteristics.

The age-of-onset distributions derived from onset information of patients are not the appropriate distributions for correcting information obtained from relatives, since one's expectation is that the relative is unaffected. The patient age-of-onset information, on the other hand, is determined from people who are in fact affected and have been seen in a hospital or clinic. These patients differ from the relatives in that their disease has progressed to an advanced level. The symptoms in individuals who are not advanced in the disease process may be less pronounced, so that the onset of the disease state may not be clear. The age-of-onset corrections utilized by most studies are appropriate for onset of severe episodes. Less severe episodes may have very different age and sex patterns. Therefore, there is need to collect the appropriate information from random individuals.

Of particular concern for these family studies is the method of ascertainment. There are several methods of recruiting families to a study: selection from a registry, clinic record, self-referral, and selection based on the presence of multiple cases among the family members. Each of these procedures leads to biases in the estimation of risks among family members. For instance, selection of families due to the presence of multiple family members who are affected certainly may improve compliance, but obviously inflates the estimation of risk to family members. Selection of young cases will yield families whose average age is younger than the total population. Therefore, the risk to relatives estimated from these data may be less for some disorders having later ages of onset and greater for other disorders having younger ages of onset. This is true even when age-of-onset corrections are employed, unless corrections are made for the affected as well as the unaffected relatives (Risch, 1983). The effects of selection bias become important, in another sense, later, in the analysis of the influence of genetic factors on familiality of a trait.

Distancing

A variant on the above prevalence studies is the indication of familiality from observed nonzero correlations between various pairs of relatives for the trait state. That is, relatives who are related more closely to the index should have larger correlations than more distant relatives. Using a variety of such pairs of relatives, inferences may be made as to the plausibility of familial (genetic and cultural) factors affecting the expression of a trait. Special types of relatives include monozygous twins and spouses. Monozygous twins are expected to be most similar, and spouses, who are largely unrelated genetically, should be least similar, if polygenic or multifactorial inheritance is important. If a single gene is largely responsible for the expression of a trait, the correlation between siblings may be smaller than that between parents and offspring. These correlations are not expected to differ under the polygenic condition. Gottesman and Shields (1982) review a long tradition of this kind of research involving schizophrenic individuals.

Recurrence Risk

The recurrence risk is the risk of the trait (disorder) in another family member. This is not to be confused with the reoccurence of a temporal trait or disorder in the index individual. For a trait to be familial, the relative risk for the trait should be greater than 1.0 for relatives as compared to controls, after correcting for confounding factors and other risk factors. Such an analysis can be done with logistic regressions or proportionals hazards models, if the appropriate assumptions hold (Weissman, Wichramaratne, Merikangas, 1984; Stancer et al., 1985). There are many risk factors which are shared by family members, but these are often ignored when recurrence risks are calculated. The most obvious, and least often ignored, familial risk factor is age. But there are also other factors which differ depending on the trait being studied. For instance, life events, athletic activities, coping behaviors, and substance use may run in families. The extent to which the latter behaviors may themselves be subject to genetic influences may be debated. However, to the extent that these are independent risk factors for other traits, such as depression, they should be accounted for in any genetic analysis.

GENETIC VULNERABILITY

Because the clustering of a trait in families can be the result of several different factors, a natural question is to what extent this clustering is due to shared genetic susceptibility. There are several kinds of observations which indicate the possibility of, but do not quantitate, the effect of genetic factors. These include an excess of consanguineous marriages in the families of index subjects as contrasted to control subjects, spouses having no increased risk for the trait, onset of the disorder independent of external events, and the demonstration of similar variation in traits in another mammalian species. However, there are other research designs and analyses that yield stronger evidence of genetic factors contributing to the familiality. The objective is to contrast the relative influence of genetic factors and other factors transmitted with the family, such as cultural factors, or genetic-environmental interactions.

Random Individuals

The distribution of a quantitative trait (phenotype) in a series of nonrelated individuals can give clues regarding the presence of genetic factors. Deviations from a normal distribution of phenotypes, especially nonzero skewness, may be consistent with the presence of a major gene—a segregating gene whose genotypes contribute in a major way to the variance in the population. To segregate means to have more than one genotype, and hence phenotype, present in the population. If one, two, or three distributions are assumed to underly the overall population phenotype distribution, the means and variances and, more importantly, the relative frequencies of individuals of each distribution can be estimated (Day, 1969). The goodness-of-fit of these models can also be evaluated. If a multiple-distribution model cannot be rejected, this may indicate presence of a segregating gene. However, such skewness in the population distribution might be due to many other factors, such as the age distribution of the sample or failure to properly transform or adjust the raw data. Because of the sensitivity of most genetic analyses to skewness, some investigators (Morton, 1982) have suggested that transforming the data to remove this skewness should always be done. Morton argues that analyzing the transformed data is the best test of the presence of a gene. This technique certainly yields a conservative analysis, if the objective of the analysis is the determination of such a gene.

Twins

The most efficient way to get an upper bound on the extent of genetic heritability for a given trait is the use of twins, monozygous (MZ) and dizygous (DZ). By comparing the concordance rates in twin pairs between these two types of twins (the classical twin study), a significant increase in MZ twins over DZ twins might be construed as evidence for genetic factors influencing the trait. However, some words of caution are appropriate. First, the concordance of DZ should be significantly different from zero. If the concordance (or correlation) of these pairs is not different from zero, then there is no clear indication of any familial clustering between these types of siblings, making the interpretation of heritability meaningless. An increase in the MZ concordance rates might then be due to other factors such as the way society treats individuals who are physically so similar.

Speaking more generally, the assumptions underlying the simple comparisons of concordance rates in twins are weak. Therefore, it is difficult to make specific predictions about the causes for concordance or generalizability to nontwins unless specific models can be posited and tested (Eaves & Eysenck, 1980). These models require partitioning the twins or evaluating other relatives of the twins (see below). However, some general statements about studying twins and simple corrections can be discussed at this time.

Because of the sex influence on many disorders, unlike-sexed DZ twins should be analysed separately (Eaves, 1977). Models can be specified which incorporate sex effects on gene expression (Eaves, & Eysenck, 1980).

Contrary to some commonly held notions, age correlations should be done with twin data. Consider a twin pair which is assessed at an age only partially through the period of risk, say an age at which half of the cases would have been diagnosed. Then the fact that one twin of the pair is unaffected does not necessarily imply that they do not share genetic vulnerability. Instead, that twin may not, as yet, have expressed the trait, as when he or she is only partially informative (McGue & Bouchard, 1984). Such individuals must be alloted for in the estimation of parameters like heritability: the proportion of the total variability of a trait which is attributable to genetic variation between individuals, calculated under restrictive assumptions using twin pairs. In practice, these assumptions do not hold, but sometimes can be shown to have minimal impact on the statistics. Among the assumptions (Gottesman & Shields, 1982) are (1) the environmental variability between members of a twin pair are similar for MZ and DZ twins as well as the population at large. This would not be true if twins tended to be exposed to or share more similar environmental situations than siblings. (2) There is no "twin factor," that is, being a twin does not alter one's vulnerability to the trait. Jackson (1960) suggested, for instance, that MZ twins would have an increased risk for schizophrenia as a result of alleged problems with confusion of identity and weak ego formation. (3) There is no artificially induced increased concordance of twins due to the identification of one twin with the cotwin. That is, the fact that twins share a unique family relationship does not result in an increased tendency to be similar. (4) There is no bias in the selection of twin pairs in favor of increasing the number of twins with both members of the pair affected. The impact of these assumptions, of course, will depend on the trait being studied.

Most analyses of twin studies involve the decomposition of variances in terms of their expected components, genetic and environmental. The appropriate linear functions of these variances allow for the estimation of the components. That is, models can be formulated which specify causes. Linear functions of these components, such as genetic factors, shared environments, and assortative mating, can be expressed for a variety of relationships. The maximum-likelihood solution of these simultaneous linear equations allows for the estimation of the proportion of variance due to genetic factors or shared environment, and so forth. However, with an increasing number of parameters to be estimated, more observed variances are required. To achieve this, twins may be separated into subgroups according to their sex (Eaves & Eysenck, 1980), or DZ twins may be separated according to the genotype at a genetic marker (Nance, 1984). Alternatively, twin studies can be expanded to include other family members, the twin family method.

Nance and his colleagues (Nance, 1984) have described the extension of these kinds of analyses to some unusual relationships. One such design focuses on the kinships of identical twins, including the twins, their offspring, and the twins' spouses. The offspring, across sibships, have the same genetic relationships as half-siblings. If the twins are male, then these offspring have an additional source of variability due to different maternal effects. Another design incorporates the multiple correlations that exist between twins and their spouses to evaluate the effects of assortative mating, mate selection, and social homogamy (Nance, 1984).

One extension of the twin studies involves longitudinal assessments of the twins. The variance between twins at different developmental periods can be used to assess the degree of genetic influence on developmental changes and the temporal effects of gene expression (Eaves, Young, Last, & Martin, 1978). The study of twin pairs over different environments can be used to estimate genotype and environment interaction (Eaves, 1982).

Adoption

Adoption studies are a powerful design for the separation of cultural effects from genetic effects. The most powerful design for this kind of study is, of course, monozygous twins reared apart. In that instance the genetic vulnerability across individuals of a twin pair is held constant and only the environment varies. However, the adoption study is also informative for siblings reared apart and for unrelated individuals who have been adopted. There are several variants to the research design (DeFries & Plomin, 1983).

The at-risk model selects parents who have had children adopted away from them (Rosenthal, Wender, Kety, Schulsinger, Welner, & Ostergaard, 1968). An increase in the prevalence of the trait among the offspring of those parents who did have it, as compared to offspring of other parents, indicates a genetic vulnerability for the trait. However, the age of adoption, foster home experience, and placement of the child are important considerations. In addition, mothers with psychiatric disorders may abuse substances. Although such abuse has never been linked to subsequent psychiatric diorders, it has been associated with various behavioral and mental changes in the offspring. Such behavior may put the individual at an increased risk for many disorders.

An extension to the at-risk model is the crossfostering design (Wender, Rosenthal, Kety, Schulsinger, & Welner, 1974). The completion of the full 2 × 2 adoption-research design is the inclusion of children who have been adopted into families in which at least one of the parents has developed the trait. One therefore, has adopted children with adopting parents with/without the trait and with biological parents with/without the trait. Of course, depending upon the nature of the trait, it may be difficult to collect a sufficient sample size for this design. Wender *et al.* (1974) did use this design for families with schizophrenia. Even though the adoption agencies try to avoid placing children in homes with a psychotic parent, some of these parents do develop psychopathology. However, this is a rare occurrence.

Another design features a classification based on the outcome (trait) of the adoptee, rather than the trait of the parents. Comparison of the adopting and biological families of affected and unaffected adoptees will yield information regarding the genetic and cultural factors. If the frequency of the trait is the same for both groups of adopting parents, but increased among the biological parents of affected adoptees, then a genetic factor can be inferred. Alternatively, if the increase in the frequency of the trait is mostly among the adopting parents of the affected adoptee, then an environmental factor can be inferred. Of importance for this design, as well as for the above designs, is that trait-status information be obtained in both of the biological parents as well as both of the adopting parents. Information in only one parent of a pair is only half the necessary information for making inferences.

Family Studies

The partitioning of variance models, noted above under twin studies, can, of course, be applied to other family studies. Harburg, Schull, Erfurt, and Schork (1970) describe a fixed family design incorporating the spouse, full sib, first cousin, and unrelated neighbor of the proband. Alternatively, Sing and Orr (1978) used selected full siblings, first cousins, and spouses to resolve a different variance components model. In their work they were careful to select only one pair per sibship so that the within-family correlation had a minimum effect on the model. Lange, Westlake, and Spence (1976) have described maximum-likelihood models which deal with the full family data. The maximum-likelihood estimation of these variance components requires complex computer algorithms, as do many of the analyses described below. A useful feature of the variance components model is that likelihoods can be calculated for each family separately. Test statistics have been proposed (Boehnke & Lange, 1984) which may be used to identify outliers that either are due to measurement error or do not conform to the polygenic model which is assumed by these models.

The methods of path analyses (Rao, Province, Wette, & Glueck, 1984) can be used with data collected on families of varying size to estimate the contribution of genetic factors relative to other specified factors. Path analysis has some similarities to the analysis of variance. Correlations between quantitative phenotypes, and even between qualitative phenotypes under certain assumptions (Rao, Morton, Gottesman, & Lew, 1984), are decomposed into the genetic and environmental causal components. However, the equations involve correlations and are generally nonlinear for the variables being estimated. These models, nevertheless, assume a linear and additive relationship between the causal factors, as to the variance components models. The path-analytic models and their maximum-likelihood algorithms have also been made more complex and generalized to include indices of the environment and multiple-correlated traits (Rao *et al.,* 1984).

A particular problem with path analyses, and with the analysis of variance models, indeed with all of the above mentioned methods of determining estimates of genetic variation, is that these estimates are population-specific (Schull & Weiss, 1980). The extent to which these variance partitions will apply to other populations is not clear. Not only are the partitions population-specific, but the latter methods depend on the assumption of linear effects and also upon the realism of the model. In many cases these may not be important restrictions. It can be argued that because most intervention strategies are themselves population-specific, this population-relative limitation does not negate the utility of estimating heritability and the application of these methods of analyses (Schull & Weiss, 1980).

NATURE OF GENETIC INFLUENCES

We now turn to the problem of the characterization of the nature of the genetic influences on a trait. In the previous section we were concerned with demonstrating that genetic factors contribute to the differences between individuals for a given trait. But exactly how that contribution is manifest is the objective of this section.

There are many, complex etiologies which involve genetic factors. However, there are only a few models of etiological processes that have been evaluated, largely because of the mathematical complexity of the analyses and the requirements of large data-sets of many kinds of individuals, such as sibs, parents and cousins, to utilize these models. The monogenetic model attributes much of the phenotypic variation to the effect of one locus. Hence this is also referred to as major-gene or single-locus in heritance. Of course, there is allowance for the rare sporatic case which might be due to new mutations or phenocopies: that is, phenotypically similar individuals who do not possess the relevant genotype. These phenocopies may be the result of environmental causes or a rare genotype at another locus. The polygenic model, on the other hand, assumes that the differences between individuals are attributable to genetic variation at many different loci, each having nearly equal and nearly additive effects on the phenotype. In practice, this is not different from the multifactorial models, which acknowledge the fact that the many sources of effects might be due to familially shared characteristics other than genes. The mixed genetic model hypothesizes a combination of both of the above models, that is, a major locus plus additional variation-in-risk due to polygenic or multifactorial factors. There are several computer algorithms available to differentiate between these hypothesized genetic etiologies. Each of the algorithms (discussed briefly below) can compare different sets of alternative models.

Other, more complicated, models, such as the two-locus or multiple-allele models have been proposed, but utilized in a more limited fashion. These have many parameters which either must be assumed or estimated. Hence, the interpretation of these results is less readily verified.

In this section we will change the pattern of the previous sections and discuss in detail the analytical procedures, rather than the sample selections. All of these analytical procedures use the data collected from family studies and pedigree studies.

Family Studies and Pedigree Studies

The distinction between family studies and pedigree studies is in large part arbitrary. Functionally, however, these distinguish between studies focused primarily on the nuclear family and studies of as many traceable relatives as possible in a few families. Rationales for the intensive study of one family includes the possibility that if the trait is heterogeneous then only one susceptibility gene will be segregating in the family, the possibility of unambiguously determining the linkage relationship between susceptibility genes and other marker gene(s), and the possibility of studying several affected members so that the presence of the susceptibility gene can be traced. However, there are disadvantages to the pedigree studies beyond the obvious problem of tracing many extended family members and obtaining their cooperation. If the susceptibility genes are not uncommon in the general population, then individuals who marry into the family bring their own susceptibility genes, potentially different from the one already segregating in the family. Further, the family members who bind various branches of the family together (e.g., great-grandparents or great-aunts), have usually died. Consequently, the co-segregation of genetic markers between the tested branches of the family must be inferred. Also, the diagnostic status of these deceased individuals must often be inferred because historical medical records are of different reliability and quality than interview information.

On the other hand, the family studies have the advantage that if the recurrence risk for the trait is low, information from several families can be combined. Further, different family structures and distribution of risk factors among families allow for the testing of hypotheses regarding the interaction of genotypes and risk factors. Comparisons between families make it possible to identify heterogeneity within the trait. The two major disadvantages of family studies are, first, that, since the data are pooled across families, heterogeneity may be missed unless it is being specifically evaluated, and, second, that the linkage-phase relationship between the gene of interest and genetic markers cannot often be determined unless extended family members are studied. In many cases, to determine linkage phase, the second degree family members such as grandparents, aunts, and uncles are required. That is, it is not always possible to determine whether the susceptibility gene is segregating on the *same* chromosome or on the homologous chromosome of a given marker (coupling or repulsion phase). In these cases, studying extended family relationships will help resolve the issue.

In a recent workshop at the American Society of Human Genetics, simulated family data were analyzed by several different groups. Several procedures were noted which improved the utility of families included in the data analyses (MacCluer, Falk, & Wagener, 1985). Families were selected for the data-set based on a minimum number of living offspring and grandparents. Further, the parents were first tested and only those families with at least one parent heterozygous for certain loci were studied further. Families were extended in a systematic fashion beyond the nuclear family based on the level of heterozygosity in the parents. These procedures insured that all of the families were minimally informative with regard to the marker loci. Of course, if the tissue samples are being collected and saved for future, as yet unidentified, markers, then these criteria cannot be applied. Such is the case in many of the current studies using DNA restriction fragment-length analyses for determination of markers. In these cases, many of the polymorphisms cannot be tested until later dates, so that one does not know if the family will be informative. Other data-reduction procedures were recommended prior to analysis of the data gathered from families. Even with the selection criteria designed to improve the information of the families, the investigators noted that many of the linkage relationships could be determined from as little as 25% of the families. Removal of untyped offspring, removal of collaterals (i.e. distant relatives), not important for the determination of segregation of common alleles, inference of untyped parents, and removal of impossible haplotypes from the data analytic programs, all serve to make the analysis of these data more efficient.

Models of Inheritance

Multifactorial inheritance is functionally not distinguishable from polygenic inheritance. This model assumes that many familial factors, including many genes, act to influence the presence of a trait or the susceptibility of an individual (Reich, Winokur, & Mullaney, 1975). Further, these factors are assumed to act in independent but identical ways to change the susceptibility. The mechanisms for this action may differ between factors, but the resultant change in the susceptibility is small and nearly identical. Therefore, a normal distribution may be assumed for the susceptibilities in the general population. Because these factors are familial, relatives of a given individual are assumed to be more similar to that individual than to the general population.

Reich *et al.* (1975) describe a way of evaluating the plausibility of the multifactorial model for a given qualitative trait. For these analyses, the nonage corrected prevalence of the trait among relatives and in the general population is utilized to obtain a maximum-likelihood estimate for parameters of the model. A goodness-of-fit statistic incorporating the expected and observed prevalences can be used to reject the model. The analyses can be extended to evaluate sex effects, random environmental effects, or generation effects. The goodness-of-fit statistics can be used to differentiate between these models, which do not, however, contrast the multifactorial hypothesis to any other specific model, such as the major-gene hypothesis.

The major-gene model, on the other hand, assumes that there is one gene, usually with two alleles, which is segregating in the population, and that an appreciable proportion of the variability of a trait between individuals is due to the segregation of alleles at this single locus. That is, the genotype of an individual at this locus can explain much about the trait of that individual. The exact relationship between the genotype and the trait status of the individual may be complex, such as dominant or, its converse, recessive, or an intermediate gene-dosage relationship. Of course, factors other than the major gene, such as the individual's environment or other loci, may alter the expression of the genotype in small ways. The expression of a genotype is referred to as its penetrance with regard to a particular phenotype. As these other familial effects become greater, the model becomes a mixed model, that is, a combination of the major-gene model and the multifactorial model.

Segregation Analysis

Segregation analysis is, then, the analysis of family data to determine the manner in which the susceptibility is inherited. The specific model of inheritance, for example, X-linked (on the X chomosone) or autosomal (on chomosomes other than the X or the Y), specifies how the susceptibility segregates in the family. A given family (mating) is said to be segregating if more than one phenotype such as affected and normal is present among a sibship of the family. Alternative models yield different risks for various classes of relatives, such as the offspring, siblings, or parents of cases. The compatibility of a particular model with the observed traits (i.e., the segregation patterns), in the families which are being analysed, is the basis of segregation analysis.

The segregation frequency, or segregation ratio, is the expected proportion of offspring in a given family who have a particular trait. The actual observed segregation frequency will depend on the mating types of the families, how the families were selected (ascertained), the frequency of sporatic cases, such as, mutation, errors in assignment or phenocopies, or heterogeneity for the trait. If families are selected through children, then the nonsegregating families (those families with no affected children) are necessarily not included. This creates a bias in the data set which must be accommodated in the analyses. Under restricted conditions the segregation ratio can be easily calculated from nuclear family data, without the use of computer algorithms (Vogel & Motulsky, 1979). The number of families required for a meaningful study will depend on these various sources of bias and on the value of the true segregation ratio. Wong and Rotter (1984) give some guidelines for sample sizes.

The transmission-probability model (Elston, 1980) is a maximum-likelihood model which is a generalization of the traditional methods for the segregation evaluation of family data to complex pedigrees. This model actually allows for tests of Mendelian segregation. The model has little power to differentiate between major gene and multifactorial (polygenic) inheritance, although it may be able to detect some kinds of non-major gene transmission, such as cultural habituation. The analyses have been extended to allow for the analysis of multivariate traits and to allow for different age-of-onset distributions, depending upon the genotype of the individual (Bucher & Elston, 1981).

The mixed model (Lalouel, 1984) is an analytic routine which includes both a single locus and a multilocus (multifactorial) component, and is, therefore, designed to distinguish between these two hypotheses. The mixed model does not estimate the transmission probabilities between generations, but utilizes Mendelian segregation frequencies with variable penetrance. It is ideal for detecting a major gene in the presence of polygenic inheritance, provided there is no other non-major gene transmission occurring. This algorithm is also a maximum likelihood procedure, originally designed for nuclear families. In fact, the calculations required for an exact implementation to extended pedigrees is so complex as to force the use of approximate numerical integration in the functioning programs for extended family data. The model has been extended to include environmental correlation between siblings.

Finally, a unified model has been developed which incorporates the mixed model with the single locus parameterized in terms of the transmission probability model (Lalouel, 1984). This is, therefore, a combination of each of the above algorithms. The model incorporates the flexibility of the transmission model to estimate segregation frequencies (transmission probabilities) other than the classic Mendelian frequencies, and also the ability to estimate the contributions of both the major gene and multifactorial inheritance. This computer model should be able to evaluate several hypotheses. However, the numbers of parameters to be estimated and the need to reduce standard errors of the estimates so that meaningful tests can be performed mean that the numbers of families and of individuals needed in a study are not trivial.

Linkage Analyses

The above methods of segregation analyses utilize only the trait phenotypes of individuals in the families to resolve the segregation patterns of these genes. However, other Mendelian inherited genes, known as markers, can be used to verify the model of genetic transmission. The principle of linkage analysis if that alleles of genes which are physically close to one another on a chomosome are usually inherited together. Therefore, if the segregation of alleles at one of the loci is unambiguously determined, then the segregation of the alleles at the linked locus may be inferred, based on the genotype at the unambiguously determined "marker" locus.

Of course, there are several circumstances under which the process is not as ambiguous as the above discussion may imply. For instance, with greater distance between the two genes, recombinations between them will occur, leaving the inference of the susceptibility locus in doubt. Any distance greater than 10 centiMorgans means that more than 20% of the time the genotype at the vulnerability gene cannot be directly inferred from the marker gene. Another complicating situation is that alleles at the marker locus may be associated with the trait, either because this locus, too, is etiologically important, or because the linkage is tight enough that the association is artifactual. Another problem arises if there are heterogeneous causes for the trait distribution at the susceptibility locus. That is, the gene linked to the marker may explain some of the susceptibility in the population, but another gene located elsewhere may be responsible for the susceptibility of many cases. Further, sporadic cases due to nongenetic factors or to new mutations also make the interpretation difficult. Nevertheless, linkage remains one of the best ways, statistically, to demonstrate the inheritance pattern of a gene for a specific trait. Understanding the mode of inheritance can contribute to the elucidation of the biochemical and physiological mechanisms of susceptibility, as well as contribute to the risk assessment of individuals within a family. The sample size needed to demonstrate linkage depends on the recombinational distance, penetrance, and family size, among other factors. Some guidelines are discussed by Skolnick, Bishop, Cannings and Hasstedt (1984).

In general, linkage analyses utilize information from all family members. However, in many situations the trait status cannot be unambiguously determined in many individuals within the family. For instance, some disorders are not expressed until the individual has reached a certain age. In such cases, all individuals in the family younger than that age have unknown trait status unless they are already affected by the trait. In these instances a method known as affected sib–pair analysis can be utilized (Louis, Thomson, & Payami, 1983). For this method, only the marker-gene information of affected siblings and probands is utilized. Of course, other family members may need to have blood tests done to help determine the segregation of the marker gene in the pairs of affected siblings. However, for the linkage analyses, only the affected siblings are used. Since these individuals are alike for the trait, they would also tend to be alike for any marker gene which is linked to the trait gene. The extent to which this is true depends on the dominance at the trait locus, distance between the two loci, and heterogeneity of the disorder.

The most frequently utilized algorithm for linkage analyses is the LIPED routine (Ott, 1974). This routine will calculate the relative likelihood of a vulnerability gene linked to a marker, given a specified model of Mendelian inheritance. That is to say, the gene frequencies, penetrances of the genotypes and other parameters are specified, not tested or estimated, for the algorithm. Other algorithms (GENPED and LINKAS) also do the linkage analyses, subsequent to segregation analyses. Therefore, the potentially linked marker is not used to refine the estimates of the segregation of the vulnerability marker. In a sense, these linkage analyses are best utilized to verify the hypothesized segregation pattern and to identify linkages so that high risk individuals can be identified. At least one algorithm (PAP) can in fact simultaneously estimate segregation patterns and linkage.

IDENTIFYING HIGH-RISK VARIABLES

Of course, the ultimate goal of all of the above analyses is the identification of the most appropriate avenues of further research to elucidate the etiological process. If a trait is shown to have a large familial component that is not consistent with generalized Mendelian principles, then factors other than genes shared by family members are the appropriate areas for further research. If, however, genetic factors are shown to be important, the biological and physiological assessments which are also shown to be inherited are the appropriate avenues.

The above is, of course, a simplified view of the implications of these analyses. Certainly, most analyses do not yield such clear-cut implications. The most important reasons for an inability to draw definitive conclusions include the poorly-specified environmental effects in these models and the inability to incorporate dynamic features into them. Some modifications to the above algorithms would make the analytical difficulties and those of estimation almost insurmountable. There have been attempts to accommodate these criticisms, however. Rao and his colleagues (1984) have incorporated indices of the environment into their path-analysis models. However, these indices are not age-dependent or genotype-dependent. Further, the index is defined by multiple regression of potential environmental factors on the trait so that the correlation between the index and the trait may be artificially inflated. Eaves and his colleagues (1978) have extended the twin variance components model over the longitudinal assessments to evaluate the changes in heritability over time. In animals, the heritability for some traits has been shown to vary quite remarkable over the lifetime of the animal (Riska, Atchley, & Rutledge, 1984). Presumably, different genes which affect the outcome of the trait, or different environmental factors affecting the expression of a trait, are influential at different stages during the lifetime of an individual. Genotype-specific age dependence has been incorporated in the transmission-probability model (Bucher & Elston, 1981). However, other factors may affect the age-specific risk (penetrance) of a trait, as demonstrated by proportional-hazard analyses of risk factors affecting relatives of depressed patients (Stancer et al., 1985; Weissman et al., 1984).

The other major utility of the genetic analyses described previously is the identification of individuals at highest risk, so that further studies of biological and environmental factors can identify specific risk factors. For instance, the study of twins discordant for a certain trait (i.e. the cotwin study), can potentially identify different experiences leading to the penetrance, or lack thereof, of vulnerability. Rieder and Gershon (1978) and Cloninger, Lewis, Rice, and Reich (1981) discuss the determination of necessary and/or sufficient factors affecting the expression of an inherited vulnerability. These strategies can be used to further define the biological or physiological factors intimately involved in the etiology of a disorder.

SUMMARY

There are several different questions that can be asked regarding a trait and etiological processes which involve family studies. The appropriate studies depend on what is known about the trait. Certainly, the search for linkage is not appropriate unless some heritability has been demonstrated. Linkage analyses are also questionable without previous segregation analyses.

The most common misconceptions regarding the results from family studies are with regard to exactly what the studies have demonstrated. The failure to understand the assumptions of the complex analytic techniques and to understand what alternatives have been ruled plausible or implausible by particular analyses will lead the reader to assume that a particular genetic influence has been "proved." In large part, complex genetic analyses are exploratory, in that, a model is assumed and the appropriate parameters are estimated. It should be remembered that the estimation of parameters is an empirical exercise. Parameters can usually be estimated, but models can only be rejected. The presentation of particular parametric estimates of a model which cannot be rejected requires the reader to search further for verification of that particular model. Verification may mean the demonstration of the same estimates in another population, the use of another procedure such as linkage analyses to verify the segregation patterns which have been concluded, or the demonstration of specific risk factors which are compatible with the model. In general, in the psychiatric literature these latter means of verification have not been productive.

The other serious failure by many investigators has been to collect comprehensive family data. No one research design is perfect or can be utilized for all of the different questions addressed earlier. However, collection of twin assessments without additional evaluations of other family members will limit the utility of that population. Furthermore, the other serious oversight is the failure to collect sufficiently large sample sizes. Although it is true that some assessments are intensive and therefore cannot be done in large populations, the failure to publish standard errors of the estimates means that conclusions from many published papers have not been put in the proper perspective. In general, large populations are required for the estimation of models with many parameters.

REFERENCES

Baldessarini, R. J., Gershon, E. S., Weissman, M. M., Kidd, K. K., & Prusoff, B. A. (1984). Letters to the editor: Risk rates for depression. *Archives of General Psychiatry, 41,* 103–106.

Baron, M., Risch, N., & Mendlewicz, J. (1983). Age at onset in bipolar related major affective illness: Clinical and genetic implications. *Journal of Psychiatry Research, 17,* 5–18.

Boehnke, M., & Lange, K. (1984). Ascertainment and goodness of fit of variance component models for pedigree data. In D. C. Rao, R. C. Elston, L. H. Kuller, M. Feinleib, C. Carter, & R. Havlik (Eds.), *Genetic epidemiology of coronary heart disease: Past, present, and future* (pp. 173–192). New York: Alan R. Liss.

Bucher, K. D., & Elston, R. C. (1981). The transmission of manic depressive illness. I. Theory, description of the model and summary of results. *Journal of Psychiatry Research, 16,* 53–63.

Cloninger, C. R., Lewis, C., Rice, J., & Reich, T. (1981). Strategies for resolution of biological and cultural inheritance. In E. S. Gershon, S. Matthysse, X. O. Breakfield, & R. D. Ciaranello (Eds.), *Genetic research strategies for psychobiology and psychiatry* (pp. 319–330). Monterey, CA, Boxwood Press.

Day, N. E. (1969) Estimating the components of a mixture of normal distributions. *Biometrika, 56,* 463–474.

DeFries, J. C., & Plomin, R. (1983). Adoption designs for the study of complex behavioral characters. In C. L. Ludlow & J. A. Cooper (Eds.), *Genetic aspects of speech and language disorders* (pp. 121–138). New York: Academic Press.

Eaves, L. J. (1977). Inferring the causes of human variation. *Journal of Royal Statistical Society, Series A (General), 140,* 324–355.

Eaves, L. J. (1982). The utility of twins. In V. E. Anderson, W. A. Hauser, J. K. Penry, & C. F. Sing (Eds.) *Genetic basis of the epilepsies* (pp. 249–276). New York: Raven Press.

Eaves, L. J., & Eysenck, H. J. (1980). New approaches to the analysis of twin data and their application to smoking behaviour. In H. J. Eysenck (Ed.), *The causes and effects of smoking,* (pp. 158–235. London: Temple Smith.

Eaves, L. J., Young, P. A., Last K. A., & Martin, N. G. (1978). Model-fitting approaches to the analysis of human behavior. *Heredity, 41,* 249–320.

Elston, R. C. (1980). Segregation analysis. In J. H. Mielke & M. H. Crawford (Eds.), *Current developments in anthropological genetics: Vol 1. Theories and Methods.* (pp. 327–354). New York: Plenum Press.

Gershon, E. S., Hamovit, J., Guroff, J. J., Dibble, E., Leckman, J. F., Sceery, W., Targum, S. D., Nurnberger, Jr., J. I., Goldin, L. R., & Bunney, Jr., W. E. (1982). A family study of schizoaffective, bipolar I., bipolar II, unipolar and normal control probands. *Archives of General Psychiatry, 39,* 1157–1167.

Gottesman, I. I. & Shields, J. (1982). *Schizophrenia: The epigenetic puzzle.* New York: Cambridge University Press.

Harburg, E., Schull, W. J., Erfurt, J. C., & Schork, M. A. (1970). A family set method for estimating heredity and stress: I. A pilot study of blood pressure among negroes in high and low stress areas, Detroit, 1966–1967. *Journal of Chronic Diseases, 23,* 69–81.

Jackson, D. D. (1960). A critique of the literature on the genetics of schizophrenia. In D. D. Jackson (Ed.), *The etiology of schizophrenia* (pp. 37–87). New York: Basic Books.

Lalouel, J. M. (1984). Segregation analysis: A gene or not a gene. In D. C. Rao, R. C. Elston, L. H. Kuller, M. Feinleib, & R. Havlik (Eds.), *Genetic epidemiology of coronary heart disease: Past, present, and future* (pp. 217–245). New York: Alan R. Liss, Inc.

Lange, K., Westlake, J., & Spence, M. A. (1976). Extensions to pedigree analysis: III. Variance components by the scoring method. *Annals of Human Genetics, 39,* 485–491.

Louis, E. J., Thomson, G., & Payami, H. (1983). The affected sib method: II. The intermediate model. *Annals of Human Genetics, 47,* 225–243.

MacCluer, J. W., Falk, C. T., & Wagener, D. K. (1985). Genetic analysis workshop III: Summary *Genetic Epidemiology, 2,* 185–198, 1985.

McGue, M., & Bouchard, Jr., T. J. (1984). Adjustment of twin data for the effects of age and sex. *Behavior Genetics, 14,* 325–344.

Morton, N. E. (1982). *Outline of Genetic Epidemiology.* Basel: S. Karger.

Nance, W. E. (1984). The relevance of twin studies to cardiovascular research. In D. C. Rao, R. C. Elston, L. H. Kuller, M. Feinleib, & R. Havlik (Eds.), *Genetic epidemiology of coronary heart disease: Past, present, and future* (pp. 325–348). New York: Alan R. Liss Inc.

Ott, J. (1974). Estimation of the recombination fraction in human pedigrees: Efficient computation of the likelihood for human linkage studies. *American Journal of Human Genetics, 26,* 588–597.

Rao, D. C., Morton, N. E., Gottesman, I. I., & Lew, R. (1981). Path analysis of qualitative data of pairs of relatives: Application to schizophrenia. *Human Heredity, 29:* 325–333.

Rao, D. C., Province, M. A., Wette, R., & Glueck, C. J. (1984). The role of path analysis in coronary heart disease research. In D. C. Rao, R. C. Elston, L. H. Kuller, M. Feinleib, C. Carter, & R. Havlik (Eds.), *Genetic epidemiology of coronary heart disease: past, present, and future* (pp. 193–212). New York: Alan R. Liss.

Reich, T., Winokur, G. & Mullaney, J. (1975). The transmission of alcoholism. In R. R. Fieve, D. Rosenthal & H. Brill (Eds.), *Genetic research in psychiatry* (pp. 259–271). Baltimore: Johns Hopkins University Press.

Rieder, R. O., & Gershon, E. S. (1978). Genetic strategies: Approaches to the etiology of psychiatric disorders. *Archives of General Psychiatry, 35,* 866–873.

Risch, N. (1983). Estimating morbidity risks with variable age of onset: Review of methods and maximum likelihood approach. *Biometrics, 39,* 929–939.

Rosenthal, D., Wender, P. H., Kety, S. S., Schulsinger, F., Welner, J., & Ostergaard, L. (1968) Schizophrenics' offspring reared in adoptive homes. In D. Rosenthal & S. S. Kety (Eds.), *The transmission of schizophrenia* (pp. 377–391). Oxford: Pergamon Press.

Riska, R., Atchley, W. R., & Rutledge, J. J. (1984). A genetic analysis of targeted growth in mice. *Genetics, 107,* 79–101.

Schull, W. J., & Weiss, K. M. (1980). Genetic epidemiology: Four strategies. *Epidemiologic Reviews, 2,* 1–18.

Sing, C. F., & Orr, J. D. (1978). Analysis of genetic and environmental sources of variation in serum cholesterol in Tecumseh, Michigan: IV. Separation of polygene from common environmental effects. *American Journal of Human Genetics, 30,* 491–504.

Skolnick, M. H., Bishop, D. T., Cannings, C., & Hasstedt, S. J. (1984). The impact of RFLPs on human gene mapping. In D. C. Rao, R. C. Elston, L. H. Kuller, M. Feinleib, C. Carter, & R. Havlik (Eds.), *Genetic epidemiology of coronary heart disease: Past, present, and future* (pp. 271–292). New York: Alan R. Liss.

Slater, E., & Cowie, V. (1971). *The genetics of mental disorders.* London: Oxford University Press.

Stancer, H. C., Persad, E., Wagener, D. K., & Jorna T. (1985). Evidence for homogeneity of major depression and bipolar affective disorder. *Journal of Psychiatric Research,* in press.

Sturt, E., Kumakura, N., & Der, G. (1984). How depressing life is—Life-long morbidity risk for depressive disorder in the general population. *Journal of Affective Disorders, 7,* 109–122.

Vogel, F., & Motulsky, A. G. (1979). *Human genetics: Problems and approaches.* New York: Springer-Verlag.

Weissman, M. M., Wichramaratne, P., Merikangas, K. R., Leckman, J. F., Prusoff, B. A., Caruso, K. A. Kidd, K. K., & Gammon, D. (1984). Onset of major depression in early adulthood: Increased familial loading and specificity. *Archives of General Psychiatry, 41,* 1136–1143.

Wender, P. H., Rosenthal, D., Kety, S. S., Schulsinger, F., & Welner, J. (1974). Crossfostering: A research strategy for clarifying the role of genetic and experiential factors in the etiology of schizophrenia. *Archives of General Psychiatry, 30,* 121–128.

Williams, R. R. (1984). The genetic epidemiology of hypertension: A review of past studies and current results for 948 persons in 48 Utah pedigrees. In D. C. Rao, R. C. Elston, L. H. Kuller, M. Feinleib, C. Carter, & R. Havlik (Eds), *Genetic epidemiology of coronary heart disease: Past, present, and future* (pp. 419–442). New York: Alan R. Liss.

Wong, F. L., & Rotter, J. I. (1984). Sample-size calculations in segregation analysis. *American Journal of Human Genetics, 36,* 1279–1297.

8

Developmental Considerations

CYNTHIA G. LAST

INTRODUCTION

Historically, adult models of psychopathology and diagnostic schemes have served as prototypes for classifying psychiatric disturbances in children and adolescents. This may be due, at least in part, to the fact that the study of child psychopathology is of relatively recent origin, lagging a century or more behind that of adult psychopathology (Achenbach, 1980; Ollendick & Hersen, 1983).

Extrapolating diagnostic constructs directly from adults to children implies several relationships between adult and child psychopathology that may or may not be accurate. First, this framework indirectly suggests that childhood is the root of most adult psychopathology. Second, it similarly implies that there is a direct relationship between symptoms manifested during childhood and those appearing during adulthood (i.e., that early psychiatric disturbances have predictive validity for later psychopathology). Third, and most importantly, it assumes that differences in level of development (e.g., cognitive, social, biological, psychosexual, educational) are unimportant for understanding child psychopathology, with children essentially representing "little adults" (see Achenbach, 1980; Ollendick & Hersen, 1983).

The diagnostic classification system of the American Psychiatric Association has, over the years, reflected this trend of applying nosological constructs derived from adult disorders to children. Indeed, it was not until publication of DSM-II (American Psychiatric Association, 1968)

CYNTHIA G. LAST • Department of Psychiatry, Western Psychiatric Institute and Clinic, University of Pittsburgh School of Medicine, Pittsburgh, PA 15213. The research of this chapter was supported in part by NIMH Grant MH 00546-01.

that childhood disorders (other than adjustment reaction and childhood schizophrenia) were recognized. While in DSM-III (American Psychiatric Association, 1980), the number and type of psychiatric disorders included for children has expanded considerably, it appears that the manual continues to reflect this theoretical bent (i.e., extrapolating from adults to children).

The tradition of applying nosological constructs derived from adult disorders to children is continued in DSM-III in two ways: (1) use of the *same criteria* for adults and children for many major psychiatric disorders (e.g., schizophrenia, major depression, phobic disorders, obsessive-compulsive disorder, somatization disorder, etc.), and (2) inclusion of diagnostic categories in the childhood and adolescence section of the manual that are *functionally equivalent* to other categories that are based on constructs derived from adult psychiatric populations (e.g., separation anxiety disorder—agoraphobia, overanxious disorder—generalized anxiety disorder, conduct disorder—antisocial personality disorder, etc.). While this approach may be valid and useful for understanding and diagnosing certain psychiatric disturbances in children (as ascertained empirically by investigating the reliability and validity of the diagnostic categories in question), its advantages for other disorders are unclear.

It is only by evaluating the reliability and validity of specific diagnostic categories with children and adolescents that the suitability of this approach to child psychopathology and classification can be assessed. In this chapter, we consider the specific issues involved in evaluating both the reliability and validity of DSM-III diagnoses in children and adolescents. In the first part of the chapter, results from DSM-III diagnostic reliability studies with children and adolescents are examined, and methodological issues pertinent to conducting this type of research discussed. Following this, methodological issues that are central to executing research on diagnostic validity are covered, with particular attention paid to family and follow-up studies.

DIAGNOSTIC RELIABILITY

One of the earliest and most comprehensive examinations of the reliability of DSM-III diagnoses in children and adolescents was conducted with the 1978 draft of the manual during a two-year field trial sponsored by the National Institute of Mental Health (Williams & Spitzer, 1980). During Phase I of the study, 71 children and adolescents were interviewed. Approximately 60% of these individuals were evaluated in two separate interviews conducted by two different clinicians, while the remainder were evaluated with both clinicians being present at the same interview. During Phase II, 55 children and adolescents were interviewed. Approximately 67% received separate evaluations, while the remainder were assessed with joint interviews. Approximately 84 clinicians evaluated the total of 126 child and adolescent patients.

Kappa coefficients for Axis I disorders during Phase I revealed good agreement (i.e., a kappa coefficient at or above .70) for only 10 of the 23 psychiatric disorders. Moreover, many of the reliability coefficients were calculated with inclusion of only one or two patients (i.e., Stereotyped Movement Disorders, Anxiety Disorders, Somatoform Disorders, and Psychosexual Disorders). Therefore, excluding those disorders that had less than three cases, good agreement was evident for only six diagnostic categories. These include: Mental Retardation, Other Disorders of Infancy, Childhood, or Adolescence, Pervasive Developmental Disorders, Substance Use Disorders, Schizophrenic Disorders, and Psychotic Disorders Not Elsewhere Classified. Very poor reliability, for diagnostic categories that contained at least three cases, was shown for three disorders: Anxiety Disorders of Childhood or Adolescence (.25), Major Affective Disorders (.36), and Other Specific Affective Disorders (.38).

During Phase II of the field trial, good agreement was obtained for six disorders. Eliminating three of these that had less than three cases, only three diagnostic categories reached the criteria of .70. These include: Mental Retardation, Other Disorders of Infancy, Childhood, or Adolescence, and Eating Disorders. Observing kappa coefficients for diagnoses that had three or more cases, unacceptably low levels of agreement were evident for five disorders: Anxiety Disorders of Childhood or Adolescence (.44), Major Affective Disorders (−.02), Other Specific Affective Disorders (−.02), Adjustment Disorder, (.36), and Psychological Factors Affecting Physical Condition (-.02). Combining results from both phases of the study, it is clear that consistently high agreement was shown only for Mental Retardation and Other Disorders of Infancy, Childhood, or Adolescence, while consistently low agreement was observed for Anxiety Disorders of Childhood or Adolescence, Major Affective Disorders, and Other Specific Affective Disorders.

Strober, Green, and Carlson (1981) evaluated the reliability of DSM-III diagnoses with a sample of 95 hospitalized adolescents. Unlike the DSM-III field trial, all patients were evaluated by the same two clinicians during joint interviews (i.e., counterbalanced interviewer–observer paradigm). Also in contrast to the field trial, patients in this study received a structured interview with the *Schedule for Affective Disorders and Schizophrenia* (SADS) (Endicott & Spitzer, 1978). DSM-III diagnoses were assigned independently by the two interviewers using the 1977 draft of the manual.

Ten Axis I categories were used for classifying the psychiatric disorders of the sample for diagnoses that had a frequency greater than one. Table 1 shows obtained levels of agreement for each of these categories. As indicated, the majority of categories (seven) obtained levels of agreement above .70, although three of these categories only contained two cases each. Relatively poor agreement emerged only for one diagnostic group—Anxiety Disorders of Childhood or Adolescence (.47).

The superior levels of agreement obtained in this study, as compared to the DSM-III field trial, probably are due to three factors. First, in the Strober, Green, and Carlson (1981) investigation, all interviews were conducted jointly, while in the Williams and Spitzer (1980) study, approximately one-third of the interviews were conducted in this manner. Joint interviews generally are considered to be a less stringent test of reliability than separate interviews because the interviewers have access to exactly the same information (Grove, Andreasen, McDonald-Scott, Keller, & Shapiro, 1981). Second, a structured diagnostic interview (SADS) was utilized by Strober and colleagues, while the field trial used unstructured clinical interviews to collect information on psychopathology. As in the case of joint interviews, use of structured psychiatric interviews has been found to increase diagnostic reliability by reducing information variance. Finally, the hospitalized adolescent sample had a smaller range of types of psychopathology, which also may have increased the probability of diagnostic agreement.

Table 1. Kappa Coefficients of Agreement for Axis I DSM-III Diagnosis for Adolescents

	Kappa	Percentage
Schizophrenic disorders	.82	15.7
Schizoaffective disorders	.63	4.2
Major affective disorders	.75	17.8
Substance use disorders	1.00	2.1
Anxiety disorders	.64	2.1
Anxiety disorders of childhood or adolescence	.47	6.3
Somatoform disorders	1.00	2.1
Eating disorders	.94	11.5
Conduct disorders	.75	22.1
Other disorders of childhood or adolescence	1.00	2.1

Note. From "Reliability of Psychiatric Diagnosis in Hospitalized Adolescents" by M. Strober, J. Green, and G. Carlson, 1981. *Archives of General Psychiatry, 38,* pp. 141–145. Copyright 1981 by the American Medical Association. Reprinted by Permission.

It is of interest that both the DSM-III field trial and Strober and colleagues obtained relatively low agreement for the same diagnostic category: Anxiety Disorders of Childhood or Adolescence. DSM-III distinguishes three anxiety disorders of childhood and adolescence, including separation anxiety disorder, avoidant disorder, and overanxious disorder. Both separation anxiety and avoidant disorders have not been included in previous versions of the DSM, while overanxious disorder ("overanxious reaction") was specified as a diagnostic category for children and adolescents in DSM-II (American Psychiatric Association, 1968). Given the fairly recent conceptualization of two of these three disorders, questions regarding diagnostic reliability (and validity) become of paramount importance.

In a preliminary investigation of the reliabiity and validity of the DSM-III diagnostic category of Anxiety Disorders of Childhood or Adolescence, Last, Hersen, Kazdin, Finkelstein, and Strauss (in press) assessed the reliability of these diagnoses using the *Interview Schedule for Children* (ISC) (Kovacs, 1978, 1983a) with 65 outpatient children and adolescents. The ISC primarily was chosen for use in this project because of its previously demonstrated interrater reliability for *anxiety symptoms,* as well as a broad range of other psychiatric symptoms or indices of psychopathology (Kovacs, 1983b).

As in the study conducted by Strober, Green, and Carlson, all patients were interviewed by the same pair of clinicians. However, here patients were evaluated during two separate interviews, using a short-term (morning-afternoon) test–retest paradigm (Grove *et al.,* 1981). A short test–retest interval specifically was used in order to minimize the likelihood of patient change over time.

Although most of the patients included in the study did receive some type of anxiety diagnosis, almost all of these children were diagnosed as having other concurrent disorders as well. Therefore, kappa coefficients of agreement are reported for 10 diagnoses (n ≤ 6 for each category). As can be observed from Table 2, almost all of the diagnostic categories (eight) showed excellent reliability (kappa > .70). Moreover, the two remaining categories closely approached this level of agreement.

In contrast to results obtained from the two investigators cited earlier, extremely high agreement was obtained for the diagnostic category Anxiety Disorders of Childhood or Adolescence (kappa = .84). Moreover, kappa coefficients for each of the three anxiety diagnoses included in this subclass also were quite good (separation anxiety disorder = .79, avoidant disorder = .64, overanxious disorder = .81).

There are several possible reasons as to why Last and colleagues obtained much higher agreement. First, their study included a much larger

Table 2. Kappa Coefficients of Agreement for Axis I DSM-III Diagnoses for Children and Adolescents

	Kappa	Percentage
Disorders usually first evident in infancy, childhood or adolescence		
Attention deficit disorder	.86	35.4
Conduct disorder	.86	14.0
Anxiety disorders of childhood or adolescence	.84	63.0
Other disorders of childhood or adolescence	.67	37.0
Other disorders with physical manifestations	.73	7.7
Affective disorders		
Major depression	.84	29.2
Dysthymic disorder	.66	17.0
Anxiety disorders		
Phobic disorder	1.00	23.0
Panic disorder	.90	9.2
Adjustment disorder	.84	12.3

number of anxious children and adolescents. For example, for Anxiety Disorders of Childhood or Adolescence, Last et al. (1985) evaluated 41 cases, while Strober et al. (1981) assessed only six cases of this type. Similarly, during the DSM-III field trial, only six children in this category were interviewed during Phase I, and nine interviewed during Phase II. It seems likely that reliability was enhanced in the Last et al. (1985) study by the large number of children who participated, providing the interviewers with considerable experience in diagnosing these types of children. Second, it should be noted that the same two interviewers assessed all of the subjects in the study. Such a procedure is likely to increase reliability because it minimizes variance due to individual differences among interviewers. In fact, a more stringent test of reliability would be to include multiple pairs of interviewers who rotate across cases. Finally, Last et al. (1985) included children only if they were suspected of having an anxiety problem. Such a method of subject recruitment may result in interviewer bias, where interviewers anticipate, and subsequently diagnose, anxiety disorders more frequently, increasing the probability of agreement. A better procedure for assessing reliability would be to include consecutive admissions with any presenting complaint.

As suggested above, the study of diagnostic reliability may be influenced by a number of methodological factors, often making comparisons between different DSM-III reliability trials difficult. The number of patients interviewed in a diagnostic category, the number of interviewers participating in the study, the type of interview utilized (clinical/structured), and the reliability paradigm included (interrater, test–retest), all greatly effect levels of agreement. As such, it is clear that further investigations are needed to clarify whether (and which) DSM-III diagnoses can be given reliably to children and adolescents. It is only after diagnostic reliability has been demonstrated that one can begin to tackle the more complicated question of diagnostic validity.

DIAGNOSTIC VALIDITY

According to Feighner, Robins, Guze, Woodruff, Winokur, Munoz (1972), the diagnostic validity of a psychiatric disorder may be established primarily through follow-up and family studies. In this section, the methodological issues involved in conducting these types of studies with children and adolescents will be discussed.

Family Studies

Family studies generally are considered to be important means for establishing the validity of a diagnostic category. This type of study allows one to assess whether an increased prevalence of the same disorder exists among the close relatives of index cases. Such findings strongly suggest that one is dealing with a valid entity, independent of the question of etiology, that is, heredity and/or environmental causes (Feighner et al., 1972; Guze, 1967). It should be noted, however, that while most psychiatric illnesses have been shown to run in families, the absence of an increased family prevalence does not necessarily negate the validity of a diagnostic category, since not all illnesses show familial aggregation (Guze, 1967).

Information concerning familial prevalence of psychiatric disorders may be obtained by either the family history method or the family study method (Andreasen, Endicott, Spitzer, & Winokur, 1977; Mendlewicz, Fleiss, Cataldo, & Rainer, 1975; Thompson, Orvaschel, & Kidd, 1982). The family history method essentially consists of obtaining information from the patient or other relatives about all family members. The family study method, on the other hand, involves direct interviewing of all available relatives concerning their own present and/or past psychiatric illnesses and symptomatology.

The family study method has been noted to be the preferred technique for studying familial prevalence, since this method yields data that is more precise and accurate than that obtained through use of the family history method. However, the family history method remains widely used because it is often difficult, or impossible, to directly interview relatives. This is especially true in family research that examines close relatives of adult probands. In these cases, relatives of adult probands often are inaccessible because of geographic location or death. These factors usually do not constitute major problems for family studies of child probands. This especially is true for first-degree relatives, that is, the parents and siblings of child probands, who usually will be residing in the same household as the proband. In addition, because of the younger age of child and adolescent probands, one may anticipate that a higher percentage of first-degree relatives will still be living and available for interview.

Unlike family studies with adult probands, the first degree relatives of child and adolescent probands include parents and siblings only, since most of these youngsters do not yet have offspring of their own. When utilizing the family study method with these family members, as well as second degree relatives, the goal usually is to assess lifetime psychiatric illness (as opposed to current psychopathology only). Lifetime diagnoses are based on information obtained through unstructured (clinical) or structured psychiatric interviews and application of diagnostic criteria (e.g., DSM-III, RDC, etc.). Structured psychiatric interviews generally are the preferred means for collecting information on psychiatric history because they yield more reliable information than unstructured interviews.

There are several interview schedules available that are appropriate for use with adult relatives. One of the most commonly used instruments in familial research is the *Schedule for Affective Disorders and Schizophrenia–Lifetime Version* (SADS-L) (Edicott & Spitzer, 1978). The SADS-L particularly is well-suited for a family study because: (1) the interview schedule is one of the few available that specifically is designed to obtain information relevant to psychiatric disorders over an entire lifespan, (2) information obtained from the SADS-L can be used readily to formulate DSM-III diagnoses, and (3) available data indicate that diagnostic reliability is high for this instrument (Andreasen, Grove, Shapiro, Keller, Hirschfield, & McDonald-Scott, 1981; Mazure & Gershon, 1979).

Another instrument recently has been developed that offers certain advantages for use in familial research. The *Structured Clinical Interview for DSM-III* (SCID) (Spitzer & Williams, 1984) is a DSM-III based structured interview which incorporates diagnostic criteria from the major DSM-III disorders. The interview is easy to learn and administer, and requires only 45 minutes to one hour. It can be used to formulate both current and past DSM-III diagnoses. The instrument appears to have good face validity; diagnostic reliability currently is being assessed by the authors (Dr. Janet Williams, personal communication), as well as other independent investigators (e.g., Last, Hersen, Kazdin, Francis, & Grubb, 1986).

While both of these instruments adequately tap adult diagnoses, they do not explore in detail certain psychiatric disorders that are specific to childhood. When conducting a family study with child probands, one may be interested to see whether relatives have a history of the same disorder that the identified patient currently presents. For example, in investigating psychiatric illness in family members of children with separation anxiety disorder, it would be of interest to know whether the mothers (or other relatives) of these children had separation anxiety disorder when they, themselves, were youngsters. (Of course, it also would be of interest to examine the prevalence of adult anxiety disorders, such as agoraphobia).

In order to obtain information needed to determine diagnoses specifically applicable to children and adolescents, it may be necessary to administer sections of other interview schedules that have been designed for children and adolescents. Some DSM-III oriented instruments that have been shown useful include the *Schedule for Affective Disorders for School-Age Children* (Chambers, Puig-Antich, & Tabrizi, 1978), the *Child Assessment Schedule* (Hodges, Stern, Cytryn, & McKnew, 1982), the *Interview Schedule for Children* (Kovacs, 1978, 1983a), and the National Institute for Mental Health *Diagnostic Interview Schedule for Children* (Costello, Edelbrock, Dulcan, Kalas, & Klaric, 1984). Specific sections of these interviews may be administered to evaluate whether adult relatives have shown certain psychiatric disorders that are specific to childhood or adolescence (e.g., separation anxiety disorder, attention deficit disorder, conduct disorder, etc.)

Unlike family studies with adult probands, the siblings of child probands usually are under 18 years of age. Thus, it is necessary to utilize diagnostic interview schedules for children with these family members. The interviews mentioned above can be used for this purpose.

When analyzing lifetime prevalence of psychiatric disorders, morbidity risks should be age-adjusted, when possible, based on age-of-onset data. The Strömgren method or the Weinberg shorter method often are used to accomplish this, with the former method employed for psychiatric disorders that have detailed data regarding age-of-onset distribution, and the latter method used when such information is not available (Slater & Cowie, 1971). Age adjustment based on age-of-onset data is of particular importance in family studies with child probands because of the larger age span of family members. More specifically, morbidity risks will vary greatly for child siblings and adult relatives for certain psychiatric disorders (e.g., somatization disorder, bipolar disorder, etc.).

Follow-up Studies

Like family studies, follow-up studies also are considered to be important means for establishing the validity of a diagnostic category. A follow-up studies with child probands. One salient issue centers on the optimal time interval between follow-up assessments. In order to closely the original patients present with the clinical features of another psychiatric disorder at a later point in time. This may be referred to as the clinical course of the disorder or the stability of the diagnostic category. If a significant number of the index cases are found to meet criteria for any other psychiatric disorder at follow-up, this finding suggests that the original patients did not comprise a homogeneous group and that the diagnostic criteria for the disorders under investigation must be modified (Feighner et al., 1972; Guze, 1967). Second, follow-up enables one to assess whether marked differences in outcome or prognosis occur (e.g., complete recovery versus chronic illness) which, again, would suggest that the group is not homogeneous and that the diagnostic criteria for the disorder should be revised (Feighner et al., 1972; Guze, 1967). As Feighner et al. (1972) point out, however, marked differences in outcome

> is not as compelling in suggesting diagnostic heterogeneity as the finding of a change in diagnosis. The same illness may have a variable prognosis, but until we know more about the fundamental nature of... psychiatric illnesses, marked differences in outcome should be regarded as a challenge to the validity of the original diagnosis. (p.57)

Several important methodological issues arise when conducting follow-up studies with child probands. One salient issue centers on the optimal time interval between follow-up assessments. In order to closely follow the course and outcome of psychiatric disorders in children, more frequent follow-up evaluations than usually conducted with adult probands are preferable, due to the marked developmental (e.g., cognitive, social, biological, psychosexual, educational, etc.) changes that occur over relatively short periods of time. In fact, it may be advisable to reevaluate child and adolescent probands every three to six months to obtain an accurate representation of diagnostic stability and prognosis.

Another important issue concerns whether to include control groups in a follow-up study of psychiatrically ill children. As discussed earlier, follow-up enables an evaluation of the validity of a diagnostic category by determining the homogeneity or heterogeneity of index cases for clinical course and outcome. That is, in attempting to establish the validity of a diagnosis, one is concerned primarily with the homogeneity of course and outcome within the original group of patients. As such, follow-up studies that have focused on validating diagnostic categories usually have not included any type of control group in their experimental designs. In those studies where a control group has been included, it typically has been a psychopathological group that has been hypothesized to be related in some way to the diagnostic category under investigation (e.g., using bipolar controls for evaluating the validity of cyclothymic disorder, Akiskal, Djenderenjian, Rosenthal, & Khani, 1977; using schizophrenic controls for evaluating the validity of schizophreniform disorder, Coryell & Tsuang, 1982). In these cases, investigators are interested in making between-group comparisons, in addition to evaluating the course and outcome of patients within the diagnostic category of interest.

In a follow-up study of children, one may wish to include a psychopathological control group that has been hypothesized to be related in some way to the diagnostic group being studied. However, a psychopathology control group that has no theoretical or conceptual relationship or link to the study group may instead be included in order to serve a different purpose. In this case, comparisons between the study and control groups will allow an evaluation of the diagnostic specificity of the study group for clinical course and outcome. In other words, the comparison will enable an assessment of whether the course and outcome of the study group is *specific* to that diagnostic category or also common to children with another form of psychopathology. This point is of particular importance for follow-up studies of child probands because of limited information available about childhood psychopathology.

Similarly, a never-psychiatrically-ill control group can add information of importance in evaluating the statistical and clinical significance of findings obtained from the study group. For children and adolescents, inclusion of a never-psychiatrically-ill group controls for normal developmental changes that occur in youngsters (during the follow-up period), as well as the effects of repeated measurement (interviewing) over time.

In addition to the above, participation of children in psychopathological and never psychiatrically ill control groups helps to guard against interviewer bias, which is likely to occur if follow-up evaluations are only conducted with probands in the study group (i.e., one diagnostic category).

This added benefit applies equally well to follow-up studies executed with adult probands.

During a follow-up investigation, clinical course (diagnostic stability) can be assessed by repeating the original interview (with new interviewers who are blind to original diagnosis), and assigning DSM-III diagnoses based on current psychopathology. For prognosis, interviewers can assign ratings of outcome and episodicity after completing each follow-up interview. Last, Hersen, and Kazdin (1985) have developed a rating scale for outcome based on a classification system proposed by Coryell and Tsuang (1982). The scale takes into consideration both symptomatology and impairment in social/role functioning in classifying outcome. Moreover, assignment of outcome ratings using this system is not dependent on prior knowledge of probands' diagnoses, symptom severity, or impairment at previous assessment sessions. Thus, interviewers who are blind to information obtained from previous interviews are able to complete the ratings. Last, Hersen, and Kazdin's classification scheme for outcome ratings is outlined below:

1. *Recovered* (both a and b)
   a. Proband currently presents with a complete absence of symptoms.
   b. No impairment in social (family/peers) or role (school) functioning due to psychopathology has been evident for at least two weeks.
2. *Improved* (a or b)
   a. Proband currently presents with symptoms but psychopathology does not impair social (family/peers) or role (school) functioning. Symptoms have been absent for at least two weeks.

   or
   b. Proband currently presents with a complete absence of symptoms but impairment continues in social (family/peers) or role (school) functioning. Symptoms have been absent for at least two weeks.
3. *Unimproved* (a or b)
   a. Proband currently presents with symptoms which impair social (family/peers) or role (school) functioning.

   or
   b. Proband does not meet criteria for either of the other categories (i.e., "recovered" or "improved").

Ratings can be applied readily to children who are psychiatrically ill, as well as those who are not psychiatrically disturbed. In order to keep interviewers blind to probands' original diagnoses, the same outcome categories can be used to classify never-psychiatrically-ill controls, although the meaning of these categories will differ for this particular group of youngsters (i.e., "recovered" indicates no change, "improved" indicates the development of symptoms or impairment, "unimproved" indicates the development of symptoms and impairment). Thus, these ratings cannot be included in analysis of psychiatrically ill groups.

In addition to rating children as "recovered," "improved," or "unimproved," Last, Hersen, and Kazdin (1985) suggest that a more detailed picture of the pattern of illness/health during follow-up intervals be obtained by having clinicians also record whether recovery, improvement, or unimprovement occurred (1) throughout the entire follow-up interval, (2) episodically throughout the follow-up period (i.e., at least one clear-cut period of recovery, improvement, or unimprovement in addition to the current period), (3) for a sustained period at the end of the follow-up interval only, or (4) on a fluctuating basis (i.e., no clear cut pattern). In order to keep interviewers blind, never-psychiatrically-ill controls also can be rated for episodicity using this system. However, the meaning of these categories will differ for this group and their ratings cannot be included in analyses of psychopathological groups.

It should be noted that while outcome ratings provide information about the level or extent of psychopathology at the time of each follow-up assessment, ratings of episodicity provide more detailed information on patterns of illness/health occurring during follow-up intervals.

One variable that often has a major impact on results obtained from a follow-up study is whether or not probands have received some type of treatment during the course of the investigation. When a project does not include a intervention component (which is the case in most follow-up studies that are evaluating the issue of diagnostic validity), clinical referrals for psychiatric treatment often are made for participating subjects.

The methodological problems inherent in conducting a prospective "naturalistic" follow-up study (i.e., where treatment is not assigned by design and is not under the control of the investigators) rarely have been addressed directly. In reviewing such studies, it appears that investigators typically have recorded information regarding treatment received by patients during follow-up, but rarely have analyzed course and outcome data with and without exclusion of treated cases. Moreover, in the few cases where separate analyses have been conducted, criteria have not been provided for determining "treated" versus "untreated" cases.

It is suggested that future investigations, with probands at any developmental level, analyze course and outcome data both with and without exclusion of treated cases. In addition, detailed information regarding treatment received during follow-up intervals should be obtained and recorded. Cases then can be classified as "treated" and "untreated" according to specific criteria. Last, Hersen, and Kazdin (1985) have proposed the following criteria for this purpose for follow-up studies with child and adolescent probands (the criteria, however, are equally suitable for use with adults):

1. *Treated* (both a and b)
   a. At some time during the follow-up period, the child proband has received some form of *psychiatric/psychological treatment* (e.g., psychotherapy, pharmacotherapy, behavior therapy, etc.) administered by a mental health professional (e.g., psychiatrist, psychologist, social worker, etc.) or pharmacotherapy administered by a physician.
   b. For *psychosocial treatments* (i.e., nondrug therapies), at least three sessions have been completed, excluding diagnostic sessions (e.g., assessment interviews, testing, etc.). For *pharmacological treatments,* a known psychotropic agent has been administered at a therapeutic dose for at least the minimum amount of time required by that drug to achieve some clinical effect.
2. *Untreated* (a or b)
   a. The child proband has not received some form of psychiatric/psychological treatment during the follow-up period.
   or
   b. The child proband does not meet criteria for having received treatment (1 a and b).

It should be noted that significant differences probably will emerge between treated and untreated children during follow-up. For course of illness, it is possible that a greater percentage of treated probands will have no diagnosis at follow-up. However, such findings essentially will not hamper an evaluation of whether probands *develop the clinical features of another psychiatric disorder over time.* If treatment prevents the development of another psychiatric illness which would otherwise typically occur in the natural history of the disorder being studied, statistical comparisons will reveal this fact. For ratings of outcome and episodicity, it is possible that treated cases overall will show greater improvement during follow-up. Again, analyses will enable determination of whether these differences emerge.

SUMMARY

As noted in the introduction to this chapter, adult models of psychopathology historically have influenced the study and classification of psychiatric illness in children and adolescents. This trend has been continued in DSM-III in two ways: (1) use of the same criteria for adults and children for many major psychiatric disorders, and (2) inclusion of diagnostic categories in the childhood and adolescence section that are functionally equivalent to and based on adult diagnostic categories. By extrapolating diagnostic constructs directly from adults to children, DSM-III implies that developmental factors are unimportant or irrelevant for understanding child psychopathology.

Given the above, study of the reliability and validity of DSM-III diagnoses for children and adolescents is of central and current importance. In this chapter we have discussed the various methodological issues that are pertinent for conducting reliability and validity research with this population. We hope that this information will be utilized for designing and executing future investigations in this area.

REFERENCES

Achenbach, T. M. (1980). DSM-III in light of empirical research on the classification of child psychopathology. *American Academy, 19,* 395–412.

Akiskal. H. S., Djenderenjian, A. H., Rosenthal, R. H., & Khani, M. K. (1977). Cyclothymic disorder: Validity criteria for inclusion in the bipolar affective group. *American Journal of Psychiatry, 134,* 1227–1233.

American Psychiatric Association (1968). *Diagnostic and statistical manual of mental disorders* (2nd ed.). Washington, DC: Author.

American Psychiatric Association (1980). *Diagnostic and statistical manual of mental disorders* (3rd ed.). Washington, DC: Author.

Andreasen, N. C., Endicott, J., Spitzer, R. L., & Winokur, G. (1977). The family history method using diagnostic criteria. *Archives of General Psychiatry, 34,* 1229–1235.

Andreasen, N. C., Grove, W. M., Shapiro, R. W., Keller, M. B., Hirschfeld, R. M. A., & McDonald-Scott, P. (1981). Reliability of lifetime diagnosis. *Archives of General Psychiatry, 38,* 400–405.

Chambers, W. J., Puig-Antich, J., & Tabrizi, M. A. (1978). The ongoing development of the Kiddie-SADS. Paper presented at the American Academy of Child Psychiatry Annual Meeting, San Diego.

Coryell, W., & Tsuang, M. T. (1982). DSM-III schizophreniform disorder. *Archives of General Psychiatry, 39,* 66–69.

Costello, A. J., Edelbrock, C., Dulcan, M., Kalas, R., & Klaric, S. H. (1984). *Report on the NIMH Diagnostic Interview Schedule for Children* (DISC). Unpublished manuscript.

Endicott, J., & Spitzer, R. L. (1978). A diagnostic interview: The Schedule for Affective Disorders and Schizophrenia. *Archives of General Psychiatry, 35,* 837–844.

Feighner, J. P., Robins, E., Guze, S. B., Woodruff, R. A., Winokur, G., & Munoz, R. (1972). Diagnostic criteria for use in psychiatric research. *Archives of General Psychiatry, 26*, 57-63.

Grove, W. M., Andreasen, N. C., McDonald-Scott, P., Keller, M. B., & Shapiro, R. W. (1981). Reliability studies of psychiatric diagnosis. *Archives of General Psychiatry, 38*, 408-413.

Guze, S. B. (1967). The diagnosis of hysteria: What are we trying to do? *American Journal of Psychiatry, 124*, 491-498.

Hodges, K., Stern, L., Cytryn, L., & McKnew, D. (1982). The development of a child assessment schedule for research and clinical use. *The Journal of Abnormal Child Psychology, 10*, 173-189.

Kovacs, M. (1978). *The Interview Schedule for Children (ISC): Form C, and the follow-up form.* Unpublished manuscript.

Kovacs, M. (1983a). *The Interview Schedule for Children (ISC): Form C, and the follow-up form.* Unpublished manuscript.

Kovacs, M. (1983b). *The Interview Schedule for Children (ISC): Interrater and parent-child agreement.* Unpublished manuscript.

Last, C. G., Hersen, M., & Kazdin, A. E. (1985). *DSM-III anxiety disorders of childhood and adolescence.* Unpublished manuscript.

Last, C. G., Hersen, M., Kazdin, A. E., Finkelstein, R., & Strauss, C. C. (in press). Comparison of DSM-III separation anxiety disorder and overanxious disorders: Demographic characteristics aid patterns of comorbidity. *Journal of the American Academy of Child Psychiatry.*

Last, C. G., Hersen, M., Kazdin, A. E., Francis, G., & Grubb, H. J. (1986) *Psychiatric Illness in the Mothers of Anxious Children.* Unpublished manuscript.

Mazure, C., & Gershon, E. S. (1979). Blindness and reliability in lifetime diagnosis. *Archives of General Psychiatry, 36*, 521-525.

Mendlewicz, J., Fleiss, J. L., Cataldo, M., & Rainer, J. D. (1975). Accuracy of the family history method in affective illness. *Archives of General Psychiatry, 32*, 309-314.

Ollendick, T. H., & Hersen, M. (1983). A historical overview of child psychopathology. In T. H. Ollendick & M. Hersen (Eds.), *Handbook of child psychopathology.* New York: Pergamon Press.

Slater, E., & Cowie, V. (1971). *The genetics of mental disorders.* New York: Oxford University Press.

Spitzer, R. L., & Williams, J. B. W. (1984). *Structured clinical interview for DSM-III - Non-patient version (SCID-NP 5/1/84).* Unpublished manuscript.

Strober, M., Green, J., & Carlson, G. (1981). Reliability of psychiatric diagnosis in hospitalized adolescents. *Archives of General Psychiatry, 38*, 141-145.

Thompson, W. D., Orvaschel, H., & Kidd, J. R. (1982). An evaluation of the family history method for ascertaining psychiatric disorders. *Archives of General Psychiatry, 39*, 53-58.

Williams, J. B. W., & Spitzer, R. L. (1980). Appendix F. In American Psychiatric Association, *Diagnostic and statistical manual of mental disorders* (3rd. ed.). Washington, DC: Author.

III

Special Topics

9

Psychometric Research on Children and Adolescents

CRAIG EDELBROCK

INTRODUCTION

The study of child psychopathology has been dominated by two major assessment paradigms, the *medical* and the *psychometric*. The medical assessment paradigm, epitomized by the *Diagnostic and Statistical Manual (DSM)* of the American Psychiatric Association (1952, 1968, 1980) is founded on the assumption that psychopathological disorders are disease entities. The purpose of psychiatric diagnosis is to relate observed signs and symptoms to underlying brain pathology. Even when a specific organic etiology cannot be identified, as in the case of most child mental health problems, the goal is still to explain observed signs and symptoms in terms of an underlying deficit or disorder. Within this paradigm, clinical interviews, physical examinations, and laboratory tests are used to determine if a patient has a given disorder or not.

The psychometric paradigm, in contrast, grew out of attempts to measure individual differences in psychological traits such as personality and intelligence. Within this paradigm, there is less concern with identifying causes of psychopathology and more concern with describing target phenomena. Rather than inferring underlying defects and deficits that explain observed symptoms, the goal is accurate description of phenotypic variations in emotional and behavioral functioning. Research within this

CRAIG EDELBROCK • Department of Psychiatry, University of Massachusetts Medical School, Worcester, MA 01605. The research for this chapter was supported in part by NIMH grant MH40599 and by a Faculty Scholar's Award from the William T. Grant Foundation.

paradigm has relied on standardized assessment instruments, including psychological tests and rating scales, and has been characterized by the use of multivariate statistical procedures such as factor analysis and discriminant analysis.

The goal of this chapter is to review psychometric research on the assessment and classification of child and adolescent psychopathology. These studies have involved the multivariate analysis of data obtained from behavioral checklists and rating scales, and the quantitative scaling and standardization of such ratings. Specific assessment instruments will not be discussed in detail (for recent reviews see Barkley, 1986; Edelbrock, 1986; Edelbrock & Rancurello, 1985; Mash & Terdal, 1981; McMahon, 1984). In this chapter, the methods and findings of psychometric research will be surveyed, with an emphasis on studies aimed at identifying behavioral syndromes. The results of psychometric studies will be compared to child psychiatric diagnoses embodied in the third edition of the DSM (DSM-III). The utility of psychometric research, including the reliability and validity of empirically derived measures, will be summarized, and the achievements and future prospects of psychometric research will then be discussed.

AN OVERVIEW OF PSYCHOMETRIC RESEARCH

The goal of much psychometric research has been to construct more reliable, valid, and empirically-based classifications of child psychopathology than those offered in the DSM and other clinically derived taxonomies (e.g., Group for the Advancement of Psychiatry, 1966; Rutter, Shaffer, & Shepherd, 1975). A major focus of psychometric research has been on the identification of behavioral syndromes via factor analysis.

Syndrome Identification

Most factor-analytic studies of child psychopathology have followed similar research steps. A checklist or rating scale covering emotional and behavioral problems is first developed, and informants such as parents or teachers rate the presence, frequency, and/or severity of each item for a sample of subjects. Responses are then factor analyzed to summarize correlations among items in terms of a few factors. Each factor represents a subset of behaviors that co-occur and form a distinct syndrome. These empirically derived syndromes can be used to construct scales for scoring the raw checklist responses. Scores on two or more scales can be portrayed on a single profile which shows how much of each type of behavior a given child manifests.

Preliminary Considerations

Although the general rationale and methods of this type of research seem clear and simple, many problems and issues arise at virtually every step in the research process. First of all, what behaviors should be assessed? Most research aimed at syndrome identification is motivated by the lack of well-established syndromes and disorders of child psychopathology. Moreover, most psychometric research is not founded on a theory of maladaptive behavior that would guide the selection of target phenomena. Choosing which items to include in a behavioral checklist is obviously crucial since it determines the range of possible syndromes that can be identified. This problem is usually solved in a practical way. Target phenomena are simply selected by the investigator and may be broad (e.g., maladaptive behavior, emotional and behavioral problems) or narrow (e.g., aggression, hyperactivity, anxiety). A pool of items is then generated. Most behavioral rating scales comprise items drawn from several sources including clinical material, consultation with parents, teachers, and mental health professionals, the research literature, previously developed measures, and the investigator's personal judgment. Items are often pilot tested before the instrument is finalized. The initial item pool for the parent version of the Child Behavior Checklist (Achenbach & Edelbrock, 1983), for example, was drawn from case histories of 1,000 children and adolescents referred for psychiatric services (Achenbach, 1966). By design, these items covered a broad range of emotional and behavioral problems. The item pool was pilot tested in clinical settings and revised on the basis of feedback from parents and mental health professionals.

Behavioral checklists and rating scales differ tremendously in the target phenomena they are designed to assess and the nature of their items. These differences affect the results of statistical analyses designed to identify behavioral syndromes. Moreover, selection of items is only the first step in the research process. Numerous other technical and methodological factors influence the final results. Edelbrock (1983) has enumerated several technical differences among rating scales. Response scaling, for instance, can vary from dichotomous alternatives (e.g., Yes/No, Present/Absent, True/False) to multi-step scales of frequency or severity. The time frame for making ratings also varies from relatively short intervals such as a day or a week up to several months (or none specified at all!). Rating scales also differ in unit of analysis. Some comprise molecular items focused on tiny bits of behavior, whereas others comprise more molar items encompassing broad behavioral categories.

Even if all factor analytic studies employed exactly the same assessment instrument, there would still be major differences in results. For one, potential informants, such as parents, teachers, trained observers, and clinicians, differ in their perceptions, biases, and expectations regarding child behavior. They also differ in the nature and amount of their contact with children, and the settings and situations in which they observe and interact with children. Due to these intrinsic differences, syndromes derived from one type of informant are likely to differ from those derived from other informants. Second, the prevalence and patterning of reported behaviors depends on the subject samples. Factor analytic studies have generally been based on very haphazard and heterogenous samples of children and subject samples vary widely in size, degree of behavioral disturbance, age range, demographic characteristics, and numerous other variables. Third, factor analysis is neither a totally automated nor a perfectly objective procedure. It involves numerous methodological alternatives and some subjective judgments. Almost all published factor analyses of child behavior problems have employed principal components and principal factor analysis with varimax rotation (see Achenbach & Edelbrock, 1978, for a review). However, some investigators have used very lenient criteria for determining a number of factors, whereas others have used stringent criteria. Furthermore, the minimum cutoff point for item loadings on each factor has varied widely, as has the minimum number of items required to constitute a factor. Researchers given *exactly the same data,* therefore, would not necessarily obtain the same factors. Agreement across studies would also be obscured by the use of different factor labels. For example, in different studies similar syndromes encompassing truancy, vandalism, stealing, running away from home, and drug abuse, have been labeled *Delinquent, Antisocial Reaction,* and *Socialized Aggression*—terms that have quite different connotations. Unfortunately, labeling empirically derived syndromes involves subjective judgments and it is almost impossible to choose terms that are free from excess meanings.

Convergence across Studies

Given all of the methodological variations between studies, agreement on identifying behavioral syndromes may seem impossible. Factor analytic studies have in fact produced very heterogenous results. Surprisingly, despite differences in assessment instruments, informants, subjects samples, and methods of analysis, two global syndromes and numerous circumscribed syndromes have been identified in two or more studies. Among studies that have identified four or more factors, there is good agreement regarding the existence of narrow-band aggressive, delinquent, hyperactive, schizoid, anxious, depressed, withdrawn, and somatic syndromes. No one study has identified all of these syndromes, and syndrome labels have varied. Syndromes characterizing immaturity, obsessions-compulsions, sex problems, sleep problems, academic difficulties, and uncommunicativeness have also been identified in two or more studies (see Achenbach & Edelbrock, 1978, 1984, for detailed reviews).

In contrast, other studies have yielded only two or three factors representing more global syndromes of psychopathology. Studies finding a few global "broad-band" syndromes do not necessarily contradict studies that yielded many circumscribed "narrow-band" factors. Second-order factor analyses have shown that narrow-band syndromes of hyperactivity, aggression, and delinquency form a broad-band *undercontrolled* or *externalizing* grouping, whereas narrow-band syndromes of anxiety, depression, somatic complaints, and obsessions-compulsions form a broadband *overcontrolled* or *internalizing* grouping (Miller, 1967; Achenbach, 1978; Achenbach & Edelbrock, 1979, 1983). In other words, narrow-band syndromes are hierarchically related to higher-order broad-band syndromes. No one level of syndrome differentiation is intrinsically correct, and global broad-band syndromes may be useful for different purposes than more circumscribed narrow-band syndromes.

Considering studies that have identified broad-band syndromes, there is good agreement regarding two global syndromes. One has comprised primarily affective and neurotic problems and has been variously labeled *Internalizing, Personality Problem, Inhibition, Shy-Anxious, Apathy-Withdrawal,* and *Anxious-Fearful.* The other has comprised primarily behavior and conduct problems and has been labeled *Externalizing, Conduct Problem, Aggression, Anger-Defiance, Acting Out,* and *Hostile-Aggressive,* (Achenbach, 1966, 1978; Achenbach & Edelbrock, 1979, 1983; Behar & Stringfield, 1974; Edelbrock & Achenbach, 1984, 1985; Clarfield, 1974; Cowen, Dorr, Clarfield, Kreling, McWilians, Pokracki, Pratt, Terrell, & Wilson, 1973; Kohn & Rosman, 1972; Miller, 1967; Peterson, 1961; Quay, 1966; Quay & Quay, 1965; Venables, Fletcher, Dalais, Mitchell, Schulsinger, & Mednick, 1983). Taken together, these studies corroborate an almost universal dichotomy between affective/neurotic problems on the one hand, and behavior/conduct problems on the other.

Syndrome Replication. The conclusion that behavioral syndromes have been replicated across studies is based primarily on similarities in item content. To see much agreement across studies, one must tolerate considerable variability in syndrome content. No syndrome has been precisely replicated in separate studies. Even syndromes given the same summary labels differ in number of items, item wording, and specific component behaviors. Is the agreement across studies more apparent than real? Do similar-looking syndromes derived in different studies actually reflect the same behavioral domains? These questions are subject to empirical test.

When the same assessment instrument is used in different studies the replication of factors can be tested by computing *congruence coefficients* (see Harmon, 1976, pp. 336-360). Congruence coefficients greater than .80, have been taken to represent factor replication. According to this criterion, the two broad-band syndromes derived from the Behavior Problem Checklist (labeled Personality Problem and Conduct Problem) have been identified in separate factor analyses on diverse samples (Paraskevopolos, & McCarthy, 1970; Quay, 1966; Quay, Morse, & Cutler, 1966).

When different assessment instruments are used in the same study, correlations between the two sets of scale scores can be used to test for similarities between syndromes. Numerous cross-instrument studies have been published (see Achenbach & Edelbrock, 1978, 1983), and they indicate considerable correspondence between syndromes tapped by different measures. Achenbach and Edelbrock (1983, pp. 53-54), for example, have shown that the Aggressive scale derived from the parent version of the Child Behavior Checklist correlates very highly ($r > .80$) with the Conduct Disorder scale of the Behavior Problem Checklist (Quay & Peterson, 1983) and the Conduct Problem scale of Conner's (1973) Parent Questionnaire. Similarly, the Somatic Complaints scale derived from the Checklist correlates highly with the Psychosomatic scale derived from Conner's measure. Several other empirically derived syndromes appear to have counterparts in these three parent measures.

In sum, there appears to be considerable consistency across studies in identifying two broad-band syndromes and several narrow-band syndromes. Studies differ in their ability to resolve global syndromes into more circumscribed patterns, but the finding of numerous narrow-band syndromes does not necessarily contradict the finding of a few broad-band syndromes. Second-order factor analyses have shown that narrow-band syndromes are hierarchically related to broad-band syndromes reflecting the dichotomy between affective/neurotic problems and behavior-conduct problems. No level of syndrome differentiation is intrinsically correct, and it is an advantage to be able to score both broad-band and narrow-band syndromes from the same measure.

Methodological Differences between Studies

This optimistic appraisal of the net results of psychometric studies suggests that "the glass is half-full." Two broad-band syndromes and several narrow-band syndromes have been identified in two or more studies. However, one could argue that "the glass is half empty." Many studies have identified syndromes that have no clear counterparts in other analyses. Precise replications of factor structures across studies are nonexistent. What accounts for disagreements across studies? Do these studies yield a cumulative body of knowledge or a hodge-podge of random noise? Are behavioral syndromes ephemeral artifacts of statistical machinations, or can differences between studies be explained? Fortunately, discrepancies between studies can largely be attributed to methodological differences.

Instrument Differences. As mentioned previously, a major difference between studies is the assessment instrument. The number of syndromes identified is largely a function of the number of items assessed. In general, checklists containing relatively few items (e.g., Behar & Stringfield, 1974; Clarfield, 1974; Peterson, 1961; Venables, et al., 1983) have yielded only two or three syndromes, whereas checklists containing many items (e.g., Achenbach, 1978; Edelbrock & Achenbach, 1984; Miller, 1967) have yielded eight or more syndromes. Some instruments are narrowly focused on specific syndromes, whereas others are designed to cover a broad range of emotional and behavioral problems. This obviously influences the number and type of syndromes that can be identified.

Conners' Revised Teacher Rating Scale (TRS), for example, is focused primarily on childhood hyperactivity and conduct problems. Factor analyses of the TRS revealed three syndromes labeled *Conduct Problem, Inattentive-Passive,* and *Hyperactivity* (Goyette, Conners, & Ulrich, 1978). In contrast, the teacher version of the Child Behavior Checklist (Edelbrock & Achenbach, 1984) has broad behavioral coverage. Factor analyses for boys aged 6-11 yielded eight narrow-band syndromes labeled *Anxious, Social Withdrawal, Unpopular, Self-Destructive, Obsessive-Compulsive, Inattentive, Nervous-Overactive,* and *Aggressive.* At first glance, these two factor-analytic studies appear to disagree: one study yielded three factors, the other eight. However, three pairs of syndromes are very similar in item content. The factors labeled *Inattentive* and *Inattentive-Passive* both encompass distractibility, short attention span, daydreaming, failure to finish things, immaturity, and difficulty learning. The factors labeled *Aggressive* and *Conduct Problems* have a common core of items reflecting arguing, disobedience, temper tantrums, sulking, moodiness, and uncooperative and oppositional behaviors. The factors labeled *Nervous-Overactive* and *Hyperactivity* both contain restless and fidgety behaviors, but the former includes items such as nervous or tense and nervous movements, whereas the lattter includes items such as demands attention, disturbs other children, and excitable or impulsive.

Edelbrock, Greenbaum, and Conover (1985) have recently examined relations between the teacher Checklist and the TRS. Teachers completed both measures for a sample of 104 disturbed boys aged 6-11. Correlations between the two measures indicated a one-to-one correspondence between the three factor- based scales of the TRS and three of the eight factor-based scales of the teacher Profile. Specifically, TRS scales labeled *Inattentive-Passive, Hyperactivity,* and *Conduct Problem* correlated highly (p. < .001) with Profile scales labeled *Inattentive, Nervous-Overactive,* and *Aggressive,* respectively. These results indicate that three behavioral syndromes have been replicated across studies that have used different measures, factoring procedures, and subject samples.

The comparison between the teacher Checklist and the TRS illustrates several other methodological points. First, the TRS contains only 28 items, compared to 118 on the teacher Checklist. This alone may account for the large discrepancy in the number of factors derived from each measure. Second, three syndromes had very similar items, but were given different summary labels. These labels can obscure similarities between syndromes and can carry different connotations. The terms "nervous-overactive" and "hyperactivity," for example, can have different meanings to different people. Third, no syndrome was precisely replicated in both studies. The Aggressive and Conduct Problems syndromes, for instance, contained many similar items and correlated very highly with one another ($r = .90, p < .001$). Nevertheless, they differed in number and wording of items and some behaviors were represented on one version, but not the other. Fourth, only three of eight syndromes derived from the teacher Checklist were replicated. The remaining five (Anxious, Social Withdrawal, Unpopular, Self-Destructive, and Obsessive-Compulsive) have no counterparts in the Revised TRS. This is certainly because the TRS is more narrowly focused on hyperactivity and conduct problems. Factors representing syndromes such as anxiety cannot be derived from the TRS, due to the scope of the item pool.

Measures also differ in unit of analysis. Some address fine-grained molecular behaviors, whereas others address more molar behavioral units. The parent and teacher versions of the Child Behavior Checklist, for example, include the item *poor schoolwork.* In contrast, other measures are more fine-grained and include items such as *math problems, numbers problems,* and *concept problems* (Clarfield, 1974); *spells poorly, reads poorly,* and *makes failing grades in arithmetic* (Dreger, Lewis, Rich, Miller, Reid, Overlade, Taffel, & Flemming, 1964); and *spells poorly, reads poorly,* and *writes poorly* (Miller, 1967). Not surprisingly, such items correlate very highly with one another and form an Academic Disability or Learning

Problems syndrome that is not derived from measures that treat poor school performance as a single problem.

Subject Samples. Differences between subject samples also influences the number and type of syndromes that are identified. Analyses based on nonclinical samples are limited in their ability to detect syndromes of extremely deviant behavior. This point has been nicely illustrated by Venables, Fletcher, Dalais, Mitchell, Schulsinger, & Mednick (1983) who performed separate factor analyses of Rutter's (1967) teacher questionnaire on samples of normal and disturbed children. Three factors, similar to those labeled Hostile-Aggressive, Anxious-Fearful, and Hyperactive-Distractible by Behar and Stringfield (1974), were derived from data on the normal sample. Analysis of the disturbed sample, however, yielded five factors, some of which represented more circumscribed and severe behavioral syndromes. It follows also that factor analyses of data on more severely disturbed children, such as inpatient samples, will not yield syndromes characterizing less severely disturbed children, such as those seen in outpatient settings, and vice versa. Sex and age differences in the prevalence and patterning of behaviors also affect factor structures. As Achenbach and Edelbrock (1984) have pointed out,

> a sample of one sex or age group cannot yield syndromes peculiar to the other sex or age groups. Conversely, analysis of a sample containing both sexes or different age groups may obscure syndromes present in only one sex or age group within the sample. (p. 233)

These points have been documented in research. Few factor analyses have been conducted separately for boys and girls or children differing in age. One exception is the development of the parent versions of the Child Behavior Profile (Achenbach and Edelbrock, 1983), where factor analyses were conducted separately for boys and girls aged 4–5, 6–11 and 12–16. Several narrow-band syndromes emerged in all analyses, but some were age- and sex-specific. A syndrome labeled *Uncommunicative,* for example, was obtained only for boys, whereas a syndrome labeled *Cruel* was obtained only for girls. For boys and girls age 6-11, a *Depressed* syndrome emerged that was not evident among boys and girls aged 12-16. Conversely, an *Immature* syndrome was identified for boys and girls age 12–16, but not for boys and girls aged 6–11. Furthermore, when sex and age groups were combined, such syndromes were obscured in the factor analysis.

Informant Differences. Separate analyses of ratings by different informants such as parents, teachers, and mental health workers have yielded broad-band syndromes corresponding to the affective/neurotic versus behavior/conduct dichotomy. In their review of empirical studies,

Achenbach and Edelbrock (1978) concluded that most narrow-band syndromes had emerged in analyses to date from different informants. However, teacher ratings have rarely yielded narrow-band syndromes. Why has this occured? One possibility is that the degree of syndrome differentiation obtainable from teachers may be limited by the lack of opportunity to observe certain child behaviors outside the school setting. An alternative explanation is that most teacher rating scales contain few items (e.g., Clarfield, 1974; Rutter, 1967) or are focused on circumscribed syndromes such as hyperactivity and conduct problems (e.g., Conners, 1969; Goyette, Conners, & Ulrich, 1978), thereby limiting the range of syndromes that can be derived. Recent research supports the latter explanation. Given a longer checklist covering a broader range of childhood behaviors, teachers produce more differentiated syndromes (Edelbrock & Achenbach, 1984, 1985).

Some syndromes derived from teachers' ratings have no counterparts in analyses of parents' ratings, and vice versa. This is illustrated in the development of parallel versions of the Child Behavior Checklist and Child Behavior Profile for parents and teachers (Achenbach & Edelbrock 1983; Edelbrock & Achenbach, 1984, 1985). The parent and teacher versions of the Checklist contain the same number of behavior problem items. There are some differences in content, but approximately 80% of the items are contained in both versions. Response scaling is identical and the same factoring procedures were used in separate analyses of parent and teacher ratings. Subject samples were also similar in size, clinical status, and demographic characteristics. The same criteria were used for choosing number of factors and similar conventions were used in selecting factor labels. These analyses are the best pure test of informant differences to date, because many potentially confounding variables were held constant.

Separate analyses of parent and teacher ratings yielded several factors that were similar enough to warrant the same summary labels: Aggressive, Delinquent, Depressed, Immature, Obsessive-Compulsive, and Social Withdrawal. Some of these syndromes were age- and/or sex-specific, but all had counterparts in analyses of parent and teacher ratings. Additionally, the Anxious syndrome derived from teachers' ratings resembled the syndrome labeled *Schizoid or Anxious* derived from parent ratings. The Inattentive and Nervous-Overactive syndromes derived from teachers' ratings also encompassed items that loaded on the *Hyperactive* factor derived from parents' ratings. It appears therefore that teachers provide somewhat greater syndrome differentiation in the area of hyperactivity than parents. A major difference between informants involved the Unpopular syndrome which emerged consistently in analyses of teachers' ratings, but did not appear in analyses of parents' ratings. This syndrome, which comprised items such as *not liked by other children, is teased, poor peer relations, fights,* and *prefers to play with younger children,* probably reflects teachers' unique opportunities to observe children's social acceptance and peer popularity. Analyses of teachers' ratings did not yield a Somatic Complaints factor like that derived from parents' ratings. This no doubt reflects parents' greater awareness of children's somatic problems. Lastly, a Delinquent factor arose consistently in analyses of parents' ratings but emerged in only one analysis of teachers' ratings. It seems likely that teachers are less aware than parents of children's delinquent behaviors such as stealing, vandalism, running away from home, firesetting, and alcohol and drug abuse, because such behaviors generally occur outside of the classroom.

Factoring Technique. Differences in factoring technique have also contributed to discrepancies between studies. It appears, for example, that the familiar "eigenvalue greater than 1.0" rule for determining number of factors is far too lenient. Factors with eigenvalues greater than 1.00 often have very few high-loading items and they may represent trivial associations between redundant pairs of items. The high correlation between pairs of items such as *overeats* and *overweight,* for instance, can result in a two-item "Obese" factor. But such a tiny factor hardly represents a behavioral syndrome and it is unlikely that a two-item scale would have predictive power over and above each item taken separately. More conservative rules for determining number of factors, such as an eigenvalue greater than 2.0 (which makes more sense statistically) or Catell's (1966) *scree test* for number of factors result in the identification of fewer but more robust factors.

Relations to DSM-III

Do empirically derived behavioral syndromes align with child psychiatric diagnoses embodied in DSM-III? Some behavioral syndromes have clear counterparts in DSM. However, some empirically derived syndromes do not correspond to DSM diagnoses, and many DSM diagnoses are not represented in the results of empirical research. The degree of agreement obtainable is obviously limited by numerous factors. Several psychiatric diagnoses applied to children and adolescents do not represent behavioral syndromes. Diagnoses such as elective mutism (refusing to talk), pica (eating dirt, paint, etc.), enuresis, encopresis, simple phobia, stuttering, sleepwalking, and minor motor tics, for example, refer to specific symptoms rather than syndromes and are represented by *items* on many checklists and rating scales. Diagnoses of extremely rare and/or severe forms of psychopathology such as anorexia (self-starvation), bulemia (extreme binge eating), Tourette's disorder (multiple vocal tics), infantile autism, pervasive developmental disorder, conversion disorder, and dissociative disorders such as psychogenic amnesia, have not been identified in multivariate studies of children and adolescents. This is probably due to the fact that child assessment instruments lack items relevant to such diagnoses. However, even when such items are represented, too few children having such rare disorders will be included in any one research sample. A few subjects having an unusual pattern of behaviors will not affect correlations between items enough to modify factor analytic results. Factor analytic studies are more attuned to identifying behavioral syndromes that represent quantitative deviations in behaviors that are relatively common in clinical samples. Extremely rare syndromes are likely to be missed even when the relevant behaviors are assessed.

Many psychiatric diagnoses, particularly those based on patterns of observable behaviors, are similar to empirically derived syndromes. Attention Deficit Disorder with Hyperactivity, which reflects inattention, impulsivity, and overactivity, has been represented in multivariate studies by syndromes labeled Hyperactive, Hyperactivity, Hyperactive-Distractible, Immature-Hyperactive, and Impulsive-Hyperactive (Achenbach, 1978; Achenbach & Edelbrock, 1979, 1983; Arnold & Smeltzer, 1974; Behar & Stringfield, 1974; Conners, 1973; Miller, 1967). Attention Deficit Disorder without Hyperactivity, which reflects inattention and impulsivity but *not* overactivity, has less empirical support but corresponds roughly to syndromes labeled Inattentive, Inattentive-Passive, Daydreaming-Inattentive Distractibility, and Immaturity (Conners, 1969; Edelbrock & Achenbach, 1984, 1985; Edelbrock, Costello, & Kessler, 1984; Quay & Quay, 1965; Walker, 1976). The diagnosis of Conduct Disorder is broken down in the DSM into four subtypes: Socialized Aggressive, Undersocialized Aggressive, Socialized Non-Aggressive, and Undersocialized Non-Aggressive. The socialized versus undersocialized distinction, which is based on whether the child has established social attachments, has not been reflected in multivariate research. However, the aggressive versus nonaggressive distinction has been supported by studies that have identified separate syndromes of *aggression* and *delinquency* (Achenbach, 1978; Achenbach & Edelbrock, 1979; 1983; Arnold & Smeltzer, 1974; Conners, 1973; Edelbrock & Achenbach, 1985; Jenkins, 1966; Miller, 1967). A Cruel syndrome, identified in factor analyses of parents' ratings of girls (Achenbach & Edelbrock, 1979, 1983), is also related to Conduct Disorder.

Several affective/neurotic disorders have also been corroborated in multivariate studies (see Achenbach & Edelbrock, 1978, 1984). Overanxious Disorder resembles empirically derived syndromes labeled Overanxious-Neurotic, Anxious, Anxiety Symptoms, Tension-Anxiety, and Anxious-Fearful. Both Dysthymia and Major Depression have been represented in syndromes labeled Depressed, Depressed Withdrawal, and Withdrawal-Depression. Social Phobia overlaps with social withdrawal syndromes identified in many studies. In a few studies (Achenbach, 1966, Achenbach & Edelbrock, 1979, 1983; Edelbrock & Achenbach, 1984, 1985) an Obsessive-Compulsive syndrome has been derived which closely resembles the diagnosis of Obsessive-Compulsive Disorder.

The central aspects of Gender Identity Disorder, particularly wishing to be the opposite sex and behaving like the opposite sex, are included in the Sex Problems syndrome derived from the parent version of the Child Behavior Checklist (Achenbach, 1978; Achenbach & Edelbrock, 1979, 1983). Likewise, some of the key features of Somatization Disorder overlap with syndromes labeled Somatic Complaints (Achenbach & Edelbrock, 1983; Arnold & Smeltzer, 1974), and Psychosomatic (Conners, 1970, 1973; Goyette, Conners, & Ulrich, 1978). Syndromes reflecting academic and learning problems (Arnold & Smeltzer, 1974; Borgatta & Fanshel, 1965; Clarfield, 1974; Dreger et al., 1964; Miller, 1967) do not align with clinical syndromes coded on Axis I of the DSM, but do correspond to Specific Developmental Disorders coded on Axis II.

Some empirical syndromes are not reflected in a single DSM diagnosies. Syndromes reflecting immaturity, unpopularity, social withdrawal, self-destructive behavior, and uncommunicativness do not have clear counterparts in the DSM. However, some diagnoses are similar to two or more syndromes and some syndromes are related to two or more diagnoses. Both anxious and immature syndromes, for example, overlap with diagnostic criteria for Separation Anxiety. Uncommunicativeness encompasses behaviors such as refusing to talk, secretive, shy, timid, and self-conscious, which resemble diagnostic criteria for Elective Mutism, Avoidant Disorder, and Social Phobia. A Sleep Problems syndrome that has emerged in some studies (Arnold & Smeltzer, 1974; Dreger et al., 1964; Miller, 1967) overlaps with diagnostic criteria for Dysthymia and Major Depression. The social withdrawal syndrome that has been identified in many studies resembles both Avoidant Disorder and Social Phobia in the DSM.

A few DSM diagnoses can draw little support from empirical studies. Oppositional Disorder, for example, encompasses temper tantrums, stubbornness, disobedience, arguing, and provocative behavior. These behaviors have usually loaded on a larger aggressive factor. Oppositional and aggressive behaviors fall on the same behavioral dimension, but the former are relative mild and the latter are more severe. To date, there has been no support for a separate oppositional syndrome apart from more general aggressiveness. As mentioned previously, Separation Anxiety has not emerged as a distinct syndrome but has been reflected in both anxious and immature syndromes.

Utility of Psychometric Research

Thus far, we have concluded that several syndromes have been identified in two or more factor analytic studies and many of these are related to DSM diagnoses. Even if "the glass is half full" as this review suggests, several questions remain. How can the results of multivariate studies be translated into useful products for clinical practice, training, and research? The results of a factor analysis do not readily lend themselves to any practical applications. The identification of empirically based behavioral syndromes is only the first step towards improving the assessment and classification of child psychopathology. Unfortunately, there have been few attempts to translate the findings from psychometric research into useful assessment materials and procedures.

Translating Statistical Results

The steps for translating statistical results into useful products are clear. First, statistically identified factors must be translated into scales. This requires that a minimum factors loading be selected for determining which highly loading items or "salients" define the factor. As discussed previously, there are methodological differences between studies which influence scale construction. A high minimum loading (i.e., .40 or higher) will result in scales comprising fewer, but more highly salient items. Conversely, a low minimum loading (i.e., .25 or lower) will result in scales comprising more items, but many will be of low salience. In other words, the key items that define the factor may be washed out by numerous other peripheral items. There are no definitive rules for translating factors into scales, but in general a higher minimum loading is preferable, providing there is a suffecent number of items on each scale.

Second, procedures for scoring raw responses must be developed. Rather than weighting items by their factor loadings, each item is usually given equal weight when computing scale scores. In most measures, the score for a scale is simply the sum of raw responses for all items scored on the scale: raw responses are *not* weighted by their factor loadings. Since each scale contains only highly loading items, differences between factor loadings are minute and probably do not reflect the relative importance of different items. It may seem surprising, but scores based on unequally weighted items are rarely superior in predictive and discriminative power to scores based on equal item weights (see Wainer, 1976). Unit weights (i.e., all items are weighted 1.00) yield more robust findings. Of course, the use of unit weights also greatly simplifies the scoring of scales. Weighting items by their factor loadings is so difficult and time-consuming that it is impractical, and the advantages of such a cumbersome procedure are questionable to boot.

The third step involves standardization of scales. Raw scale scores rarely have intrinsic meaning, but can be used for comparing criterion groups and for plotting change over time. Standardization of scores greatly increases their utility and interpretability. The purpose of standardization is to locate scores on a continuum relative to some reference group. The most common reference group is children considered normal by some independent criteria. Inclusion criteria for normative standardization samples vary across studies. In some studies, a randomly selected community sample is used for standardization purposes, whereas in others additional criteria, such as lack of referral for mental health services or clinical judgments, are employed. To increase the precision of normative comparisons, norms can be stratified by major demographic characteristics such as age and sex. However it is done, normative standardization provides benchmarks for inferring whether behavior problem scores are within the "normal range" or are abnormally high. This makes scale scores much more useful in screening and diagnostic efforts, and provides a means of "social validation" in treatment and outcome studies (see Edelbrock, 1984, pp. 28-30).

These three steps are necessary, but not sufficient, for successful translation of factor-analytic results into a useful assessment device. Assessment materials, administration and scoring procedures, and guidelines for interpretation and use in clinical and research applications must also be developed. Few behavioral rating scales have been developed sufficiently for clinical and research applications. Among the best standardized measures are the parent and teacher versions of the Child Behavior Profile (Achenbach & Edelbrock, 1983; Edelbrock & Achenbach, 1984, 1985), Conners' Revised Parent and Teacher Rating Scales (Goyette, Conners, & Ulrich, 1978), The Revised Behavior Problem Checklist (Quay & Peterson, 1983), and the Preschool Behavior Questionnaire (Behar & Stringfield, 1974). Even when an assessment instrument has been developed sufficiently to be placed in the hands of clinical and research consumers, many research questions remain. The key issues, of course, are whether empirically based behavioral measures are reliable and valid indices of child psychopathology.

Reliability. Many psychometric studies have focused on determining the reliability of empirically-based measures. Different types of reliability have been explored. The *internal consistency* of scales is obtained by "correlating a scale with itself". A common procedure is to split the scale in two (e.g., odd items versus even items) and compute the correlation between both subscales. Various statistical procedures have been developed for estimating internal consistency, including corrections for restricted range such as the Spearman-Brown formula and the coefficient *alpha,* which represents the mean of all possible split half reliabilities for a given scale (see Kerlinger, 1973, pp. 442-455). Using these procedures, the internal consistency of most child behavior rating scales has been very high (i.e., .80 - .95). However, indices of internal consistency are computed from only one administration of a measure, so they sidestep major sources of error variance that arise in actual use. Differences over time and between raters, for example, are not reflected in internal consistency estimates. Internal consistency is therefore a very weak form of reliability and high internal consistency does not guarantee that scores will generalize across time, settings, or informants.

Test–retest reliability reflects stability of scores over time. Most parent and teacher rating scales yield high test–retest reliabilities (r = .80 to .90) over one-week to one-month intervals (see Achenbach & Edelbrock, 1978; Barkley, 1986 for detailed reviews). Reliabilities are generally lower (r = .50 to .70) for intervals from one to six months, but this may be due to true change in behavior over time rather than measurement error. The reliability of self-ratings by children and adolescents are generally lower than ratings by adults, but are still moderately high (r = .60 to .70). A recent study also indicates that the reliability of children's self-reported psychopathology increases with age and is much higher for adolescents than young children (Edelbrock, Costello, Dulcan, Kalas, & Conover, 1985).

Interrater reliability, which reflects agreement between different raters, depends upon similar exposure to the target child. Mothers and fathers, who observe and interact with their children in similar settings and situations, tend to agree pretty well when rating child psychopathology (r = .60 to .80). Parents and teachers do not agree highly on the presence and severity of child problem behaviors (r = .30 to .40), but this is probably due to true differences in children's behavior beween home and school. Parent–child agreement on child symptoms is generally low, but consistent patterns of disagreement have emerged. Several studies have shown that parents report more overt, annoying child behaviors, such as hyperactivity, disobedience, and aggression, than their children report about themselves. Conversely, children report more fears, anxieties, and affective disturbances about themselves, than parents report about their children (Edelbrock, Costello, Dulcan, Conover, & Kalas, 1986; Herjanc

& Reich, 1982; Kazdin, Esveldt-Dawson, Unis, & Rancurello, 1983; Kovacs, 1983; Leon, Kendall, & Garber, 1980; Weissman, Orvaschel, & Padian, 1980). The consistency with which these patterns of disagreement have been identified across studies suggests the existence of differing perceptions and biases between parents and children, rather than psychometric flaws in the measures.

Validity. Validation of behavioral measures is complicated by the lack of a definitive criterion for child psychopathology. Empirically derived measures cannot be validated against child psychiatric diagnoses because in most studies the latter have questionable reliability and validity themselves. In fact, the inadequacies of child psychiatric diagnoses have been a major stimulus for the development of empirically based measures in the first place. Validation of behavioral rating scales is therefore a complex task, involving numerous problems and issues. No one criterion can either prove or disprove the validity of a behavioral measure. Validation rests on a cumulative body of findings which relate the measure to a variety of criteria, each recognized as fallible.

The most common first step when validating measures of child psychopathology has been to evaluate their ability to discriminate between normal and disturbed children. Operational definitions of normality and disturbance vary from study to study, and any definition is fallible. Nevertheless, almost all empirically-based measures of child psychology discriminate well ($p < .001$) between normal and disturbed groups. Statistical significance alone, however, is a poor index of discriminative power. With large samples, it is possible for a scale to discriminate significantly between criterion groups, despite substantial overlap in scores. Unfortunately, only a few investigators have reported the degree of overlap (e.g., Achenbach & Edelbrock, 1981). The criterion-related validity of behavioral measures has been supported by their ability to discriminate between subgroups of children. The scales developed by Conners, for example, have been repeatedly shown to discriminate between hyperactive and nonhyperactive children (see Edelbrock & Rancurello, 1985). The recently developed teacher version of the Child Behavior Profile has been shown to discriminate between children independently classified as learning disabled versus emotionally disturbed (Harris, King, Reifler, & Rosenberg, 1984) and between diagnostic subgroups of disturbed children (Edelbrock, Costello, & Kessler, 1984). Validation efforts have also involved assessing relations between different measures that tap similar syndromes (Achenbach & Edelbrock, 1983; Edelbrock, Greenbaum, & Conover, 1985; Cowen et al., 1973; Kohn & Rosman, 1972; Lessing & Zagorin, 1971). In general, similar syndromes scored from different rating scales have manifested moderately high correlations with one another ($r = .50$ to $.80$), which lends some support to their validity. Rating scales have also been shown to correlate significantly with observational assessments of children's behavior (e.g., Kazdin, Esveldt-Dawson, & Loar, 1983; Reed & Edelbrock, 1983).

SUMMARY

The major achievement of psychometric research has been to provide stronger empirical support for the existence of numerous behavioral syndromes of child psychopathology. The results of psychometric studies have also been translated into assessment materials and procedures that have had widespread applications within the field of child mental health. These measures have improved the quantitative description of children's emotional and behavioral functioning and have been particulary useful in epidemiologic and screening efforts aimed at identifying disturbed children in nonreferred populations (e.g., Trites, Dugas, Lynch, & Ferguson, 1979). Behavioral checklists and rating scales have also played central roles in the evaluation of treatment effects, particularly in the area of childhood hyperactivity (see Edelbrock & Rancurello, 1985). Clinically, empirically based measures have been useful in (a) initial evaluations of children referred for mental health services, (b) formulation of diagnoses, (c) determining treatment priorities and goals, and (d) monitoring treatment effects. They are also useful for evaluating programs within clinical settings, agencies, and schools. Several emerging trends are likely to guide future psychometric research. First, there have been several appeals to reduce the proliferation of new child behavior rating scales and to concentrate on building a cumulative body of findings based on a few well-established measures (Achenbach & Edelbrock, 1978; Barkley, 1986). In the future, most investigators are likely to adopt one of the handful of highly developed measures, rather than developing their own. One exception may be in the area of self-report measures for older children and adolescents, where few omnibus instruments have been developed and where the need for solid psychometric work is clear.

Second, there has been a recent trend towards the development of coordinated assessment batteries comprising parallel instruments for different informants such as parents and teachers (e.g., Goyette, Conners, & Ulrich, 1978; Achenbach & Edelbrock, 1983). Such measures will be very useful in future research aimed at determining ways of optimally integrating disparate data from multiple informants into a comprehensive assessment of a child's emotional and behavioral functioning.

Third, the translation of empirically derived syndromes into taxonomic distinctions among disturbed children has received little research attention. Only a few studies have used taxometric procedures such as cluster analysis to construct empirically based classifications of child psychopathology (e.g., Edelbrock & Achenbach, 1980; Spivack, Swift, & Prewitt, 1971; Eisenberg, Gersten, Langner, McCarthy, & Simcha-Fagan, 1976). Quantitative methods for describing and classifying child psychopathology are the most promising alternative to categorical approaches such as the DSM.

Lastly, synergistic research combining both medical and psychometric paradigms hopefully will become more common. Neither the medical or psychometric paradigms have offered definitive achievements and both approaches have acknowledged strengths and weaknesses. There is equal need to determine the diagnostic correlates of behavioral measures *and* the behavioral correlates of psychiatric diagnoses. A major goal for the future is contributing to the evolution and refinement of psychiatric diagnoses of children and adolescents. The current effort to revise the third edition of the DSM (DSM-III-R) has drawn heavily on findings from psychometric research. This interim revision will not solve all of the problems of child psychiatric diagnosis, but it does represent an incremental advance, and more attention has been paid to empirical research than ever before.

REFERENCES

Achenbach, T.M. (1966). The classification of children's psychiatric symptoms: A factor-analytic study. *Psychological Monographs, 80,* (7, Whole No. 615).

Achenbach, T.M. (1978). The Child Behavior Profile: I. Boys aged 6-11. *Journal of Consulting and Clinical Psychology, 46,* 478–488.

Achenbach,T.M., & Edelbrock, C.S. (1978). The classification of child psychopathology: A review and analysis of empirical efforts. *Psychological Bulletin, 85,* 1275–1301.

Achenbach, T.M., & Edelbrock, C.S. (1979). The Child Behavior Profile: II. Boys aged 12–16 and girls aged 6-11and 12–16. *Journal of Consulting and Clinical Psychology, 47,* 223–233.

Achenbach, T.M., & Edelbrock, C.S. (1981). Behavior problems and competencies reported by parents of normal and disturbed children aged 4 through 16. *Monographs of the Society for Research in Child Development, 46,* (1, Serial No. 188).

Achenbach, T.M., & Edelbrock, C.S. (1983). *Manual for the Child Behavior Checklist and Revised Child Behavior Profile.* Burlington, VT: Author.

Achenbach, T.M. & Edelbrock, C.S. (1984). Psychopathology of childhood. *Annual Review of Psychology, 35,* 227–256.

American Psychiatric Association. (1952). *Diagnostic and statistical manual of mental disorders.* Washington, D.C.: Author.

American Psychiatric Association. (1968). *Diagnostic and statistical manual of mental disorders* (2nd edition). Washington, DC: Author.

American Psychiatric Association. (1980). *Diagnostic and statistical manual of mental disorders* (3rd edition). Washington, DC: Author.

Arnold, L.E., & Smeltzer, D.J. (1974). Behavior checklist factor analysis for children and adolescents. *Archives of General Psychiatry, 30,* 799-804.

Barkley, R. (1986). A review of child behavior rating scales and checklists for use in research on child psychopathology. In M. Rutter, A.H. Tuma & I. Lann (Eds.) *Assessment and diagnosis in child and adolescent psychopathology.* New York: Guilford.

Behar, L.B., & Stringfield, S. (1974). A behavior rating scale for the preschool child. *Developmental Psychology, 10,* 601-610.

Borgatta, E.F., & Fanshel, D. (1965). *Behavioral characteristics of children known to psychiatric outpatient clinics.* New York: Child Welfare League of America.

Cattell, R.B. (1966). The scree test for the number of factors. *Multivariate Behavioral Research, 1,* 245-276.

Clarfield, S.P. (1974). The development of a teacher referral form for identifying early school maladaption. *American Journal of Community Psychology, 2,* 199-210.

Conners, C.K. (1969). A teacher rating scale for use in drug studies with children. *American Journal of Psychiatry, 126,* 884-888.

Conners, C.K. (1970). Symptom patterns in hyperkinetic, neurotic, and normal children. *Child Development, 4,* 667-682.

Conners, C.K. (1973). Rating scales for use in drug studies with children. *Psychopharmacology Bulletin,* (special issue), 24-84.

Cowen, E., Dorr, D., Clarfield, S., Kreling, B., McWilliams, S.A., Pokracki, F., Pratt, D.M., Terrell, D., & Wilson, A. (1973). The AML: A quick screening device for early identification of school maladaption. *American Journal of Community Psychology, 1,* 12-35.

Dreger, R.M., Lewis, P.M., Rich, T.A., Miller, K.S., Reid, M.P., Overlade, D.C., Taffel, C., & Flemming, E.L. (1964). Behavioral classification project. *Journal of Consulting Psychology, 28,* 1-13.

Edelbrock, C. (1983). Problems and issues in using rating scales to assess child personality and psychopathology. *School Psychology Review, 12,* 293-299.

Edelbrock, C. (1984). Developmental considerations. In T. H. Ollendick and M. Hersen (Eds.) *Child behavioral assessment: Principles and procedures* (pp. 20-37). New York: Pergamon.

Edelbrock, C. (1986). Behavioral checklists and rating scales. In J.D. Noshpitz (Ed.) *Basic handbook of child psychiatry* (Vol. 5). New York: Basic Books.

Edelbrock, C., & Achenbach, T.M. (1980). A typology of Child Behavior Profile patterns: Distribution and correlates for disturbed children aged 6-16. *Journal of Abnormal Child Psychology, 8,* 441-470.

Edelbrock, C., & Achenbach, T.M. (1984). The teacher version of the Child Behavior Profile: I. Boys aged 6-11. *Journal of Consulting and Clinical Psychology, 52,* 207-217.

Edelbrock, C., & Achenbach, T.M. (1985). *The teacher version of the Child Behavior Profile: II. Boys aged 12-16 and girls aged 6-11 and 12-16.* Unpublished manuscript.

Edelbrock, C., & Rancurello, M. D. (1985). Childhood hyperactivity: An overview of rating scales and their applications. *Clinical Psychology Review, 5,* 429-445.

Edelbrock, C., Costello, A.J., & Kessler, M.K. (1984). Empirical corroboration of Attention Deficit Disorder. *Journal of the American Academy of Child Psychiatry, 23,* 285-290.

Edelbrock, C., Costello, A.J., Dulcan, M.K., Kalas, R., & Conover, N.C. (1985). Age differences in the reliability of the psychiatric interview of the child. *Child Development, 56,* 265-275.

Edelbrock, C., Greenbaum, R., & Conover, N.C. (1985). Reliability and concurrent relations between the teacher version of the Child Behavior Profile and Conners' Revised Teacher Rating Scale. *Journal of Abnormal Child Psychology, 13*, 295–304.

Edelbrock, C., Costello, A.J., Dulcan, M.K., Conover, N.C., & Kalas, R. (1986). Parent–child agreement on child psychiatric symptoms assessed via structured interview. *Journal of Child Psychology and Psychiatry, 27*, 181–190.

Eisenberg, J.G., Gersten, J.C., Langner, T.S., McCarthy, E.D., & Simcha-Fagan, O. (1976). A behavioral classification of welfare children from survey data. *American Journal of Orthopsychiatry, 46*, 447–463.

Goyette, C.H.,Conners,C.K., & Ulrich, R. (1978). Normative data on Revised Conners Parent and Teacher Rating Scales. *Journal of Abnormal Child Psychology, 6*, 221–236.

Group for the Advancement of Psychiatry (1966). *Psychopathological disorders in childhood: Theoretical considerations and a proposed classification* (GAP Report No. 62). New York: Author.

Harmon, H.H. (1976). Modern factor analysis (3rd edition revised). Chicago: University of Chicago Press.

Harris, J.C., King, S.L., Reifler, J.P., & Rosenberg, L.A. (1984). Emotional and learning disorders in 6–12 year-old boys attending special schools. *Journal of the American Academy of Child Psychiatry, 23*, 431–437.

Herjanic, B., & Reich, W. (1982). Development of a structured psychiatric interview for children: Agreement between child and parent on individual symptoms. *Journal of Abnormal Child Psychology, 10*, 307–324.

Jenkins, R.L. (1966). Psychiatric syndromes in children and their relation to family background. *American Journal of Orthopsychiatry, 36*, 450–457.

Kazdin, A.E., Esveldt-Dawson, K., & Loar, L. (1983). Correspondence of teacher ratings and direct observations of classroom behavior of psychiatric inpatient children. *Journal of Abnormal Child Psychology, 11*, 549–564.

Kazdin, A.E., Esveldt-Dawson, K., Unis, A.S., & Rancurello, M. D. (1983). Child and parent evaluations of depression and aggression in psychiatric inpatient children. *Journal of Abnormal Child Psychology, 11*, 401–413.

Kerlinger, F. N. (1973). *Foundations of behavioral research* (2nd edition). New York: Holt, Rinehart, & Winston.

Kohn, M., Rosman, B.L. (1972). A social competence scale and symptom checklist for the preschool child: factor dimensions, their cross-instrument generality, and longitudinal persistence. *Developmental Psychololgy, 6*, 430–444.

Kovacs, M. (1983). *The Interview Schedule for Children: Inter-rater and parent–child agreement.* Unpublished manuscript.

Leon, G.R., Kendall, P.C., & Garber, J. (1980). Depression in children: Parent, teacher, and child perspectives. *Journal of Abnormal Child Psychology, 8*, 221–235.

Lessing, E.E., & Zagorin, S.W. (1971). Dimensions of psychopathology in middle childhood as evaluated by three symptom checklists. *Educational and Psychological Measurement, 31*, 175–198.

Mash, E.J., & Terdal, L. (1981). *Behavioral assessment of childhood disorders.* New York: Guilford.

McMahon, R.J. (1984). Behavioral checklists and rating scales. In T.H. Ollendick and M. Hersen (Eds.) *Child behavioral assessment: Principles and procedures* (pp. 80–105). New York: Pergamon.

Miller, L.C. (1967). Louisville Behavior Check List for males 6–12 years of age. *Psychological Reports, 21*, 885–896.

Paraskevopoulos, J., & McCarthy, J.M. (1970). Behavior patterns of children with special learning disabilities. *Psychology in the Schools, 7,* 42–46.

Peterson, D. R. (1961). Behavior problems of middle childhood. *Journal of Consulting Psychology, 25,* 205–209.

Quay, H.C. (1966). Personality patterns in pre-adolescent delinquent boys. *Educational and Psychological Measurement, 26,* 99–110.

Quay, H.C., Morse, W.C., & Cutler, R.L. (1966). Personality patterns of pupils in special classes for the emotionally disturbed. *Exceptional Children, 32,* 297–301.

Quay, H.C., & Peterson, D. (1983). *Manual for the Revised Behavior Problem Checklist.* Coral Gables, FL: Author.

Quay, H.C., & Quay, L. C. (1965). Behavior problems in early adolescence. *Child Development, 36,* 215–220.

Reed, M.L., & Edelbrock, C. (1983). Reliability and validity of the Direct Observation Form of the Child Behavior Checklist. *Journal of Abnormal Child Psychology, 11,* 521–530.

Rutter, M. (1967). A children's behavior questionnaire for completion by teachers: Preliminary findings. *Journal of Child Psychology and Psychiatry, 8,* 1–11

Rutter, M., Shaffer, D., & Shepherd, M. (1975). *A multiaxial classification of child psychiatric disorders: An evaluation of a proposal.* Geneva: World Health Organization.

Spivack, G., Swift, M., & Prewitt, J. (1971). Syndromes of disturbed classroom behavior: A behavioral diagnostic system for elementary school. *Journal of Special Education, 5,* 269–292.

Trites, R.L., Dugas, E., Lynch, G., & Ferguson, H.B. (1979). Prevalence of hyperactivity. *Journal of Pediatric Psychology, 4,* 179–188.

Venables, P.H., Fletcher, R.P., Dalais, J.C., Mitchell, D.A., Schulsinger, F., & Mednick, S.A. (1983). Factor structure of the Rutter Children's Behavior Questionnaire in a primary school population in a developing country. *Journal of Child Psychology and Psychiatry, 24,* 213–222.

Wainer, H. (1976). Estimating coefficients in linear models: It don't make no never-mind. *Psychological Bulletin, 83,* 213–217.

Walker, H.M. (1976). *Walker problem behavior identification checklist.* Los Angeles: Western Psychological Services.

Weissman, M., Orvaschel, H., & Padian, N. (1980). Children's symptom and social functioning self-report scales: Comparison of mothers' and children's reports. *Journal of Nervous and Mental Disease, 168,* 736–740.

10

Computer Generated Diagnosis

JAMES L. HEDLUND and BRUCE W. VIEWEG

INTRODUCTION

A search for more reliable psychiatric diagnosis has been largely responsible for the development of an increasing number of symptom checklists, clinical rating scales, structured or semistructured diagnostic interviews, and computer algorithms to process such information as diagnostic aids. The specific body of literature in the 1950s and 60s which suggested that many clinical judgments could be made with information about relatively few variables, combined in relatively simple ways (see, e.g., Goldberg, 1968), and that actuarial (or "mechanical") prediction models could virtually replicate many clinical judgments (see, e.g., Meehl, 1954; Sawyer, 1966; Sines, 1970), was also clearly influential in promoting computer diagnosis research.

Valid computer diagnosis systems could potentially enhance the value of clinical diagnoses in mental health treatment decisions, help insure the proper selection of homogeneous groups for clinical research, facilitate better controlled epidemiologic and cross-cultural studies of mental illness, and provide a more objective tool for certain kinds of peer review or quality assurance functions.

The purpose of this chapter is to describe the types of computer models that have been most frequently used in psychiatric diagnosis, to summarize the evidence for their effectiveness (validity), to discuss a number of special research applications, and to explore some of the problems, issues, and limitations of computer diagnosis. Although some attention will be given to other computer classification systems, this chapter will

JAMES L. HEDLUND and BRUCE W. VIEWEG • Department of Psychiatry, University of Missouri—Columbia, at the Missouri Institute of Psychiatry, St. Louis, MO 63139.

principally focus on research having to do with standard psychiatric nomenclatures. Other general discussions of computer diagnosis in mental health may be found in Glueck and Stroebel (1980), Spitzer and Endicott (1975), Hedlund, Evenson, Sletten, and Cho (1980), and Stroebel and Glueck (1972).

STATISTICAL VERSUS DECISION TREE MODELS

Computer diagnosis models in mental health have generally been referred to as either "statistical" or logical "decision tree" models. The most frequently used statistical models have utilized Bayesian or discriminant function methods.

Bayesian Models

Bayesian models utilize the axioms of elementary probability theory to estimate the likelihood that a particular patient or individual belongs to a particular diagnostic group (see, e.g., Birnbaum & Maxwell, 1960; Gulbinat, Hirschfeld, Jablensky, Sartorius, & Shapiro, 1980; Hirshfeld, Spitzer, & Miller, 1974; Overall, & Gorham, 1963; Smith, 1966). In general terms, the probability of membership in a specific diagnostic group is related to the joint probability of a given individual's symptoms (or other characteristics) belonging to that diagnostic group. Separate probabilities are calculated for each possible diagnosis, and the patient is usually assigned to the diagnostic category with the highest probability value.

In order to develop a Bayesian model for psychiatric diagnosis, it is therefore usually necessary to have a large, representative sample of psychiatric patients with "known" psychiatric diagnoses and symptoms. Relative frequencies of each symptom are then calculated for each possible diagnosis, and these conditional probabilities are later used to compute the likelihood of any patient belonging to the same diagnostic groups that were used in the development of the model. The very nature of this procedure has a number of important implications: (a) the more explicit and reliable the initial diagnostic procedure and nomenclature, the more likely that the initial diagnostic groups will form homogeneous reference (normative) groups; (b) standard definitions and procedures for determining whether symptoms (or other characteristics) are present will help insure the reliability and validity of such observations not only in the initial reference group, but for subsequent patients with whom the computer model is to be used; and (c) the "validity" of the results of the Bayesian model cannot exceed the reliability of the initial (developmental) diagnostic procedure. Inasmuch as the frequencies of patients in each diagnostic group, and the relative frequencies of symptoms for each diagnostic group, are likely to be somewhat different for different samples of individuals or patients, the importance of a large, representative development group should also be clear. One would expect the validity of such a computer model to diminish if it were applied to individuals or groups that differ greatly from the developmental sample. That is why validation procedures for such statistical models should use a sample other than the development group itself, and cross-validation studies should be conducted for virtually all different types of applications or application groups.

Technically, the Bayesian model requires independence of the observed symptoms—that is, that presence or absence of any specific symptom will not affect the presence or absence of any other symptom. Because this assumption can rarely be met in behavioral observations, there has been some tendency to use factor analytic symptom scores that are somewhat more independent than raw observations and ratings. Smith (1966), however, found poorer results with factor scores than with original clinical ratings, and Hirschfeld et al. (1974) seem to imply that it is not a very critical assumption. Whatever the effect, it will be reflected in any end-result validity measures.

Although the Bayesian model is especially suited for categorical variables such as the presence or absence of symptoms, or demographic variables which can often be expressed in several mutually exclusive categories, it "can also be applied to numeric data by treating each interval as a qualitative category, ignoring both the interval's original quantitative value and ordinal position" (Fleiss, Spitzer, Cohen, & Endicott, 1972).

A Bayesian computer diagnosis model was developed by Fleiss et al. (1972), based on the clinical diagnoses of 454 psychiatric patients and conditional probabilities of 17 symptom factors of the Current and Past Psychopathology Scales (CAPPS) (Endicott & Spitzer, 1972) as the independent observational measures. The chance-corrected agreement (Weighted Kappa) between clinical and Bayesian computer diagnoses for 8 diagnostic categories was .56 for the development group ($N = 454$), .43 for an independent validation with psychiatric patients ($N = 286$), and .20 for a very different sample of maternity patients ($N = 435$) who were involved in a prospective study of the offspring of mothers with a high or low likelihood of schizophrenia. In a similar study, Hirschfeld et al. (1974) reported chance-corrected agreement (Kappa) on 11 diagnostic categories was .59 for 212 U.S. psychiatric patients of the development group ($N = 417$), .28

for a "completely separate" U.S. psychiatric validation group (N = 107), .30 for an Italian psychiatric group (N = 106), and .25 for maternity patients (N = 277) who had scored high in a screening test for schizophrenia (*absolute percentages* of diagnostic agreement for these various groups were 69, 55, 51, and 42, repectively).

In each instance, the "shrinkage" in diagnostic agreement from the development to a similar-but-separate validation group was apparent. Even greater shrinkage was evident for cross-validation with patients who were quite different from the development group. The lesser amount of shrinkage in diagnostic agreement for the psychiatric validity group in the Fleiss *et al.* (1972) study, as compared with the psychiatric validity groups of the Hirschfeld *et al.* (1974) study, is associated with the fact that the clinical diagnosis distribution of that validation sample was much more similar to that of its developmental counterpart: in the former study, the development and validation groups were random samples of the same population of patients, whereas in the latter study, both the U.S. and Italian psychiatric validation samples were drawn from very different psychiatric settings than their developmental counterpart. (Indeed, the U.S. and Italian psychiatric validation groups had only *one* or *no* patients with clinical diagnoses in half of the eight possible diagnostic categories).

As indicated above, validation of two Bayesian computer diagnosis models with general psychiatric patients provided chance corrected clinical and computer agreements (Kappa or Weighted Kappa) of .43, .28, and .30. That level of agreement is very similar to the chance-corrected agreement which is reported for clinicians, themselves, for similar types of patients and diagnostic categories. Kappa and Weighted Kappa values for diagnostic agreement among clinicians, as reported in a number of studies (Fleiss *et al.*, 1972; Melrose, Stroebel, & Glueck, 1970; Spitzer & Endicott, 1968, 1969, 1974a; Spitzer, Endicott, Cohen, & Fleiss, 1974) have ranged from .25 to .80, with a median value of about .45, for general psychiatric patients.

Instead of using large groups of patients to empirically derive conditional probabilities for symptoms in his Bayesian model, Smith (1966) had 14 expert clinicians rate how characteristic each of 41 symptoms of psychopathology were in 38 different psychiatric disorders. He then computed the average relative frequency of these symptom judgments for each diagnosis, and used those values as the conditional probabilities for computer generating diagnoses in his Bayesian model. He found 86% absolute agreement between the computer and clinical diagnoses in a small validation group of psychiatric patients (N = 30).

Discriminant Analysis Models

Developing a *discriminant function model* for computer diagnosis also involves the use of special statistical procedures (see, e.g., Overall, 1963), usually entailing a large development group with known diagnoses and symptoms. Instead of using the relative frequency (conditional probability) of each symptom for each possible diagnosis, however, as in the case of the Bayesian model, the discriminant function method takes into account the correlations among the various symptom measures, and computes for each diagnostic category of the development group a set of discriminant functions so as to maximize the separation among diagnostic categories. Each patient is then given a composite score (the sum of the patient's symptom scores multiplied by discrimination weights) for each diagnostic category, and these are converted into the patient's likelihood of belonging to each diagnostic group.

The same caveats that were noted for Bayesian diagnostic models are applicable to discriminant function models—that is, concerning the importance of explicit and reliable initial (clinical) diagnostic procedures, and the role of standard definitions and procedures for making independent observations about patient sypmtoms. Because both of these statistical models usually derive their prediction parameters from a developmental sample, they also both capitalize on chance characteristics of the group, and therefore require validation with separate, independent samples.

In the Fleiss *et al.* (1972) study previously cited, a discriminant function computer diagnosis model was also developed, based on the same 454 psychiatric patients and their CAPPS symptom factor scores. The chance corrected agreement (Weighted Kappa) between clinical and the discriminant function model diagnoses for 8 diagnostic categories was .56 for the development group (N = 454), .47 for their independent validation with psychiatric patients (N = 286), and .28 for the maternity patients (N = 435). Using a randomized split-half development-validation paradigm with 3, 278 psychiatric patients, Altman, Evenson, and Cho (1976) also developed and tested a discriminant function computer diagnosis model. They utilized the "best 20" demographic, mental status, and admission checklist items as independent variables, and reported chance corrected agreement (Weighted Kappa) values of .59 and .57 for their development and validation groups, respectively, across 10 diagnostic categories. In a third study, by Melrose *et al.* (1970), a discriminant function model was developed with 413 psychiatric patients and 70 CAPPS symptom items, and validated on 255 psychiatric patients "from the same clinical sources" as the development sample (but with a very different distribution of clinical diagnoses); they report a chance corrected agreement (Kappa) of only .18 for their validation group, over 14 diagnostic categories.

Again, the shrinkage of diagnostic agreement from development to validation groups is obvious, except where the two groups had clearly come from the same patient population (as in the Altman *et al.* study); and chance corrected agreement between clinical and computer diagnoses compares favorably with diagnostic agreement among clinicians.

Decision Tree Models

Logical decision tree diagnostic models are generally nonstatistical and nonmathematical. They rely on a systematic, rational analysis of a given diagnostic schema or nomenclature, and compare the basic definitional requirements of each diagnostic category with standard clinical observations or other patient characteristics (the independent variables). The exact comparative procedure may vary considerably, depending on the rules of the diagnostic schema and the author of the model. Normally, however, that procedure

> is similar to the differential diagnostic model used by clinicians in making a psychiatric diagnosis .... [In the logical decision tree model] the computer program consists of a sequence of questions, each of which is either true or false. The truth or falsity of each question rules out one or more diagnoses and determines which question is to be examined next. Some questions may specify the presence of a single sign or symptom, others may specify that a numeric score is in a certain range, and still others may specify a complex pattern of both signs and scores. (Spitzer & Endicott, 1974a, p. 74)

The two best known logical decision tree diagnostic models in mental health are DIAGNO, developed in the U.S. by Spitzer and Endicott (1968, 1969, 1974a), and CATEGO, developed by Wing and his associates (Wing, 1980b, 1983; Wing, Cooper, & Sartorius, 1974; Wing, Nixon, von Cranach, & Strauss, 1977, 1980) in England.

DIAGNO has gone through three major stages or revisions. The output of DIAGNO I (Spitzer & Endicott, 1968) was one of 25 standard American Psychiatric Association diagnoses (from the first edition of the *Diagnostic and Statistical Manual of Mental Disorders* [DSM], 1952), based on 39 psychopathology scale scores derived from a structured interview, the Psychiatric Status Schedule (PSS) (Spitzer, Endicott, Fleiss, & Cohen, 1970), as well as age, sex, and number of previous psychiatric hospitalizations. Independent variables for DIAGNO II (Spitzer & Endicott,

1969), which was programmed to "recognize" 44 standard DSM diagnoses, were age, sex, and 94 scaled judgments. These were taken from another structured interview, the Current and Past Psychopathology Scales (CAPPS) (Endicott & Spitzer, 1972). DIAGNO III (Spitzer & Endicott, 1974a,b), using input data from the Mental Status Examination Record (MSER) and case history information from the Psychiatric Anamnestic Record (PAR) (Spitzer & Endicott, 1971; Laska & Bank, 1975), was programmed to make as many as 75 standard psychiatric diagnoses from DSM-II (1968); and it was later modified to make as many as 42 diagnoses with only mental status (MSER) findings as the independent variables. Chance corrected agreement (Kappa or Weighted Kappa) between clinical and DIAGNO computer-generated diagnoses, as reported in a number of studies (Fleiss et al., 1972; Hirschfeld et al., 1974; Melrose et al., 1970; Spitzer & Endicott, 1968, 1969, 1974a; Spitzer et al., 1974; Johnson, Klingler, Giannetti, & Williams, 1980), has ranged from .22 to .56, with a median value of .38, very similar to the range of diagnostic agreement among clinicians for similar types of patients.

CATEGO, which has been used in a number of cross-cutural research studies, is a computerized logical decision tree diagnostic system that utilizes a semistructured interview guide, the Present State Examination (PSE) (Wing et al., 1974), as the principal basis for entry of its independent variables. It can classify subjects into 50 subclasses or 20 major classes of psychopathology (Wing, 1980b), and then in conjuction with information from the Aetiology Scale, which includes clinical ratings concerning possible organic, social or psychological, intellectual, or premorbid personality factors, an ICD (International Classification of Diseases) diagnosis can be reached.

> The final steps of reaching a diagnosis have not been programmed for the computer but they are very simple to apply. The main aim of the Catego procedure is not to reach a ICD diagnosis, since this classification itself needs much improvement. The main aim is to reach a categorization by steps that are communicable and repeatable, so that the same procedure carried out in different parts of the world will yield groups that are in some specifiable sense comparable. (Wing et al., 1974, p.87)

The use of CATEGO for classifying large numbers of psychiatric patients in many different countries, however, has resulted in agreement between clinical and CATEGO- derived diagnoses averaging 82–90% for the three broad diagnostic categories of schizophrenic and paranoid psychoses versus manic psychoses versus depressive illnesses (Duckworth & Kedward, 1978; Wing & Nixon, 1975; World Health Organization, 1975), and 73–95% for schizophrenic and paranoid psychoses versus manic psychoses versus other diagnoses (Duckworth & Kedward, 1978; Fischer, 1974; Wing &

Nixon, 1975). Agreement for clinical and CATEGO-related diagnoses for schizophrenic versus affective psychoses, alone, has been reported by Scharfetter, Moerbt, and Wing (1976) to be 82%, with chance corrected agreement (Kappa), .62, for 115 Swiss psychiatric patients with functional psychoses. Schmid, Bromisch, and von Zerssen (1982) have also obtained average values of .56 to .60 and .50 to .53 for chance corrected agreement (Kappa) between clinical and CATEGO diagnoses for 100 psychiatric patients in Germany, for 4 and 10 diagnostic categories, respectively.

Comparative Efficacy

Results from studies prior to 1980 indicated that statistical and decision tree models for computer diagnosis were about equal in their agreement with clinical diagnoses for general psychiatric patients, and that both were essentially limited by the amount of diagnostic agreement among clinicians, themselves. This is evidenced both in the general level of clinical-computer agreement for studies involving individual models and in the few studies (Fleiss et al., 1972; Gulbinat et al., 1980; Hirschfeld et al., 1974; Melrose et al., 1970) which compared the results of different computer diagnosis models on the same patients. The Fleiss et al. (1972) study, for example, compared Baynesian, discriminant function, and decision tree (DIAGNO II) models on the same samples of psychiatric and maternity patients. Clinical and computer diagnostic agreement (Weighted Kappa) for both statistical models was .56 for the development group of 454 psychiatric patients, .43 to .47 on the validity group of 286 psychiatric patients, and .20 for the maternity group. Chance corrected agreement for clinical and DIAGNO II diagnoses was .42 and .48 for the two psychiatric groups, and .36 for the maternity patients. As already noted, average chance corrected agreement among clinicians, themselves, was about .45 for general psychiatric patients.

The principal difference between the statistical and decision tree models, insofar as comparative efficacy is concerned, has to do with their generalizability to different patient groups. As previously noted, the statistical models are particularly sensitive to sampling "errors," and tend to evidence a reduction in validity (i.e., agreement with clinical diagnoses) when the application groups are quite different from the development group. Since the decision tree model does not rely on a development sample for its diagnostic rules, it tends to be less sensitive to differences in patient groups, as may be seen in the Fleiss et al. (1972) data (i.e., clinical-computer diagnostic agreement was .20 for the statistical models versus .36 for DIAGNO II, for the maternity patients, as compared with .42 to .48 for psychiatric validation groups).

Since 1980, however, when operational definitions with explicit inclusion and exclusion rules were provided by DSM-III for standard American Psychiatric Association diagnoses, there has been much less interest in statistical models for computer diagnosis. As long as standard psychiatric diagnoses were defined in general descriptive terms (as with pre-DSM-III standards), there was a relatively clear conceptual difference between statistical and decision tree models: statistical models, in effect, took as their standard the collective or "average" interpretation of practicing clinicians; decision tree models take as their standard the interpretations of an "expert," the author of the model. As diagnostic criteria and decision rules become more explicit, as with DSM-III, differences between these two conceptual approaches diminish—because the "interpretations" of practicing clinicians and the expert author should have less room for idiosyncratic difference. In essence, then, diagnostic decisions become "a matter of definition," with variability (unreliability) occurring principally in the areas of clinical observation (i.e., deciding what symptoms a patient has), rather than in the application of diagnostic rules, themselves. Thus, along with a reduced interest in statistical models—because diagnostic rules have become more explicit and may no longer need some sort of collective interpretation—there has been an increased interest in standardizing and objectifying observational input for computer models.

SPECIAL RESEARCH APPLICATIONS

Computer Diagnosis as Interactive Consultation

Advances in computer technology have also had an impact on computer diagnosis models. Early models involved collection of patient symptoms (and/or other characteristics) with paper-and-pencil forms, keypunch entry, batch processing, usually on a large mainframe computer, and delayed delivery of some type of computer-generated report. With the advent and increasing availability of mini- and micro-computers—and, indeed, even of on-line terminals to mainframe systems—more timely and responsive ("interactive") diagnosis systems have emerged.

As early as 1976, Greist, Klein, and Erdman reported an on-line, interactive computer diagnosis system which was based on decision tree logic associated with the Research Diagnostic Criteria (RDC) (Spitzer, Endicott, & Robins, 1975), a forerunner to DSM-III. Clinicians interacted directly with a computer terminal by reading questions or statements on a video screen and responding by pressing keys (usually a single number) on a typewriter keyboard. Branching logic that was dependent upon prior responses determined questions to be asked, so that the amount of information required was kept to a minimum. Using this consultation program, which included 25 RDC diagnoses, typically took a clinician 10–15 minutes. Although no quantitative evaluation information is available, this system was reported to be well received by clinicians in preliminary trials.

A more comprehensive interactive computer diagnosis system, the Physician Interview Program (PIP) (Erdman, Greist, Klein, Jefferson, Olson, & Salinger, 1980, 1981), was developed subsequently, to consult on DSM-III diagnoses. In this direct computer consultation system, the clinician describes his/her patients in much the same way as outlined for the RDC diagnosis program. PIP, however, utilizes DSM-III decision trees and diagnostic criteria to cover all DSM-III diagnoses, including subtypes of both adults and children, and all five diagnostic axes. This consultation system was also developed to serve as a teaching tool, and can provide immediate feedback not only about likely DSM-III diagnoses for each patient, but an explanation of why, the inclusion and exclusion criteria for any specific diagnosis, and an indication of which criteria were met (or not met). PIP computer programs are available in MIIS and MUMPS standard programming languages, and can even be run on widely available microcomputers such as the IBM PC/XT (Greist, Mathisen, Klein, Benjamin, Erdman, & Evans, 1984). Although this diagnosis consultation system would appear to have considerable promise for clinical practice, training, and research, preliminary reports of incomplete evauation studies have estimated average chance-corrected agreement (Kappa) between computer and clinical diagnoses of only .35 (Erdman et al., 1980, 1981), despite lack of independence of the computer and clinical diagnoses (i.e., the clinician who entered data for the computer program also made the clinical diagnoses).

Direct Patient Interviews and Computer Diagnosis

As previously noted, the explicitness of DSM-III diagnostic rules has also encouraged further objectification and standardization of clinical observations that drive computer models. Earlier attempts to systematize clinical observations took the form of standardized symptom checklists and rating scales, and increasingly since the mid-1960s, the form of semistructured and structured psychiatric interviews (see, e.g., reviews by Hedlund & Vieweg, 1981; Helzer, 1983). The Psychiatric Status Schedule (PSS) (Spitzer et al., 1970), already mentioned in relation to DIAGNO I, the Current and Past Psychopathology Scales (CAPPS) (Endicott & Spitzer, 1972), used with DIAGNO II, and the Present State Examination (PSE) (Wing et al., 1974), used with CATEGO, are examples of such diagnostic interviews.

One of the most recent and comprehensive diagnostic interviews in the National Institute of Mental Health (NIMH) Diagnostic Interview Schedule (DIS) (Robins, Helzer, Croughan, & Ratcliffe, 1981). This highly structured, standardized interview, with over 250 items, is the most recent in a series of interviews developed at Washington University. It is intended for use by lay interviewers or physicians, and is designed so that its results yield computer-generated psychiatric diagnoses in accordance with DSM-III (1980), Research Diagnostic Criteria (RDC) (Spitzer et al., 1975), or Feighner research criteria (Feighner, Robins, Guze, Woodruff, Winoker, & Munoz, 1972). Although the DIS was specifically developed under NIMH contract for use in an extensive series of epidemiologic studies (see later section on Diagnosis in Cross-Cultural Research and Epidemiological Surveys), it can be used in clinical settings as well. The fact that DIS provides detailed wording for all symptom questions and for all follow-up probes—in terms that can be understood by nonclinicians— has also made it an instrument that could be translated into a computerized, direct patient interview.

Greist, and his associates (Greist, Klein, Erdman, & Jefferson, 1983; Greist, Klein, Erdman, Bires, Bass, Machtinger, & Kresge, 1985) have developed and are evaluating such an automated DIS patient interview and diagnosis system. In one study (Greist et al., 1985), 150 general psychiatric patients completed both the automated DIS interview and a personally administered DIS with a well-trained lay interviewer. Although the computer DIS took an average of two hours and fifteen minutes to complete (almost an hour longer than the personally administered DIS), patients generally reported in postinterview evaluations that both personal and computer DIS interviews were quite acceptable. There were no significant differences in the patient's reports for liking or preferring one of the procedures, or for feeling that communication of ideas and feelings were better in one procedure, as opposed to the other. These evaluation responses appeared to be unrelated to sex, age, inpatient versus outpatient status, or diagnosis, except that more female patients did express a preference for the computer interview and more embarrassment in the personal interviews. Chance corrected agreement (Kappa) between computer and personal DIS diagnoses was .55, across all DSM-III primary diagnoses. It was only .25 and .26, however, between clinical (final dis-charge) diagnoses and the computer DIS or the personal DIS diagnoses, respectively, and where there were discrepancies between clinical and DIS diagnoses, a medical chart review by an experienced clinician most fre-quently favored the clinical diagnosis. Greist and his associates conclude that "it seems likely that the DIS cannot compete on an equal footing with clinicians who have access to significant others and to important informa-tion not collected by the DIS, such as the patient's medical history, res-ponse to previous treatment and family history" (p. 28). They note, however, that for some diagnoses, such as alcohol and other drug abuse, the computer appears to obtain more accurate information than the clini-cian, that there are a number of cost advantages to computer interviewing, and that, especially with improvements that are under development (e.g., shortening of the DIS interview and extending its diagnostic coverage), the DIS interactive interview can efficiently and effectively *augment* patient evaluations for both clinical and research applications.

In another study of the DIS computer interview, involving 135 general psychiatric patients in a different setting, Mathisen and his asso-ciates (Mathisen, Evans, Meyers, Rockford, & Wilson, 1984; Mathisen, Evans, & Meyers, 1984) have corroborated the ability of such patients to successfully use the computer terminal, and their general acceptance of the computerized DIS interview. They also report that participating psy-chiatrists ($N=23$) have generally responded positively to it—with 61% in-dicating the DIS computer diagnoses were "somewhat" or "very" accurate, 54% that the results were "somewhat" or "very" helpful, and nearly half that the results provided some additional insight into their diagnostic for-mulation for at least some patients. Chance corrected agreement (Kappa) between clinical and DIS computer diagnoses was .47. The authors point out, however, that this measure of agreement was attenuated because DIS computer programs did not provide a diagnosis for 25 of their 135 patients; if these were eliminated, DIS chance corrected agreement with clinical diagnoses rose to .67. Thus, their results evidenced considerably better agreement between clinical and DIS computer diagnoses than Greist et al. (1985). They indicated, however, that the DIS diagnostic coverage needs to be extended, and that the interview, itself, could be shortened by branching out of diagnostic sections as soon as the program could exclude given diagnoses. They concluded that computerized patient interviewing can provide valuable diagnostic information, and that an im-proved DIS interview could serve as an effective screening instrument as well as "a rapid and cost-effective second opinion in the diagnostic pro-cess" (Mathisen *et al.,* 1984, January, p. 9).

Other Multivariate Classification Research

Although this chapter is primarily concerned with computer diagnosis systems which involve standard psychiatric nomenclature, some attention should also be given to more general multivariate classification and computer-modeling research having to do with the nature of psychopathology. One of the most systematic and productive programs of research in this area has been that of Overall and his associates, involving the Brief Psychiatric Rating Scale (BPRS) (Overall & Gorham, 1962).

The BPRS, which consists of 18 symptom constructs, each rated on a 7-point scale of severity ranging from "not present" to "extemely severe," is one of the most widely used standard instruments for the description, measurement, and classification of psychopathology (see, e.g., reviews or summaries by Guy, 1976, pp. 157–159; Hedlund & Vieweg, 1980; Overall & Hollister, 1968; Overall & Klett, 1972; Overall, 1974). Early studies with the BPRS (Overall, 1963; Overall & Gorham, 1963; Overall & Hollister, 1964) evaluated ratings for 13 functional psychotic diagnostic categories in an effort to identify a minimal set of dimensions "required to represent most of the objectively measurable differences among hospitalized psychiatric patients" (Overall & Hollister, 1968, p. 278). BPRS profiles were constructed for the 13 diagnostic stereotypes, and multivariate analyses were conducted that yielded four distinct major diagnostic groupings: "paranoid," "schizophrenic," "depressive," and "manic." These four core profile patterns have held up well in cross-cultural research, and assignment of patients to these groups, especially to the paranoid, schizophrenic, and depressive profile types, has enhanced the understanding of specific drug responses in many psychopharmacologic research studies.

Overall (1974), however, noted that actual patient profiles were not always well represented by diagnostic stereotypes, and he therefore conducted a series of empirical profile cluster analyses "to identify the most frequently occurring profile patterns, without regard for clinical diagnostic classification" (p. 69). This next phase of BPRS classification and treatment model research began with a study (Overall, Hollister, Johnson, & Pennington, 1966) that differentiated three BPRS depressive subtypes ("anxious," "hostile," and retarded") and related these to differential drug treatment effects. Additional work with more heterogeneous, general psychiatric patients (Overall, 1974; Overall & Hollister, 1968, 1982; Overall & Rhoades, 1982; Overall & Woodward, 1975) has led to the development of BPRS profiles for eight phenomenological clusters of general psychiatric patients: Anxious Depression; Retarded Depression; Agitated Depression; Hostile Depression; Florid Thinking Disorder; Withdrawn-Disorganized; Agitation-Excitement; and Paranoid Hostile-Suspiciousness. Mean BPRS symptom construct scores have been provided for each of these eight phenomenological subgroups (Overall, 1974; Overall & Hollister, 1982), and patients with BPRS ratings may be computer classified into one of the subtypes by calculating an index of the similarity of an individual profile to each of the eight prototypes, or by calculating eight optimally weighted sums (discrimination functions) of the individual's BRPS ratings (Overall & Hollister, 1982).

Computer classification of patients into the eight phenomenological types has been used principally to obtain greater sensitivity in evaluating treatment changes (see, e.g., Henry, Overall, & Woodward, 1976; Overall, 1974; Overall & Henry, 1973; Overall, Henry, Markett, & Emken, 1972; Overall, Henry, & Woodward, 1976; Overall & Hollister, 1972; Woodward, Henry, & Overall, 1975). Typical of this work, Overall and Henry (1973) conclude that "the application of computer profile classification in this research once more emphasizes the feasibility of utilizing powerful statistical models and computer techniques as *aids* in psychiatric practice" (p. 88).

Other examples of complex multivariate classification research in psychiatric diagnosis which may be of interest to the reader include that of Beenen, Frankenhuysen, & Veldkauns (1972), Blashfield and associates (see, e.g., Blashfield & Morey, 1979; Morey & Blashfield, 1981; Skinner & Blashfield, 1982), Lorr (1966), Markin (1975), Mezzich (1978), and Strauss and associates (see e.g., Carpenter, Bartko, Carpenter, & Strauss, 1976; Bartko, Carpenter, & Strauss, 1981; Strauss, Bartko, & Carpenter, 1973; Strauss, Gabriel, Kokes, Ritzler, Van Ord, & Tarana, 1979). Such computer classification studies are often concerned with the nature of structure of specific diagnostic groups, as well as with the nature of psychopathology, more generally.

Computer Diagnosis in Cross-Cultural Research and Epidemiological Surveys

As noted earlier, CATEGO has been extensively involved in cross-cultural research studies of psychopathology, typified by the World Health Organization's International Pilot Study of Schizophrenia (see, e.g., World Health Organization, 1973, 1979). In such studies, translations of the Present State Examination provide the standard base for observing and recording clinical symptoms, and CATEGO, the common diagnostic logic. The importance and effectiveness of using common (computer) diagnostic logic in cross-cultural studies—over and above standardized observation and recording procedures—is most clearly demonstrated by results of the United States-United Kingdom study of psychiatric diagnosis in New York and London (Cooper, Kendell, Gurland, Sharp, Copeland, & Simon, 1972). In this study, involving 366 general psychiatric inpatients, 192 from New York and 174 from London, *clinical* diagnoses evidenced a strong predilection for schizophrenic disorders in New York, as opposed to affective illness in London. Careful analysis of Present State Examination and Psychiatric Status Schedule findings between the US-UK groups, however, failed to substantiate such diagnostic differences, and both CATEGO and DIAGNO computer-generated diagnoses were generally in accord with *consensus project diagnoses* in correcting the diagnostic biases of the two clinical settings (Cooper, 1970; Cooper, Kendal, Gurland, Sartorius, & Farkas, 1969; Wing, 1973).

Computer diagnosis has also been used quite extensively in epidemiological survey research concerned with the prevalence of mental illness in the general population. PROBE (Benfari & Leighton, 1970), a discriminant analysis computer model, was one of the earliest of these. It utilized data from field survey questionnaires to classify the "caseness" of 290 survey respondents, with chance corrected agreement (Kappa) of .61 and an absolute 70% agreement between computer and psychiatric judgments in the validation sample of 102 individuals. The authors conclude that "the crossvalidation results indicated that the PROBE computer program had levels of agreement with consensual ratings of two psychiatrists equal to or greater than any two psychiatrists agree with their independent ratings of either detailed symptom patterns or 'caseness' " (p. 358). Similar results were obtained for a multiple regression computer model described by Singer, Cohen, Garfinkel, and Srole (1976) for 695 Midtown Manhattan respondents ($r=.83$, with 69% agreement between computer-derived and psychiatrists' mental health ratings).

A computer model, CASE, constructed by Benfari, Leighton, Beiser, and Coen (1972), involved a computerized symptom dictionary and the natural language processing of Stirling County epidemiologic survey notes for 120 respondents. Chance corrected agreement (Kappa) between computer and psychiatric judgments concerning 34 symptom patterns was .67 (91% absolute agreement) for their validation group.

Papers by Spitzer, Cohen, Miller, and Endicott (1969), Spitzer, Endicott, Cohen, and Nee (1980), Yamamoto, Lamp, Choi, Reese, Lo, Hahn, and Fairbanks, (1982), and Yamamoto, Korestsune, and Reese (1982) have described the use of DIAGNO in epidemiological survey research. Although the Psychiatric Status Schedule (PSS), which provides the standardized input to DIAGNO, has been criticized by Dohrenwend, Yager,

Egri, and Mendelsohn (1978) on the grounds that some of the PSS variables yielded low internal consistency reliability in their community samples, Spitzer *et al.* (1980) correctly noted that Dohrenwend *et al.* were inappropriately concerned with internal consistency measures and demonstrated that "the low internal consistency found by Dohrenwend *et al.* for most of these scales did not prevent them from showing good case-noncase discrimination" (p. 1197).

Wing and associates (see, e.g., Orley, Litt, & Wing, 1979; Sturt, Bebbington, Hurry, & Tennant, 1981; Wing, 1976, 1980a; Wing, Mann, Leff, & Nixon, 1978) have also described the use of the PSE and CATEGO in general population surveys.

The most recent and ambitious use of computer diagnosis in epidemiological survey research involves the NIMH Diagnostic Interview Schedule (DIS) (Robins *et al.,* 1981), administered by lay interviewers to a total of approximately 20,000 survey respondents in five geographic locations throughout the United States (New Haven, Baltimore, St. Louis, Los Angeles, and North Carolina). This extensive Epidemiologic Catchment Area (ECA) Program (see, e.g., Regier, Meyers, Kramer, Robins, Blazer, Hough, Eaton, & Locke, 1984; Eaton, Molzer, Von Korff, Anthony, Helzer, George, Burnam, Boyd, Kessler, & Locke, 1984), which is intended to provide precise estimates of the incidence and prevalence of specific mental disorders in the United States (see, e.g., Robins, Helzer, Weissman, Orvaschel, Gruenberg, Burke, Jr., Regier, 1984); Myers, Weissman, Tischler, Holzer III, Leaf, Orvaschel, Anthony, Boyd, Burke, Kramer, & Stoltzman, 1984), batch processes the DIS data for each survey respondent through a decision tree computer model (Boyd, Robins, Helzer, Jordan, Escobar, 1985) that was designed to simulate DSM-III diagnoses as well as those associated with the Research Diagnostic Criteria (RDC) (Spitzer et al., 1975) and Feighner research criteria (Feighner *et al.,* 1972). In a study of 216 subjects, most of whom were psychiatric patients (Robins, Helzer, Ratcliff, & Seyfried, 1982), the median chance corrected agreement (Kappa) between DIS computer-generated lifetime diagnoses for lay and psychiatrist interviewers was .65, with a range of .40 to 1.00 over 20 DSM-III diagnostic categories. Although 63% of all diagnoses in the medical charts were identified by the psychiatrists' DIS computer diagnoses, as compared with 55% by the lay interviewers' DIS computer diagnoses, only about one quarter of the psychiatric or lay DIS diagnoses were confirmed by the chart. Overall, the authors concluded that results from the lay administered DIS agreed well with those of the psychiatrist-administered DIS (even when the psychiatrist was instructed to use his clinical experience in scoring and pursuing respondent answers). They expressed some concern, however, about generalizing these results—based principally on psychiatric patients—to general population surveys, because of the fact that "current disorders and severe disorders are more accurately diagnosed than disorders in remission or borderline conditions" (Robins et al., 1982, p. 869).

In an ECA-related study (Helzer, Robins, McEvoy, Spitznagel, Stoltzman, Farmer, & Brokington, 1985), where 370 selected survey respondents were independently interviewed by both a lay interviewer and a psychiatrist, the median chance-corrected agreement (Kappa) between lay and psychiatrist DIS computer diagnoses was .38, with a range of .21 to .68, and the median chance-corrected agreement between the lay interviewers' DIS computer diagnoses and the psychiatrists' "clinical" diagnoses was .41, with a range of .12 to .63 over 10 DSM-III categories. The authors note there was evidence "that most disagreement on specific disorders is on cases near the threshold of the diagnostic definition, and as expected in a sample drawn from the general population, that there was a relatively high proportion of these borderline cases" (Helzer et al., 1985, p. 665). Thus, the reduced level of DIS diagnostic agreement in this study, as compared with that for an essentially clinical sample, confirmed their prior expectation. Despite the somewhat lower diagnostic concordance, however, the authors conclude that DIS lay interviewer rates provide acceptable, essentially unbiased estimates of the prevalence of psychiatric illness in the general population.

PROBLEMS AND ISSUES IN COMPUTER DIAGNOSIS

Reliability of Computer Diagnosis

There is a tendency to refer to the reliability (i.e., the reproducibility) of computer diagnosis as "perfect." This, of course, is only true in a very narrow sense. If exactly the same patient symptoms (or other characteristics) are entered into the computer program, the same diagnosis will be generated. In effect, the computer program completely eliminates variability associated with *interpreting the rules* for combining clinical observations into diagnostic categories. In a broader sense, however, computer diagnoses are only as reliable as the clinical observations which drive them. Inasmuch as almost all current computer diagnosis systems are linked with some sort of structured or semistructured diagnostic interview, their diagnostic reliability is essentially defined by the reliability of those interview schedules. Detailed reliability data—involving individual items, symptom scales, and end-result diagnoses—for such interview schedules (including the PSS, CAPPS, PSE, and DIS) have been summarized in a recent review article (Hedlund, & Vieweg, 1981). Suffice it to note here that average chance-corrected diagnostic agreement that has been reported with use of scheduled interviews since the implementation of DSM-III has tended to be in the .60s and .70s, even somewhat higher for some studies reporting RDC diagnoses (Hedlund & Vieweg, 1981; Matarazzo 1983). These values are considerably above the average of .45 reported by Fleiss *et al.* (1972) for the chance corrected diagnostic agreement among well-trained clinicians, and the median chance corrected agreement of .44 for all clinical diagnoses, averaged over six reliability studies (Spitzer & Fleiss, 1974). Such increases in diagnostic reliability are apparently related to the more explicit diagnostic criteria (e.g., RDC and DSM-III), use of the standardized diagnostic interviewing procedures, and, perhaps, as Grove, Andreason, McDonald-Scott, Keller, & Shapiro (1981) note, to the special training and experience which has tended to be associated with diagnosticians involved in recent reliability studies (for further discussion of these as well as other issues related to diagnostic reliability, the reader is referred to Cloninger, Miller, Wette, Martin, & Guze, 1979; Grove et al., 1981; Helzer, Clayton, Pambakian, Reich, Woodruff, & Reveley, 1977; Helzer, Robins, Taibleson, Woodruff, Reich, & Wish, 1977; Matarazzo, 1983).

Validity of Computer Diagnosis

Coupling explicit diagnostic criteria, structured interviews, and computer diagnosis models has quite clearly provided a quantum improvement in the *reliability* of psychiatric diagnosis. This is important because, although the diagnostic procedures can be made more reliable without necessarily making it more valid (i.e., more "accurate"), the validity of a procedure cannot be greater than its reliability (i.e., a procedure, generally, cannot correlate more highly with something else than with itself). The validity of pre-DSM-III structured interviews and computer diagnosis systems, for example, could not achieve a demonstrated level of validity any higher than the level of diagnostic agreement among clinicians, themselves (see e.g., Spitzer *et al.,* 1974).

This brings us full square to the fundamental criterion problem for computer diagnosis. What should be the validity criterion for computer diagnosis? Washinton University psychiatric researchers (see, e.g., Helzer & Robins, 1981; Helzer, Robins, Croughan, & Welner, 1981; Helzer *et al.,* 1986; Robins *et al.,* 1981; Robins et al., 1982), Spitzer (1983), and Greist et al. (1985) have all drawn recent attention to this issue, and have taken a position that the earlier standard of "clinical diagnosis" is no longer the best standard of diagnostic accuracy. They seem to agree that at present the "best" diagnoses—the ones most likely to be "accurate"—are diagnoses which have been made by experienced, well-trained clinicians who have utilized, *as a part of their diagnostic procedure,* a carefully developed, structured or semistructured interview, as well as all other kinds of available information (e.g., the medical chart, collateral, and longitudinal information) about the individual patients involved.[1]

In evaluating the Renard Diagnostic Interview (RDI) and its computer-derived diagnoses (Helzer *et al.,* 1981), the Washington University group therefore assessed its validity by examining diagnostic concordance between RDI diagnoses and the "results achieved by the traditional structured psychiatric interview that has been used in our department for many years" (p. 393). They referred to this as "procedural validity," a term suggested by Spitzer and Williams (1980) for situations where "the question being asked concerns the extent to which diagnostic procedure yields results similar to the results of an established diagnostic procedure that is used as a criterion" (p. 1039). Similarly, the Washington University researchers have used *psychiatrists'* DIS computer diagnoses (Robins et al., 1982; Helzer, *et al.,* 1985) or psychiatrists' DIS-based "clinical" diagnoses (Helzer *et al.,* 1985) as their principal criterion for the validity of lay administered DIS computer diagnosis. Although some (see, e.g., Endicott,

---

[1]Indeed, Spitzer (1983) has even proposed a new, *semi-structured* interview, the Structured Clinical Interview Schedule (SCID), to be used by expert diagnosticians, as a future criterion for the validity of diagnostic procedures. This interview schedule involves many open-ended questions, encouragement to rephrase scheduled questions whenever subjects have difficulty understanding them, the use of longitudinal and other relevant information from outside the interview, and an interviewer who "is expected to be familiar with DSM-III, assess the DSM-III criteria as the interview progresses, and make a provisional DSM-III diagnosis during the course of the interview, pending other diagnostic information that may become available" (p. 406). Spitzer believes that such a procedure, i.e., clinical experts using SCID, will be more sensitive to specific psychiatric disorders and subjects with ambiguous or confusing presentations, and will minimize false positive diagnoses by focusing on the *intent* of the diagnostic criterion rather than on the presence or absence of symptoms as determined by overly simplified self-report procedures. Spitzer, in the absence of the ultimate "gold standard" diagnosis criterion, refers to and recommends this procedure as a "modest LEAD standard" (p. 409). He admits that data is not yet available to test his "clinical biases" regarding SCID, but a quotation from Helzer et al. (1986) may be of particular interest in this regard:

> At the present time, we do not know if 1) the physician's opportunity to apply that indefinable quality called clinical judgment enables him to more accurately identify true cases of illness and if that perhaps is the reason for the low sensitivity for many lay diagnoses compared to clinicians or if, alternatively, 2) many of the cases are simply at the threshold of definition and the sensitivity of one physician relative to another physician would have been similar to what we found between physicians and lay interviewers here. If 1) is the case, we expect that in our one- and five-year follow-ups clinicians' diagnoses will predict outcomes and other illness validators better than will the lay interviewers' diagnoses. If 2) is true, outcomes and illness validators should be predicted as well by one as by the other.

1981) have been concerned that these procedures, particularly the concordance of psychiatrist and lay DIS computer diagnoses, are more akin to
reliability than validity, the Washington University group (Helzer *et al.*,
1985; Helzer & Robins, 1981; Robins et al., 1981) emphasize that the critical difference here has to do with the fact that the comparative procedures
were not simply a repetition of each other (as in the case of reliability), but
that the two examiners (psychiatrist and lay interviewers) differed greatly
in their training and experience, and that except for the DIS interview,
proper, the psychiatrists did bring their expertise to bear on exploring
questionable areas and pursuing diagnostic uncertainties.

The effect of such criterion changes on the actual values of validity
coefficients may be quite dramatic. For psychiatric patient samples, for
example, the average chance corrected agreement (Kappa) between lay
and psychiatrist interviewers, using either the Renard Diagnostic Interview (RDI) or the DIS, was .65 (Helzer *et al.*, 1981; Robins, et al., 1982), as
compared with chance-corrected concordance between structured-inter-
view computer diagnosis and general clinical diagnostic procedures that
have generally averaged in the .30s and .40s. Presumably, comparable
measures of agreement for RDI versus Washington University traditional
diagnosis procedures (Helzer *et al.*, 1981), and for lay DIS versus
clinically-modified psychiatrists' DIS diagnoses (Robins *et al.*, 1982),
would have been somewhere in between, although that data was not
provided.

Utilization and Clinical Acceptance

Although virtually all computer diagnosis systems described here
have been essentially *research* applications of one type or another, some
have been used operationally in clinical settings. Multiple discriminant
models were elements of the Missouri Department of Mental Health's
Standard System of Psychiatry (see, e.g., Altman, Evenson, Hedlund, &
Cho, 1978; Hedlund, Sletten, Evenson, Altman, & Cho, 1977) and of the
clinical information system at the Institute of Living (see, e.g., Glueck,
1974); DIAGNO III (Spitzer & Endicott, 1974a) was a Multi-State Information System (MSIS) application (see, e.g., Laska & Bank, 1975); and the
Erdman *et al.*, (1980, 1981) interactive DSM-III diagnosis system has been
included in the Veterans Administration Mental Health Information System Package, being disseminated to its 172 field sites (Hammond &
Gottfredson, 1984).

Even when computer diagnosis has been available in clinical settings, however, few operating clinicians have chosen to use such systems

routinely (see, e.g, Griest *et al.,* 1983; Hedlund *et al.,* 1980; Taintor, 1980), despite the findings of some positive attitudes during evaluation studies. An increased interest in and use of microcomputers, however, together with the availability of DSM-III consultation programs for them (see, e.g., Greist, Mathisen, Klein, Benjamin, Erdman, & Evans, 1984; Swartz, & Pfohl, 1981), may be changing some of this "resistance."

Gelenter and Gelenter (1984) have also suggested that a different approach to computer-supported diagnostic consultation may be more effective. They propose an

> *online diagnostic monitor,* which is a diagnostic expert system designed for interactive use by a clinician during the course of a patient interview. The exchange between a diagnostic monitor and its clinician user is guided by the user, not the system, and the monitor functions as a passive advisor rather than an active decision-maker. (p. 45)

Mathiesen *et al.* (1984, January) suggest that "The question is no longer whether computer technology will contribute to clinical care but rather how it will be integrated into the psychiatric setting" (p. 10). They, like Greist and his associates (see, e.g., Greist et al., 1983, 1984, 1985), think of computer diagnosis as a potential *aid* to the clinician, both in the systematic collection of necessary information and in organizing, processing, and comparing that data to standard diagnostic rules. While there is ample evidence that such *consultative* and support functions could be beneficial, there is no attempt to usurp clinicial prerogatives—as Greist et al. (1983) note, "Clinicians remain critically important in the diagnostic process. The goal of computer diagnosis is not to replace clinicians but to extend and enhance their capabilities" (p. 791). Similarly, Helzer et al. (1986) indicate that,

> The DIS is not an attempt to eliminate the need for psychiatrists or to obviate clinical judgment in making psychiatric diagnoses. But in many types of clinical and epidemiologic studies, there is a necessity to use non-psychiatrists for gathering diagnostic information. The DIS is a response to the desire to have an instrument which will, as closely as possible, replicate a psychiatrist's diagnoses for situations when the use of psychiatrists is impractical or impossible. (p. 31)

Use of computer diagnosis as a research tool is well documented. Although it is beyond the scope of this chapter to comprehensively review specific research applications, some attention has been given to its use in selecting or verifying the diagnosis of research subjects, in studying the nature of psychopathology, and in epidemiological and cross-cultural studies of mental illness. Another application area of special relevance to issues in diagnostic research has to do with the results or impact of using different diagnostic criteria in various studies; the work of Overall and his associates (see, e.g., Cobb & Overall, 1981; Overall, Cobb & Click, 1982; Overall & Zisook, 1980; Overall & Hollister, 1979) is of particular interest in this regard.

SUMMARY

This chapter has briefly described a number of computer diagnosis models and applications that have been developed and tested for potential use in mental health clinical or research settings. Evidence was presented to indicate that such applications, whether using statistical or rational decision tree models, have agreed with clinical diagnoses at about the same level as clinicians agreed with each other. The implementation of standard psychiatric nosologies with explicit inclusion and exclusion criteria for each diagnostic category (i.e., DSM-III, Research Diagnostic Criteria, and Feighner's research criteria), advances in computer technology, and the development of structured interviews that specifically target the explicit diagnostic criteria, however, has permitted and encouraged the development of a newer breed of decision tree computer diagnosis applications: interactive diagnostic consultation with the clinician; a potentially more precise lay administered interview and diagnosis system, the NIMH Diagnostic Interview Schedule (DIS); and a direct patient interviewing and diagnostic system which utilizes the basic DIS structure. It would appear that such carefully defined diagnostic systems can significantly improve diagnostic reliability, and that the use of a potentially better diagnostic criterion may break prior constraints associated with the relative unreliability of unstructured clinical diagnosis for evaluating the validity of such computer applications. Despite a number of issues, including the relative lack of enthusiasm of operating clinicians for such systems, there is considerable evidence that computer diagnosis applications *can* provide useful and cost-effective consultation in mental health clinical settings, and strong support for clinical and epidemiologic research.

Aknowledgments

The authors gratefully acknowledge the valuable comments and suggestions of Drs. Paul R. Binner, Doug W. Cho, Richard C. Evenson, Allen L. Hammer, and Scott T. Meier, all members of the Mental Health Systems Research Unit at the Missouri Institute of Psychiatry, following their review of an earlier draft of this manuscript.

REFERENCES

Altman, H., Evenson, R. C., & Cho, D. W. (1976). New discriminant functions for computer diagnosis. *Multivariate Behavioral Research, 11,* 367–376.

Altman, H., Evenson, R. C., Hedlund, J. L., & Cho, D. W. (1978). The Missouri Actuarial Report System (MARS). *Comprehensive Psychiatry, 19,* 195–192.

Bartko, J. J., Carpenter, W. T., & Strauss, J. S. (1981). Statistical basis for exploring schizophrenia. *American Journal of Psychiatry, 138,* 941–947.

Beenen, F., Van Frankenhuysen, J. H., & Veldkamp, J. G. (1972). The construction of a descriptive diagnostic system in psychiatry: First experiences with a computer simulation. *Behavioral Science, 17,* 278–287.

Benfari, R. C., & Leighton, A. H. (1970). PROBE: A computer instrument for field surveys of pschyiatric disorder. *Archives of General Psychiatry, 23,* 352–358.

Benfari, R. C., Leighton, A. H., Beiser, J., & Cohen, K. (1972). CASE: Computer Assigned Symptom Evaluation—An instrument for psychiatric epidemiological application. *Journal of Nervous and Mental Disease, 154,* 115–124.

Birnbaum, A., & Maxwell, A. E. (1960). Classification procedures based on Bayes' formula. *Applied Statistics, 9,* 152–169.

Blashfield, R. D., & Morey, L. C. (1979). The classification of depression through cluster analysis. *Comprehensive Psychiatry, 20,* 516–527.

Boyd, J. H., Robins, L. N., Holzer, C. E., Jordan, K. B., & Escobar, J. (1985). Making diagnoses from DIS data (pp. 209–231). In W. W. Eaton & L. G. Kessler (Eds.), *Epidemiologic field methods in psychiatry: The NIMH Epidemiologic Catchment Area Program.* New York: Academic Press, Inc.

Carpenter, W. T., Bartko, J. J., Carpenter, C. L., & Strauss, J. S. (1976). Another view of schizophrenia subtypes: A report from the International Pilot Study of Schizphrenia. *Archives of General Psychiatry, 33,* 508–516.

Cloninger, C. R. Miller, J. P. Wette, R., Martin, R. L., & Guze, S. B. (1979). The evaluation of diagnostic concordance in follow-up studies: I. A general model of causal analysis and a methodological critique. *Journal of Psychiatric Research, 15,* 85–106.

Cobb, J. C., & Overall, J. E. (1981). Computer simulation and comparison of specific diagnostic concepts for schizophrenia and depression. In. H. G. Hefferman (Ed.), *Proceedings of the Fifth Annual Symposium on Computer Applications in Medical Care* (pp. 412–416). New York: Institute of Electrical & Electronics Engineers.

Cooper, J. E. (1970). The use of a procedure for standardizing psychiatric diagnosis. In E. H. Hare, & J. K. Wing (Eds.), *Psychiatric epidemiology.* London: Oxford University Press.

Cooper, J. E., Kendell, R. E., Gurland, B. J., Sartorius, N., & Farkas, T. (1969). Cross-national study of diagnosis of the mental disorders: Some results from the first comparative investigation. *American Journal of Psychiatry, 125,* (10, Suppl.), 21–29.

Cooper, J. E., Kendell, R. E., Gurland, B. J., Sharpe, L., Copeland, J. R. M., & Simon, R. (1972). *Psychiatric diagnosis in New York and London.* London: Oxford University Press.

Dohrenwend, B. P., Yager, T. J., Egri, G., & Mendelsohn, S. (1978). The Psychiatric Status Schedule as a measure of dimensions of psychopathology in the general population. *Archives of General Psychiatry, 35,* 731–737.

Duckworth, G. S., & Kedward, H. B. (1978). Man or machine in psychiatric diagnosis. *American Journal of Psychiatry, 135,* 64–68.

Eaton, W. W., Holzer, C. E., Von Korff, M. Anthony, J. C., Helzer, J. E., George, L., Burnam, M. A., Boyd, J. H., Kessler, L. G., Locke, B. Z. (1984). The design of the Epidemiologic Catchment Area surveys. *Archives of General Psychiatry, 41*(10), 942–948.

Endicott, J. (1981). Diagnostic Interview Schedule: Reliability and validity (Letter to the editor). *Archives of General Psychiatry, 38,* 1300.

Endicott, J., & Spitzer, R. L. (1972). Current and Past Psychopathology Scales (CAPPS): Rationale and validity. *Archives of General Psychiatry, 27,* 678-687.

Erdman, H. P., Greist, J. H., Klein, M. H., Jefferson, J. W., Olson, W., & Salinger, R. (1980). Computer consultation for psychiatric diagnosis. In J.T. O'Neill (Ed.), *Proceedings of the Fourth Annual Symposium on Computer Applications in Medical Care* (pp. 923-927). New York: Institute of Electrical and Electronics Engineers.

Erdman, H. P., Greist, J. H., Klein, M. H., Jefferson, J. W., Olson, W., & Salinger, R. (1981). Clinical usefulness of a computer program for psychiatric diagnosis. In B. Shriver, R. Walker, & R. Grams (Eds.), *Proceedings of the Fourteenth Hawaii International Conference on System Sciences* (pp. 802-817). North Hollywood, CA: Wester Periodicals.

Feighner, J. P., Robins, E., Guze, S. B., Woodruff, R. A., Winokur, G., & Munoz, R. (1972). Diagnostic criteria for use in psychiatric research. *Archives of General Psychiatry, 26,* 57-63.

Fischer, M. (1974). Development and validity of a computerized method for diagnoses of functional psychoses (DIAX). *Acta Psychiatrica Scandinavica, 50,* 243-288.

Fleiss, J. L., Spitzer, R. L., Cohen, J., & Endicott, J. (1972). Three computer diagnosis methods compared. *Archives of General Psychiatry, 27,* 643-649.

Gelernter, D., & Gelernter, J. (1984). Expert systems and diagnostic monitors in psychiatry. In G.S. Cohen (Ed.), *Proceedings of the Eighth Annual Symposium on Computer Applications in Medical Care* (pp. 45-48). Silver Springs, MD: Institute of Electrical & Electronics Engineers.

Glueck, B. C. (1974). Computers at the Institute of Living. In J. L. Crawford, D. W. Morgan, & D. T. Gianturco (Eds.), *Progress in mental health information systems: Computer Applications* (pp. 303-316). Cambridge, MA: Ballinger Publishing Company.

Glueck, B. C., & Stroebel, D. F. (1980). Computers and clinical psychiatry. In H. I. Kaplan, A. M. Freedman, & B. J. Sadock (Eds.), *Comprehensive textbook of psychiatry:* Vol. 1 (3rd ed., pp. 413-428). Baltimore: Williams & Wilkins.

Goldberg, L. R. (1968). Simple models or simple processes? Some research on clinical judgments. *American Psychologist, 23,* 483-496.

Greist, J. H., Klein, M. H., & Erdman, H. P. (1976). Routine on-line psychiatric diagnosis by computer. *American Journal of Psychiatry, 133,* 1405-1408.

Greist, J. H., Klein, M. H., Erdman, H. P., & Jefferson, J. W. (1983). Computers and psychiatric diagnosis. *Psychiatric Annals, 13,* 785, 789-792.

Greist, J. H., Mathisen, K. S., Klein, M. H., Benjamin, L. S., Erdman, H. P., & Evans, F. J. (1984). Psychiatric diagnosis? What role for the computer? *Hospital and Community Psychiatry, 35,* 1089-1090, 1093.

Greist, J. H., Klein, M. H., Erdman, H. P., Bires, J., Bass, S., Machtinger, P., & Kresge, D. (1985). *Psychiatric diagnosis by direct patient-computer interview.* Unpublished manuscript. Department of Psychiatry, University of Wisconsin-Madison.

Grove, W. M., Andreason, N. C., McDonald-Scott, P., Keller, M. B., Shapiro, R. W. (1981). Reliability studies of psychiatric diagnosis: Theory and practice. *Archives of General Psychiatry, 38,* 408-413.

Gulbinat, W., Hirschfeld, R. M. A., Jablensky, A., Sartorius, N., & Shapiro, R. (1980). Bayes' theorem and methods of classification in psychiatry. In. J.J. Bartko & W. Gulbinat (Eds.), *Multivariate statistical methodologies used in the international pilot study of schizophrenia* (pp. 54-67). (National Institute of Mental Health, Series GN No. 1, DHHS Publication No. (ADM) 80-630). Washington, D.C.: Superintendent of Documents, U.S. Government Printing Office.

Guy, W. (1976). *Assessment manual for psychopharmacology* (DHEW No. [ADM] 76-338). Rockville, MD, National Institute of Mental Health.

Hammond, K. W., & Gottfredson, D. K. (1984). The VA Mental Health Information System Package: Version I. *Computer Use in Social Network, 4,* 6-7.

Hedlund, J. L., Sletten, I. W., Evenson, R. C., Altman, H., & Cho, D. W. (1977). Automated psychiatric information sytems: A critical review of Missouri's Standard System of Psychiatry (SSOP). *Journal of Operational Psychiatry, 8,* 5-26.

Hedlund, J. L., Evenson, R. C., Sletten, I. W., & Cho, D. W. (1980). The computer and clinical prediction. In J. B. Sidowski, J. H. Johnson, & T. A. Williams (Eds.), *Technology in mental health care delivery systems* (pp. 201-235). Norwood, NJ: Ablex.

Hedlund, J. L., & Vieweg, B. W. (1980). The Brief Psychiatric Rating Scale (BPRS): A comprehensive review. *Journal of Operational Psychiatry, 11,* 48-65.

Hedlund, J. L., & Vieweg, B. W. (1981). Structured psychiatric interviews: A comparative review. *Journal of Operational Psychiatry, 12,* 41-67.

Helzer, J. E. (1983). Standardized interviews in psychiatry. *Psychiatric Developments, 2,* 161-178.

Helzer, J. E., & Robins, L. N. (1981). Diagnostic Interview Schedule: Reliability and validity (Letter to the editor, in reply to J. Endicott). *Archives of General Psychiatry, 38,* 1300-1301.

Helzer, J. E., Clayton, P. J., Pambakian, R., Reich, T., Woodruff, R. A., & Reveley, M. A. (1977). Reliability of psychiatric diagnosis: II. The test-retest reliability of diagnostic classification. *Archives of General Psychiatry, 34,* 136-141.

Helzer, J. E., Robins, L. N., Taibleson, M., Woodruff, R. A., Reich, I., Wish, E. D. (1977). Reliability of psychiatric diagnosis: I. A methodological review. *Archives of General Psychiatry, 34,* 129-133.

Helzer, J. E., Robins, L. N., Croughan, J. L., & Welner, A. (1981). Renard Diagnostic Interview: Its reliability and procedural validity with physician and lay interviewers. *Archives of General Psychiatry, 38,* 393-398.

Helzer, J. E., Robins, L. N., McEvoy, L. T., Spitznagel, E. L., Stoltzman, R. K., Farmer, A. & Brokington, I.F. (1985). A comparison of clinical and DIS diagnoses: Physical reexamination of lay interviewed cases in the general population. *Archives of General Psychiatry, 42*(7), 657-667.

Henry, B. W., Overall, J. E., Woodward, J. A. (1976). Actuarial justification for choice of drug treatment for psychiatric patients. *Diseases of the Nervous System, 37,* 555-557.

Hirschfeld, R., Spitzer, R. L., & Miller, R. G. (1974). Computer diagnosis in psychiatry: A Bayes approach. *Journal of Nervous and Mental Diseases, 158,* 399-407.

Johnson, J. H., Klingler, D. E., Giannetti, R. A., & Williams, T. A. (1980). The reliability of diagnoses by technicians, computer, and algorithm. *Journal of Clinical Psychology, 36,* 447-451.

Laska, E. M., & Bank, R. (Eds.), (1975). *Safeguarding psychiatric privacy: Computer systems and their uses.* New York: John Wiley & Sons.

Lorr, M. (1966). *Exploration in typing psychotics.* Oxford, England, Pergamon Press.

Markin, R. A. (1975). Information, decision-making, and the diagnostic process. *Comprehensive Psychiatry, 16,* 557-572.

Matarazzo, J. K. (1983). The reliability of psychiatric and psychological diagnosis. *Clinical Psychological Review, 3,* 105-145.

Mathisen, K. S., Evans, F. J., & Myers, K. (1984, August). *Reliability of an interactive computerized DSM-III diagnostic interview.* Paper presented at the 92nd Annual Convention of the American Psychological Association, Toronto, Canada.

Mathisen, K. S., Evans, F. J., Meyers, K., Rockford, J. M., & Wilson, G. F. (1984, January). *An evaluation of computerized DSM-III diagnosis in a private psychiatric hospital*. Paper presented at the 51st Annual Meeting of the National Association of Private Psychiatric Hospitals, Palm Springs, CA.

Meehl, P. E. (1954). *Clinical versus statistical prediction*. Minneapolis, MN: University of Minnesota Press.

Melrose, J. P., Stroebel, C. F., & Glueck, B. C. (1970). Diagnosis of psychopathology using stepwise multiple discriminant analysis. *Comprehensive Psychiatry, 11,* 43–50.

Mezzich, J. E. (1978). Evaluating clustering methods for psychiatric diagnosis. *Biological Psychiatry, 13,* 265–281.

Morey, L. C., & Blashfield, R. K. (1981). A symptom analysis of the DSM-III definition of schizophrenia. *Schizophrenic Bulletin, 7,* 258–268.

Myers, J. K., Weissman, M. M., Tischler, G. L., Holzer III, C. E., Leaf, P. J., Orvaschel, H., Anthony, J. C., Boyd, J. H., Burke, J. D., Kramer, M., & Stoltzman, R. (1984). Six-month prevalence of psychiatric disorders in three communities. *Archives of General Psychiatry, 41*(10), 959–970.

Orley, J., Litt, B. & Wing, J. K. (1979). Psychiatric disorders in two African villages. *Archives of General Psychiatry, 36,* 513–520.

Overall, J. E. (1963). A configural analysis of psychiatric diagnostic stereotypes. *Behavioral Science, 8,* 211–219.

Overall, J. E. (1974). The Brief Psychiatric Rating Scale in psychopharmacology research. In P. Pichot (Ed.), *Psychological measurements in psychopharmacology, Modern problems of pharmacopsychiatry,* Vol. 7. Basel: S. Karger.

Overall, J. E., & Gorham, D. R. (1962). The Brief Psychiatric Rating Scale. *Psychological Reports, 10,* 799–812.

Overall, J. E., & Gorham, D. R. (1963). A pattern probability model for the classification of psychiatric patients. *Behavioral Science, 8,* 108–116.

Overall, J. E., & Henry, B. W. (1973). Decisions about drug therapy: III. Selection of treatment for psychiatric inpatients. *Archives of General Psychiatry, 28,* 81–89.

Overall, J. E., Hollister, L. E. (1964). Computer procedures for psychiatric classification. *Journal of the American Medical Association, 187,* 583–588.

Overall, J. E., & Hollister, L. E. (1968). Studies of quantitative approaches to psychiatric classification. In M. M. Barton, J. O. Cole, & W. E. Barton (Eds.), *The role and methodology of classification in psychiatry and psychopathology,* Washington, D.C.: U.S. Department of Health, Education & Welfare.

Overall, J. E., & Hollister, L. E. (1972). Decisions about drug therapy: II. Expert opinion in a hypothetical situation. *Behavioral Science, 17,* 349–360.

Overall, J. E., & Hollister, L. E. (1979). Comparative evaluation of research diagnostic criteria. *Archives of General Psychiatry, 36,* 1198–1205.

Overall, J. E., & Hollister, L. E. (1982). Decision rules for phenomenological classification of psychiatric patients. *Journal of Consulting and Clinical Psychology, 50,* 535–545.

Overall, J. E., Klett, C. J. (1972). *Applied multivariate analysis.* New York: McGraw-Hill.

Overall, J. E., & Rhoades, H. M. (1982). Refinement of phenomenological classification in clinical psychopharmacology research. *Psychopharmacology, 77,* 24–30.

Overall, J. E. & Woodward, J. A. (1975). Conceptual validity of phenomenological classification of psychiatric patients. *Journal of Psychiatric Research, 12,* 215–230.

Overall, J. E., Hollister, L. E., Johnson, M. & Pennington, V. (1966). Nosology of depression and differential response to drugs. *Journal of the American Medical Association, 195,* 946–948.

Overall, J. E., Henry, B. W., Markett, J. R., & Emken, R. L. (1972). Decisions about drug therapy: I. Prescriptions for adult psychiatric outpatients. *Archives of General Psychiatry, 26,* 140–145.

Overall, J. E., Henry, B. W., & Woodward, J. A. (1976). Models derived from diagnostic frequency patterns. *Journal of Psychiatric Research, 13,* 77–89.

Overall, J. E., Cobb, J. C., & Click, M. A. (1982). The reliability of psychiatric diagnoses based on alternative research criteria. *Journal of Psychiatric Evaluation, 4,* 209–220.

Overall, J. E., & Zisook, S. (1980). Diagnosis and the phenomenology of depressive disorders. *Journal of Consulting & Clinical Psychology, 48,* 626–634.

Regier, D. A., Myers, J. K., Kramer, M., Robins, L. N., Blazer, D. G., Hough, R. L., Eaton, W. W., & Locke, B. Z. (1984). The NIMH Epidemiologic Catchment Area program. *Archives of General Psychiatry, 41*(10), 934–941.

Robins, L. H., Helzer, J. E., Croughan, J., & Ratcliff, K. S. (1981). National Institute of Mental Health Diagnostic Interview Schedule: Its history, characteristics, and validity. *Archives of General Psychiatry, 38,* 381–389.

Robins, L. H., Helzer, J. W., Ratcliffe, K. S., & Seyfried, W. (1982). Validity of the Diagnostic Interview Schedule, Version II: DSM-III diagnoses. *Psychological Medicine, 12,* 855–870.

Robins, L. N., Helzer, J. E., Weissman, M. M., Orvaschel, H., Gruenberg, E., Burke, Jr., J. D., & Regier, D. A. (1984). Lifetime prevalence of specific psychiatric disorders in three sites. *Archives of General Psychiatry, 41*(10), 949–958.

Sawyer, J. (1966). Measurements and prediction, clinical and statistical. *Psychological Bulletin, 66,* 178–200.

Scharfetter, C., Moerbt, H., & Wing, J. K. (1976). Diagnosis of functional psychoses: Comparison of clinical and computerized classifications. *Archiv für Psychiatrie und Nervenkrankheiten, 222,* 61–67.

Schmid, W., Bronisch, T., Von Zerssen, D. (1982). A comparative study of PSE/CATEGO and DiaSiKa: Two psychiatric diagnostic systems. *British Journal of Psychiatry, 141,* 292–295.

Sines, J. O. (1970). Actuarial versus clinical prediction in psychopathology. *British Journal of Psychiatry, 116,* 129–144.

Singer, E., Cohen, S. M., Garfinkel, R., & Srole, L. (1976). Replicating psychiatric ratings through multi-regression analysis: The midtown Manhattan restudy. *Journal of Health and Social Behavior, 17,* 376–387.

Skinner, H. A., & Blashfield, R. D. (1982). Increasing the impact of cluster analysis research: The case of psychiatric classification. *Journal of Consulting and Clinical Psychology, 50,* 727–735.

Smith, W. G. (1966). A model for psychiatric diagnosis. *Archives of General Psychiatry, 14,* 521–529.

Spitzer, R. L. (1983). Psychiatric diagnosis: Are clinicians still necessary? *Comprehensive Psychiatry, 24,* 399–411.

Spitzer, R. L., & Endicott, J. (1968). DIAGNO: A computer program for psychiatric diagnosis utilizing the differential diagnostic procedure. *Archives of General Psychiatry, 18,* 746–756.

Spitzer, R. L. & Endicott, J. (1969). DIAGNO II: Further development in a computer program for psychiatric diagnosis. *American Journal of Psychiatry, 125,* (7 Suppl.), 12–21.

Spitzer, R. L., & Endicott, J. (1971). An integrated group of forms for automated psychiatric case records: A progress report. *Archives of General Psychiatry, 24,* 540–547.

Spitzer, R. L., & Endicott, J. (1974a). Computer diagnosis in automated recordkeeping systems: A Study of clinical acceptability. In J. L. Crawford, D. W. Morgan, & D. T. Gianturco (Eds.), *Progress in mental health information systems: Computer applications* (pp. 73–105). Cambridge, MA: Ballinger.

Spitzer, R. L., & Endicott, J. (1974b). Can the computer assist clinicians in psychiatric diagnosis? *American Journal of Psychiatry, 131,* 523–530.

Spitzer, R. L., & Endicott, J. (1975). Computer applications in psychiatry. In D. A. Hamburg & E. H. Brodie (Eds.), *American handbook of psychiatry: New psychiatric frontiers:* Vol. 6 (2nd ed., pp. 811–839). New York: Basic Books.

Spitzer, R. L., & Fleiss, J. L. (1974). A re-analysis of the reliability of psychiatric diagnosis. *British Journal of Psychiatry, 125,* 341–347.

Spitzer, R. L., & Williams, J. B. W. (1980). Classification of mental disorders and DSM-III. In H. Kaplan, A. Friedman, & B. Sadock (Eds.),*Comprehensive Textbook of Psychiatry* (3rd Ed., pp. 1035–1072). Baltimore: Williams & Wilkins.

Spitzer, R. L., Cohen, G., Miller, J. E., & Endicott, J. (1969). The psychiatric status of 100 men on Skid Row. *International Journal of Social Psychiatry, 15,* 230–234.

Spitzer, R. L., Endicott, J., Fleiss, J. L., & Cohen, J. (1970). The Psychiatric Status Schedule: A technique for evaluating psychopathology and impairment in role functioning. *Archives of General Psychiatry, 23,* 41–55.

Spitzer, R. L., Endicott, J., Cohen, J., & Fleiss, J. L. (1974). Constraints on the validity of computer diagnosis. *Archives of General Psychiatry, 31,* 197–203.

Spitzer, R. L., Endicott, J., Robins, R. E. (1975). *Research Diagnostic Criteria.* New York: New York State Psychiatric Institute.

Spitzer, R. L., Endicott, J., Cohen, J., & Nee, J. (1980). The Psychiatric Status Schedule for epidemiological research. *Archives of General Psychiatry, 37,* 1193–1197.

Strauss, J. S., Gabriel, K. R., Kokes, R. F., Ritzler, B. A., Van Ord, A., & Tarana, E. (1979). Do psychiatric patients fit their diagnoses? Patterns of symptomatology as described with the biplot. *Journal of Nervous & Mental Disease, 167,* 105–113.

Strauss, J. S., Bartko, J. J., & Carpenter, W. T. (1973). The use of clustering techniques for the classification of psychiatric patients. *British Journal of Psychiatry, 122,* 531–540.

Stroebel, C. F., & Glueck, B. C. (1972). The diagnostic process in psychiatry. Computer approaches. *Psychiatric Annals, 2,* 58–77.

Sturt, E., Bebbington, P., Hurry, J., & Tennant, C. (1981). The Present State Examination used by interviewers from a survey agency: Report from the MRC Camberwell community survey. *Psychological Medicine, 11,* 185–192.

Swartz, C. M., & Pfohl, B. (1981). A learning aid for DSM-III: Computerized prompting of diagnostic criteria. *Journal of Clinical Psychiatry, 42,* 359–361.

Taintor, Z. C. (1980). Computers and diagnosis (Editorial). *American Journal of Psychiatry, 137,* 61–63.

World Health Organization (1973). *The International Pilot Study of Schizophrenia.* Geneva, Switzerland: Author.

World Health Organization (1975). Schizophrenia: A multinational study: A summary of the initial phase of the International Pilot of Schizophrenia. *WHO Public Health Paper No. 63* (11–150). Geneva: Author.

World Health Organization (1979). *Schizophrenia: An international follow-up study.* New York: John Wiley.

Wing, J. K. (1973). International variations in psychiatric diagnosis. *Triangle, 12,* 31–36.

Wing, J. K. (1976). A technique for studying psychiatric morbidity in in-patient and out-patient series and in general population samples. *Psychological Medicine, 6*(4), 665–671.

Wing, J. K. (1980a). The use of the Present State Examination in general population surveys. *Acta Psychiatrica Scandinavica, 61,* 230–240.

Wing, J. K. (1980b). Standardizing clinical diagnostic judgments: the PSE-CATEGO system. *Australian and New Zealand Journal of Psychiatry, 14,* 17–20.

Wing, J. K. (1983). Use and misuse of the PSE. *British Journal of Psychiatry, 143,* 111–117.

Wing, J. K., & Nixon, J. M. (1975). Discriminating symptoms in schizophrenia: A report from the International Pilot Study of Schizophrenia. *Archives of General Psychiatry, 32,* 853–854.

Wing, J. K., Cooper, J. E., & Sartorius, N. (1974). *The description and classification of psychiatric symptoms: An instruction manual for the PSE and CATEGO system.* London: Cambridge University Press.

Wing, J. K., Nixon, J., von Cranach, M., & Strauss, A. (1977). Further developments of the Present State Examination and CATEGO system. *Archiv fur Psychiatrie und Nervenkrankheiten, 224,* 151–160.

Wing, J. K., Mann, S. A., Leff, J. P., & Nixon, J. M. (1978). The concept of 'case' in psychiatric population surveys. *Psychological Medicine, 8*(2), 203–217.

Wing, J. J., Nixon, J., von Cranach, M., & Strauss, A. (1980). Further developments of the PSE and CATEGO system. In J. J. Bartko & W. Gulbinat (Eds.), *Multivariate statistical methodologies used in the International Pilot Study of Schizophrenia* (pp. 46–50) (National Institute of Mental Health, Series GN NO. 1, DHHS Publication No. [ADM] 80–630). Washington, D. C.: Superintendent of Documents, U.S. Government Printing Office.

Woodward, J. A., Henry, B. W., & Overall, J. E. (1975). Patterns of symptom change in anxious depressed outpatients treated with different drugs. *Diseases of the Nervous System, 36,* 125–129.

Yamamoto, J., Koretsune, S., & Reese, S. (1982). The application of the Psychiatric Status Schedule to the Japanese and Japanese-American psychiatric patients in Los Angeles. *The American Journal of Social Psychiatry,* II, 24–27.

Yamamoto, J., Lam, J., Choi, W. I., Reese, S., Lo, S., Hahn, D. S., & Fairbanks, L. (1982). The Psychiatric States Schedule for Asian Americans. *American Journal of Psychiatry, 139,* 1181–1184.

11

Differential Diagnosis of Medical and Psychiatric Disorders

JAMES M. STEVENSON and MELINDA C. MULLINS

INTRODUCTION

Psychiatry stands as a medical specialty on its own, but the distinction between psychiatry and the other specialties, particularly internal medicine and neurology, begins to blur when patients present with diseases which are diagnostic challenges to all. Clinicians appreciate the discovery of tests and methods by which rapid, accurate diagnoses can be reached. Conversely, research performed without attention to the potentially confounding factor of coexistent illness will almost certainly be less valuable than data which has been collected and analyzed with cautious regard for other influences.

Hall, Gardner, Stickney, LeCann, and Popkin (1980), Engel and Margolin (1941), and many others have written of the importance of recognizing medical illnesses within the psychiatric population, as well as the significant amount of psychiatric disease in the general medical population. Less than a day spent in the office of a primary care physician is enough to demonstrate the truth of the maxim that 50-70% of the patients seen will have some psychiatric component of their illness, and between 5% and 20% of all patients will have significant psychiatric disorders (Fauman, 1981).

Mental health professionals are often those with whom psychiatric patients have the most contact, and may be the initial persons to whom

JAMES M. STEVENSON and MELINDA C. MULLINS • Departments of Behavioral Medicine and Psychiatry and Internal Medicine, West Virginia University Medical Center, Morgantown, WV 26506.

symptoms are reported. Knowledge of common medical conditions and their presenting symptoms can be helpful in providing optimum care to these patients. Additionally, inappropriate resource allocation may be avoided by accurate diagnoses of medical conditions presenting as psychiatric disorders.

Thus, the differential diagnosis of medical and psychiatric disorders becomes of utmost importance to diagnostic research. If research is to have validity, fulfillment of positive diagnostic criteria must be complemented by consideration of potentially confounding conditions. Clinical usefulness of data obtained through such research is enhanced and leads to improved patient care.

Our chapter on the differential diagnosis of medical and psychiatric disorders is organized by broad categories of psychiatric presenting complaints or syndromes. Diagnostic and Statistical Manual of Mental Disorders, 3rd Edition (DSM-III) nomenclature and criteria are used throughout.

ORGANIC BRAIN SYNDROMES

Impaired intellectual function is an abnormal state, the diagnosis of which is often a puzzle for either the psychiatrist or the internist. Many manifestations of cognitive impairment may accompany medical disorders. It has also been clearly shown that part of the presentation of psychiatric disorders may be intellectual dysfunction (McAllister, 1983).

Unraveling this Gordian knot requires many elements. Careful mental status examination and recording of serial results of mental status examinations should be performed. Complete physical examination, including rectal and genital exams, is mandatory.

Even the most experienced clinician, operating under the best of conditions, may upon occasion be unable to separate dementing syndromes, such as Primary Degenerative Dementia, from primary psychiatric illnesses, such as Major Depressive Disorder, and a therapeutic trial may be undertaken. Additionally, many elderly patients have multiple coexisting problems; multiple pathology may muddle the overall clinical picture.

Well-known demographics underline the importance of work with organic brain syndromes to clinical practice as well as to research efforts. In the next 50 years the elderly population of the United States will double, resulting in more than one in five citizens being over 65 years of age (Rowe & Besdine, 1982). DSM-III estimates (although epidemiologic data are poor) that between 2 and 4% of the population over the age of 65 has Primary Degenerative Dementia.

Organic Mental Disorders

Organic mental disorders are described in DSM-III as a constellation of behavioral signs and symptoms for which the etiology is known or presumed. The organic brain syndromes are grouped into six categories: (1) delirium and dementia, where cognitive impairment is relatively global; (2) amnestic syndrome and organic hallucinosis, with relatively selective areas of impaired cognition; (3) organic delusional syndrome and organic affective syndrome, which often resemble thought disorders or affective disorders; (4) organic personality syndrome; (5) intoxication and withdrawal, in which the disorder is associated with ingestion or reduction in use of a substance, and (6) atypical/mixed organic brain syndrome, a residual category.

Dementia, delirium, intoxication, and withdrawal, the most common organic brain syndromes, will be discussed here. Organic affective and personality syndromes usually present less potential for confusion with medical illnesses—most often the diagnostic problem encountered is in differentiation from functional psychiatric disorders.

Dementia

Dementia is characterized by a loss of intellectual abilities manifested in many spheres, in the absence of clouding of consciousness. (See Table 1).

The classic mental status examination of the demented patient demonstrates changes in some or all of these areas, and may also be remarkable for lability and shallowness of mood. Early in the course of the illness, these signs may be absent, although foreshadowed by vague symptoms. Often the early demented patient will have many somatic complaints—perhaps reflecting the awareness that "something isn't right." Irritability and lowered frustration tolerance may be noted, and some degree of memory impairment may be found by careful examination. The patient may struggle to perform tasks which were previously completed with ease. Avoidance of novel tasks may not be noted initially by the family, or its significance may only be recognized in retrospect.

Impaired judgment, memory, and impulse control are evident in the middle stages of dementia, as well as continued deterioration in abstract thinking. Personality alterations, either changes in or accentuations of premorbid traits, may become prominent. Later in the course, the individual becomes totally oblivious of his or her surroundings, may be virtually mute, and requires constant care.

Insidious and gradual progression is the rule in dementia, especially

Table 1. DSM-III Criteria for Dementia

A. A loss of intellectual abilities of sufficient severity to interfere with social or occupational functioning
B. Memory impairment
C. At least one of the following:
   (1) impairment of abstract thinking
   (2) impaired judgement
   (3) other (specified) disturbances of higher cortical function
   (4) personality change
D. State of consciousness not clouded
E. Either (1) or (2):
   (1) Evidence from history, physical exam, or laboratory tests of a specific organic factor judged to be etiologically related
   (2) In the absence of such evidence, an organic factor necessary for the development of the syndrome can be presumed if conditions other than Organic Mental Disorders have been reasonably excluded and if the behavioral change represents cognitive impairment in a variety of areas.

Note. From *Diagnostic and Statistical Manual of Mental Disorders* (p. 111) by the American Psychiatric Association, 1980, Washington, DC. Copyright 1980 by the American Psychiatric Association. Adapted by permission.

Primary Degenerative Dementia (DSM-III, 290.XX). Multiple infarct dementia has many of the same clinical features, but the deterioration is said to be more abrupt and stepwise, with "patchy" distribution of deficits. Periodic vascular insults are thought to cause the deficits, which may include pseudobulbar palsy and affect, dysarthria, dysphagia, and other focal neurologic signs. The most significant factor in pathogenesis is arterial hypertension, but cardiac enlargement, cardiac valvular disease and/or arrhythmias (predisposing to emboli), or generalized arteriosclerotic disease may be present. Computerized tomographic scanning may or may not be helpful in differentiation of these two entities. The laboratory evaluation suggested in Table 2 would be expected to discover the estimated 15% of patients presenting with potentially reversible causes of dementia (Wells & Duncan, 1980). Additionally, it is suggested that some measure which will improve functioning can be found in 20-25% of patients, even if complete functioning cannot be restored.

Pseudodementia, or, alternatively, the "dementia syndrome of depression," is a clinical reality which may confound the most rigorous of diagnostic efforts. In his authoritative review of the subject, McAllister (1983) points out the difficulty in diagnosis of patients presenting with functional psychiatric disorders who appear to have the diffuse cerebral dysfunction characteristic of dementia. In addition, with an increasing population of elderly patients, pseudodementia is more likely to occur in the setting of coexisting cerebral dysfunction, further complicating dif-

Table 2. Laboratory Evaluation for Dementia

Complete blood count with differential
Automated metabolic screening, with electolytes, calcium, hepatic enzymes, renal function
tests, *etc.*
T4, T3RU, and TSH
VDRL
Vitamin B 12 and folate levels
Urinalysis
Chest x-ray
Cranial computerized tomographic scanning
Lumbar puncture
Others as indicated: may include blood levels of drugs (including ethanol and therapeutic
drugs), tuberculosis skin testing, arterial blood gases, electroencephalogram, neuro-
psychological testing, *etc.*

---

ferentiation. Depression is the most common psychiatric disorder causing pseudodementia, although it has been reported across the entire spectrum of psychiatric disease.

Clinical features which are helpful in the differentiation of pseudodementia from true dementia include a previous history of psychiatric illness, symptoms of short duration before help is sought, rapid progression of symptoms, strident complaining of cognitive deficits, "don't know" answers, and variability of performance. All of these factors are said to be more common in pseudodementia. Laboratory studies may be helpful in differentiation if they are diagnostic of an organic illness, but add nothing if they are normal. The dexamethasone suppression test, the EEG, and even amobarbital interviewing may not aid in differentiating the two (McAllister, 1983).

Serial bedside mental status evaluations should be performed on each patient, as well as a standardized neuropsychological testing battery. Ancillary diagnostic aids, such as lumbar puncture, should be used where appropriate. Ultimately, a trial of somatic therapy such as tricyclic antidepressants or ECT may be necessary before the issue is decided. The obvious difficulties presented for the researcher, as well as the clinician dealing with these differentiations, can be minimized by strict attention to either DSM-III or RDC criteria for diagnosis and to physical signs and symptoms of disease requiring investigation.

Delirium

While the diagnosis of dementia implies a slow, insidious onset and often precedes a stepwise, paced evaluation, the diagnosis of delirium

Table 3. Differential Diagnosis of Dementia
_____
Primary central nervous system dysfunction

Diffuse parenchymatous diseases of the central nervous system
    Alzheimer disease (senile or presenile form)
    Pick disease
    Parkinson's disease
    Huntington's disease

Trauma
    Open and closed head injuries
    Subdural hematoma

Brain tumors (primary or metastatic)

Vascular disorders
    Atherosclerosis
    Multiple cerebral emboli
    Prolonged sustained hypertension

Normal pressure hydrocephalus

Infections
    Postmeningitis or encephalitis
    Jakob-Creutzfeldt disease
    Syphilis
    Cryptococcal meningitis

Secondary central nervous system dysfunction

Metabolic disorders
    Hypo- or hyperthyroidism
    Hypo- or hyperglycemia
    Chronic liver or renal failure
    Hypoxia or anoxia

Deficiency diseases
    Wernicke-Korsakoff syndrome
    Vitamin B 12 or folate deficiency

Toxins and drugs
    Chronic alcohol abuse
    Chronic abuse of sedatives or tranquilizers
    Dialysis dementia
_____

almost always implies a neuropsychological emergency. Often, causes of delirium lie outside the central nervous system, and may include systemic infections, metabolic disorders, respiratory imbalances, and substance intoxication and withdrawal. It may also be seen in patients with seizures, encephalopathy from any cause, or focal lesions of the parietal or occipital lobes. The association of delirium with acute illness is highlighted by the fact that 10 to 15% of acute medical inpatients develop a degree of organic brain syndrome, which is usually delirium (Wells & Duncan, 1980).

Clouding of consciousness is the classic feature of the delirious patient, in addition to the disorientation and memory impairment characteristic of organic brain syndromes. Table 4 contains DSM-III criteria for the diagnosis. Increased susceptibility to delirium seems to occur in nervous tissue with preexisting abnormalities—children, the elderly, or those with previous injuries.

Differentiation of delirium must often be made from schizophrenic or schizophreniform disorders, or other psychotic disorders, but the alteration in the level of consciousness, and signs of organic brain syndrome on careful mental status testing, lend clues to the diagnosis. Additionally, the electroencephalogram (EEG) often has a characteristic pattern of diffuse slowing which is of aid. Differentiation from dementia is more difficult, but is helped by a history of preexisting cognitive deficit.

An active search for organic causes of the dysfunction is mandatory (See Table 5). Intoxication with or withdrawal from drugs or alcohol should always be suspected and evaluated.

Table 4. DSM-III Criteria for Delirium

A. Clouding of consciousness (reduced clarity of awareness of the environment, with attention deficit)
B. At least two of the following:
   (1) perceptual disturbance
   (2) speech at times incoherent
   (3) disturbance of sleep-wakefulness cycle
   (4) increased or decreased psychomotor activity
C. Disorientation and memory impairment
D. Clinical features developing over a short period of time (hours to days) and tending to fluctuate over the course of a day
E. Evidence, from the history, physical examination, or laboratory tests, of a specific organic factor judged to be etiologically related

---

Note. From *Diagnostic and Statistical Manual of Mental Disorders* (p. 107) by the American Psychiatric Association, 1980, Washington DC. Copyright 1980 by the American Psychiatric Association. Adapted by permission.

Table 5. Laboratory Evaluation for Delirium

Electrolytes
Serum glucose
Blood urea nitrogen
Arterial blood gases
Urinalysis
Electrocardiogram
Other studies as indicated (chest x-ray, liver function tests, *etc.*)

Intoxication

Drug intoxication is used in DSM-III to denote a substance-specific syndrome, due to the recent use and presence in the body of a substance causing maladaptive behavior, with the clinical picture not corresponding to any of the specific organic brain syndromes. In psychiatric practice, the drugs most often dealt with include opioids, sedative-hypnotics, alcohol, hallucinogens, stimulants, and inhalants.

Additionally, a large number of drugs used for treatment of medical illnesses, while not strictly fitting the leaning of DSM-III toward the use of the term in reference to substances used purposefully for intoxication, can yield significant behavioral disturbances when used in excess (or even, on occasion, in therapeutic doses). Categories of these drugs that must be considered in the evaluation of the patient with an apparent organic brain syndrome include anticonvulsants, anti-inflammatory agents, hormones (thyroid, corticosteroids, estrogens, progesterones, androgens), anticholinergics, antihypertensives, bronchodilators, cardiac drugs (digitalis, beta-blockers, antiarrhythmics), sympathomimetics, L-dopa, hypoglycemics (insulin and oral agents), antibiotics (particularly isoniazid), and antineoplastic agents. Over-the-counter medications which might not be reported by patients or families in the drug history could be of significance. For instance, a use of scopolamine-containing hypnotics or sympathomimetic proprietary diet aids could nicely explain an apparent toxic psychosis, and could lead to appropriate diagnostic testing.

Withdrawal

Drug withdrawal is described in DSM-III as development of a substance-specific syndrome following cessation or a reduction in intake of a substance that was previously regularly used by the individual to induce a state of intoxication, which does not correspond to any of the specific organic brain syndromes. Often the identity of the substance is known from the history, or perhaps from laboratory tests. Although the

Table 6. Symptoms and Signs of Common Drug Intoxications

Opioids
   symptoms—apathy, drowsiness, difficulty with concentration
   signs—pupillary construction, slurred speech, respiratory depression, sterile abscesses
   (meperidine), reversal with narcotic antagonists

Sedative-hypnotics
   symptoms—slurred speech, stupor, emotional dysinhibition
   signs—ataxic gait, incoordination, lateral nystagmus, respiratory depression

Hallucinogens
   symptoms—hallucinations or distortions of perception occurring in a clear sensorium,
   often with the sense of profound insight (PCP may produce a grandiose or paranoid
   state difficult to differentiate from functional psychiatric disorders)
   signs—tachycardia, pupillary dilitation, palpitations, diaphoresis, tremor (PCP can produce hypertension, nystagmus, decreased pain sensitivity and seizures as well)

Stimulants
   symptoms—hyperalertness, restlessness, pressured speech
   signs—tachycardia, hypertension, pupillary dilitation, insomnia

Inhalants
   symptoms—mild euphoria or confusion, disorientation
   signs—toxic psychosis, seizures, coma (chronic lead intoxication can result from long-
   term inhalation of leaded gasoline fumes)

---

withdrawal syndrome is different for differing substances of abuse, common features of many include anxiety, restlessness, irritability, insomnia, and impaired attention.

Sedative-hypnotic (including alcohol) withdrawal is the most dangerous of the abstinence syndromes, with anxiety and apprehension in the initial stages, succeeded by delirium, tremulousness, visual and tactile hallucinations, hyperreflexia, hyperpyrexia, and seizures. Most of the other withdrawal syndromes are not life-threatening, although they can be quite uncomfortable. Withdrawal disorders should always be considered in the hospitalized patient who develops a delirium after a short period of time in the hospital.

ANXIETY

A precise definition of anxiety is difficult, for the term has been applied to a wide range of emotional responses. The similarities between the individual with an anxiety disorder and a normal person experiencing an anxious mood further blur exactness in diagnosis. Anxiety can be the predominant disturbance as in Panic Disorder and Generalized Anxiety Disorder. Also, anxiety can be experienced as an individual attempts to overcome symptoms, as in confronting a feared object or situation in a phobic disorder or resisting the obsessions or compulsions of Obsessive Compulsive Disorder.

Anxiety and fear are related in their physiologic manifestations. Both are accompanied by increased activity of the autonomic nervous system (ANS) with such physical signs as sweating, tachycardia, tremor, hyperventilation and gastrointestinal distress (Allen & Allen, 1978). Consequently, the differential diagnosis of anxiety disorders requires vigilance for organic phenomena that are manifested, as well, by hyperautonomic nervous responses. As psychological events, fear and anxiety differ greatly, in that fear is a normal reaction to consciously recognized external danger and its sources. By contrast, anxiety involves apprehension (and often terror) about danger unassociated with any rationally perceived threat.

Although anxiety as a psychological concept has existed from the earliest times of medical history, current understanding remains limited. Clinical research in the area of anxiety disorders has been greatly enhanced in the past several years with the introduction of a new anxiolytic (alprazolam), which has been found to control panic symptoms (the acute awareness of fear and its physiologic result) and to relieve anticipatory anxiety. Further study of certain tricyclic antidepressants and monoamine oxidase inhibitors has resulted in similar excellent results, especially in relieving the panic component. Recently, progress has been made in understanding the basic mechanisms underlying the phenomena of anxiety with the production of anxiety-like states in man by lactate infusions (Kelly, Michell-Heggs, Sherman, 1971) and by the discovery of benzodiazepine receptors in the human brain (Braestrup, & Squires, 1978; Mohler, & Okada, 1977). Importantly, it is estimated that approximately 5% of the population suffers from symptoms of anxiety persistent and severe enough to warrant diagnosis and treatment. Approximately 10-15% of patients seeking care from a primary care provider suffer some form of recurrent anxiety. Anxiety is a common occurrence in many physical illnesses; consequently, researchers as well as clinicians must be comfortable in assigning the etiology to anxiety complaints before proceeding with either research protocol admission or definitive treatment.

The DSM-III category of anxiety disorders contains ten entities recognized currently as distinct and free standing illnesses. Most recent research has focused on two, Panic Disorder and Generalized Anxiety Disorder.

Panic Disorder

The primary feature of a Panic Disorder is the precipitous occurrence of anxiety with a concomitant flush of ANS symptoms. The subjective response on the part of the individual expressing the panic can be so severe that frequent emergency medical evaluations are common. At least three panic episodes must occur within a three week period for a Panic Disorder diagnosis to be made. Repeated episodes can lead frequently to a chronic anxiety (anticipatory) condition as the person attaches significance to the physical and/or psychological surroundings of the panic events. A common complication of this disorder is Agoraphobia, which develops as the individual avoids particular surroundings as a presumptive defense of the acute panic. At the point where many of these situations are avoided, thus limiting the individual's lifestyle, the diagnosis of Agoraphobia with Panic Attacks should be made.

The differential diagnosis of Panic Disorder includes certain medical conditions, depression, intoxication, and withdrawal phenomena, and the schizophrenic spectrum disorders. If a psychiatric disorder predates a panic episode or condition, the presumptive diagnosis is that of the pre-

Table 7. DSM-III Criteria for Panic Disorder

A. At least three panic attacks within a three-week period in circumstances other than during marked physical exertion or in a life-threatening situation. The attacks are not precipitated only by exposure to a circumscribed phobic stimulus.
B. Panic attacks are manifested by discrete periods of apprehension or fear, and at least four of the following symptoms during each attack.
   1. dyspnea
   2. palpitations
   3. chest pain or discomfort
   4. choking or smothering situation
   5. dizziness, vertigo, or unsteady feelings
   6. feelings of unreality
   7. paresthesias (tingling in hands or feet)
   8. hot and cold flashes
   9. sweating
   10. faintness
   11. trembling or shaking
   12. fear of dying, going crazy, or doing something uncontrolled during an attack
C. Not due to a physical disorder or another mental disorder, such as Major Depression, Somatization Disorder, or Schizophrenia
D. The disorder is not associated with Agoraphobia.

Note. From *Diagnostic and Statistical Manual of Mental Disorders* (p. 231) by the American Psychiatric Association, 1980, Washington DC. Copyright 1980 by the American Psychiatric Association. Adapted by permission.

existing psychiatric disorder. Acute anxiety frequently accompanies the schizophrenic spectrum disorders, especially in the prodromal phase. However, in this group, these symptoms are followed rapidly by a breakdown in the individual's ability to test reality (i.e., psychosis). Major depression can be accompanied by acute panic episodes also. Historically, the mood disorder precedes any sudden subjective sense of fearfulness and should be the primary diagnosis.

Table 8 contains a listing of the medical conditions that can complicate a diagnostic approach to Panic Disorders. These disorders are so diverse that great care must be taken in soliciting adequate historical documentation of the illness as well as in a thorough physical examina-

Table 8. Panic Attacks Due to Medical Conditions

Neurologic conditions
    Partial complex seizures
    Tumors
    Fever

Metabolic conditions
    Hypocalcemia
    Hypoglycemia
    Ketoacidosis

Endocrine conditions
    Hyperthyroidism
    Hyperadrenalism

Respiratory conditions (alkalosis)
    Excessive mechanical ventilation (hyperventilation syndrome)
    Salicylate poisoning
    Pulmonary embolism

Cardiac conditions
    Mitral valve prolapse
    Hyperdynamic beta-adrenergic syndrome

Other
    Pheochromocytoma
    Sedative withdrawal
    Muscular exercise
    Hypotension
    Chronic renal insufficiency
    Marijuana
    Hallucinogens
    Carcinoid Syndrome

tion. Various laboratory studies may be helpful in revealing the source of the anxious behavior. An especially high index of suspicion should be maintained for drug use and abuse, with specific laboratory screening to rule out these states. Several interesting medical conditions to consider include pheochromocytoma, mitral valve prolapse, and hyperventilation syndrome.

Pheochromocytomas occur rarely, yet can mimic precisely a panic state, as the primary pathology occurs in the adrenal gland with a secondary production of excess catecholamines (Jefferson, & Marshall, 1981) inducing ANS symptomatology. An associated hypertension may be either paroxysmal or sustained but is nearly always found.

Mitral valve prolapse (MVP) is a fairly common incidental finding on auscultation of normal individuals. One study suggests that as many as 15% of the population may have a prolapsed mitral valve with findings of a click in late systole and perhaps an associated murmur of mild mitral regurgitation. Confirmation of this condition is made by the echocardiogram. These individuals complain of anxiety frequently, many of sudden onset fear and panic feelings. Several studies find a disproportionately high percentage of MVP individuals in the Panic Disorders category. However, this is a highly controversial concomitant finding and must be considered carefully when developing a pure population for research purposes.

Hyperventilation syndrome is a mechanically induced state of panic based on excessive, self-induced ventilation. This rapid overbreathing results in excess carbon dioxide output and respiratory alkalosis producing the panic state. Rebreathing (into a paper bag) corrects the chemical condition and normalizes the feeling state. This condition occurs spontaneously, although inconsistently. It can be precipitated by a stressful event and is most commonly found in individuals with a histrionic disorder. (Usdin & Lewis, 1979).

Generalized Anxiety Disorder

The anxiety component of generalized anxiety is persistent and of at least one month's duration. Generally, there are signs of motor tension, autonomic hyperactivity, apprehensive expectation, and vigilance and scanning. The differential diagnosis includes Schizophrenia, Affective Disorders, Hypochondriasis, and Obsessive Compulsive Disorders, as well as several medical conditions. Generalized anxiety can occur in Panic Disorders, but if panic attacks occur the latter diagnosis is confirmed. This diagnosis is not made if the anxiety is judged to be due to another of the mental disorders.

Table 9. DSM-III Criteria for Generalized Anxiety Disorder

A. Generalized, persistent anxiety is manifested by symptoms from three of the following four categories:
1. motor tension: shakiness, jitteriness, jumpiness, trembling, tension, muscle aches, fatigability, inability to relax, eyelid twitch, furrowed brow, strained face, fidgeting, restlessness, easy startle
2. autonomic hyperactivity: sweating, heart pounding and racing, cold, clammy hands, dry mouth, dizziness, light-headedness, paresthesias (tingling in hands or feet), upset stomach, hot or cold spells, frequent urination, diarrrhea, discomfort in the pit of the stomach, lump in the throat, flushing, pallor, high resting pulse and respiration rate
3. apprehensive expectation: anxiety, worry, fear, rumination, and anticipation of misfortune to self or others
4. vigilance and scanning: hyperattentiveness resulting in distractibility, difficulty in concentrating, insomnia, feeling "on edge", irritability, impatience
B. The anxious mood has been continuous for at least one month.
C. Not due to another mental disorder, such as a Depressive Disorder or Schizophrenia.
D. At least 18 years of age.

Note. From *Diagnostic and Statistical Manual of Mental Disorders* (p. 233) by the American Psychiatric Association, 1980. Washington DC. Copyright 1980 by the American Psychiatric Association. Adapted by permission.

Giannini, Black, and Goettsche (1978) listed 91 medical entities which can produce signs and symptoms of anxiety. The disorders are so diverse that a differential diagnostic approach is best made on the basis of thorough history-taking and a good physical examination coupled with a high index of suspicion for certain of the more commonly appearing medical conditions. Table 10 presents a listing of many of these medical conditions.

Two specific conditions warrant mentioning, as they are always major considerations in differentiating a generalized anxiety state. Hyperthyroidism frequently produces anxiety, restlessness, and emotional lability. Clues to this condition include the presence of diarrhea and palpitations with tachycardia, weight loss, and a tremor (Thorn, 1977). Use of stimulants is the most frequent cause of a medically induced anxiety state. Substances such as caffeine, contained in coffee, tea, and various cola containing beverages, are commonly abused. Chronic use results in anxiety indistinguishable from a generalized anxiety state. Careful questioning of everyday eating, drinking, and drug use habits can define caffeinism. Amphetamines, other stimulant drugs, and aspirin also generate significant anxiety symptomatology when used frequently.

Table 10. Generalized Anxiety due to Medical Conditions.

Cardiovascular conditions
  Angina pectoris
  Cardiac arrhythmia
  Recurrent pulmonary emboli
  Myocardial infarction

Metabolic and endocrine conditions
  Hyperthyroidism
  Hypoglycemia
  Hypoparathyroidism
  Cushing's syndrome

Toxic conditions
  Amphetamines
  Caffeine
  Aspirin
  Alcohol
  Cocaine
  PCP
  THC

Other
  Medication side effects
  Withdrawal—sedatives, hypnotics, barbiturates

DEPRESSION

Depression, the most common of psychiatric symptoms, is another symptom complex often seen in the offices of psychiatrists and primary care physicians. Experienced clinicians know that an increased focus on seeking medical care many times signals a depressive illness (Widmer & Cadoret, 1978).

Conversely, depressions resulting from physical illness or as symptoms of physical illness are frequently seen. Iatrogenic depressions, particularly those caused by drugs, are important medical causes of mood disturbance responsive to intervention (Rowe & Besdine, 1982).

Even with the exclusion of organic causes, the symptom of depression requires differential diagnostic consideration. On the list of considerations are Dementia, Schizophrenia or Schizoaffective Disorders, Dysthymic and Cyclothymic Disorders, Obsessive Compulsive Disorder, Alcohol Dependence, Psychologic reactions to physical illness, and Uncomplicated Bereavement.

Table 11. DSM-III Criteria for Depression.

A. Dysphoric mood or loos of interest or pleasure in all or almost all usual activities and
   pastimes. The dysphoric mood is characterized by symptoms such as the following: depressed, sad, blue, hopeless, low, down in the dumps, irritable. The mood disturbance
   must be prominent and relatively persistent, but not necessarily the most dominant
   symptom, and does not include momentary shifts from one dysphoric mood to another
   dysphoric mood, e.g., anxiety to depression to anger, such as are seen in states of acute
   psychotic turmoil. (For children under six, dysphoric mood may have to be inferred from
   a persistently sad facial expression.)
B. At least four of the following symptoms have each been present nearly every day for a
   period of at least two weeks (in children under six, at least three of the first four).
   (1) poor appetite or significant weight loss (when not dieting) or increased appetite or
       significant weight gain (in children under six, consider failure to make expected
       weight gains)
   (2) insomnia or hypersomnia
   (3) psychomotor agitation or retardation (but not merely subjective feelings of restless-
       ness or being slowed down)
   (4) loss of interest or pleasure in usual activities, or decrease in sexual drive not limited to
       a period when delusional or hallucinating (in children under six, signs of apathy)
   (5) loss of energy; fatigue
   (6) feelings of worthlessness, self-reproach, or excessive or inappropriate guilt (either
       may be delusional)
   (7) complaints or evidence of diminished ability to think or concentrate, such as slowed
       thinking, or indecisiveness not associated with marked loosening of associations
       or incoherence
   (8) recurrent thoughts of death, suicidal ideation, wishes to be dead, or suicide
       attempt
C. Neither of the following dominate the clinical picture when an affective syndrome (i.e.,
   criteria A and B above) is not present, that is, before it developed or after it has
   remitted:
   (1) preoccupation with mood-incongruent delusion or hallucination
   (2) bizarre behavior
D. Not superimposed on either Schizophrenia, Schizophreniform Disorder, or a Paranoid Disorder.
E. Not due to any Organic Mental Disorder or Uncomplicated Bereavement.

Note. From *Diagnostic and Statistical Manual of Mental Disorders* (p. 213) by the American Psychiatric
Association, 1980, Washington DC. Copyright 1980 by the American Psychiatric Association. Adapted
by permission.

Endocrine Causes

Many endocrine causes for depression have been recognized. One of
the most common endocrine disorders presenting as depression is hypothyroidism. The hypothyroid patient may have many of the features of the
depressed patient, including lack of energy, weight gain, depressed affect,
constipation, cold intolerance, menorrhagia, and apathy. Physical signs

of inadequate thyroid function include dry, puffy skin, coarsening of the voice and facial features, goiter, slowed relaxation of deep tendon reflexes, and thinning of the lateral third of the eyebrows. With progression of the thyroid deficiency, the patient may become more withdrawn and develop psychotic features ("myxedema madness").

Differentiation from depressed patients is made by laboratory findings of a low serum thyroxine level, high thyroid stimulating hormone (TSH) levels, and/or an abnormal response to a thyrotropin-releasing hormone (TRH) stimulation test. Other laboratory abnormalities which may be found include increased serum creatine phosphokinase (CPK), increased serum cholesterol, and bradycardia and low voltage on the electrocardiogram.

Hyperthyroid patients, especially in the younger and middle-aged groups, are less likely to be diagnosed as depressed. Clues to the hyperfunction are found in the physical examination and history, and include diarrhea, anxiety, palpitations, and irritability; the examiner confirms tachycardia, a goiter, brisk reflexes, and a tremor.

Atypical depression with confusion may herald thyroid dysfunction in the elderly. "Apathetic thyrotoxicosis" may present with "failure-to-thrive" with weight loss, lethargy, depression, and confusion. Physical signs may include new onset of atrial fibrillation, congestive heart failure, unexplained weight loss, or new onset hypertension. Many of the elderly will not have a goiter. Laboratory evaluation demonstrating elevated T4 or T3 levels is confirmatory.

Adrenal gland dysfunction is another category to be considered. Hypercortisolism contributes to depressive symptoms. Intriguing recent work with the hypothalamic-pituitary-adrenal (HPA) axis and use of the dexamethasone suppression test in the diagnosis of depression makes the distinction between "medical" and "psychiatric" HPA dysfunction somewhat blurry, and points to the need for further research.

Hypercortisolism is signaled in the history by symptoms of obesity, diabetes mellitus, hypertension, osteoporosis, hirsuitism, and amenorrhea, easy fatigue, emotional lability, and somatic delusions. Physical examination may demonstrate the typical habitus, hypertension, easy bruisability, pink striae, plethora, and hirsuitism. Laboratory findings include hypokalemia, low eosinophils, osteoporosis on x-rays, and evidence of diabetes mellitus. Usually urinary and plasma 17-hydroxycorticoid levels are elevated, and further diagnosis depends on the demonstration of increased cortisol production in the absence of stress.

Adrenocortical insufficiency, classically caused by Addison's disease, may be mistaken for depression on cursory examination. The predominant symptom with these patients is asthenia—progressive fatigue, listlessness, and lack of energy. Marked personality changes, usually involving irritability and restlessness, may further misdirect diagnostic efforts. Other symptoms include anorexia, nausea and vomiting, weight loss, cutaneous and mucosal pigmentation, hypotension, and hypoglycemia. Routine laboratory screening may be normal, or may show reduced levels of serum sodium, chloride, and bicarbonate with elevated serum potassium. There may be an anemia, a lymphocytosis, and moderate eosinophilia. Studies of adrenal stimulation with adrenocorticotrophic hormone (ACTH) will demonstrate abnormalities even early in the disease.

Diabetes mellitus, a disease of absolute or relative deficiency of insulin from the pancreas, is a disease with worldwide distribution. Symptoms of polyuria, polydipsia, and polyphagia prompt diagnostic efforts. Very occasionally, diabetes may present as a depressive syndrome, es-

Table 12. Medical Problems Associated with Depression

Endocrine
    Hypothyroidism
    Hyperthyroidism
    Hypercortisolism (for example, Cushing's syndrome)
    Addison's disease
    Diabetes mellitus
    Hypoparathyroidism
    Hyperparathyroidism

Deficiency Diseases
    Pernicious anemia

Neoplasia
    Pancreatic carcinoma
    Brain tumors
    Meningeal carcinomatosis
    Other tumors

Infectious Diseases
    Chronic meningitis
    Mononucleosis

Drugs
    Antihypertensives
    Steroids

Other
    Myasthenia gravis
    Normal pressure hydrocephalus
    Acute intermittent porphyria

pecially in patients presenting with complaints of apathy, fatigue, or impotence. Another clinical syndrome which is beyond the scope of this discussion, but nonetheless important to clinicians, is the secondary depression seen in many longterm diabetics who have complications of their disease including neuropathy, nephropathy, and retinopathy.

Hypo- and hyperparathyroidism are noted as potential causes of a depressive syndrome, usually manifested by weakness, irritability, apathy, anorexia, or fatigue. Hyperparathyroidism is often associated with patients who have kidney stones, polyuria, abdominal pains, or ulcers. Diagnosis of these disorders is made primarily on clinical grounds, supplemented by serum calcium and phosphate determinations and parathyroid hormone measurements.

Deficiency Disorders

Pernicious anemia, a disorder arising from the failure of the stomach to secrete adequate amounts of intrinsic factor for absorption of vitamin B-12, is the premier deficiency disease which may present with depression as a psychiatric syndrome. Irritability or memory disturbances may also be seen. Disease onset is generally insidious, and symptoms may include the classic triad of weakness, sore tongue, and numbness and tingling in the extremities, or may only consist of nonspecific gastrointestinal or neurologic complaints.

Physical findings include a glazed-appearing beefy red tongue, and loss of vibratory sense and incoordination of the lower extremities. The laboratory abnormalities are an often severe anemia with enlarged red blood cells and hypersegmented nuclei of white blood cells. Postgastrectomy patients are predisposed to pernicious anemia, as well as those who have had damage to gastric mucosa from corrosive ingestion. Malabsorption syndromes will also increase the incidence of the disease.

Neoplasia

Cause and effect is sometimes unclear for patients who have neoplasms diagnosed and also manifest depression. More intriguing are those patients who have depression as a presenting symptom. Weight loss or new onset of psychiatric symptoms in patients without a previous history mandates careful consideration and screening.

Carcinoma of the pancreas is the outstanding example of this, where depression, apathy, anxiety, and a sense of doom may precede the diagnosis. Some speculation has been put forth that an unidentified substance produced by the tumor is responsible for the mood disturbance. This is anecdotally supported by the clinical observation that the depression often worsens with progression of the disease, but no such substance has been identified (Fras, Litin, & Bartholomew, 1968).

Early diagnosis is difficult, as weight loss, pain, and unremitting jaundice are the main symptoms, but may not all be present. More frequently, the patient has vague abdominal distress and fullness. Laboratory evaluation can be equally unrevealing, with abnormal serum amylase and lipase in only 10% of patients. Although glucose tolerance tests are frequently abnormal, in the over-60 age group abnormal glucose tolerance tests are not sufficiently unusual to be useful in diagnosis. Computerized tomographic scanning of the pancreas is a simple test which can aid in the visualization of even small tumors.

Adrenal carcinomas may present with depressive manifestations in the same manner as other states of hypercortisolism. Other carcinomas will, though less frequently, have depression as a presenting symptom. Brain tumors or meningeal carcinomatosis are considerations in the appropriate setting.

Infectious Diseases

The acuteness of many infectious diseases and their characteristic clinical pictures of fever, elevated white blood cell counts, and other signs usually preclude the misassignment of patients with these diseases to a diagnostic category of depression. However, some infectious causes must be included in differential diagnosis.

Chronic meningitis can present with apathy, psychomotor retardation, and personality alterations, with or without physical signs of disease or organic brain syndrome. Tuberculous meningitis, chronic fungal meningitis, or even (uncommonly) parasitic CNS infections may present with the appearance of depression.

Underlying immunosuppression, including AIDS, Hodgkin's disease, lymphatic malignancies, leukemia, or diabetes, should alert the clinician to the possibility of an infection as causative. Diagnosis is made by cerebrospinal fluid examination.

Mononucleosis, caused by the Epstein-Barr virus, has long been known to produce the so-called "post-mono syndrome," which includes depression and lassitude. A recent paper (Jones et al., 1985) has pointed out evidence for a chronic mononucleosis syndrome which may also have associated depressive features. Although still poorly-defined, this syndrome may assume some importance in the future in patients with the appearance of a chronic infectious disease and depression.

Syphilis should be mentioned in any discussion of medical causes of psychiatric disease, and certainly may be manifested as a chonic depressive syndrome as well as a chronic organic brain syndrome. The VDRL is a cheap and simple screen.

Drugs

Many drugs may produce depression as a side effect. The prototype of these is reserpine, which has been used for many years as an antihypertensive and antipsychotic drug. Most antihypertensive drugs may produce depression in their side effects profile; important among these are alphamethyldopa, clonidine, and beta-blockers.

Exogenously administered steroids may also cause a depressive constellation. Hypnotics and antianxiety drugs may also be culprits.

Miscellaneous

History and physical examination provide clues to some of the more uncommon organic causes of a depressive syndrome. Myasthenia gravis may present with listlessness and irritability, but should also be associated with muscle weakness, easy fatiguability, and perhaps ptosis. Normal pressure hydrocephalus patients may have depressive affect initially, but with progression will develop the classic triad of gait ataxia, dementia, and incontinence. Ten to fifteen percent of patients with acute intermittent porphyria will initially present with psychiatric symptoms, among them anxiety, irritability, emotional outbursts, depression, and acute psychosis; most of these will also have a history of abdominal pain, constipation, and neuromuscular disturbances.

"Depression" can be considered as a descriptive label for a symptom complex produced by a multitude of causes, many of them organic in origin. The preceding discussion has highlighted the most frequent causes for this complex.

SCHIZOPHRENIA

Schizophrenic syndromes and psychoses are among the most difficult of psychiatric disorders to diagnose, particularly during the initial presentation phase. The etiology of psychotic thinking is ubiquitous, ranging from stress-induced psychological origins to the purely medical. The inability of the individual to test reality, manifested by hallucinatory and delusional phenomena, identifies the person as psychotic. This cognitive impairment, over time and ingrained, separates the schizophrenic from the others, who at most are at risk for periodic, limited episodes of disordered thinking only. Virtually all of the disorders with psychotic features are treatable with good prognoses.

Although psychotic/disordered thinking can be found in psychiatric conditions other than schizophrenia, it is the schizophrenic disorders that are highly variable in their treatment outcome and mostly with a seriously guarded prognosis. It is those individuals who suffer from a schizophrenic spectrum illness who are most apt to develop into the well-recognized chronic mental patient. Reliable estimates predict that in the United States of America one in every 100 individuals will be hospitalized at some point in his life for the treatment of schizophrenia. Further, approximately 2 million new cases occur around the world each year (Goldman, 1984).

The schizophrenic disorders represent a varied group with prominent psychotic features, early age of onset, and a natural course of illness marked by chronicity and social deterioration.

Controversy exists as to the precise diagnosis of schizophrenia. In the past, making the diagnosis of schizophrenia was determined often by the philosophic orientation of the practitioner rather than the symptomatology of the patient. Kraepelin's model followed the natural course of the illness, while Bleuler, focused attention on the variability of symptoms and to the psychological significance of those symptoms. The DSM-III diagnostic criteria for schizophrenia reflects the current conceptualization in the area. Applying the schizophrenia disorder label to the psychotic patient indicates the absence of organic (medical) illness or preexisting affective disorder.

Differential Diagnosis of Schizophrenia

Three broad categories of disorders need to be considered when the diagnosis of schizophrenia is entertained: functional psychiatric disorders, personality disturbances, and organic mental disorders, particularly secondary to drug reaction or intoxication.

Paranoid disorders are distinguished by the absence of prominent hallucinations or bizarre delusions, such as delusions of being controlled or thought broadcasting. The thought processes of these individuals are organized and coherent as well.

Affective disorders present with mood alteration first. Bipolar affective disorders may present as a hostile, agitated and psychotic state but with a previous history of mood disturbance or a course of illness of less than 6 months' duration.

Schizophreniform disorders meet all of the criteria for schizophrenia except for duration, lasting less than 6 months. Schizoaffective disorder is a controversial diagnostic grouping which indicates difficulty in assigning primary etiologic responsibility to either the schizophrenic or the affective spectrum illness category. Psychotic thinking in the face of marked mood disturbance, recurrent and limiting, is a feature.

The personality disorders that may be included in a differential diagnosis of schizophrenia differ from that disorder mainly in the severity of symptoms and in the rapid return to normal behavior.

Table 14 lists most medical conditions that can present as a psychotic state, complicating both clinical management and research diagnostic attempts. In both instances a high index of suspicion for medical causes should be maintained, as a quick search of the literature highlights convincingly the evidence that physical illness frequently presents as disturbances in thinking (Koranyi, 1979). In particular, a detailed listing with a complete documentation of substance use will discount two major categories of toxic conditions: alcohol and hallucinogen abuse. Acutely, these states (and particularly the latter) can be indistinguishable from an acute schizophrenic episode. Disulfiram is an additional drug that can cause schizophrenic-like episodes with chronic use. This is a frequent event as this medication is being used commonly to help maintain abstinence in the alcohol-addicted patient. Anderson (1980) outlines a sensible approach to delineating organic states with psychotic features.

EATING DISORDERS

The diagnostic category of eating disorders is a relatively new consideration in psychiatry. Although recognized traditionally as symptomatic of other disorders, this category has only recently been able to withstand scrutiny as containing discrete diagnostic considerations. In particular, the category of anorexia nervosa has a long history of psychodynamic exploration as well as physiologic investigation. It has been with the institution of the DSM-III that a vigorous evaluation of this population has occurred. A second major category for consideration is bulimia. A recently recognized disorder with a discrete behavior pattern, Bruch (1973) suggests that it may actually reflect a subgrouping of anorexics. Unfortunately, these two disorders, anorexia nervosa and bulimia, have appeared at a startingly high rate over the past five years, especially among the adolescent and young adult female population. Obesity is an additional grouping of eating patterns that can be considered aberrant but is poorly organized currently for diagnostic purposes.

Table 13. DSM-III Criteria for Schizophrenia

A. At least one of the following during a phase of the illness:
  1. bizarre delusions (content is patently absurd and has no possible basis in fact), such as delusions of being controlled, thought broadcasting, thought insertion, or thought withdrawal.
  2. somatic, grandiose, religious, nihilistic, or other delusions without persecutory or jealous content
  3. delusions with persecutory or jealous content if accompanied by hallucinations of any type
  4. auditory hallucinations in which either a voice keeps up a running commentary on the individual's behavior or thoughts, or two or more voices converse with each other
  5. auditory hallucinations on several occasions with content of more than one or two words, having no apparent relation to depression or elation
  6. incoherence, marked loosening of associations, markedly illogical thinking, or marked poverty of content of speech if associated with at least one of the following:
      a. blunted, flat, or innappropriate affect
      b. delusions or hallucinations
      c. catatonic or other grossly disorganized behavior
B. Deterioration from a previous level of functioning in such areas as work, social relations, and self-care.
C. Duration: Continuous signs of the illness for at least six months at some time during the person's life, with some signs of the illness at present. The six-month period must include an active phase during which there were symptoms from A, with or without a prodromal or residual phase, as defined below.
  Prodromal phase: A clear deterioration in functioning before the active phase of the illness not due to a disturbance in mood or to a Substance Use Disorder and involving at least two of the symptoms noted below.

  Residual phase: Persistence, following the active phase of the illness, of at least two of the symptoms noted below, not due to a disturbance in mood or to a Substance Use Disorder.

Prodromal or residual symptoms:
  1. social isolation or withdrawal
  2. marked impairment in role functioning as wage-earner, student or homemaker
  3. markedly peculiar behavior (e.g., collecting garbage, talking to self in public, or hoarding food)
  4. marked impairment in personal hygiene and grooming
  5. blunted, flat, or inappropriate affect
  6. digressive, vague, over-elaborate, circumstantial, or metaphorical speech
  7. odd or bizarre ideation, or magical thinking, e.g., superstitiousness, clairvoyance, telepathy, "sixth sense," "others can feel my feelings," overvalued ideas, ideas of reference.
  8. unusual perceptual experiences, e.g., recurrent illusions, sensing the presence of a force or person not actually present

  Examples: Six months of prodromal symptoms with one week of symptoms from A; no

---

(continued)

Table 13 (continued)

prodromal symptoms with six months of symptoms from A; no prodromal symptoms with two weeks of symptoms from A and six months of residual symptoms; six months of symptoms from A, apparently followed by several years of complete remission, with one week of symptoms from A in current episode.

D. The full depressive or manic syndrome (criteria A and B of major depressive or manic episode), if present, developed after any psychotic symptoms, or was brief in duration relative to the duration of the psychotic symptoms in A.

E. Onset of prodromal or active phase of the illness before age 45.

F. Not due to any organic mental disorder or mental retardation.

Note. From *Diagnostic and Statistical Manual of Mental Disorders* (p. 188) by the American Psychiatric Association, 1980, Washington DC. Copyright 1980 by the American Psychiatric Association. Adapted by permission.

Table 14. Differential Diagnosis of Schizophrenic Disorders

Neurologic conditions
  Epilepsy
    Temporal lobe epilepsy
    Postictal states
  Degenerative states: senile and presenile psychosis
    Huntington's Disease
  Infections of the central nervous system
  Vascular lesions: infarcts, hemorrhages, collagen disorders, aneurysms
  Space-occupying lesions
    Tumors: primary and metastatic
    Brain abscesses
    Subdural hematoma
  Normal pressure hydrocephalus

Toxic conditions
  Hallucinogens
    Lysesrgic acid diethylamide (LSD)
    Phencyclidine (PCP)
    Mescaline
    Marijuana (THC)
  Amphetamines
  Opiates (cocaine)
  Barbiturates, intoxication and withdrawal
  Alcohol
    Alcoholic hallucinations
    Alcohol withdrawal states: delirium tremens
  Steroids
  Anticholinergics
  Bromides
  Heavy metals
  Disulfiram

(continued)

Table 14 *(continued)*

Metabolic Endocrine Conditions
  Thyroid: hyperthyroidism, hypothyroidism
  Addison's disease and Cushing's syndrome
  Porphyria
  Fluid & Electrolyte Imbalances
  Wilson's Disease
  Diabetes mellitus

Nutritional Deficiency Conditions
  Niacin: pellagra
  Thiamin: Wernicke-Korsakoff's syndrome
  Pernicious anemia
  Pyridoxine deficiency

Iatrogenic conditions
  Antipsychotics
  Sedative-hypnotics
  Antidepressants
  Lithium
  Levodopa
  Anticonvulsants
  Antitubercular drugs
  Anti-inflammatory drugs
  Antihypertensive agents
  Cardiac drugs
  Idiosyncratic reactions to nearly any medication

Anorexia Nervosa

The essential features of anorexia nervosa include self-imposed dieting with a 25% weight loss, severe disturbance in body image and amenorrhea in females. Individuals with this disorder report gross distortions in their appearance, stating they "look (feel) fat," even though grotesquely emaciated. Stubbornly maintaining this misperception, anorexic patients will tremendously reduce dietary intake, often developing strange and ritualistic eating habits, especially cutting into their protein and carbohydrate food groups. Frequently the anorexic will exercise compulsively, use laxatives, and induce vomiting to maintain or further reduce her weight.

Some anorexics cannot maintain strict dietary self-control and abstinence and will occasionally resort to binge eating (bulimic episodes) with frequent self-induced purges. This individual may develop a propen-

Table 15. DSM-III Criteria for Anorexia Nervosa.

A. Intense fear of becoming obese, which does not diminish as weight loss progresses.
B. Disturbance of body image, e.g., claiming to "feel fat" even when emaciated.
C. Weight loss of at least 25% of original body weight or, if under 18 years of age, weight loss from original body weight plus projected weight gain expected from growth charts may be combined to make 25%.
D. Refusal to maintain body weight over a minimal normal weight for age and height.
E. No known physical illness that would account for the weight loss.

Note. From *Diagnostic and Statistical Manual of Mental Disorders* (p. 69) by the American Psychiatric Association, 1980, Washington DC. Copyright 1980 by the American Psychiatric Association. Adapted by permission.

sity to feed, literally, those around them by planning and cooking elaborate meals, yet denying themselves participation in the meal, while occasionally hoarding foodstuffs. The anorexia nervosa patient denies assiduously that she has an illness and is highly resistant to intervention. Recent reports indicate that as much as 1% of the population may have some form of the illness (Crisp, Palmer, & Kalucy, 1976).

Differential Diagnosis of Anorexia Nervosa

The principal differential must be made between certain medical disorders and anorexia nervosa, although several psychiatric states should be considered as well.

In schizophrenia, bizarre eating behavior may occur related to the individual's delusional perceptions. However, the full syndrome of anorexia nervosa is rarely present and the patient will show generalized thought impairment.

In depression, weight loss may occur; however, the fear of obesity or body image disturbances are not present. Also, these patients have a primary mood disturbance that they acknowledge while the anorexic will deny any mood problem and, in fact, react positively to most interchanges. In bulimia rarely is weight loss in excess of 25% of the body weight, if there is much weight loss at all. Bulimia can accompany anorexia nervosa rarely; if so, both should be diagnosed.

The differential diagnostic possibilities for anorexia nervosa and medical illnesses are intriguing. Table 16 lists these possibilities. None of these patients will show the intense fear of becoming obese that is a hallmark of anorexia nervosa, however. These medically ill patients accurately perceive their nutritional states and show appropriate concern. The differentiation between these disorders can be made readily from a thorough history and adequate physical examination. A laboratory ex-

Table 16. Differential Diagnosis of Medical Disorders and Anorexia Nervosa

Brain tumors
Hypothalamic area
Area of the third ventricle
Inflammatory bowel disease
Panhypopituitarism
Hyperthyroidism
Neoplasms of almost any type

amination of the neuroendocrine axis can delimit physiologic response. CT scan may be necessary to rule out as a possibility a central, space-occupying lesion.

Bulimia

This disorder is one of the newer psychiatric entities, described in the late 1950's as a behavior pattern noted in some obese individuals. Primarily, the bulimic displays episodic binge eating accompanied by an awareness that the eating pattern is abnormal. These individuals fear not being able to stop eating voluntarily, with depressed mood and self-depreciating thoughts following the eating binges. Within the past few

Table 17. DSM-III Criteria for Bulimia.

A. Recurrent episodes of binge eating (rapid consumption of a large amount of food in a discrete period of time, usually less than two hours).

B. At least three of the following:
   (1) Consumption of high-caloric, easily ingested food during a binge.
   (2) Inconspicuous eating during a binge.
   (3) Termination of such eating episodes by abdominal pain, sleep, social interruption, or self-induced vomiting.
   (4) Repeated attempts to lose weight by severely restrictive diets, self-induced vomiting, or use of cathartics or diuretics.
   (5) Frequent weight fluctuations greater than 10 pounds due to alternating binges and fasts.

C. Awareness that the eating pattern is abnormal and fear of not being able to stop eating voluntarily.

D. Depressed mood and self-deprecating thoughts following eating binges.

E. The bulimic episodes are not due to anorexia nervosa or any known physical disorder.

Note. From *Diagnostic and Statistical Manual of Mental Disorders* (p. 70) by the American Psychiatric Association, 1980, Washington DC. Copyright 1980 by the American Psychiatric Association. Adapted by permission.

years this disorder has become one of the most commonly reported psychological phenomena among college women (Bruch, 1985). Recently, it has been identified as a distinct disorder occurring in nonobese individuals who do not suffer from anorexia nervosa (See Table 17).

The eating binges may be planned and usually consist of high caloric (high carbohydrate) foods. The binge can proceed over an extended period of several hours, usually surreptitiously and without a feeling of loss of control. Often, a purge phase follows to decrease the pain from abdominal distention (Hamilton, Gelwick, & Meade, 1984). Individuals with bulimia almost always display intense concern for their weight and may use self-induced vomiting as a conscious means of weight control. A frequent concomitant finding in bulimics is poor dentition (especially enamel erosion), which is caused from the continued exposure of the teeth to regurgitated stomach acid.

Differential Diagnosis of Bulimia

Few functional disorders can be confused with bulimia. Anorexia nervosa requires a severe weight loss and is life-threatening, unlike bulimia. Schizophrenic patients may have unusual eating patterns but the full syndrome of bulimia is rare.

It may be necessary to rule out several neurologic entities including epileptic-equivalent seizures, CNS tumors, Kluver-Bucy-like syndromes, and Kleine-Levin syndrome. Although these are extremely unusual conditions, their consideration should be entertained.

Kluver-Bucy syndrome includes hyperphagia, visual agnosia, compulsive licking and biting, exploration of objects by mouth, and hypersexuality. This is an extremely rare condition and unlikely to present a problem in diagnosis. Kleine-Levin syndrome includes hyperphagia and periods of hypersomnia lasting 2-3 weeks. This is mainly a condition of males which represent a minute fraction of the total population of bulimics.

MISCELLANEOUS

Seizure disorders may require differentiation from functional psychiatric disease in the evaluation of patients. Certainly, the grand mal seizure sequence will be evident to the nonmedically-trained observer, but other seizures may be more subtle. Patients with psychomotor epilepsy may experience complex hallucinations or illusions as part of the aura preceding their seizure. Somatic sensory seizures nearly always indicate a parietal lobe lesion. Auditory hallucinations are rare as manifestations of seizures, but have been reported. Somewhat more common are vertiginous sensations, visceral sensations, or even olfactory or gustatory hallucinations.

Psychic phenomena, including depersonalization and derealization, as well as compulsive thought or behavior, hyperreligiosity, hypergraphia, or even frank psychoses are frequently seen with temporal lobe foci.

Systemic lupus erythematosus, while a rheumatologic disease, is frequently the focus of psychiatric attention. The problems may range from those of adjustment to a chronic, disabling disease, to those of frank delirium or psychosis from vasculitic, hypertensive, uremic, or even iatrogenic (steroid) effects on nervous tissue. It has been estimated that 50 percent of patients with SLE will experience neuropsychiatric complications at some time during the course of their disease.

Multiple sclerosis is another disease which may frustrate initial attempts at diagnosis, especially in the young adult experiencing a first attack where central nervous system lesions separated in time and space have not yet become evident. Vague symptoms accompanied by only slight objectively demonstrable dysfunction may convince the clinician of hysteria rather than a demyelinating disorder. A high index of suspicion combined with serial examinations, as well as the finding of elevated CSF gamma globulin, leads to greater diagnostic certainty.

SUMMARY

This chapter has been an attempt to present common psychiatric syndromes which may be caused by medical conditions, and to point out factors which should be considered in their differentiation.

Patients at the interface of internal medicine, psychiatry, and neurology frequently present difficulties in diagnosis. Workers in each field must have familiarity with related fields if they are to avoid errors.

Every differential diagnosis of behavioral symptoms should include physical illness, with medical assessment a priority before diagnostic formulations are solidified. Serial physical examinations, additional history taking, appropriate laboratory testing, and timely consultations cannot help but maximize diagnostic validity and patient care.

REFERENCES

Allen, J. R., & Allen, B. A. (1978). *Guide to psychiatry.* New York: Medical Examination Publishing Company, Inc.

Anderson, W. H. (1980). The physical examination in office practice. *American Journal of Psychiatry, 137,* 1188–1192.

Braestrup, C., & Squires, R. (1978). Brain specific benzodiazepine receptors. *British Journal of Psychiatry, 133,* 249.

Bruch, H. (1973). *Eating disorders: Obesity, anorexia nervosa and the person within.* New York: Basic Books.

Bruch, H. (1985). Four decades of eating disorders. In D. M. Garner & P. S. Garfinkel (Eds.), *Anorexia nervosa and bulimia* (pp.7–18). New York: Guilford Press.

Crisp, A. H., Pamer, R. L., & Kalucy, R. S. (1976). How common is anorexia nervosa? A prevalence study. *British Journal of Psychiatry, 129,* 549–554.

Engel, G. L., & Margolin, S. G. (1941). Neuropsychiatric disturbances in internal disease. Archives of Internal Medicine, 70, 236–259.

Fauman, M. A. (1981). Psychiatric components of medical and surgical practice: A survey of general hospital physicians. *American Journal of Psychiatry, 138,* 1298–1301.

Fras, I., Litin, E. M., & Bartholomew, L. G. Mental symptoms as an aid in the early diagnosis of carcinoma of the pancreas. *Gastroenterology, 55,* 191–198.

Giannini, A. J., Black, H. R., Goettsche, R. L. (1978). *Psychiatric, psychogenic, and somatopsychic disorders handbook.* New York: Medical Examination Publishing.

Goldman, H. H. (1984) *Review of General Psychiatry.* Los Altos: Lange.

Hamilton, M. K., Gelwick, B. P., & Meade, C. J. (1984). Differential diagnosis: Bulimia, anorexia nervosa, and obesity. In R. C. Hawkins, W. J. Fremouw, & P. F. Clement (Eds.), *The binge-purge syndrome* (pp. 3–27). New York: Springer.

Jefferson, J. W., & Marshall, J. R. (1981). *Neuropsychiatric features of medical disorders.* New York: Plenum.

Jones, J. F., Ray, C. G., Minnich, L. L., Hicks, M. J., Kibler, R., & Lucas, D. O. (1985). Evidence for active epstein-barr virus infection in patients with persistent unexplained illnesses. *Annals of Internal Medicine, 102,* 1–7.

Kelly, D., Mitchell-Higgs, N., & Sherman, D. (1971). Anxiety and the effects of sodium lactate assessed clinically and physiologically. *British Journal of Psychiatry, 119,* 129–141.

Koranyi, E. K. (1979). Morbidity and rate of undiagnosed physical illness in a psychiatric clinic population. *Archives of General Psychiatry, 36,* 414–419.

McAllister, T. W. (1983). Pseudodementia. *American Journal of Psychiatry, 140,* 528–533.

Mohler, H., & Okada, T. (1977). The benzodiazepine receptor in normal and pathological human brain. *Science, 1977, 198,* 849.

Rowe, J. W., & Besdine, R. W. (1981). *Health and Disease in Old Age.* Boston: Little, Brown.

Thorn, G. W., Adam, R. D., Baunwald, E., Isselbacher, K. J., & Petersdorf, R. G. (1977). *Harrison's principles of internal medicine* (8th edition). New York: McGraw-Hill.

Usdin, G., & Lewis, J. (1979). *Psychiatry in General Medical Practice.* New York: McGraw-Hill.

Wells, C. E., & Duncan, Gary W. (1980). *Neurology for Psychiatrists.* Philadelphia: F. A. Davis.

12

DSM-III and Behavioral Assessment

ROSEMERY O. NELSON

INTRODUCTION

The main focus of this chapter is the relationship between behavioral assessment and the third edition of the *Diagnostic and Statistical Manual of Mental Disorders* (DSM-III: American Psychiatric Association, 1980). Introductory topics include the advantages and disadvantages of classification systems in general, and a brief description of DSM-III, along with its strengths and weaknesses. The pros and cons of DSM-III from the vantage of behavioral assessors are emphasized. The utility of the manual in achieving the goals of behavioral assessment is discussed, with the conclusion that it offers useful suggestions to behavioral assessors, but that it cannot replace behavioral assessment. Finally, a particular, proposed contribution of behavioral assessment to DSM-IV is described.

CLASSIFICATION AND DIAGNOSIS

The Greek origins of "diagnosis" are "dia" (through, between, here used in the sense of "through") and "gnosis" (knowledge or investigation); to know something thoroughly includes distinguishing it from other things (Matarazzo, 1983). Diagnoses are assigned to individuals and/or to their problems based on a classification schema. Of relevance here are classification systems for mental disorders and/or behavior problems.

ROSEMERY O. NELSON • Department of Psychology, University of North Carolina, Greensboro, NC 27412.

Brief History of Classification

The diagnostic classification of mental disorders and behavior problems has had a long history (Matarazzo, 1983; Singerman, 1981). Some of
its outstanding figures are: Hippocrates, who in the fifth century B.C.
created one of the first recorded categorizations of mental illnesses;
Phillipe Pinel, who in the 19th century devised a classification system for
the psychotic states that he observed at La Bicetre Hospital in Paris; Emil
Kraepelin, who at the turn of the 20th century divided mental illnesses
into three categories: organic psychoses, endogenous psychoses—including dementia praecox and manic depressive psychosis, and deviations of
personality and reactive states; William Menninger, whose work in World
War II was incorporated by the American Psychiatric Association into
DSM-I (1952) and DSM-II (1968); J. Feighner, who, with Eli Robins at
Washington University, developed the Feighner diagnostic criteria for
several mental illnesses (Feighner, Robins, Guze, Woodruff, Winokur, &
Munoz, 1972); Robert Spitzer, Jean Endicott, and, again, Eli Robins, who
modified the Feighner criteria into the Research Diagnostic Criteria
(1978); and, again, Robert Spitzer, who chaired the American Psychiatric
Association's task force that produced DSM-III in 1980.

Advantages of Classification

Among the many advantages of descriptive classifications (Adams &
Haber, 1984; Bannister, Salmon, & Lieberman, 1964), reflecting their long
and noble tradition, are the following. First, a classification system,
organizing data into meaningful and precise concepts, is necessary for the
development of a clinical science (Adams & Haber, 1984). These concepts,
enhancing communication among scientists, allow recognition of common features among phenomena in several dimensions: behavior or
symptoms, etiology, prognosis, and responses to particular types of treatment. Classification systems provide labels for these features, which,
along with precise definitions, facilitate contributions to a research literature. Data can be compiled and hypotheses generated about phenomena
identified to be the same from one scientist to the next. The alternative, elaborate individual case descriptions, would be much more cumbersome.

The remaining advantages are related to the communication function of widely accepted classification systems. As a second advantage, professionals can more easily develop, and have easier access to, a research
literature related to particular mental or behavioral problems when they

are identified by shorthand labels. Third, referrals from one professional to another are facilitated by diagnostic labels, providing a "ball park" description of the client. Fourth, classification systems assist in record-keeping and in statistical compilation, such as epidemiological records or tallies of types of service-recipients in different agencies. Fifth, diagnoses allow communication between service providers and third-party payers of those services (Miller, Bergstrom, Cross, & Grube, 1981).

Disadvantages of Classification

Despite the obvious advantages of classification systems for mental or behavioral problems, such systems are not without drawbacks. The iatrogenic effects of diagnostic labelling have been widely recognized (e.g., Hobbs, 1975; Stuart, 1970; Szasz, 1960). Among these iatrogenic effects are the social stigma of being labeled "mentally ill," the passivity of waiting for a cure of one's "mental illness," a pessimistic belief that some or many types of mental illnesses cannot be cured, and the exaggeration or stereotyping of symptoms produced by diagnosis labels, in the manner of a self-fulfilling prophesy.

Another concern raised about diagnostic systems is their psychometric properties. Is the system reliable, valid, and useful? Reliability here refers to the extent of agreement among clinicians in assigning a diagnostic label to the same patient. While poor reliability can surely result from an inadequate diagnostic system, other contributing factors include differences among clinicians in training, expertise, and prejudices; client characteristics other than behavior, like gender or socioeconomic status; and the fact that diagnosis frequently occurs in hospital or clinic settings, where some abnormal behavior is seldom observed (Stuart, 1970). In a thorough review of the reliability of psychiatric and psychological diagnosis, Matarazzo (1983) reached two conclusions. First, intensive research from 1930 to 1965 revealed that interclinician reliability was typically low. Second, diagnostic reliability has greatly improved recently due to the use of structured interviews to obtain information about patients and the development of diagnostic systems including operational criteria for different disorders.

Validity here refers to the content of the diagnostic system. Does it have some basis in reality? For instance, some believe that mental problems are more validly depicted by continuous dimensions than the discontinuous typologies that underlie most diagnostic systems (Draguns & Phillips, 1971; Vaillant, 1984).

Utility refers to the usefulness of the system in providing information about the etiology, prognosis, and/or treatment of a particular disorder. To illustrate, Stuart (1970) notes that diagnoses contribute only about 10% of the variance in determining if a patient is released from a mental hospital (Turner & Cummings, 1967). More important determinants are the patient's family situation and socioeconomic status. The utility for treatment planning of descriptive classification systems has been of major concern (Singerman, 1981). For example, based on a statistical analysis of 1,000 cases, Bannister et al. (1964) conclude that diagnosis and treatment are significantly related for some categories of disorders, but that there is no such statistical association for many other categories.

A final type of criticism is logical inconsistency within the classification system (Bannister et al., 1964; Draguns & Phillips, 1971). Categories are criticized as not being mutually exclusive (Zigler & Phillips, 1961). Similarly, categories within the same system are criticized as not being derived from a single logical basis; instead, they are based on body, behavior, and mind (Szasz, 1957).

DSM-III

Brief History of DSM-III

A classification schema for mental and behavioral disorders is necessary for the development of a clinical science, and also facilitates other types of communication among professionals. Nonetheless, abundant criticism was directed at the two diagnostic systems created by the American Psychiatric Association, the first (1952) and second (1968) editions of the Diagnostic and Statistical Manual of Mental Disorders. The third edition, known as DSM-III (1980), was designed to provide major improvements over DSM-I and DSM-II, and is radically different from its predecessors.

The history of the development of DSM-III has been summarized by Kazdin (1983), Matarazzo (1983), Millon (1983), Spitzer, Endicott, and Robins (1978), and Taylor (1983), and in DSM-III itself. Several factors contributed to its development. One factor was the preparation and publication in 1979 of the ninth edition of the international Classification of Diseases (ICD-9) by the World Health Organization. This classification system for diseases, injuries, impairment, and causes of death is used world-wide and is revised about every ten years. However, the section on clinical or mental disorders in ICD-9 was judged too sparse for adequate clinical use. Thus, a clinical modification of ICD-9 (ICD-9-CM) was prepared by the Council on Clinical Classification, for United States use.

DSM-III was intended to elaborate and modify that portion of ICD-9-CM that dealt with mental disorders, but to remain compatible with ICD-9-CM. An explicit "crosswalk" between DSM-III and ICD-9-CM is described by Thompson, Green, and Savitt (1983).

A second factor contributing to the development of DSM-III was the creation of classification systems that provided operational criteria for each diagnosis, namely, the Feighner Criteria devised by the Washington University group (Feighner *et al.,* 1972) and the Research Diagnostic Criteria (Spitzer *et al.,* 1978). While both were developed primarily for research purposes, and included only a limited number of diagnostic categories, because of the improved diagnostic reliability resulting from the operational criteria, such criteria for diagnostic categories were to be included in DSM-III.

Thus, in 1974, the American Psychiatric Association appointed a Task Force on Nomenclature and Statistics, with Robert Spitzer as chairperson, to revise DSM. The Task Force was aided by 14 advisory committees on specific disorders, the members of which are listed in the opening pages of DSM-III. Liaisons were established with other related groups (e.g., American Psychological Association, American Psychoanalytic Association). Draft forms of DSM-III were tried out in field trials between 1976 and 1980 that involved hundreds of clinicians. The final version (APA, 1980) contains explicit criteria for 16 major diagnostic categories and 187 subcategories (Matarazzo, 1983).

Assets of DSM-III

There is strong consensus that DSM-III is a great improvement over DSM-I and DSM-II. Among its specific assets, the following have been noted.

First, there is the open process by which DSM-III was developed (Spitzer *et al.,* 1978), with many individuals and groups involved in its evolution. The process was not always smooth. Great controversy was generated, for example, by these issues: a draft introduction identifying mental disorders as a subset of medical disorders, the elimination of the term "neurosis," and the inclusion or exclusion of homosexuality as a sexual deviation. Nonetheless, a more or less acceptable consensus emerged, permitting publication of the document.

Second, and relatedly, there are the field trials which permitted input into DSM-III by on-line clinicians (Klerman, 1984; Spitzer *et al.,* 1978). The final field trial involved hundreds of clinicians across the country, and was sponsored by the National Institute of Mental Health. This was the first time that a classification system for mental disorders had been modified in a systematic manner before its formal adoption (Spitzer *et al.,* 1978).

A third asset is the operational criteria, both inclusive and exclusive, provided for each diagnostic category (Kazdin, 1983; Klerman, 1984; Millon, 1983; Spitzer *et al.,* 1978), such criteria having historically been shown to increase diagnostic reliability.

A fourth asset is the improved diagnostic reliability of DSM-III over its predecessors (Spitzer *et al.,* 1978). Diagnostic reliability was evaluated in two phases, Phase One using the 1978 draft of DSM-III, and Phase Two using the final version. The reliability statistic was kappa, a conservative measure that corrects for chance agreement. Overall kappa reliability for Axis I for adults was .68 and .72 in Phases One and Two, respectively. Overall kappa reliability for Axis I for children was .68 and .52 in the two respective phases (APA, 1980). Matarazzo (1983) notes that these reliability figures are even more impressive because no standardized method, such as a structured interview, was used to elicit patient information.

A sixth asset is the multiaxial format of DSM-III (Kazdin, 1983; Klerman, 1984; Millon, 1983; Spitzer *et al.,* 1978). These axes are thought to be somewhat independent of each other, and to help portray the clinical complexity of the individual. One or more of the specific diagnostic codes of DSM-III are entered on Axis I. On Axis II, personality disorders are diagnosed for adults, and specific developmental disorders for children. On Axis III are coded physical disorders and conditions. Ratings (1-7) are provided for Axes IV and V, indicating, respectively, severity of psychological stressors and highest level of adaptive functioning in the last year.

A seventh asset is the generally atheoretical nature of DSM-III (Kazdin, 1983). The focus is on presenting symptoms rather than presumed etiology. The rationale was to increase the acceptability of the diagnostic system, since clinicians are more likely to agree on symptomatology than etiology.

An eighth asset of DSM-III is that it provides a rather comprehensive description of individual disorders (Kazdin, 1983; Millon, 1983). Several characteristics of a disorder are described, including its essential and correlated features, age of onset, course, impairment, complications, predisposing factors, prevalence, sex ratio, familial patterns, and criteria for differential diagnosis.

A ninth asset is that the focus is on diagnosing disorders, and not individuals (Kazdin, 1983). A tenth asset is the advancement of the recognition of personality disorders by their diagnosis on a separate axis, Axis II (Millon, 1983). An eleventh asset is the realization that DSM-III can presage a DSM-IV with further improvements (Klerman, 1984; Millon, 1983).

Criticisms of DSM-III

Despite the many assets of DSM-III, criticisms have also abounded. In January, 1977, the American Psychological Association created the Task Force on Descriptive Behavioral Classification. The Task Force concluded that the approach used in DSM-III was unsatisfactory for these reasons: (a) its disease-based model is used inappropriately to decribe problems in living; (b) its specific categories show consistently high levels of unreliability; (c) it is a mixed model that bases the groupings variously on symptom clusters, antisocial behaviors, theoretical considerations, or developmental influence; (d) categories have been either created or deleted on committee vote rather than on hard scientific data; (e) the labels have assumed strong judgmental qualities that frequently result in bias and social injustice; and (f) it offers low capability for indicating treatment modality or predicting clinical outcome (Smith & Kraft, 1983). Some of these criticisms are elaborated on below, and a few additional criticisms are noted.

One criticism of DSM-III is that it continues to endorse, at least implicitly, a disease model of mental and behavioral disorders. The statement in an earlier draft of DSM-III that mental disorders are a subset of medical disorders was recanted in the heat of political battle (Millon, 1983; Spitzer et al., 1978). Nonetheless, many are concerned that the spirit of the medical model continues to permeate DSM-III (e.g., Taylor, 1983). The nature of the concerns are twofold. One is the lack of validity in considering mental or behavioral problems as medical problems. In survey results reported by Smith and Kraft (1983), nearly three-fourths of the 556 respondents (members of Division 29 of the American Psychological Association) agreed that most conditions that DSM-III labels as mental disorders can best be described as nonmedical problems in living. Thomas Szasz's view (1960) prefers a sociobehavioral classification of behavioral disturbance, rather than a medical classification. McLemore and Benjamin (1979) believe that the interpersonal basis of diagnosis should be more explicitly recognized. Another concern about the implicit incorporation of mental and behavioral disorders within the medical model is the economic and political impact on nonmedical personnel who deal with mental and behavioral disorders (Schact & Nathan, 1977; Smith & Kraft, 1983). If these disorders are considered to be medical problems, then they should be treated by medical personnel.

A second criticism of DSM-III is that its categories were not empirically derived. Instead, "truth" was determined by committees and by political compromise (Schact, 1985). Examples include the diagnosis of homosexuality and the inclusion or exclusion of mental disorders as medical disorders.

A third criticism of DSM-III is that it not only continues the iatrogenic effects of diagnostic labeling, but that it does so in a way that is biased against women (Kaplan, 1983). Kaplan argues that healthy behaviors are determined using masculine-based assumptions, and that the diagnosis of particular personality disorders are prejudicial against women (i.e., histrionic and borderline personality disorders).

A fourth criticism of DSM-III is that it has little treatment utility (Singerman, 1981). This concern has led to proposals of a sixth axis to be added to the present five axes of DSM-III. Schact and Nathan (1977) suggest as a sixth axis "response to treatment," on which would be coded both the treatment offered to the patient and his or her response to it. Karasu and Skodol (1980) suggest "psychodynamic evaluation" as a sixth axis, one suggesting both the psychotherapeutic approach by which the patient is likely to derive maximal benefit, and the problems he or she might be expected to encounter with a particular therapeutic venture.

A fifth criticism of DSM-III focuses on particular diagnostic categories, such as the disorders usually first evident in infancy, childhood, or adolescence. For instance, the proliferation of categories for children's disorders (Kazdin, 1983) go far beyond the bounds of the two major factors generally resulting from factor analyses of children's behavior problems: acting-out problems or conduct disorders, and withdrawal or emotional problems (Quay, 1979). Likewise, rather mild problems that children may experience have been promoted to the status of mental disorders (Harris, 1979). Such problems include stuttering and enuresis. Problems typically within the sphere of education, such as delays in reading or arithmetic, have been brought within the purview of psychiatry (Kazdin, 1983).

A sixth criticism of DSM-III relates to the specificity or lack of specificity of diagnostic criteria, and related concerns about reliability. Frequently, clinicians are forced to assign Axis I and Axis II diagnoses within a very limited time frame, even when inadequate data are available (Schact & Nathan, 1977). In fact, the reliability of Axis II diagnoses was found to be lower in everyday clinical settings than in the DSM-III field trials (Mellsop, Varghese, Joshua, & Hicks, 1982). Concerns about the reliability of ratings assigned to Axis IV and V are even stronger (Schact & Nathan, 1977). Taylor's concerns (1983) lie in a related but opposite direction, that of the arbitrariness and pseudospecificity of the diagnostic criteria. The operational criteria appear to be specific or quantifiable, but in many cases require inference or subjective judgment.

DSM-III FROM A BEHAVIORAL PERSPECTIVE

Much of the praise and criticism directed at diagnostic classification in general, and at DSM-III in particular, as summarized earlier, is shared by behavioral assessors. Because of behavioral assumptions, however, diagnostic classification and DSM-III present some unique liabilities and assets to behavioral assessors.

Liabilities of Diagnostic Classification and DSM-III from a Behavioral Perspective

The concerns described here are directed by behaviorists at diagnostic classification in general. Since DSM-III is presently "the state of the art" in diagnostic classification, the concerns are directed also at DSM-III.

Historical Focus on Single Target Behaviors

One assumption of behaviorism is that behavior is important in and of itself, constituting a sample of what a person *does* in a particular situation, rather than a sign of what he *has*–trait, personality, disease (Goldfried & Kent, 1972; Goodenough, 1949). As applied to clinical psychology, this view can be summarized in Eysenck's frequently quoted aphorism: "get rid of the symptom and you have eliminated the neurosis" (1960).

In the early days of behavior therapy, this emphasis on behavior *qua* behavior was translated into monosymptomatic assessment and treatment of client's problems (Evans, 1985; Kanfer, 1985; Kazdin, 1985; Mash, 1985). Quite literally, the client's target behavior (note the singular) was identified and modified. One example is Ayllon's approach to the treatment of psychotic patients. Using different interventions, these specific target behaviors were modified in individual patients: eating problems, stealing food, towel hoarding, and the wearing of excessive clothing (Ayllon, 1963, 1965). Another example was the choice of a very slow speech rate as the target behavior in a chronically depressed man (Robinson & Lewinsohn, 1973).

This monosymptomatic approach to assessment and treatment was relatively successful in the history of behavior therapy, and hence it was continued. There was no need to assess syndromes or constellations of behavior, which are at the heart of diagnostic classification schemes. At this point, the behavioral approach had no need for diagnoses.

Moreover, the monosymptomatic approach was compatible with other aspects of behaviorism. The target behavior could readily be operationalized in terms of observable behavior, and could readily be measured (Kazdin, 1985). Alterations in the target behavior could be monitored and accounted for through single-subject experimental designs, in which typically a single target behavior serves as a dependent variable (Evans, 1985).

Eschewing of Constructs

Another characteristic of behavioral assessment is that it is generally noninferential. Behavior is thought to be situation-specific and response mode-specific, so inferences are not made to other situations or to other response modes without evidence. Even more absolutely, inferences are not made to hypothesized entities sometimes presumed to underlie behavior, such as traits and illnesses (Goldfried & Kent, 1972). As noted above, behaviorists prefer the *sample* approach over the *sign* approach in interpreting behavior.

Many behaviorists believe that the level of inference inherent in classification systems is too great. Kazdin (1983) attempts to draw parallels between DSM-III concepts and behavioral concepts in the following way. On a first level, *symptom* in psychiatric parlance refers to a particular overt behavior, affect, cognition, or perception. In behavioral terms, the symptom corresponds closely to target behavior or the focus of intervention. A second level is a *syndrome*. In psychiatric terms, a syndrome is a constellation of symptoms occuring together and covarying over time. In behavioral terms, a syndrome might refer to response covariation (discussed later in this chapter). A third level is *disorder*. For a syndrome to be considered a disorder in psychiatry, more information is needed than merely the clustering of symptoms, such as the natural course of the disorder, family history, possible biological correlates, and response to treatment. Kazdin notes: "In behavior therapy, there is no clear analogue to the concept of disorder. Indeed few proponents of behavior modification might even agree that this level of concept would be useful" (1983, p. 86). A fourth level of conceptualization is *disease*. In psychiatric terms, the notion of disease is invoked for a disorder when there is a specific known etiology and an identifiable underlying (pathophysiological) process. Kazdin comments: "Needless to say, the notion of disease is not embraced in describing behavioral dysfunctions in behavior therapy. However, neither is the concept of great use in the classification of mental disorders . . . DSM-III focuses on syndromes and disorders" (1983, pp. 86–87).

Behaviorists might generally feel comfortable with the behavioral equivalent of symptoms and of syndromes (elaborated on later in this chapter). The concepts of disorders and of diseases, however, would be considered too inferential, as well as incompatible with other behavioral assumptions (e.g., the behavioral emphasis on environmental causes for behavioral problems). The main focus of DSM-III, to the contrary, is on the classification of mental disorders, which might be considered as hypothetical constructs, in the sense of MacCorquodale and Meehl: "The distinction is between constructs which merely abstract the empirical relationships . . . and those constructs which are 'hypothetical' (i.e., involve the supposition of entities or processes not among the observed)" (1948, pp. 106–107).

Hypothetical constructs are not acceptable to many behaviorists, who thus tend to reject a diagnostic system for mental disorders. For example, Kozak and Miller (1982, p. 350) write: "More generally, it could be claimed that all hypothetical constructs (with their associated spectre, reification) should be barred from behavioral science entirely". The proper subject matter of behavioral assessment is behavior, and not behavioral constructs (Barrett, Johnston, & Pennypacker, 1986). What some would judge as a narrow definition of behavior is provided by Johnston and Pennypacker (1980, p. 48): "The behavior of an organism is that portion of the organism's interaction with its environment that is characterized by detectable displacement in space through time of some part of the organism that results in a measurable change in at least one aspect of the environment". According to many behaviorists, assessment should occur at the level of behaviors and not at the level of constructs, including disorders.

Classification is Nomothetic

A behaviorist assumption is that the appropriate level of analysis is the individual and not the group (Cone, 1986). In other words, an idiographic approach is preferred to a nomothetic approach. In behavioral science, general principles are built inductively, from the level of the individual to the level of generalizations across individuals. In behaviorist practice, the emphasis is on the individual client.

In contrast to this sort of focus, the basis of classification systems is the identification of common features within groups of individuals (within-group homogeneity), and the identification of differences between groups of individuals (between-group heterogeneity) (Nelson & Hayes, 1986). The focus is nomothetic—on groupings of individuals.

In discussing the DSM-III diagnosis of anxiety disorders in particular, Turner and Michelson (1984) note that this diagnostic category perpetuates a myth of uniformity. Not all clients diagnosed as having an anxiety disorder are the same. Some may have other disorders, as well, markedly altering the clinical picture. The severity of the anxiety disorder might differ dramatically within the same diagnostic category. Anxious clients might vary in their behavioral avoidance, physiological reactivity, and cognitive styles. These concerns about variability among clients assigned a diagnosis of anxiety disorder might well be extended to clients assigned to other diagnostic categories.

To be sure, concerns about the nomothetic nature of diagnosis are not the exclusive domain of behaviorists. Carl Rogers notes that "therapists must lay aside their preoccupation with diagnosis . . . [and recognize that] diagnosis is a process which goes on in the experience of the client, rather than in the intellect of the clinician" (Rogers, 1951, pp. 219, 223). More generally, "humanistic psychologists maintain that every person should be considered in his own uniqueness and individuality, and that no one should be stripped of his dignity by being assigned classificatory labels that represent general characteristics more or less shared by groups of people" (Weiner, 1972). Existentialists like Laing hold that diagnostic categorizing and labeling is inherently dehumanizing and incompatible with psychotherapy (Draguns & Phillips, 1971).

Diagnosis Is Structural and Not Functional

As used in biology, structuralism examines the structure of an organ or tissue, whereas functionalism asks what the function of the organ or tissue is in the life of the organism. As used in psychology, structuralism focuses on *how* people behave, that is, on the form or topography of behavior, whereas functionalism focuses on *why* people behave.

Behaviorism stems largely from a functionalist tradition (Nelson & Hayes, 1986). Behavior is defined and understood in terms of its relationship to a given context. In a behavioral view, understanding involves the degree to which behavior can be predicted and controlled in a variety of settings. In order to predict and control, the contextual events that produce behavior must be identified.

A distinction between topographic (or structural) analysis and functional analysis has been made by Ferster (1965). Diagnosis provides a topographic or structural or static analysis because it relies on the *form* of the behavior, ignoring the environmental events of which behavior is a function. Identification of these environmental events, that is, a functional analysis, is necessary to control behavior, according to many behaviorists. The variables controlling the target behavior are identified in assessment and are subsequently modified in treatment (Goldfried & Pomeranz, 1968). In Ferster's words: "Such a functional analysis of behavior has the advantage that it specifies the causes of behavior in the form of explicit environmental events that can be objectively identified and that are potentially manipulable" (Ferster, 1965, p. 11). In other words, the functional analysis is thought to lead to treatment in a way that the structural analysis does not.

The same behavior, topographically speaking, might be occurring for different reasons, functionally speaking. Different treatments might be required in each case to alter the same behavior. As a hypothetical example used by Nelson (1984), three children in a classroom might show similar disruptive behaviors, but with different controlling variables. One child may receive teacher attention contingent on disruptive behavior, and benefit from a "praise-and-ignore" intervention program, in which the teacher praises appropriate behavior and ignores inappropriate behavior. A second child may receive peer attention contingent on disruptive behavior, and benefit from the "Good Behavior Game," which involves peer contingencies for appropriate behavior. The third child might be disruptive in response to curriculum materials that are too difficult for the child, and would benefit from more appropriate curriculum materials.

In an empirical example of the importance of correct functional analyses, Carr and Durand (1985) compare treatment outcomes when interventions were based on different functional analyses. Their assumption is that children's behavior problems (e.g., self-injury, tantrums, aggression) may serve a communicative function. Assessments were conducted for individual children to hypothesize whether behavior problems serve either an escape function (by observing children's behavior under easy vs. difficult task conditions) or an attention-seeking function (by observing children's behavior under conditions involving frequent vs. infrequent adult attention). Children were subsequently taught two phrases: "Help me," which was believed to communicate the need for task assistance, and "Am I doing good work?," which was believed to communicate the wish for attention. For children whose behavior problems were assessed as serving an escape function, such problems were reduced when the children were taught "Help me," but not when they were taught "Am I doing good work?" In contrast, for children whose behavior problems were assessed as serving an attention-seeking function, such problems were reduced when the children were taught "Am I doing good work?," but not when they were taught "Help me." Thus, many behaviorists believe that a correct functional analysis is needed for successful treatment, and not merely a topographical diagnosis.

The concern that diagnosis is overly structural and not sufficiently functional is not limited to behaviorists. Psychodynamically oriented professionals are concerned that DSM-III emphasizes symptom description at the expense of the dynamics underlying the symptom (Frances & Cooper, 1981; Vaillant, 1984). According to this view, treatment should be focused on the dynamics and not the symptoms; therefore, DSM-III has limited treatment utility.

Assets of Diagnostic Classification and DSM-III from a Behavioral Pespective

DSM-III has been criticized by professionals of various theoretical persuasions, and its assumptions seem to be incompatible with traditional behavioral views. Nonetheless, in reporting their survey results, Smith and Kraft (1983) note that behaviorally oriented psychologists were among the most positive responders to DSM-III. The next section of this chapter examines aspects of classification in general, and DSM-III in particular, that may appeal to behaviorists.

Recognition of Response Covariation

The single strongest factor in the increasing acceptance by behavioral assessors of diagnostic classification in general, and of DSM-III in particular, is the recognition of response covariation within the behavioral repertoires of individuals. Far from the monosymptomatic approach espoused by early behaviorists is the current emphasis on interrelationships among behaviors (Baer, 1982; Evans, 1985; Kanfer, 1985; Kazdin, 1982, 1983, 1985; Mash, 1985; Mash & Terdal, 1981; Voeltz & Evans, 1982; Wahler & Fox, 1982).

One of the first acknowledgments of response interrelationships by behaviorists was the concept known as the triple response system (Lang, 1968). Initially, the triple response system referred to motor, cognitive, and physiological responses that occur in fear or anxiety. The system was extended to other disorders, such as sexual deviations or depression. The triple response system has been criticized, however, as being inadequate to represent response interrelationships in all disorders, and as drawing artificial response boundaries (e.g., is speech considered a cognitive or a motor response?) (Evans, 1986).

Thus, expanded views of response interrelationships have emerged. These views, however, are squarely within a behavioral framework. Response interrelationships are described in terms of response chains, response generalization, response hierarchy, concurrent responses, keystone behavior, and response class (Baer, 1982; Voeltz & Evans, 1982; Wahler & Fox, 1982). There is no need to describe or to account for response interrelationships in terms of traditional concepts such as personality, disease, syndrome, or symptom substitution.

At times, response relationships are examined in a structural manner. In other words, the frequencies of several behaviors are measured, and the correlations among the frequencies are determined. To illustrate, 19 behaviors of two boys were observed at home and at school for three years; the behavior categories were intercorrelated, but the groupings differed at home and at school (Wahler, 1975).

At other times, response relationships are examined in a functional manner. In other words, aspects of the environment are deliberately manipulated, and the effects on several behaviors are measured. As Baer (1982, p. 218) describes this approach: "In the analytic study of behavior, we inevitably find ways to make structures, remake them, and unmake them". In one example by Wahler and Fox (1980), contingency contracts were in effect at different times for solitary play and for social play with four boys who showed aggressive and oppositional behavior. Only the contract for solitary play resulted in reduced oppositional behavior during the observation sessions and fewer reports from parents of low-rate problem behaviors. Thus, solitary play, but not social play, covaried inversely in a functional manner with oppositional and aggressive behavior.

The diagnostic criteria for the disorders listed in DSM-III can be viewed as covarying behaviors (Nelson & Barlow, 1981). When a client appears with a particular problem, a wise clinician generally assesses other problems that are likely to covary. Suggestions for typical covarying response patterns can be found in the diagnostic criteria of the disorders in DSM-III. Although there is no systematic empirical basis for these response covariations (i.e., the diagnostic criteria were derived from committees and not from factor analyses or other multivariate statistics), the concept of response interrelationships is now compatible with the current thinking of many behaviorists. The acceptability of DSM-III to behaviorists has been enhanced by the recognition of response covariation.

Recognition of Diagnosed-Based Treatment Success

The functional analysis, as described earlier, has been the classic strategy used by behaviorists to link assessment and treatment. Using this strategy, the controlling variables identified in assessment are subsequently modified in treatment. An alternative strategy is to base treatment on a diagnosis (Nelson, in press). After the person is diagnosed, he or she is administered the treatment that has been found to be most effective with other people who have been diagnosed with the same disorder. Nathan (1981) has suggested that a diagnosis is sufficient for treatment choice for the psychotic disorders because of the success of medication in treating these disorders. Conversely, he has suggested that a behavioral assessment (presumably a functional analysis) may be needed for nonpsychotic disorders, because of the range of behavioral treatments that are effective with them. Even for nonpsychotic disorders, a diagnostic or topographical strategy may be sufficient for effective treatment selection, if there is sound research evidence that a particular treatment has been effective for others with this disorder (Nelson, in press). Thus, a phobic might receive exposure therapy (Barlow & Wolfe, 1981), a depressive might receive cognitive therapy (Beck, Rush, Shaw, & Emery, 1979), and an exhibitionist might receive covert sensitization (Maletzky, 1980). Thus, the evidence of successful treatment, based on a diagnosis, contributes to the acceptability of DSM-III among behaviorists (Taylor, 1983).

Lack of an Acceptable Alternative

Several classification systems have been developed by behaviorists, but not in response to DSM-III. Two of these systems focus on classifying behavioral responses: Cautela and Upper (1973) and Adams, Doster, and Calhoun (1977). A third system is based on a more functional approach (Bandura, 1968). The major categories in this last system are: difficulties in the stimulus control of behavior, aversive self-reinforcing systems, deficient behavioral repertoires, aversive behavioral repertoires, and difficulties with incentive systems (reinforcers).

The American Psychological Association also considered the development of a "descriptive behavioral classification" that could serve as an alternative to DSM-III. The project was eventually judged to be infeasible (Horai, 1981). A more limited project directed at the behavioral classification of children's disorders was instead initiated (e.g., Edelbrock & Achenbach, 1984).

As a conclusion to the description of their survey data, Smith and Kraft (1983) assert that psychologists have expressed the desire for a classification alternative to DSM-III. Nevertheless, clinicians rely heavily on the manual. Among the explanations that Smith and Kraft pose for this discrepancy are: The DSM system is too entrenched to be challenged; the financial outlay and time expenditures prohibit the development of alternatives; and there is an economic fear that insurance companies would find an alternative unacceptable. Miller *et al.* (1981) similarly report that DSM-III was used mainly due to agency and insurance company requirements.

Thus, behaviorists may prefer an alternative classification system to DSM-III, and indeed have developed some alternatives. The contingencies are such, however, that DSM-III continues to be frequently used, even by behaviorists. As Hersen and Turner (1984) note, no alternative system has "caught on."

Specific Attractive Features of DSM-III

Some specific features of DSM-III enhance its appeal for behavioral clinicians. First, DSM-III is explicitly atheoretical. While it is not pro-behavioral, neither is it antibehavioral. Second, the diagnostic criteria are stated in operational terms, which is certainly compatible with behaviorism. Although Taylor (1983) complains of the "pseudospecificity" of the diagnostic criteria and the degree of inference required to judge their presence or absence, they are a step in a more behavioral direction. Third, the rather extensive information that is provided in DSM-III about each disorder might suggest controlling variables to the behavior assessor (Nelson & Barlow, 1981). In other words, both biological and environmental variables contributing to the problematic behavior might be suggested. A more individualized assessment can determine the presence or absence of those variables in a particular instance. For example, when a client exhibits schizophrenic behaviors, assessment should contain questions about familial history of schizophrenia or of institutionalization, age when the first schizophrenic behaviors were evidenced, and a description of premorbid behavior. In another example, depressive behavior may suggest both environmental variables (e.g., loss of reinforcers, sudden environmental changes) and organismic variables (e.g., familial history of bipolar affective disorder, an inadequate repertoire of social skills to obtain or maintain sufficient reinforcers). Fourth, although the diagnostic categories are nomothetic, some room is allowed for individual differences. Many of the diagnostic criteria are prefaced by the statement that the patient must exhibit X of the following Y symptoms. An acknowledgement is thus made that not all patients within a particular diagnostic category will behave in the same manner. This flexible approach is compatible with the idiographic emphasis of behaviorists. Fifth, DSM-III explicitly acknowledges the role of the environment in mental disorders. Axis IV allows the clinician to rate the severity of psychosocial stressors; the role of the environment in contributing to mental disorders is thus acknowledged. Axis V allows the clinician to rate the patient's highest level of functioning the past year, and the effects of mental disorders upon the environment are thus acknowledged.

DSM-III AND BEHAVIORAL ASSESSMENT

It is clear that the model and assumptions underlying diagnostic classification are largely incompatible with the behaviorist model and assumptions. Diagnosis is inferential. Moreover, the nature of the constructs to which inferences are made is generally medical or trait-like, both of which underplay the role of the environment in behavioral causation. Classification systems emphasize similarities and differences across groups of people, instead of focusing on their idiographic behaviors and situations. Diagnosis is structural or topographic, rather than functional. It describes behavior, rather than controlling variables or treatment implications.

Utility of Classification for Behavioral Assessors

Despite the incompatibility of the diagnostic classification model with behavioral assumptions, classification, and especially DSM-III, are useful for behavioral assessors. In the words of Hersen and Turner:

> Indeed, if we are to have a science of human behavior, a system of classification is essential. Moreover, at the practical level, if reinbursement by third-party payers for clinical service is to occur, some type of categorization is necessary such that a decision can be made as to what type of disorders will be covered for reimbursement and which ones will not.... Although DSM-III was conceived in a relatively nonempirical fashion, and represents a traditional approach to assessment, it probably is as effective as any other system of classification available at this time. (Hersen & Turner, 1984, pp. 497–498)

The communication functions of classification and of DSM-III are stressed by Nelson and Barlow (1981, p. 27): "Thus, in order to communicate with others, it is important in describing our clients in journal articles or professional referrals, in classifying clients for insurance or accountability purposes and in grant proposals." In this manner, classification, and DSM-III as the current classification system, are useful for behavioral assessors.

DSM-III and the Goals of Behavioral Assessment

Behavioral assessment can be defined as "the identification and measurement of meaningful response units and their controlling variables (both environmental and organismic) for the purposes of understanding and altering human behavior" (Nelson & Hayes, 1981, p. 3). This definition becomes more concrete when we cite the triple goals of behavioral assessment: (a) to identify target behaviors; (b) to select treatment strategies; and (c) to evaluate the effectiveness of the treatment (Nelson & Hayes, 1979, 1981).

While classification is useful to behavioral assessors for some purposes, the relationship between DSM-III and the goals of behavioral assessment merits further exploration. DSM-III is somewhat useful to behavioral assessors in identifying target behaviors. The diagnostic criteria of DSM-III suggest behaviors that tend to covary. When a client appears with a particular problem, it is wise to investigate whether typically covarying problem behaviors also occur. To use the words of Nelson and Barlow (1981, p. 27): "Nomothetic response covariations do seem to describe the clinical reality of clients. Thus, when a client begins to describe or to show some of the behaviors characteristic of a depressive episode, for example, he or she is sufficiently likely to show other related characteristics" to make questioning about other depressive diagnostic criteria worthwhile. The diagnostic criteria aid in *suggesting* target behaviors, but they do not *replace* behavioral assessment in identifying the target behaviors for the individual client, and in determining the quantitative parameters of their occurrence (frequency, duration, intensity).

The second goal of behavioral assessment is treatment selection. Hersen and Turner (1984) have noted that classification generally does not lead to treatment selection. There are, however, circumstances in which DSM-III may contribute to it for behavioral assessors. Nelson (in press) has identified three strategies used by behavior therapists to link assessment and treatment: (a) the functional analysis; (b) keystone behavior strategy: and (c) the diagnostic strategy. In the functional analysis, the variables controlling the target behavior are identified in assessment, and are modified in treatment (Goldfried & Pomeranz, 1968). As described earlier, the ancillary material provided in DSM-III about diagnostic categories sometimes gives suggestions of typical controlling variables for particular response patterns (Nelson & Barlow, 1981). Both environmental and organismic controlling variables are suggested. Again, DSM-III aids in suggesting controlling variables, but it certainly does not replace behavioral assessment, especially in identifying environmental controlling variables.

Behavioral assessment emphasizes the situation-specificity of behavior (Kazdin, 1979). It has a wide range of techniques available that help identify the situational determinants of target behaviors (Nelson & Hayes, 1981), their environmental controlling variables, leading to a functional analysis upon which treatment can be based. Conversely, diagnosis, generally made on the basis of an interview or informal in-office or in-hospital observations, usually emphasizes intra-organism determinants of behavior, and no systematic attempt is made to include situational determinants in the diagnostic process.

A second treatment selection strategy is the keystone behavior strategy (Nelson, in press). Here, particular behaviors are selected that are thought to be a keystone in altering a problematic response class. An example might be the modification of irrational cognitions in Beck's view of depression (Beck et al., 1979). DSM-III does not seem to be particularly useful for this strategy, because the identification of keystone behaviors for different response classes and for different individuals is in its infancy.

A third treatment selection strategy is the diagnostic strategy (Nelson, in press). Diagnosis may be a useful basis for choosing treatment from a medical perspective, that is, a certain diagnosis implicates a certain drug for effective treatment (Hersen & Turner, 1984; Nathan, 1981). Diagnosis may also be a useful basis for choosing treatment from a behavioral perspective, especially under these conditions outlined by Haynes (1986): (a) if clients within a particular diagnostic category are relatively homogeneous; (b) if a powerful treatment is available to treat the disorder; and (c) if the cost of an idiographic assessment outweighs its additive benefits.

The third and final goal of behavioral assessment is evaluation of treatment outcome. Classification can serve this purpose only in a very molar dichotomous sense, that is, where a treatment moved the client from an abnormal to a normal classification. This molar evaluation might be useful on a pre-post basis to help establish the clinical or substantive significance of a treatment. Classification would not be useful for repeated measurement that provides ongoing feedback to the clinician regarding treatment progress. For this purpose, more molecular and more sensitive measures are needed, of which behavioral assessment offers a plethora (Nelson, 1981).

In summary, DSM-III offers suggestions to behavioral assessors to help accomplish the goals of behavioral assessment. But it cannot replace behavioral assessment in identifying target behaviors, in selecting treatment, and in evaluating treatment outcome.

A Possible Contribution of Behavioral Assessment to DSM-III

It is clear that DSM-III is used by and is acceptable to many behavioral clinicians. Inversely, it is also possible that behavioral assessment can make a contribution to the DSM systems. This contribution, perhaps in DSM-IV, would involve using behavioral diagnostic criteria that are more operationally and more specifically defined.

A workshop that might presage this development was organized by Drs. Jack Maser and Robert Hirshfeld of the National Institute of Mental Health on September 26 and 27, 1985. The topic of the workshop was the behavioral assessment of depression, and this writer was a fortunate participant. Behavioral assessment was viewed by the participants in a rather limited manner, as the systematic observation of overt motor behavior. This contrasts with a broader view that behavioral assessment is a behavioral *approach* to assessment (Nelson & Hayes, 1986). The overt motor behaviors that are thought to be critical to depression were presented orally and in written papers by experts: Aron Siegman on speech characteristics, Klaus Scherer on vocal characteristics, Allen Dittmann on body movements, and Paul Ekman and Alan Fridlund on facial behavior. This writer's understanding of the conclusions of this workshop are that particular behaviors characteristic of depression can be identified, and that behavioral observations can be used to quantify these behaviors. Both of these aspects, more specific diagnostic criteria and the methodologies to assess them, could be included in DSM-IV.

SUMMARY

The central topic of this chapter is the relationship between behavioral assessment and DSM-III. First, the pros and cons of diagnostic classification systems in general were reviewed, because some of the positive and negative features of classification systems are applicable to DSM-III. Second, a brief history of DSM-III was presented, along with its chief assets and liabilities, often recognized as such by both behavioral and nonbehavioral clinicians. Third, diagnostic classification in general, and DSM-III in particular, were evaluated specifically from a behavioral perspective. Main deterrents from such a perspective are: the historical emphasis by behaviorists on singular target behaviors; the inferential nature of a diagnostic system of mental disorders; the nomothetic nature of diagnosis; and the structural nature of diagnosis. Main attractions are: increasing recognition by behaviorists of response covariation and of diagnosis-based treatment efficacy; lack of an acceptable alternative to DSM-III; and several positive features of DSM-III itself. Regarding the goals of behavioral assessment, DSM-III was judged as offering useful suggestions in identifying target behaviors, selecting treatment, and evaluating treatment outcome, but as not replacing behavioral assessment in fulfilling these goals. A possible contribution of behavioral assessment to DSM-IV was suggested: behavioral observation to quantify more precise diagnostic criteria.

REFERENCES

Adams, H. E., & Haber, J. D. (1984). The classification of abnormal behavior: An overview. In H. E. Adams & P. B. Sutker (Eds.), *Comprehensive handbook of psychopathology* (pp. 3–25). New York: Plenum.

Adams, H. E., Doster, J. A., & Calhoun, K. S. (1977). A psychologically based system of response classification. In A. R. Ciminero, K. S. Calhoun, & H. E. Adams (Eds.), *Handbook of behavioral assessment*. New York: Wiley.

American Psychiatric Association (1952). *Diagnostic and statistical manual of mental disorders* (1st ed.). Washington, D. C.: Author.

American Psychiatric Association (1968). *Diagnostic and statistical manual of mental disorders* (2nd ed.). Washington, D. C.: Author.

American Psychiatric Association (1980). *Diagnostic and statistical manual of mental disorders* (3rd ed.). Washington, D. C.: Author.

Ayllon, T. (1963). Intensive treatment of psychotic behavior by stimulus satiation and food reinforcement. *Behaviour Research and Therapy, 1,* 53–61.

Ayllon, T. (1965). Some behavior problems associated with eating in chronic schizophrenic patients. In L. P. Ullmann & L. Krasner (Eds.), *Case studies in behavior modification* (pp. 73–77). New York: Holt, Rinehart, & Winston.

Baer, D. M. (1982). The imposition of structure on behavior and the demolition of behavioral structures. In D. J. Bernstein (Ed.), *Response structure and organization: 1981 Nebraska symposium on motivation* (pp. 217–254). Lincoln: University of Nebraska Press.

Bandura, A. (1968). A social learning interpretation of psychological dysfunctions. In P. London & D. Rosenhan (Eds.), *Foundations of abnormal psychology*. New York: Holt, Rinehart, & Winston.

Bannister, D., Salmon, P., & Lieberman, D. M. (1964). Diagnosis–treatment relationships in psychiatry: A statistical analysis. *British Journal of Psychiatry, 110,* 726–732.

Barlow, D. H., & Wolfe B. E. (1981). Behavioral approaches to anxiety disorders: A report of NIMH-SUNY, Albany, research conference. *Journal of Consulting and Clinical Psychology, 49,* 448–454.

Barrett, B. H., Johnston, J. M., & Pennypacker, H. S. (1986). Behavior: Its units, dimensions, and measurement. In R. O. Nelson & S. C. Hayes (Eds.), *Conceptual foundations of behavioral assessment*. New York: Guilford.

Beck, A. T., Rush, A. J., Shaw, B. F., & Emery, G. (1979). *Cognitive therapy of depression*. New York: Guilford.

Carr, E. G., & Durand, V. M. (1985). The social-communicative basis of severe behavior problems in children. In S. Reiss & R. Bootzin (Eds.), *Theoretical issues in behavior therapy*. New York: Academic Press.

Cautela, J. R., & Upper, D. (1973). A behavioral coding system. Unpublished manuscript available from J. Cautela, Dept. of Psychology, Boston College, Chestnut Hill, Boston, MA.

Cone, J. D. (1981). Psychometric considerations. In M. Hersen & A. S. Bellack (Eds.), *Behavioral assessment* (pp. 38–68). New York: Pergamon.

Cone, J. D. (1986). Idiographic, nomothetic, and related perspectives. In R. O. Nelson & S. C. Hayes (Eds.), *Conceptual foundations of behavioral assessment*. New York: Guilford.

Draguns, J. G., & Phillips, L. (1971). *Psychiatric classification and diagnosis: An overview and critique*. Morristown, N. J.: General Learning Press.

Edelbrock, C., & Achenbach, T. M. (1984). The teacher version of the child behavior profile: I. Boys aged 6–11. *Journal of Consulting and Clinical Psychology, 52,* 207–217.

Evans, I. M. (1985). Building systems models as a strategy for target behavior selection in clinical assessment. *Behavioral Assessment, 7,* 21–32.

Evans, I. M. (1986). Response structure and the triple response mode concept in behavioral assessment. In R. O. Nelson & S. C. Hayes (Eds.), *Conceptual foundations of behavioral assessment.* New York: Guilford.

Eysenck, H. J. (Ed.). (1960). *Behaviour therapy and the neuroses.* London: Pergamon.

Feighner, J. P., Robins, E., Guze, S. B., Woodruff, R. A., Winokur, G., & Munoz, R. (1972). Diagnostic criteria for use in psychiatric research. *Archives of General Psychiatry, 26,* 57–63.

Ferster, C. B. (1965). Classification of behavior pathology. In L. Krasner & L. P. Ullmann (Eds.), *Research in behavior modification* (pp. 6–26). New York: Holt, Rinehart, & Winston.

Frances, A., & Cooper, A. M. (1981). Descriptive and dynamic psychiatry: A perspective on DSM-III. *American Journal of Psychiatry, 138,* 1198–1202.

Goldfried, M. R., & Kent, R. N. (1972). Traditional versus behavioral assessment: A comparison of methodological and theoretical assumptions. *Psychological Bulletin, 77,* 409–420.

Goldfried, M. R., & Pomeranz, D. M. (1968). Role of assessment in behavior modification. *Psychological Reports, 23,* 75–87.

Goodenough, F. L. (1949). *Mental testing.* New York: Rinehart.

Harris, S. L. (1979). DSM-III—Its implications for children. *Child Behavior Therapy, 1,* 37–46.

Haynes, S. N. (1986). The design of intervention programs. In R. O. Nelson & S. C. Hayes (Eds.), *Conceptual foundations of behavioral assessment.* New York: Guilford.

Hersen, M., & Turner, S. M. (1984). DSM-III and behavior therapy. In S. M. Turner & M. Hersen (Eds.), *Adult psychopathology and diagnosis* (pp. 485–502). New York: Wiley.

Hobbs, N. (1975). *The futures of children: Categories, labels, and their consequences.* San Francisco: Jossey-Bass.

Horai, J. (1981). A brief history of the descriptive behavioral classification project. Washington, D.C.: American Psychological Association.

Johnston, J. M., & Pennypacker, H. S. (1980). *Strategies and tactics of human behavioral research.* Hillsdale, N. J.: Erlbaum.

Kanfer, F. H. (1985). Target selection for clinical change programs. *Behavioral Assessment, 7,* 7–20.

Kaplan, M. (1983). A woman's view of DSM-III. *American Psychologist, 38,* 786–792.

Karasu, T. B., & Skodol, A. E. (1980). Sixth axis for DSM-III: Psychodynamic evaluation. *American Journal of Psychiatry, 137,* 607–610.

Kazdin, A. E. (1979). Situational specificity: The two-edged sword of behavioral assessment. *Behavioral Assessment, 1,* 57–75.

Kazdin, A. E. (1982). Symptom substitution, generalization, and response covariation: Implications for psychotherapy outcome. *Psychological Bulletin, 91,* 349–365.

Kazdin, A. E. (1983). Psychiatric diagnosis, dimensions of dysfunction, and child behavior therapy. *Behavior Therapy, 14,* 73–99.

Kazdin, A. E. (1985). Selection of target behaviors: The relationship of the treatment focus to clinical dysfunction *Behavioral Assessment, 7,* 33–47.

Klerman, G. L. (1984). The advantages of DSM-III. *American Journal of Psychiatry, 141,* 539–542.

Kozak, M. J., & Miller, G. A. (1982). Hypothetical constructs versus intervening variables: A re-appraisal of the three-systems model of anxiety assessment. *Behavioral Assessment, 4,* 347–358.

Lang, P. J. (1968). Fear reduction and fear behavior: Problems in treating a construct. In J. M. Schlien (Ed.), *Research in psychotherapy, Vol. 3,* (pp. 90–102). Washington, D. C.: American Psychological Association.

MacCorquodale, K., & Meehl, P. E. (1948). On a distinction between hypothetical constructs and intervening variables. *Psychological Review, 55,* 95–107.

Maletzky, B. M. (1980). Self-referred versus court-referred sexually deviant patients: Success with assisted covert sensitization. *Behavior Therapy, 11,* 306–314.

Mash, E. J. (1985). Some comments on target selection in behavior therapy. *Behavioral Assessment, 7,* 63–78.

Mash, E. J., & Terdal, L. G. (1981). Behavioral assessment of childhood disturbance. In E. J. Mash & L. G. Terdal (Eds.), *Behavioral assessment of childhood disorders* (pp. 3–76). New York: Guilford.

Matarazzo, J. D. (1983). The reliability of psychiatric and psychological diagnosis. *Clinical Psychology Review, 3,* 103–145.

McLemore, C. W., & Benjamin, L. S. (1979). What happened to interpersonal diagnosis? A psychosocial alternative to DSM-III. *American Psychologist, 34,* 17–33.

McReynolds, W. T. (1979). DSM-III and the future of applied social science. *Professional Psychology, 10,* 123–131.

Mellsop, G., Verghese, G., Joshua, S., & Hicks, A. (1982). The reliability of Axis II of DSM-III. *American Journal of Psychiatry, 139.* 1360–1361.

Miller, L. S., Bergstrom, D. A., Cross, H. J., & Grube, J. W. (1981). Opinions and use of the DSM system by practicing psychologists. *Professional Psychology, 12,* 385–390.

Millon, T. (1983). The DSM-III: An insider's perspective. *American Psychologist, 38,* 804–814.

Nathan, P. E. (1981). Symptomatic diagnosis and behavioral assessment. In D. H. Barlow (Ed.), *Behavioral assessment of adult disorders* (pp. 1–11). New York: Guilford.

Nelson, R. O. (1981). Realistic dependent measures for clinical use. *Journal of Consulting and Clinical Psychology, 49,* 168–182.

Nelson, R. O. (1984). Is behavioral assessment the missing link between diagnosis and treatment? Address presented at the Meeting of the Association for Advancement of Behavior Therapy, Philadelphia, November, 1984.

Nelson, R. O. (in press). Relationships between assessment and treatment within a behavioral perspective. *Journal of Psychopathology and Behavioral Assessment.*

Nelson, R. O., & Barlow, D. H. (1981). An overview of behavioral assessment with adult clients: Basic strategies and initial procedures. In D. H. Barlow (Ed.), *Behavioral assessment of adult disorders* (pp. 13–43). New York: Guilford.

Nelson, R. O., & Hayes, S. C. (1979). Some current dimensions of behavioral assessment. *Behavioral Assessment, 1,* 1–16.

Nelson, R. O., & Hayes, S. C. (1981). An overview of behavioral assessment. In M. Hersen & A. S. Bellack (Eds.), *Behavioral assessment: A practical handbook* (2nd. ed., pp. 3–37). New York: Pergamon.

Nelson, R. O., & Hayes, S. C. (1986). Nature of behavioral assessment. In R. O. Nelson & S. C. Hayes (Eds.), *Conceptual foundations of behavioral assessment.* New York: Guilford.

Quay, H. D. (1979). Classification. In H. C. Quay & J. S. Werry (Eds.), *Psychopathological disorders of childhood* (2nd ed., pp. 1–42). New York: Wiley.

Robinson, J. C., & Lewinsohn, P. M. (1973). Behavior modification of speech characteristics in a chronically depressed man. *Behavior Therapy, 4,* 150–152.

Rogers, C. R. (1951). *Client-centered therapy*. Boston: Houghton-Mifflin.

Schact, T. E. (1985). DSM-III and the politics of truth. *American Psychologist, 40*, 513–521.

Schact, T., & Nathan, P. E. (1977). But is it good for psychologists? Appraisal and status of DSM-III. *American Psychologist, 32*, 1017–1025.

Singerman, B. (1981). DSM-III: Historical antecedents and present significance. *Journal of Clinical Psychiatry, 42*, 409–410.

Smith, D., & Kraft, W. A. (1983). DSM-III: Do psychologists really want an alternative? *American Psychologist, 38*, 777–785.

Spitzer, R. L., Endicott, J., & Robins, E. (1978). Research diagnostic criteria. *Archives of General Psychiatry, 35*, 773–782.

Stuart, R. B. (1970). *Trick or treatment*. Champaign, IL: Research Press.

Szasz, T. (1960). The myth of mental illness. *American Psychologist, 15*, 113–118.

Szasz, T. S. (1957). The problem of psychiatric nosology: A contribution to a situational analysis of psychiatric operations. *American Journal of Psychiatry, 114*, 405–413.

Taylor, C. B. (1983). DSM-III and behavioral assessment. *Behavioral Assessment, 5*, 5–14.

Thompson, J. W., Green, D., & Savitt, H. (1983). Preliminary report on a crosswalk from DSM-III to ICD-9-CM. *American Journal of Psychiatry, 140*, 176–180.

Turner, R. J., & Cummings, J. (1967). Theoretical malaise and community mental health. In E. L. Cowen, W. A. Gardner, & M. Zax (Eds.), *Emergent approaches to mental health problems* (pp. 40–62). New York: Appleton-Century-Crofts.

Turner, S. M., & Michelson, L. (1984). Conceptual, methodological, and clinical issues in the assessment of anxiety disorders. *Journal of Behavioral Assessment, 6*, 265–279.

Vaillant, G. E. (1984). The disadvantages of DSM-III outweighs its advantages. *American Journal of Psychiatry, 141*, 542–545.

Voeltz, L. M., & Evans, I. M. (1982). The assessment of behavioral interrelationships in child behavior therapy. *Behavior Assessment, 4*, 131–165.

Wahler, R. G. (1975). Some structural aspects of deviant child behavior. *Journal of Applied Behavior Analysis, 8*, 27–42.

Wahler, R. G., & Fox, J. J. (1980). Solitary toy play and time out: A family treatment package for children with aggressive and oppositional behavior. *Journal of Applied Behavior Analysis, 13*, 23–39.

Wahler, R. G., & Fox, J. J. (1982). Response structure in deviant child-parent relationships: Implications for family therapy. In D. J. Bernstein (Ed.), *Response structure and organization. 1981 Nebraska symposium on motivation* (pp. 1–46). Lincoln: University of Nebraska Press.

Weiner, I. B. (1972). Does psychodiagnosis have a future? *Journal of Personality Assessment, 36*, 534–546.

Zigler, E., & Phillips, L. (1961). Psychiatric diagnosis and sympomatology. *Journal of Abnormal and Social Psychology, 63*, 69–75.

13

DSM-III-Revised and Child Psychiatry

JUDITH L. RAPOPORT

INTRODUCTION

The third edition of the American Psychiatric Association's *Diagnostic Statistical Manual of Mental Disorders* (DSM-III, APA, 1980) had a particularly dramatic effect upon child psychiatry. It highlighted a descriptive approach to diagnosis, drawing new attention to phenomenology, and to the relationships among childhood disorders, as no other classifications (e.g., the manual's second edition [DSM-II, APA, 1968], or Group for Advancement of Psychiatry—1966) had done. DSM-III has facilitated the development of numerous structured interviews for research in child psychiatry, and its atheoretical approach and operational definitions have been a radical departure from DSM-II.

The number of childhood diagnoses increased from DSM-II to DSM-III by 200%, clearly a "splitting" approach, and the introduction of the multiaxial diagnostic system has encouraged the multiple recording of independent dimensions of pathology, a crucial need in childhood psychopathology, as discussed in detail elsewhere (Rapoport and Ismond, 1984; Rutter and Shaffer, 1980). The atheoretical approach will be particularly useful for the genetic, psychopharmacological, developmental, and epidemiologic research in which the system is currently in use. Most important, the multiaxial system permitted simultaneous recording of concurrent developmental disabilities and medical conditions, in addition to the behavioral syndrome. Previous systems led to arbitrary decisions, resulting in poor diagnostic reliability in multiply handicapped

JUDITH L. RAPOPORT • National Institute of Mental Health, Laboratory of Clinical Science, Bethesda, ME 20205.

children (Rutter, Shaffer, and Shepherd 1975). In spite of the care and effort that went into DSM-III, the APA Task Force often relied on clinical opinion rather than research data for many definitions of the childhood disorders. Increased clinical and research use brought many criticisms. Consequently, a number of revisions are being made for DSM-III, to be published as an interim report (DSM-III-R), and the APA Task Force for revising DSM-III has met throughout 1984 to identify clinical and, where possible, research data, indicating problems with the present system. This chapter summarizes those deliberations related to the disorders of childhood and adolescence. However, as revision of DSM-III are not complete at the time of this chapter's writing, these proposals are provisionary.

Relatively little research has addressed diagnosis *per se* of childhood disorders. By providing an operational system, DSM-III makes research more possible, giving more specific subcategories to be validated or "relumped." Because research in child psychiatry is at an early phase of development, perhaps 25 years behind the parent field, DSM-III is particularly important for child psychiatry. There is less agreement on the major diagnostic groupings than in adult psychiatry, and comparison of research results has been severely limited by the lack of validated rating methods.

While a dimensional approach to diagnosis is addressed elsewhere in this book (Chapter 10), this review is confined to the DSM-III categorical, dichotomous approach. The dimensional measures seem most useful as predictors or reflectors of change, while major episodic, and rare, disorders would seem to be the least well-served by this approach.

Most clinical research has utilized a categorical model, with exclusion and inclusion criteria, and a combination of onset, age, time course, duration, and so on. On the other hand, much of the diagnosis of attention deficit disorder represents chronic, high frequency behavior, for which both dimensional and categorical diagnoses would at least partially agree.

The point of this chapter is to highlight the current debates about DSM-III childhood entities, for which at least some research has been carried out. It is clear that major questions remain, particularly for attention deficit conduct, depressive, pervasive developmental, and affective disorders.

ATTENTION DEFICIT DISORDER/CONDUCT DISORDER

A major question about the DSM-III group of attention deficit disorders (the former hyperkinetic reaction of childhood) has been the relative rarity of the diagnosis in European countries, where the International

Classification of Disease, 9th edition (ICD-9) is used. In Europe, the diagnosis of "Conduct Disorder" has subsumed many of the cases labeled "ADD" in the U.S. and Canada.

There have been few comparisons of DSM-III and ICD-9 for any childhood disorders. The controversial DSM-III category "Attention Deficit Disorder," was the focus of a study carried out by the Maudsley Hospital in London and the National Institute of Mental Health (NIMH) Child Psychiatry Branch in Bethesda. In this study, 40 case histories of grade school-age boys with restless, inattentive, and/or aggressive-impulsive behaviors were categorized by clinicians both in London and in the United States, using both the ICD-9 and DSM-III classification schemes. Almost all cases would entail problems differentiating between conduct disorder and attention deficit disorder.

It seems probable that the differences in diagnostic rates stem from the weighting of symptoms into categories, rather than from lack of recognition of symptoms. Preliminary data show that when the 40 cases were compared on Axis I of DSM-III, the research teams obtained a kappa of .69 (for 3 digit agreement). For Axis I of ICD-9 the equivalent figure was .60; this corresponds to a perfect agreement on better than 80% of cases.

Most disagreement came from deciding where to place a mixed case. That is, in three cases where the British team diagnosed ICD-9 conduct disorder and the American team diagnosed hyperkinetic syndrome, there was complete agreement between the teams with DSM-III, where both diagnoses were given all three of these cases. In another three cases, the British diagnosed emotional disorder while the Americans diagnosed hyperkinesis; again, in each of these the British also recognized "Attention Deficit Disorder with Hyperactivity" (ADDH) in their DSM-III list, and in two of the three the Americans had also diagnosed emotional disorder in DSM-III. It is clear, however, that agreement *can* be reached in the subdivision of this group. It is also clear that ICD-9, which permits only one Axis I choice, will have the most difficulty with mixed cases.

Most research in this area addresses the validity of the attention deficit disorders: what are the core features of these disorders, and, most important and relevant, their distinction from conduct disorder? There is already more written on these subtopics than can be easily summarized.

First, let us address the independence of hyperactivity or attention deficit disorder and conduct disorder. The factor analytic work of Loney and others clearly indicates independent factors of hyperactivity and conduct disorder/aggression (Langhorn and Loney, 1979). A series of studies elegantly summarized by Taylor (1984) indicates that these independent factors are more often replicated than not, and that they also have somewhat different correlations with background variables, and somewhat different prediction for followup status. Not surprisingly, delinquent status, aggressive behavior, and drug use were predicted in part from the presence of antisocial and aggressive behaviors on initial evaluation.

For these reasons, there are some groups interested in having the criteria for attention deficit disorder with hyperactivity "purified" to reflect the inattention/hyperactivity dimension, leaving out the more general-impulsive items from ADD, and relegating these behaviors to the "Conduct Disorder" subsections. In support of this approach are the epidemiological and clinically based studies of Taylor (1984). Taylor demonstrated, in an epidemiological, teacher report-based study, that, while mixed "cases" are the rule, "pure" hyperactivity was not infrequent. Of almost 400 children who were clinical cases, the overlap between hyperactive/inattentive clusters and aggressive/defiance behavioral clusters was also great, with a small number of his sample narrowly defined as having "cross-situational" hyperactivity. The converse, those children with "pure" conduct disorders, was clearly a rarity. The largest fraction of both clinical and epidemiological studies showed a mixed picture. Thus, Taylor's work suports separation of "Hyperkinetic" and "Conduct Disorder" subgroups.

On the other hand, Gittelman's (1984) 10 year prospective followup study indicates that, along with the already well-recognized continuity of hyperactive/inattentive symptomatology (in about 50% of the grade school samples followed into adolescence), about 15% of her cases became conduct problems, some with serious antisocial behaviors at followup. The importance of the Gittelman study is that, of several prospective studies of childhood hyperactivity, this was the most careful to select children who were *not* conduct-disordered at baseline. Moreover, there was close association between continuation of attention/restless problems and development of conduct disorder/antisocial personality. This is the best demonstration of what clinicians have long speculated: that some cases of hyperactivity in childhood may represent a milder or an early form of conduct disorder. The mediators of this change are not known (e.g., environmental interaction, genetic factors, etc.). However, Gittelman's work blurs any simple distinction between ADDH and conduct disorder. Even Taylor's studies, while supporting some distinction, stress that mixed cases are the rule, both clinically and epidemiologically. Finally, biological studies indicate more broad-band correlates with delayed, restless, and impulsive behaviors, and also do not support a distinction (Rapoport & Ferguson, 1983).

For those advocating separate diagnoses, a further problem is the relative significance of attention deficit *per se*. The DSM-III committee in 1976 leaned heavily on the studies of Douglas and coworkers (Douglas,

1974), indicating that attention deficit was a major distinguishing feature between hyperactive children and controls. Other studies about that time had suggested that stimulant drugs exerted their effectiveness primarily through their effect on attention span. Both of these notions are now in question.

In the first place, Sargeant (1984) and others have not found a clear distinction in sustained attention between attention-deficit disordered children and controls, even when tested over very long time periods. Second, a provocative clinical study (Lahey, Schaughency, Strauss, & Frame, 1984) suggests that those children who are diagnosed as having "pure" attention deficit *without* hyperactivity may represent a different clinical population altogether, one that is primarily anxious, shy, and socially withdrawn. Such children seem to comprise quite a different population, and one not continuous with the mild forms of ADDH, as had been hypothesized when ADD without hyperactivity was added to DSM-III. Maurer and Stuart (1980) similarly found that, according to parent data, children diagnosed as ADD without hyperactivity are a heterogenous group, discontinuous with the hyperactive-impulsive population. Moreover, successful treatment with stimulant medication appears to be mediated, at least in part, by direct motor effects, and *not* solely by attention (Porrino, Rapoport, Ismond, Sceery, Behar, & Bunney, 1983). In addition, the cognitive and behavioral effects of stimulants are not significantly correlated (Gittelman, 1975).

Motor activity *per se* is also still a contender as a core deficit for ADD. As Porrino and colleagues (1984a,b) have shown, when measured mechanically on a 24 hour basis, hyperactive children have significantly greater motor activity than controls, even in activities not demanding sustained attention, such as during sleep! Finally, the Gittelman followup study (1984) found as many cases with residual restlessness as with residual inattention, indicating no clear evidence for inattention as the core deficit.

The upshot of this research is that hyperactive *and* impulsive *and* inattentive behaviors probably all equally characterize children with ADD. There is still considerable discussion of this point, however. A key issue remaining is to what degree the impulsivity factor, generally seen as common to *both* conduct disorders and ADD as understood currently, should be separated to allow for yet greater research distinction between the groups. That is, should impulsivity be more generally relegated to conduct disorder, or, acknowledging the overlap, should impulsive items be kept within the ADDH diagnostic group, representing current clinical use? In order to achieve greater discriminant validity between ADD and Conduct Disorder, one runs the danger of lessening that between hyperactive children and children with other disorders, including normal controls. There clearly is not sufficient data for making a decision at this time, and even provisional revisions for DSM-III-R are in flux over this point.

For the moment, any major changes seem premature. In fact, it is likely that DSM-III-R will have less "splitting" and return to a more simple list of items, including impulsivity, inattention, and motor restlessness for ADDH.

There is better empirical data and somewhat greater agreement about Conduct Disorder (Robins, 1978). As reviewed by Robins, the major problems are with the subtyping of conduct disorders as they stand, and with the lack of items more appropriate for young children and for girls. Few studies have substantiated the distinction between aggressive/unaggressive or socialized/unsocialized subtypes. For example, Quay (1979) reviews the literature and finds that children with conduct disorder are ubiquitously unpopular, not supporting the socialized/unsocialized distinction except as related to gang membership and sociocultural acceptance.

It is probable that socialized conduct disorder is a very specific phenomenon, limited to only some urban settings and generally not useful in clinical settings.

Similar limitations are apparent, more surprisingly, with the aggressive/unaggressive distinction. Predictive studies indicate, not only a continuum between agressive and covert behaviors, but that the total number of symptoms has greater predictive usefulness by far than any *pattern* of particular symptoms. Moreover, in some cases covert behavior may be more predictive of later delinquency than overt behavior. Finally, a number of investigations fail to obtain good agreement on diagnostic subtypes, finding three-digit reliability adequate o nly for Conduct Disorders.

Other difficulties appear to be that DSM-III criteria are not appropriate for girls—perhaps because of the absence of items dealing with precocious sexual activity (sexual misbehavior)—and that the criteria are too stringent for young children who physically cannot accomplish some of the present items of behavior such as breaking and entering, and so forth.

Because of the relative lack of controversy over this research data and its interpretation, it is likely that subtypes of conduct disorder will be dropped and all items simply listed under the general Conduct Disorder heading. Additional items will be added for females, and for some milder criteria to be employed with younger children.

The research that will be most influential for DSM-IV will be that targeted for the most instructive groups, probably representing the rarer cases with "pure" disorders as they are presently defined. Specifically, the group of conduct-disordered children not motorically restless or inattentive will be particularly instructive, as will be children with attention deficit who are not "impulsive" or motorically restless. Other groups of interest are those motorically restless but attentive children, and studies of younger children for whom conduct-disorder diagnoses are difficult to make, but who turn out at a later age to be severely conduct-disordered. Identification and followup of such groups would be important contributions to diagnostic clarification. Study of these groups will be more instructive than further examination of the large samples of mixed groups representing most clinic populations, who tend to have the associations of conduct-disorder syndromes (Stewart, Cummings, Singer, & deBlois, 1981), although some replication of this finding is important. In a categorical model, mixed disorders will have the association of one condition or another, while a dimensional model will predict associations of both. A categorical model predicts bimodality, while a dimensional model does not. This area requires careful collaborative studies across groups with uniform assessment methods.

DEPRESSIVE DISORDERS

DSM-III's development coincided with a greatly increased interest in childhood depression. Thus, a relatively large number of recent studies have focused on the use of modified and unmodified adult criteria in either pharmacological or biological studies of pediatric populations (e.g., sleep physiology, endocrine response, etc.).

Depression in childhood had become an increasingly "legitimate" entity (Puig-Antich, 1980), with increasing evidence that unmodified Research Diagnostic Criteria identify at least one valid group of depressed children, those with major depression. Similarly, using unmodified DSM-III diagnoses, studies with both inpatient and outpatient, prepubertal and pubertal children, conducted in different research sites, have shown that major depression is relatively well handled with the current version of DSM-III (Kovacs 1983).

The DSM-III diagnosis of major depression has been studied prospectively by Kovacs, who found a characteristic duration and a high frequency of concurrent disorders (i.e., dysthymia, anxiety, and conduct disorders). Furthermore, Kovacs' research indicated that within five years, diagnosis major depressive disorder predicts a high probability (.72) of a second episode. Thus, current research indicates that major depression is a well founded concept, for even prepubertal children. There are some interesting differences from the adult counterpart, however, such as the striking association of major depression in children with conduct disorder, which require further investigation.

More interesting have been the recent studies by Kovacs and her colleagues, in which the diagnostic category of "Dysthymic Disorder" in childhood appears both reliable and valid, with a surprisingly chronic and malignant course. Dysthymic disorder predicted subsequent major depressive episodes within 5 years (69%), and the occurrence of both dysthymic disorder and major depression carried with it a greater likelihood of recurrence of MDD than for those children with major depression alone.

The main area of research concern appears to be the developmental modifications necessary in the diagnosis of depression. Attempts to relate cognitive depression to a Piagetian framework have not been successful (Kovacs, 1980). However, other measures of development patterns in dysthymic states/depressive disorder need a great deal of work as well.

In this regard, Rutter has reviewed diagnostic systems as applied to childhood depression (Rutter, 1984). In spite of the advances in diagnosis and research in the diagnosis of depression, it is clear that DSM-III still does not address the possible age-related differences in diagnosis, particularly in young children wo cannot or will not report information necessary for the current DSM-III diagnosis. Also, DSM-III was not devised with young children in mind, and it is questionable to what extent the current criteria apply below the age of 6 or 7 years.

Children's ability to report their own feelings as depressive (meta-cognition) are probably not adequate for reliable DSM-III diagnostic reports up to about the age of 8. Similarly, their awareness of time will limit reports of past depressive episodes, both as to existence and duration.

DSM-III has not only focused attention on the diagnosis of childhood depression, but the reporting of the "multiple diagnosis" has made clear other major differences in depressed populations of children, even for those for whom unmodified adult criteria for major depressive disorder seem to apply. These differences include the fact that about one third of children with major depression also meet DSM-III criteria for conduct disorder, and the majority also show significant separation anxiety.

At this point in time, it seems unlikely that there will be any changes from DSM-III in the area of diagnosing childhood depression. Research is lacking on how expression of depression varies with age, at least in a systematic enough manner to apply this to DSM-III-R. The current status of research in developmental expression and/or true incidence of depression is frustrating, as clinical criteria await validation studies which, in turn, are dependent upon appropriate clinical criteria. Nevertheless, followup/descriptive, genetic, biological, and epidemiological studies will provide useful data comparing for example, anxiety, depression, and their combination in the child. Similar studies are required to examine the background of children with both conduct disorder and depression, in contrast to those children with either condition alone.

PERVASIVE DEVELOPMENTAL DISORDERS

A great deal of research has directly or indirectly addressed the DSM-III category of "Pervasive Developmental Disorders (PDD)." While this may seem surprising in light of the relative rarity of the condition, the abundance of studies may be due to the general agreement that this is one of the most valid categories of disorder within the childhood onset group (Rutter, 1978), that there is certainly a biological basis for the disorder which may be researchable, and that, in view of the lifelong handicap that the disorder presents, PDD is certainly a public health problem.

Almost every aspect of the PDD section of DSM-III has been questioned. Some studies have specifically addressed whether DSM-III is appropriate for use with clinic populations (Volkmar, et al., 1986), while others have addressed the need for the return to the DSM-II category of "Childhood Schizophrenia" (Cantor, Pearce, Greene et al., 1984).

Infantile autism, as defined in DSM-III, is an early-onset (before 30 months) disorder characterized by (1) pervasive lack of responsiveness to other people, (2) gross deficits in language development, (3) peculiar speech patterns, (4) bizarre responses to the environment, and (5) absence of delusions, hallucinations, loosening of associations, and incoherence, as in schizophrenia. Childhood onset PDD begins after 30 months of age and before age 12, and is characterized by impaired social relatedness and an absence of delusions, hallucinations, and so forth, and at least three of the following: (1) resistance to change, (2) inappropriate or constricted affect, (3) sudden excessive anxiety, (4) peculiar movements, (5) abnormal speech patterns, (6) under-or oversensitivity to sensory stimuli, and (7) self-mutilation. Therefore, criteria for the two disorders differ primarily in age of onset, but also somewhat in descriptors.

The age of onset criteria have been questioned by several researchers in this area. While most autistic individuals exhibit symptoms early in life, a smaller number do not.

A number of critics have pointed out that clinical groups diagnosed as autistic on clinical behavioral grounds contain a small but significant number of children with onset later than 30 months of age. For example, Volkmar, Cohen, and Paul (1986) found that while the mean age of onset for 50 cases was 1.5 years, six subjects were reported to have had the onset of the disorder after three years of age. These findings are further complicated by the fact that it was the older subjects for whom the later age of onset was reported by their parents, suggesting that retrospective error might account for the large number of "late onset" individuals in this sample. However, even if such is the case, Wing (1984) points out that it is frequent that these children are brought to the clinic some years after the difficulties first arose, and that therefore it is unreasonable for a major criteria to be unverifiable so often. It is interesting, however, that while Volkmar's data suggest that, in fact, most of the six "late onset" cases were probably of earlier onset, DSM-III is a practical nomenclature designed primarily for clinical use, and only secondarily with research settings in mind.

The criteria of pervasive unrelatedness, the most generally agreed-upon core criteria for this group of disorders, has also proved problematic. Systematic questioning of parents indicates that perhaps half of autistic children do indeed show some social responsiveness, for example, cuddled somewhat when held, and were somewhat aware of mother's absence when infants. Thus, the slightly less-restrictive criterion of "gross and sustained impairment in social relations," as included in the diagnosis of Childhood Onset PPD, would have been more appropriate for the infantile autistic sample as well.

A great deal of discussion has focused on the clinical difficulties in ascertaining whether or not a nonverbal child is having hallucinations or delusions. The problem stems primarily from the difficulty of employing these criteria, although there is general agreement that infantile autism and schizophrenia are not related.

Another issue still unresolved is the question of whether the diagnosis can be made when the IQ is extremely low. There are those who feel that when an IQ is untestable, or even below 50, stereotyped movements and social abnormalities are so frequent that the diagnosis should not be attempted.

Wing, however, has argued strongly for the absence of such a cutoff and, at least for the present, the factor of IQ will not be part of the diagnostic criteria. However, it has been agreed that the IQ of any group should be reported as part of a sample description, and that for many studies higher-functioning autistics are more relevant.

A number of comments have emerged about the "Childhood Onset" and "Atypical" categories of PDD. Series of children with PDD include up to one third who msut be classified as "Atypical" under the existing criteria. For example, those who meet other criteria for Autism, but with a later age of onset, must be classified as "Atypical." This group could be handled by increasing the presently too strict age-of-onset criteria for PDD. However, many atypical cases are so categorized because of either the milder nature of the symptoms or the possible presence of thought disorder. Particularly in older children, thought disorder is inferred, or at least it is felt that inner life takes the place of reality. As the presence of delusions or hallucinations is an exclusionary criterion for infantile autism and childhood onset of PDD, this latter issue proves perhaps the most difficult in the group of issues surrounding this diagnosis.

Even more difficult is our lack of guidelines about the variations in childhood onset schizophrenia. There is no doubt that such variations occur and a recent report suggests that in many cases DSM-III criteria are inadequate (Green et al., 1984). There is controversy over the categorization of other groups in which routine motoric disturbances and/or early "autistic-like" phases have been described. Cantor et al., (1982) for example describe a group of 30 children having good eye contact, but with motoric disturbance, and signs of schizophreniform thought disorder. Some of these children had onset before 30 months of age, and most had abnormal language development.

Others, such as Noll and Benedict (1981), have argued for a subgroup of children who show the early developmental pattern of autism followed by schizophrenia. Petti, Ornitz, and Michelman (1984) have also argued for such a group, although their case number was small, and the childhood data retrospective.

Finally, the status of categories for disintegrative disorders, that is, disorders with definate disintegration and Asperger's syndrome, are still under discussion, but some trial descriptions of these entities will be attempted. It is striking that "Autism," perhaps child psychiatry's most valid category, has provoked the most discussion, and will be subject to considerable change. It is likely that some categories will be collapsed into "Autistic Disorder" which will subsume at least infantile autism and childhood onset PDD in DSM-III-R.

MULTIAXIAL CLASSIFICATION AND CHILD DIAGNOSIS

There is general agreement that the multiaxial scheme will be particularly beneficial to child psychiatry, because of the associations between developmental disabilities and some behavioral syndromes (for example, between conduct disorder and reading disability) have too often been obscured by the previous diagnostic schemes. The placement of specific developmental disabilities on Axis II has clearly been advantageous.

The specific developmental disabilities need reworking. It is not clear for which age-range specific grade cutoffs are useful in definition. While this is acknowledged in the text, it would be helpful if more specific guidelines could be given. Moreover, there is a need for a specific motor development delay ("Clumsy Child Syndrome") to be added, as in ICD-9. Even with Axis II, several additional changes are likely. It is generally agreed that IQ should be on a separate axis from Axis I, although it is not clear whether it should be on Axis II (child version) or have a separate axis.

A major source of confusion is that mental retardation in DSM-III, and in the United States in general, is defined by both IQ and adaptive functioning. If mental retardation is placed on Axis II, there is still a problem in noting IQ when relevant. One option for "borderline" functioning is to use the V-code. In ICD-9, mental retardation is defined by IQ alone, simplifying the issue at least diagnostically.

A current proposal is to move Pervasive developmental disorders to Axis II, the point being to have Axis II unified conceptually by developmental problems.

Axis IV (psychosocial stressors) needs to be better articulated for pediatric cases; it may be more helpful if stressors were rated independent of their presumed etiological significance. The specific situation, in addition to coding for severity, may prove more useful, although data is lacking at present for the clinical utility of a spceific listing. In spite of moderate Kappa scores for reliability reported in the field trials, the NIH research team has had very poor reliability in coding even written cases, and multiple stressors are present because of arbitrary choice of category. Certainly, for research purposes, work is needed to provide a more reliable coding scheme.

Axis V (highest level of adaptive functioning) is also inappropriate for children as worded. In young children, the time period of one year may be inappropriate. In older children, developmental issues may cloud the question of functioning, which generally is not a useful concept in pediatric cases, for whom level of functioning is hard to judge and usually requires a much shorter time span. A more specific statement about developmental level of functioning might prove useful, although here, too, there is no data comparable to that for adult patients to support the usefulness of this axis in predicting the outcome of in-treatment planning.

In spite of relatively good reliability reported for Axis II and IV for child cases in the DSM-III field trials, other experience has been less promising. Rapoport and Taylor, in an unpublished NIMH-Maudsley Hospital cross-national study, rated 40 written pediatric bases in which academic testing, social stressors, and developmental history were recorded in a uniform manner. Agreement on Axis II was poor (kappa = .40), and below the marginal DSM-III field-trial kappa of .51. Axis IV was considerably more difficult to rate, owing to the multiplicity of categories into which a particular stressor could fall, and the subjective nature of the rating.

It is clear, therefore, that considerable work is needed to make the multiaxial approach feasible and relevant for children. It is conceivably that an entirely different approach will be needed for pediatric cases, in particular.

SUMMARY

There are several major issues to be considered in the DSM-III revision for disorders of childhood and adolescence. The discussions of the APA Task Force have pointed out the need for more focused research, and hopefully such studies will be conducted prior to the publication of DSM-IV.

However, compared with the preparation of DSM-III, current issues are much more specific, and there is considerable consensus on priority areas for future research. This represents important gains, and a major contribution to the study of childhood psychopathology.

REFERENCES

Cantor, S, Pearce, J., & Pearce, T. (1982). Childhood schizophrenia: Present but not accounted for. *American Journal of Psychiatry, 139,* 758–762.

Douglas, V. (1974). Differences between normal and hyperactive children. In C. Conners (Ed.), *Clinical use of stimulant drugs in children.* Amsterdam: Excepta Medica.

GAP. (1966) *Psychopathological disorders in childhood: Theoretical considerations and a proposed classification.* New York: Group for the Advancement of Psychiatry.

Gittelman, R. (1975). Are behavioral and cognitive effects of stimulants correlated? *International Journal of Mental Health, 41,* 182–198.

Gittelman, R. (1984). A ten year followup of Attention Deficit Disorder with Hyperactivity. Paper presented at NIMH workshop on Treatment of Adolescents with Attention Deficit Disorder, Washington, D. C.

Green, W., Campbell, M., Hardesty, A., Grega, D., Padron-Gayal, M., Shell, & J., Ellenmeyer-Kimling, L. (1984). A comparison of schzophrenic and autistic children. *Journal of the American Academy of Child Psychiatry, 23,* 399–409.

Kovacs, M. (1983) DSM III: The Diagnoses of Depressive Disorders in Children: An interim appraisal. Paper presented at the American Psychiatric Association Conference on: "DSM-III An Interim Appraisal," Washington, D.C.

Lahey, B., Schaughency, E., Strauss, C., & Frame, C. (1984). Are attention deficit disorder with and without hyperactivity similar or disimilar disorders? *Journal of the American Academy of Child Psychiatry, 23,* 302–309.

Langhorne, J. & Loney, J. A. (1979). A fourfold model for subgrouping the hyperkinetic/MBD syndrome. *Child Psychiatry and Human Development, 9,* 153–159.

Loney, J. (1983). Diagnostic research criteria for childhood hyperactivity. In S. Guze, F. Earls, & J. Barrett (Eds.), *Childhood Psychopathology and Development.* New York: Raven Press.

Maurer, R. & Stewart, M. (1980). Attention deficit disorder without hyperactivity in a Child Psychiatry Clinic. *Journal of Clinical Psychiatry, 41,* 232–233.

Noll, R. B. & Benedict, H. (1982). Differentiations within the classifications of childhood psychoses: a continuing dilemma. *Merrill Palmer Quarterly, 27,* 176–199.

Petty, L. K., Ornitz, E., & Michelman, J. D. (1984). Autistic children who become schizophrenic. *Archives of General Psychiatry, 41,* 129–135.

Porrino, L., Rapoport, J., Ismond, D., Sceery, W., Behar, D., & Bunney, W. (1983a). Twenty four hour motor activity in hyperactive children and controls. *Archives of General Psychiatry, 40,* 681–687.

Porrino, L., Rapoport, J., Ismond, D., Sceery, W., Behar, D., & Bunney, W. (1983b). Twenty-four hour motor activity of hyperactive children II. Effects of dextroamphetamine. *Archives of General Psychiatry, 40,* 688–696.

Puig-Antich, J. (1980). Affective disorders in childhood: A review and perspective. Psychiatric Clinics of North America, 3, 403–424.

Quay, H. (1979). Classification. In H. C. Quay & J. D. Werry (Eds.). *Psychopathological disorders of childhood* (2nd ed., P.P. 1–42). New York: Wiley.

Rapoport, J. & Ferguson, B. (1981). Biological validation to Hyperkinetic Syndrome. *Medical Child Newsletters, 23,* 667–682.

Rapoport, J. & Ismond, D. (1984). *DSM-III Training Guide for Diagnosis of Childhood Disorders.* New York: Bruner/Mazel.

Rapoport, J. & Taylor, E. *National Institute of Mental Health-Maudsley Hospital cross-national study.* Unpublished Manuscript.

Robins, L. (1984). An evaluation of the DSM-III Diagnosis of conduct disorder. Paper presented at The American Psychiatric Association workshop on ADD and Conduct Disorder, New York.

Robins, L. (19   ) Sturdy childhood predictors of adult antisocial behavior from longitudinal studies. *Psychological Medicine, 8,* 611–622.

Rutter, M. (1984). Depressive disorders in childhood and adolescence: Nosological considerations. Paper presented at workshop in assessment diagnosis and classification in Child and Adolescent Psychopathology, Washington, D.C.

Rutter, M. (1978). Diagnostic validity in child psychiatry. *Advances in Biological Psychotherapy, 2,* 2–22.

Rutter, M. & Shaffer, D. (1980). DSM-III—A step forward or back in terms of the classification of child psychiatric disorders? *Journal of the American Academy of Child Psychiatry, 19,* 371–394.

Rutter, M., Shaffer, D., & Shepherd, M. (1975). A multiaxial classification of child psychiatric disorders. Geneva: World Health Organization.

Sargeant, J. (1984). Cognitive Measures. Paper presented at the Annual Highpoint Hospital Symposium on Attention Deficit Disorder, Toronto, Canada.

Stewart, M., Cummings, C., Singer, S. & de Blois, C. S. (1981). The overlap between hyperactive and unsocialized aggressive children. *Journal of Child Psychology and Psychiatry, 22,* 35–46.

Taylor, E. (1984). Nosology of Attention Deficit Disorder and Conduct Disorder Syndromes. Paper presented at NIMH Workshop on Assessment, Diagnosis and Classification in Child and Adolescent Psychopathology, Washington, D.C.

Volkmar, F., Cohen, D., & Paul, R. (1986). An evaluation of DSM-III criteria for infantile autism. *Journal of the American Academy of Child Psychiatry,* 1986.

Wing, L. (1984). Comments on the Pervasive Developmental Disorders section of DSM-III. Paper presented at The American Psychiatric Association workshop on DSM-III Disorders, New York.

Index